Matthew Condon is an award-winning author of several novels, works of non-fiction, and is the two-time winner of the Steele Rudd Award for short fiction. His novels include *The Motorcycle Café*, *The Pillow Fight* and *The Trout Opera*. His non-fiction titles include *Brisbane* and, as editor, *Fear, Faith and Hope: Remembering the Long Wet Summer of 2010–2011*. His bestselling first volume of the Lewis Trilogy – *Three Crooked Kings* – won the John Oxley Library Award 2013, and was shortlisted for the Queensland Literary Awards Queensland Book of the Year and the Waverley Library NIB Award for non-fiction. He lives in Brisbane.

PRAISE FOR *THREE CROOKED KINGS*

'*A fascinating account of the corruption and the power struggles within the Queensland Police.*' WEEKEND AUSTRALIAN

'Three Crooked Kings *paints a compellingly dark picture.*' SYDNEY MORNING HERALD

'*Hailed as the most explosive book of 2013 – a riveting epic and unrelenting tour-de-force which will shock a nation. And it's all true.*' THE CHRONICLE

JACKS AND JOKERS

MATTHEW CONDON

UQP

First published 2014 by University of Queensland Press
PO Box 6042, St Lucia, Queensland 4067 Australia
Reprinted 2015

www.uqp.com.au
uqp@uqp.uq.edu.au

Cover design by Design by Committee
Cover photo illustration by Josh Durham
Author photo © Russell Shakespeare
Typeset in 11.5/16 pt Bembo by Post Pre-press Group, Brisbane
Printed in Australia by McPherson's Printing Group

Quotes from *Sometimes Gladness: Collected Poems* by Bruce Dawe
reprinted by permission of the author.

Quotes from *The Bagman* by Jack Herbert and Tom Gilling
reprinted by permission of Tom Gilling.

Quotes from *Trial and Error* by Don Lane
reprinted by permission of Boolarang Press.

Quotes from *Joh* by Hugh Lunn
reprinted by permission of the author.

Quotes from *The Man They Called a Monster* by Paul Wilson
reprinted by permission of the author.

All attempts have been made to contact copyright licensees for
permission to reproduce material. If you believe material for which
you hold rights is reprinted here, please contact the publisher.

National Library of Australia cataloguing-in-publication
data is available at http://catalogue.nla.gov.au/

Jacks and Jokers / Matthew Condon
ISBN 978 0 7022 4996 9 (pbk)
ISBN 978 0 7022 5198 6 (pdf)
ISBN 978 0 7022 5199 3 (epub)
ISBN 978 0 7022 5200 6 (Kindle)

University of Queensland Press uses papers that are natural, renewable and recyclable
products made from wood grown in sustainable forests. The logging and manufacturing
processes conform to the environmental regulations of the country of origin.

For the gang – Katie, Finnigan, Bridie Rose and
little Oliver George – with love

SHE DISCOVERED, SHORTLY AFTER, that the man who had just raped her was a policeman.

To add to the humiliation, when he had finished with her, several of his colleagues emerged from closets and doorways where they had been hiding, watching while their friend degraded her.

He thought it was funny. So did his mates. He produced his identification badge and she tried to read his name. She wanted to memorise it, because she was about to do the unthinkable. She was going to report the incident to the police. She didn't want this to happen to other working girls.

Her name was Mary Anne Brifman, the eldest daughter of the former prostitute, brothel madam and police whistleblower Shirley Margaret Brifman, who had been found dead of a suspected drug overdose on 4 March 1972.

It was Mary Anne who had discovered the twisted corpse of her mother on that Saturday in the small room of the family flat in Bonney Avenue, in the Brisbane suburb of Clayfield. It was Mary Anne who only a year before her mother's untimely death was being groomed against her will to take over her mother's brothels in Sydney, before Shirley was charged with soliciting her own child for the purposes of prostitution. When the charge failed to disappear, even though Shirley had been paying off corrupt police like Glen Patrick Hallahan, Tony Murphy and Fred Krahe for more than a decade, she went on live national television and snitched on the whole rotten lot of them.

Following Shirley's live-to-air interview the Brifmans had returned to Brisbane to hide, to disappear, to keep safe. Shirley and her husband Sonny had lived in the sub-tropical city from the late 1950s until 1963, when the

National Hotel inquiry into police misconduct at the famous city watering hole got started. Shirley had been a star witness at the inquiry. At the time she had denied being a prostitute. She rejected any intimate association with Murphy and Hallahan. And no, she claimed, there was most definitely not a prostitution ring working out of the National. It was a classy joint. And what would she know of it anyway? She wasn't a working girl.

Having perjured herself, Shirley then moved the family to Sydney. Almost ten years later, after blowing the whistle, she returned to Brisbane. Nine months after that she was dead.

Now Shirley's daughter, Mary Anne, was in her twenties with two children of her own. She was working as a call-out prostitute for an independent outfit called Quality Escorts. The job on this particular night was slightly unusual. The client had asked to meet Brifman in an auto repair shop north of the Brisbane CBD. She accepted the job, but was unaware she was walking into a sexual ambush.

They didn't know her real identity, of course. They didn't know she was a Brifman. If they did, and word got back to headquarters, alarm would have spread through the building. It might have been several years earlier, but the stench of the Brifman 'suicide' still haunted the corridors of the Queensland Police Force. The tall, gangly officer Shirley knew from the Consorting Squad when she worked in the Killarney brothel over in South Brisbane, Terry Lewis, would rise to become Commissioner. And her friend and lover, Tony Murphy, would stand as the most powerful detective in the force.

In an eerie replica of another time, another Brifman was being used and abused by police. Mary Anne lodged an official complaint against the officer who had raped her and later gave a formal, detailed statement. She too, in a small way, was standing up to those who had disrespected her, just as her mother had done.

For a week internal police investigators visited her home to counsel and placate her. It was clear that while they appeared genuinely concerned for her wellbeing, they also didn't want the press to get wind of the incident. The constable who raped you, they told Mary Anne, was engaged to be married and had since lost his fiancé because of his actions. He would be exiled to a police station in a remote part of the state.

Mary Anne Brifman didn't proceed with charges. She didn't want the world to know she was the daughter of the deceased Shirley Brifman. She didn't want to live with the shame, so she stepped back into the shadows. From that moment on, for as long as she worked as an escort in Brisbane, she never heard from or came to the attention of the police again. They didn't dare go near her, the daughter of the ghost of Bonney Avenue.

1970s

The Year of the Dragon

By mid-1976 Inspector Terence (Terry) Murray Lewis of Charleville, a dusty town in western Queensland, should already have known that he was in for a stellar year. To begin with, it was a leap year, and he finally got to celebrate his birthday – 29 February – on the actual date. Also, he was born under the Chinese astrological sign of the Dragon, and 1976 was coincidentally the Year of the Dragon. Lewis would be turning 48.

He may not have been familiar with the characteristics of the revered Dragon in Chinese astrology: inflated self-assurance, tyrannical with a stern demeanour, impressed by prestige and rank, devoted to work and lucky with money-making schemes – the Dragon was renowned for leaving a trail of wealth.

By winter Lewis had already had a frank and lengthy discussion with Queensland premier Joh Bjelke-Petersen on the airstrip at Cunnamulla following a country cabinet meeting of the ruling National Party, and he would soon be making a flurry of political contacts. He also wasted not a single opportunity – like his friend Anthony (Tony) Murphy up in Longreach – to disparage the administration of Police Commissioner Raymond (Ray) Wells Whitrod.

The day after Bjelke-Petersen flew back to the big smoke of Brisbane, Lewis returned to his desk in downtown Charleville, in the wooden police station beside the stone bank in the main street. It was a timely visit by the premier. Lewis had had enough of being stuck in western Queensland, and had actually applied for a vacancy in the Commonwealth Police. The Dragon could be stubborn and impetuous at times, and did not like taking orders – they could express flexibility and be amenable to life around them; but only to a point.

'It crossed my mind to leave – that's when I applied for a job in the Commonwealth [Police],' Lewis recalls. 'I made an application … I think there were two vacancies, one for an Assistant Commissioner somewhere, and a Superintendent. They flew me to Sydney.'

Lewis was picked up at the airport by New South Wales police officer Dick Lendrum who had married Yvonne Weier – one of Lewis's favourites from his days in the Juvenile Aid Bureau (JAB) in Brisbane in the 1960s.

After his interview (he would later find out that he didn't get the job), Lendrum arranged for Lewis to meet the New South Wales Police Commissioner Fred 'Slippery' Hanson, a foundation member of the legendary '21 Division' unit, formed to smash post-war hoodlum gangs. Hanson had become Commissioner in 1972, succeeding the corrupt Norm Allan.

Hanson had made his views on policing very clear not long after he took the top job. 'Every cop should have a good thumping early in his career to make him tolerant,' he told the press. 'A good thumping teaches a young policeman how to get along with people. It's no use getting police recruits from university, the ones who have never knocked around the lower levels.'

It was rumoured Hanson had been corrupt New South Wales Premier Robert Askin's organiser of paybacks from illegal casinos, as had Allan.

'[Dick] took me and introduced me to Fred Hanson, whom I'd never met,' Lewis says. 'He's the one who said [of Whitrod], "Oh yeah, how's that fat little bastard up there who should be charged with assuming the designation of a police officer?"'

Meanwhile, retired detective and former Rat Packer Glendon (Glen) Patrick Hallahan was trying to make a fist of the farming life. He had left Brisbane under a cloud following his abrupt resignation from the force in 1972, although for a while continued to live at Kangaroo Point before shifting to acreage in the Sunshine Coast hinterland.

He and the land would be an awkward fit. The big, powerful Hallahan, plagued with bouts of ill-health since the late 1950s, was a city creature, a habitué of bars, wine saloons and restaurants – he relished the bright lights of Sydney. Well into his thirties, he continued to enjoy the nightlife.

In the aftermath of his departure from the force, his good friend – newspaper reporter from the 1950s and now editor of the *Sunday Sun* newspaper Ron Richards – offered Hallahan an alternative career.

Hallahan, one-time crack detective, receiver of graft from prostitutes, accomplice to criminals in both Brisbane and Sydney and associate to drug dealer John Edward Milligan, would try his hand as a specialist writer and break exclusive stories about crime and corruption. Richards believed that Hallahan could utilise his extensive police (and criminal) contacts, both state and federal, and drum up some rollicking Sunday crime reads.

Despite the fact that the office of the *Sun* was located in very familiar territory to Hallahan – the heart of Fortitude Valley – life as a reporter didn't work out. 'He produced a story using Federal Police intelligence about the arrival of the phenomenon of the car bomb in Australia,' recalls Des Houghton, then a young journalist on the *Sunday Sun*, based in Brunswick Street. 'It caused a bit of a drama and there were questions asked about where he got his intelligence from.

'Hallahan was aloof. He was a hit with the women in the office. Most of the time he asked for help in how to fill out his expenses.'

After the car bomb scoop, Hallahan virtually disappeared, resuming residence with his wife, Heather, in Obi Obi on the north coast, growing fruit and vegetables and toying with the idea of selling farm machinery. Despite the distance between them he was not lost to his old mate Tony Murphy. The two men remained in regular contact.

During this time in the state's capital, the classified advertisements in the *Courier-Mail* newspaper were featuring – in the Beauty and Health section – a relatively new phenomenon to the Brisbane scene – the massage parlour.

In the preceding few years parlours such as the Brisbane Health Studio, The Oriental Bathhouse, The Coronet and others, actually dispensed what they advertised – qualified massages. Each was equipped with bona fide massage tables.

The first Brisbane 'health studio' to be prosecuted as a premises used for prostitution was the Carla–Deidre Health Studio in Enogerra in June 1970. A man called Bernard John Pack was prosecuted. The case against Pack established that 'relief massages' given to men fell under the prostitution umbrella.

Quaintly, staff of the Temple of Isis were charged in 1971 with breaching the *Physiotherapists Act* by misleadingly calling themselves qualified masseurs or masseuses.

Police from the Licensing Branch, Drug Squad, Consorting Squad, the Valley Crime Intelligence Unit and even Commonwealth Police regularly visited the parlours, trying to catch prostitutes in the act of sexual congress. On some occasions officers confiscated parlour towels.

If prostitution was detected, the girls were immediately breached. There were no tip-offs about raids, no protection money payments, no charging on rotation. But by 1976, the entire parlour scene had changed.

As Lewis toiled in Charleville, and Premier Joh Bjelke-Petersen jetted out on an overseas trade mission, hoping to convince both the British and the Japanese to invest in Queensland's limitless reserves of coal, and state Cabinet debated sand mining on Moreton Island, gentlemen were being invited to explore the pleasures of female 'masseuses' across Brisbane city.

There was the Penthouse Health Studio at 141 Brunswick Street, Fortitude Valley. There was the Kontiki at 91 Gympie Road, Kedron. 'Have you met our pretty and talented girls at Kontiki? Well they're just longing to entertain you the way you enjoy the best.'

There was the Fantasia Health Spa at 187 Barry Parade, Fortitude Valley. And the Golden Hands Health Salon at 1145 Ipswich Road, Moorooka. 'Come and meet our lovely talented girls ...'

In the Year of the Dragon, a lot of money was changing hands in Brisbane after dark, and men like corrupt former Licensing Branch officer Jack Reginald Herbert picked up the scent.

The luck of the Dragon would touch Lewis not once, but twice, in just a matter of months. Coming events – an act of police brutality in far-off Brisbane, and a bungled drug raid in even remoter Far North Queensland – would trigger Commissioner Ray Whitrod's demise. They would also, as if by magic, open a clear path for Lewis to the summit of the Queensland Police Service.

A Lemonade in Blackall

Just as Police Commissioner Ray Whitrod and Police Minister Max Hodges had paid a visit to Inspector Terry Lewis in Charleville in the winter of 1976, taking morning tea in the station and keeping tabs on the banished Rat Packer, they continued their tour 300 kilometres north to remote Blackall.

A grazing town perched on the Barcoo River and home to the historic Blackall Woolscour, the township evolved mainly as a service centre to surrounding properties. On one of those – Alice Station – in 1892, shearer Jack (Jackie) Howe broke colony records when he shore with hand shears 321 sheep in seven hours and 40 minutes and cata- pulted himself into folklore.

As was the custom, Whitrod and Hodges' visit necessitated a

function in one of the local hotels, which was attended by 30 to 40 dignitaries, graziers and of course the local police. The Blackall police station was operated by sergeant in charge Les Lewis and four other officers. At the event, Les Lewis was sipping a glass of lemonade when he was approached by Minister Hodges.

'What are you drinking, sergeant?' Hodges asked him.

'Lemonade,' Sergeant Lewis replied.

'What would you usually drink?'

'Beer,' he replied. 'But I never drink [alcohol] in uniform.'

Hodges pointed out that even the Commissioner of Police was drinking a glass of wine in full uniform, and said to the barman: 'Give the sergeant a beer.'

As the two men engaged in conversation, the Minister immediately expressed his dislike of the inspector in charge of the Longreach district (which took in Blackall, 213 kilometres away), Tony Murphy.

'Murphy's got a chip on his shoulder,' Hodges remarked. 'So has [Terry] Lewis.' Hodges went on to tell him that Whitrod planned to transfer Terry Lewis from Charleville to Innisfail in Far North Queensland, 'to keep him as far away as possible from Brisbane and the Commissioner', and that Murphy would be staying put in Longreach 'until he learned to smile'.

Sergeant Les Lewis, who worked well with Murphy and believed the famous detective from Brisbane had done a good job in Longreach, told Hodges that Murphy was expecting a transfer to Toowoomba where his wife and children had settled.

Hodges said it wasn't going to happen. 'Hodges was very firm,' recalls Lewis. 'He was the boss.'

A few days later, Murphy's car pulled into the police yard in Blackall. He was on his way down to Toowoomba to see his wife, Maureen, and the kids. The drive – over 1200 kilometres – also took him en route through Charleville.

Sergeant Les Lewis felt compelled to relay to his boss details of the meeting with Hodges and Whitrod. 'I've got something to tell you if you promise not to take it further,' he said. He told of Hodges' refusal to move Murphy out of Longreach until he 'learned how to smile'.

Murphy immediately got out of the car in a rage and repeatedly kicked the tyres of the vehicle. 'Those bloody bastards,' he shouted.

Murphy then 'took off out of the yard' and headed for Terry Lewis in Charleville. In Murphy's mind, Hodges' remarks about himself and Terry Lewis constituted the persecution of senior officers in the Queensland Police Force.

He would most certainly be taking the matter forward.

Love in the Lido

Down in the mean streets of Kings Cross, Sydney, once plied so successfully by former Brisbane madam Shirley Margaret Brifman, another young prostitute, Anne Marie Tilley, was working the lanes and backstreets.

Tilley, even before she hit her teenage years, was steeped in the business of prostitution. Her foster father had once been a driver for the legendary Sydney madam Matilda (Tilly) Devine of the Razor Gang era in the 1920s and 1930s. He told her many stories through her girl-hood. At the age of 11, Tilley was entranced by the popular 1963 Billy Wilder film, *Irma La Douce*, a musical comedy about a policeman who falls for a prostitute in Paris. In the movie, honest gendarme Nestor Patou (Jack Lemmon) unwittingly begins arresting call girls who are favoured by corrupt senior police and is thrown out of the force. By fate he becomes close friends with prostitute Irma (Shirley MacLaine) and eventually declares his love. Tilley adored the luxuriant lifestyle of the on-screen prostitutes. She adored Irma's fluffy white dog. She knew this was the life for her.

At the age of 16, in a Kings Cross nightclub – the Lido in Roslyn Street, a notorious haunt for gangsters and callgirls – Tilley met her very own Nestor Patou. His name was Hector (Hec) Hapeta, not an honest policeman, but a retailer of pet meat based in the distant suburbs of western Sydney.

Hapeta was hanging out with a prostitute 'keeper' called Bob. Tilley and a girlfriend wanted to get on the game. Bob threw some money on the table and asked young Tilley to go buy him and Hec a drink at the bar. She refused – ladies didn't go to the bar – and Hapeta, dressed as he habitually was in a three-piece suit, told Bob to leave her alone. Hec would get the drinks.

Hapeta was a 'smiler'; he had a happy demeanour and a cheeky sense of humour. Tilley thought he was a gentleman. They would soon move in together in a flat in Liverpool, and Tilley would begin her notorious career as a prostitute and brothel madam.

It would have been inconceivable to both Hapeta and Tilley that by the late 1970s they would find themselves drifting north to the sun and warmth of Queensland. There, with astonishing speed, they would build a vice empire of gargantuan proportions that would make them wealthy.

It could have been a plot from one of the film-loving Tilley's matinees, but this time a western. Two savvy operators ride into a hick town, take over the saloons and the houses of ill-repute, and laugh all the way to the bank. And they wouldn't need to worry about the sheriff. Because very quickly, the sheriff would be handsomely remunerated to turn a blind eye.

A Stellar Career

Meanwhile, in the Queensland capital, Gerald (Tony) Fitzgerald, QC, aged 34 (and born in the Year of the Snake), was not only one of the busiest and most respected lawyers in town but was also juggling a young family – three children under the age of five. The Fitzgeralds lived on the Brisbane River in Rosebery Terrace, Chelmer, just across the Walter Taylor Bridge from Indooroopilly.

Having taken silk the year before – one of the youngest to do so in the state – Fitzgerald had carved a lucrative niche for himself in commercial law. A Catholic, and son to a senior public servant, he had been something of a prodigy. He was called to the Bar in 1964 and for a time worked out of chambers above Cassells' frock shop in Queen Street, dubbed the 'Outs of Court' (as opposed to the official home of Brisbane's legal fraternity, the Inns of Court up on North Quay.)

By the mid-1960s he was being mentored by the legendary lawyer Gerard Brennan and moved up to the Inns, on the same floor as knockabout barrister and South Brisbane MP Colin Bennett. Brennan was the epitome of ethics and fairness in the law. A Catholic himself, he was also a champion of gentlemanly distance between the courts and government. The son of Justice Frank Brennan, he, like Bennett, believed strongly in social justice for all. He had a profound impact on Tony Fitzgerald. Brennan's father had died when he was just 21. Fitzgerald had lost his mother, Doris, to a kidney ailment when he was six years old. Both had risen out of humble financial circumstances.

Fitzgerald, like many of his young contemporaries, had heard of the police practice of 'verballing' or fabrication of evidence. And like the rest of Brisbane, knew the gossip that former police commissioner Frank Bischof was corrupt and that his bagmen in the 1960s were known as the Rat Pack.

Fitzgerald most likely heard much of the local tittle-tattle in the rooms of the Johnsonian Club in Adelaide Street. A beacon for barristers and journalists, the place was often packed with members for weekday lunch. It served a mean steak and offered the hottest English mustard in town. There, Fitzgerald rubbed shoulders with some of Brisbane's most colourful legal practitioners, including the cigar-smoking Jack

Aboud. The old barrister would often leave a burning cigar on a stairwell outside court and pick it up again on his way out. Aboud, his taste buds dead from smoking, adored lashings of the Johnsonian mustard.

Fitzgerald also got to know the best legal minds of the day – Eddie Broad, Wally Campbell, Des Sturgess, John Macrossan, Bill Pincus and Paul de Jersey. Within such a small pool of lawyers, it was hard not to notice that those who allied themselves with Joh Bjelke-Petersen's government and its legal work found themselves on the path to a successful career.

Fitzgerald, however, had little interest in day-to-day politics, though his attitude to police corruption may have been a little different. His grandfather, Casey, had been a Queensland police officer. Fitzgerald was, by choice, a lawyer who kept a low profile and treasured his privacy. He might have a regular game of tennis with a few close and trusted mates, but he did not court the social set nor did he have any interest in seeing his name in the newspapers.

Ironically, his future included a couple of years where he would become perhaps the best known legal practitioner in Australia and would embed his name in Queensland history.

The Key Club

Across town, some enterprising entrepreneurs like the petty criminal Roland Short were starting some new business ventures in the skin trade.

The city had a few illegal gambling dens and some fledgling massage parlours and 'health studios', but Short was taking things to a whole new level. Short already had the Penthouse Health Studio in Brunswick Street, and another parlour in suburban Indooroopilly, west of the CBD. His centrepiece, though, was the new Key Club at 584 Stanley Street, Woolloongabba, within sight of the Brisbane Cricket Ground.

Short had asked his friend, barman and parlour manager Geoff Crocker, to pop around and take a look in mid-1976: 'I'd never seen anything like it before in my life, lovely ladies there and everything,' Crocker said later.

Crocker checked out the club. There was gambling in two gaming rooms, pornographic movies being screened in a bar, separate areas with spa tubs and women coming out of the saunas with 'their boobs hanging out of the towels'. It was a scene from a Roman orgy.

Short told Crocker that if he looked after the parlour for him and did a good job, he would eventually end up running the place. 'So that was a bit of incentive for me, I liked the place, it looked good, you know?'

Uniquely, Short had instituted a special membership subscription to the Key Club. It cost $500 to be a member, and you put another $500 on an account card. Cash changed hands only in the gaming rooms. As a member, you were identified by your Key Club number and your birthdate. It cost $100 an hour to be with a girl.

Crocker observed that the club was 'a class above' anything else he'd seen in Brisbane. '[There were] no rough-spoken ones,' he said of the women employed at the Key Club. 'No tattoos, we couldn't employ a girl if she had a tattoo, it was Roland's orders … if their hair wasn't right or their dress wasn't up to standard, I'd say go home and get changed or do something with your hair and come back … if you do it again I won't let you in.'

The gaming side of the operation was run by a man called Luciano Scognamiglio, who had games going right across the city. The thin, sickly-looking 'Luci' was also known to punters as 'Louis'. Crocker estimated that Short was making $25,000 to $30,000 each week off the illegal games at the Key Club.

Private investigator John Wayne Ryan was called in to fit out the club's security. 'Roland always had the latest technology,' he recalls. 'If he wanted closed-circuit television, he'd order the latest from the United States.

'Roland was a bit of a heavy. He had a reputation. And he was fairly well connected. He had something to do with a couple of coppers and he'd help them out on stuff. Because of the people who were coming into his clubs – magistrates, parliamentarians, lawyers – he had a lot of potential blackmail material. He also had a lot of things on a lot of cops.'

According to Ryan, Short was an associate of both Tony Murphy and former detective Glen Hallahan. He claimed that when Hallahan had been facing corruption charges in October 1972, Short had compiled damaging material on the judge set to hear Hallahan's case – Eddie Broad. In the end the Crown offered no evidence against Hallahan and the case was dismissed. Hallahan resigned from the force shortly after.

Still, the incident highlighted that Short – though he had a well-known detestation of police – worked with them when required. As for the Key Club, Ryan befriended some of the girls working there and they called on him on several occasions to help them with personal security.

'I did a couple of favours for the girls,' Ryan says. 'They were receiving threats for money. One of the threats came from Glen Hallahan, though he was no longer in the police force. The cops at the Gabba were weighing in too, asking for favours and money.

'The girls were under a lot of pressure. They were working the parlours by day and then coming into the Key Club at night. Most of the time they were carrying huge sums of money and I'd escort them to their cars. Or I'd grab their money and put it in the night safe. Then when the cops pressed them, they could say to them they were running a bit short on money that night.'

Ryan, who had been intimately connected with Brisbane's club and vice scene since the 1960s, was walking a fine line. And Brisbane city was more volatile than anyone in the suburbs could have imagined.

Following the supposed suicide by drug overdose of the prostitute Shirley Brifman in her flat in Clayfield, the murder of Jack Cooper, manager of the National Hotel in Queen Street, and the Whiskey Au Go Go bombings that killed 15 people, it emerged that Brisbane had a dangerous underworld.

'I was walking around with two guns,' Ryan reflected. 'I was in the middle of everybody. Billy Phillips [tattooist, petty gangster, stolen goods fence and former informant or 'dog' to Hallahan] would give me a hug like I was his brother, but I was keeping an eye out for him pinning my arms and being stabbed by someone.

'When I helped some of my police contacts, I'd be thanked personally for the work I'd done and wait for my arms to be grabbed and another copper to shoot me. That's what it was like.'

Detective Saunders

The face of the future of the Queensland Police Force, Lorelle Anne Saunders, a former army sergeant, had joined the force just weeks after the death of brothel madam Shirley Margaret Brifman in 1972. Less than three years later she was appointed by Police Commissioner Ray Whitrod as Queensland's first female detective. She was just 26.

In a profession dominated by men, the Saunders appointment was big news. SHE BEAT MEN FOR DETECTIVE VACANCY, said one newspaper headline. And another: GENTLEMEN WHEN LAW IS A LADY.

'Even hardened criminals have been known to melt when arrested by Detective Constable Lorrelle [sic] Saunders,' a local Brisbane newspaper reported. 'It's amazing – they can be really polite,' Saunders was quoted in the article. 'You get a hard, rough crim yet he will talk to you, open doors and pull out chairs for you.'

Detective Constable Saunders could also stand on her record. She had a prodigious work ethic, effecting more than 650 arrests and her bravery in the line of duty was evident. In July 1974 a man threatened to blow up a building in Brisbane's Fortitude Valley if he wasn't paid $10,000. Saunders was used as a decoy. (The extortionist was apprehended before any rendezvous with Saunders.)

Saunders was the embodiment of modern Whitrod reform. He wanted more women in the force and he wanted them in senior positions. It was a measure that he hoped would go a long way towards tempering an old-fashioned, ill-educated and misogynist police force. She was not an ornament but a bona fide detective.

Yet soon after her historic appointment Saunders would upset the Rat Pack, and in particular the legendary detective Tony Murphy. Coupled with her powerful advocacy for women's rights in the force, a sense of justice and a knowledge of entrenched police corruption, she would soon suffer the same games exercised by corrupt members of the force against perceived enemies – public and professional humiliation, intimidation, direct death threats, concocted evidence, verballing and, incredibly, time in prison courtesy of a fabricated charge that she attempted to secure a hitman to kill a fellow police officer.

Dozens of promising police careers had been destroyed by the Rat Pack and its supporters, but nothing approached the venom directed at Saunders. 'As long as I can remember I have wanted to be in the force,' she told a newspaper following her elevation to detective.

As long as she could remember, too, she had had an acquaintance with Terence Murray Lewis. Interestingly, in the first week of his duties as head of the new Juvenile Aid Bureau back in the winter of 1963, Lewis had paid a visit to 25 Alamine Street, Holland Park, the home of a Mrs Lindall Rose Saunders and her daughter, Lorelle, then 15.

Lorelle had been in some minor trouble involving some undesirable young local boys and a teacher at her school, Cavendish Road State High, when the head of the JAB and his sidekick, policewoman Yvonne Weier, turned up to help set the girl on the straight and narrow.

Just over a decade later Saunders would be one of Whitrod's bright young hopefuls. A decade after that she would be in solitary confinement in prison, wondering where it all went wrong, suspended from duty and awaiting a charge of attempted murder.

Keeping an eye on every movement of her case was her boss, the kindly officer who had come to the door of her family home all those years before, Inspector Terry Lewis.

Politicking

Out west, the campaign against Commissioner Whitrod continued unabated.

Labor Opposition leader Tom Burns was touring western Queensland towns with his private secretary Malcolm McMillan when they turned up in Charleville. Burns, a popular working-class knockabout who had been elected to the Brisbane bayside seat of Lytton in 1972, loved to get among the people. An ALP powerbroker, he had been quickly elevated to leader of the Opposition and in a short time had had some memorable stoushes with Premier Bjelke-Petersen and his National Party cronies in Parliament House. He was quick on his feet and cunning of mind.

In Charleville, they of course made the acquaintance of Inspector Lewis.

'He came to see Burns,' remembers McMillan. 'The essence of the discussion was that [Police Minister Max] Hodges was no good and had to go, and Whitrod was no good and had to go. Lewis was discreet, polite, deferring, diplomatic. Lewis quite clearly understood the make-up of government and opposition.'

The next day Burns and McMillan continued on to Longreach. That night, both men were working late in Burns' motel room when there was a knock at the door.

'It was Tony Murphy,' says McMillan. 'He apologised for arriving unannounced. He repeated verbatim what Terry Lewis had told us the day before. This was clearly a concerted campaign [against Whitrod] going on right around the state.'

While it was not unusual for members of parliament to meet civic leaders and law enforcement officials while touring rural areas, Murphy's tete-a-tete was memorable. How did he know precisely where Burns and McMillan were staying that night in Longreach? And what was so urgent that a police inspector felt impelled to track down the leader of a state opposition political party late at night and share his opinions about a minister of the Crown and the number one police officer in Queensland?

The war against Ray Whitrod had become brazen.

In Brisbane, some strange machinations were also at play. Edgar Bourke, a career public servant and staff clerk to the Commissioner of Police, had seen and heard a lot of things since becoming attached to the police department as a young man in 1948.

As Lewis and Murphy were trying to sway politicians in the bush, Bourke was in a meeting with several other colleagues at head-quarters when the phone rang. 'It was Stan Wilcox from the Premier's Department,' Bourke recalls. 'He wanted to know what sort of bloke Terry Lewis was, and would we ask around.'

Bourke says the staff remembered Lewis well from his lengthy secondment to the JAB under former commissioner Frank Bischof. But the call from Wilcox was a bolt out of the blue. 'We thought Terry was quite good but we had no idea where all of this was leading,' Bourke remembers.

Incredibly, Premier Bjelke-Petersen was also making secret enquiries about how Whitrod might be legally removed for breach of contract. He ordered his press secretary Allen Callaghan to seek advice on the possibility of terminating Whitrod's tenure. A memo came back offering Bjelke-Petersen a number of options on how to eject the Commissioner.

Meanwhile, Lewis, on leave in the city several days after meeting with Bjelke-Petersen in Cunnamulla, dropped into the Premier's Department and added to his private file (# 246) a sheaf of documents. Among other things, the file contained rumour and innuendo about Whitrod that had been gathered from six years earlier: '31 August, 1970. Mr G. [Gough] Whitlam visited Mr Whitrod at police head-quarters.' And: 'On 22/12/70. Inspector Ron Eddington [sic] said the ALP not only liked Mr Whitrod, they love him.'

In the dossier Lewis also included a list of people who could provide glowing character testimonies on his behalf. The list starred two Supreme Court judges, six District Court judges and five members of parliament. Lewis then noted to the Premier: 'If Mr Whitrod hears I have spoken to you he will immediately engage in the character assassination that he learned so well from his ALP friends in Canberra.'

The irony that Lewis himself was assassinating Whitrod's character with his secret missives to the Premier seems to have escaped the inspector.

Without Whitrod's knowledge, and coming from several quarters, the grooming of Lewis for higher rank had begun in earnest.

The Shooter

James (Jim) Slade, from the small town of Kyogle in the Northern Rivers region of New South Wales, and not far south of the Queensland border, was seemingly born for intelligence work. His great-grandfather emigrated from Ireland and became a New South Wales police officer, one of many who hunted the notorious bushranger Ben Hall in the 1860s. His father, Edward, had worked undercover in Occupied Greece during World War II.

Bearing the laconic traits of a rural upbringing as part of a large Catholic family, Slade moved to Canberra in 1971 and joined the

Commonwealth Police before heading to the Document Examination Bureau based at North Head in Manly, Sydney. Over the next three years he became an expert in forensic document examination. He then specialised in photographic intelligence gathering.

When Cyclone Tracy hit on Christmas Eve and into Christmas Day in 1974, police from across Australia were mobilised. The catastrophic storm killed 71 people. Terry Lewis was there as part of the Queensland contingent. So too was Jim Slade, who landed in Darwin on Boxing Day.

'It was my job to photograph everything that normal police would have done in relation to dead bodies and forensic work,' Slade remembers. 'It was also to provide a good visual photographic record of what happened up there. I was up there for a few months. I had a Bolex [camera] and hundred-foot rolls of 16 mm film coming out my arse.'

After Tracy, the ambitious, perhaps impetuous, Slade wanted to move forward with his career. 'I had a very big interest in intelligence and I really wanted to pursue that,' he says. 'I wasn't interested in political intelligence like ASIO, I was very interested in crime intelligence.'

At the same time he was also raising a growing family with wife Chris; their three children – Tanya, Paul and Mark – all suffered from asthma. A family doctor suggested they move north to the sub-tropical climes of Queensland.

Jim Slade was sworn in as a constable of the Queensland Police Force in late July 1976. He had unwittingly joined a force rife with political in-fighting and low on morale. In addition, the war between the Police Union and Commissioner Ray Whitrod was about to hit fever pitch. Premier Bjelke-Petersen was secretly trying to remove Whitrod, and Inspector Terry Lewis of Charleville was lobbying the Premier and politicians against the Whitrod regime.

Slade, the forensic shooter, had no interest in politics. He was just itching to gather intelligence on crooks, to get out into the field, to work undercover and bring some substantial kills to the table. He was initially posted to the working-class suburb of Woodridge and it was there that he rode out, from a distance, the great battle of Whitrod.

Within months, he would be hand-picked to work in a squad in headquarters that would bring him face to face, many times over, with some of the biggest criminal cases of the 1970s. He would go on to be anointed by none other than one of Queensland's finest ever detectives, and later one of its most notorious – Tony Murphy.

Town and City

Brisbane's activist students had been relatively quiet since the Springbok apartheid demonstrations, which had rocked the city five years earlier, but by July 1976 something again stirred their ire. Prime Minister Malcolm Fraser refused to increase student allowances across the country, and it was enough to fire up students on campus at the University of Queensland in St Lucia.

Student Union president Richard Spencer – studying law and economics – began mobilising recruits in June. A half-page advertisement in the 22 June issue of the university magazine *Semper Floreat* declared: 'Protest Demand Against Federal Government Education Cuts. Student Strike! Thurs 29 July 10 am – 3 pm. March into Town. Rally City Square 1 pm.'

About 1000 students marched with cloth banners and placards affixed to timber sticks from the campus, down Sir Fred Schonell Drive, up Gailey Road then around the bend of the river at Toowong, along Coronation Drive, and into the city to King George Square. Their protest signs were innocuous. 'Save Education', some of them read.

Spencer recalls: 'I was committed to doing it grandly and, using the portable megaphone, collected a bumper crop of students to rally and "march" from campus. [It was] more fun than lectures.

'Off we strode, chanting, enjoying the camaraderie, a sunny day ... along Gailey Road where we waved at the Special Branch officers photographing from a strategic block of units, on past the Regatta [Hotel] and straight down Coronation Drive.'

At the head of the march was diminutive student Rosemary Severin, 27, of Bardon. Severin worked as a part-time cleaner to support her studies. It was her first ever protest march. As the group progressed alongside the river, police stood prepared to block the march beneath the cream stone arches of the William Jolly Bridge. At the forefront of the police blockade was the burly Brisbane Metropolitan Traffic Superintendent Inspector Michael Beattie.

High on the bridge were stationed news cameramen from the city's television stations up on Mount Coot-tha. They had the perfect vantage point to witness the protest if violence broke out.

'I went to the rear to drive the march forward in case there was any nonsense,' Spencer recalls. 'Inspector Beattie and his colleagues moved in and broke up the bannered frontline. In the melee Rosemary Severin was assaulted. I pushed the column from the rear in the manner of *Rawhide/ Bonanza* and returned to the front ... with the rear moving forward [and] the re-grouping ... an amorphous unstoppable tank ... basically we ran over/through/around the police ... Rosemary was brought to my attention and I felt a large egg contusion on her head.'

As the *Courier-Mail* reported: 'Police, shepherding them in cars, stopped the march in Coronation Drive near Grey Street and confiscated large banners and some posters mounted on sticks. There was a brief tug of war. The students claimed police brutality. A girl said she was hit with a baton.'

That girl was Severin. 'Whoever hit me gave me a hard hit,' she later said. 'And I think he did it on purpose. I can't believe it was an accident.'

It transpired that it was Beattie who struck Severin on the back of the head. He claimed it was unintentional. He said he drew his baton to wrap students on the knuckles and force them to relinquish their 'illegal' banners, when 'a head got in the way'.

After the fracas the students finally gathered in King George Square. 'There the rally settled into some rambling political speeches,' says Spencer. 'I caught up with University Librarian Derek Fielding and told him I would be making [a] complaint to the Police Commissioner. He promised to inform Zelman Cowen [UQ Vice-Chancellor].

'Then I gave my speech – it was short, to the point: the march had been ambushed and attacked by the police, a student injured and I would be making [a] complaint. This was the bite which appeared on the TV news that night.'

The following day Cowen telephoned Spencer and offered to accompany him to the office of Commissioner Whitrod at police headquarters where the complaint would be formally lodged.

'Whitrod was glum,' remembers Spencer. 'I made [the] complaint, Zelman supported … Whitrod readily yet resignedly promised to investigate, at once admitting the process would be challenging due to the "old guard". We got word the press was gathering outside and it was arranged we would leave by a back entrance, which we did.'

Commissioner Whitrod, on further advice from his minister, Max Hodges, ordered an inquiry into the Beattie assault. In a memo to Hodges dated 30 July, Whitrod wrote:

At the request of the President of the Queensland Students Union, MR. RICHARD SPENCER, who called on me today, accompanied by the Vice-Chancellor of the University of Queensland, Sir Zelman Cowen, I have agreed to enquire into the conduct of police on duty on Thursday, 29th July 1976 in relation to a demonstration by University Students.

I have detailed Chief Superintendent Becker, who is the Senior Officer responsible for FORCE discipline, and Inspector W. Galligan, Officer-in-Charge, CRIMINAL INVESTIGATION

BRANCH, who is also President of the Police Officers Union.

They are to begin their investigation on Monday next and complete it at the earliest opportunity. R.W. Whitrod, Commissioner of Police.

The scenario was, in microcosm, the distillation of all of Whitrod's problems since coming to Queensland. Here he was faced with an old-school member of the force using violence against a young, defenceless university student. Here an ugly, ill-educated brutality clashed with academia. It underlined everything he had been working for and cherished, both morally and intellectually.

It was the perfect storm for Premier Bjelke-Petersen. With everything he thought he knew about the growing chaos in the police force and the disenchantment of the rank and file, picked up on his aerial zig-zagging across the state, it gave the Premier the ideal opportunity to slap down his Police Minister and Commissioner.

On Sunday 1 August the *Sunday Mail* revealed the Premier's fury in a page-one story: JOH DELAYS INQUIRY ON STUDENT CLASH. Bjelke-Petersen stated that the so-called inquiry would be referred to state Cabinet. He, not the Police Commissioner, would decide if an inquiry would be held.

In his defence, Whitrod said he had acted under 'certain instructions' from Hodges. 'I cannot reveal what these instructions were,' he told the press. 'The only person who can tell you is the Minister himself.' Hodges could not be contacted for comment.

On Tuesday 3 August, a petite Severin was pictured on page one of the *Courier-Mail*, nursing her still sore head. Over in George Street, Cabinet met to thrash out the issue. To the shock of observers at that meeting, the brawl between Bjelke-Petersen and Hodges turned into a real 'dog fight'.

'We decided that if there is an inquiry, it should be into those who broke the law,' said a defiant Premier.

That afternoon, Hodges released his own press statement. 'I was standing up for a principle. I was trying to find out what happened and who was at fault.' Regarding the rumours he was about to be removed as Police Minister, Hodges said he'd 'tough it out'.

Two days later, unbeknown to Hodges and Whitrod, Bjelke-Petersen received a letter from former National Party candidate for the seat of Ryan (encompassing western suburban Brisbane and in particular, Bardon, and Lewis's residence at 12 Garfield Drive), Doug Mactaggart.

Mactaggart came from a well-known Queensland family of respected stock and station agents. He was archetypal country and deemed 'a good bloke'.

MP for Landsborough, Mike Ahern, knew the Mactaggart family well. 'He [Doug] would judge you by the strength of your handshake,' says Ahern. 'He got conned [by Lewis]. He didn't know. Lewis put it over him very well.'

In fact years earlier, when Lewis was removed as head of the JAB, promoted to commissioned rank and was about to be exiled in Charleville, a farewell party for Lewis was held at the National Hotel.

The function was also an opportunity for the incoming head of the JAB, Ron Edington, to be introduced to the troops. 'I'll never forget it,' Edington recalls. 'They asked me to come down to the National Hotel and introduced me to everyone as taking Terry's place. I waited outside the pub for a good while then I went in and had a couple of beers. Bischof was there. They introduced me and told me they had a big night [planned] that night, they were [going down] to Mactaggart's, the family that had the wool store. They had a penthouse. They went down there and finished the night there.'

It was typical of Lewis to see someone like Mactaggart as a potential conduit to the Premier – he had both the ear of Bjelke-Petersen and sitting members of the National Party – if there was an opportunistic crack, Lewis would find it.

How then could it hurt if Lewis offered to help Mactaggart in his election campaign and hand out flyers and how-to-vote cards for the man who may become the member for Ryan? If Mactaggart won, it might pay off dividends somewhere down the track.

Mactaggart's letter to the Premier was virtually a character reference for Lewis. It read: 'I know that he has no religious bias whatsoever. His honesty is unquestionable. He is loyal to your Government and incidentally he supported my Ryan campaign.'

By the following Tuesday, Hodges was out of the Police Ministry, replaced by Tom Newbery. In the cabinet reshuffle, Hodges was given Tourism.

The Premier said of Hodges' removal: 'I've known for a long time that the Police Union has had disagreements with Mr Hodges and the Police Commissioner. This is the opportunity to give a change of drivers. A change is good. A change of climate for your health is good.'

To his surprise, student protestor Richard Spencer was contacted by a disappointed Hodges: 'I was to receive, out of the blue, a telephone call from Police Minister Max Hodges. He was disturbed that he was being replaced. He did not agree with the course taken by Bjelke[-Petersen]. I think he wanted to reach out and say it was not his doing. It was like talking to the glum Whitrod, only more agitated ...'

Two days after Hodges was dumped, the Premier wrote back to Mactaggart: 'Rest assured I will be closely watching future promotions to see if there is any way I can help Terry.'

As the letter attested, there was little question Bjelke-Petersen had Lewis in mind for higher rank during the Hodges drama. And with Hodges gone, Whitrod had lost his most important ally.

Even Queensland Police Union chief Ron Edington had heard of the Mactaggart connection. 'Lewis, being smart, socially, he got onto this bloody wool broker bloke, Mactaggart,' says Edington. 'Mactaggart was strong with Joh so he said, "Promote Lewis".'

Simultaneously, out in Charleville, Lewis's duties, (since his verbal altercation with Hodges at the civic function in Cunnamulla, and after both Hodges and Whitrod had made their surprise visit to town), were taking on a slightly more politicised hue.

His diaries recorded that he acted on a complaint issued to Minister Ron Camm (his ally at the civic dinner just a few months earlier). Then, at the urging of local member Neil Turner, Lewis was asked to address a meeting of the Young National Party on 'Crime in the Community'.

A short time later, he recorded that he went to the Charleville airport with Turner and 'met Hon. K. Tomkins, Minister for Lands; Mr J.Corbett, MHR, member for Maranoa' and others, and conveyed them to the Charleville Motel. On that same night he 'met Mr Sparkes … [State] President … National Party'.

Almost overnight, Inspector Terence Lewis was mixing with some extremely influential political high-flyers.

Back in Brisbane, Whitrod was a commissioner alone and defenceless.

In the Foul Wake of Frank Bischof

For a few short years in the late 1950s and early 1960s, Mrs Mary Margaret Fels, farmer's wife of Underwood Road, Eight Mile Plains, lived a life of excitement and luxury that she could not have imagined. As the lover of former Police Commissioner Frank Bischof, she was treated to holidays on the Gold Coast, hobnobbing with the likes of the Roberts boys from the National Hotel and the rest of Brisbane high society who partied in their holiday houses along Hedges Avenue at Mermaid Beach. Sometimes she took her youngest son Ross along for the trip. It was a world away from the Fels family's little vegetable farm on the fringe of the Brisbane CBD.

By the mid-1970s, a decade after the scandal blew up, and the mother of six was demonised in the Brisbane gossip rags and sued for defamation by Bischof, her marriage to husband Alonzo was all but over. She moved to the little township of Buderim on the Sunshine Coast, 90 kilometres north of Brisbane, and home to the largest ginger factory in the Southern Hemisphere. There she settled into a de facto relationship that, under the circumstances, brought her and her children some happiness.

Alonzo, however, never stopped loving Mary. They both refused to talk to anyone, inside or outside the family, about the Bischof scandal. Alonzo also moved on, selling the Underwood Road farm. He never took up another relationship.

Nobody knew the truth at the heart of the Fels scandal – not the press and not the public. No one was aware of the depth of Bischof's depravity that had destroyed a good, hard-working Brisbane family, and would continue to wreak havoc for many years.

In the late 1950s one of the Fels boys, Geoff, had come to the attention of police for a silly teenage prank – he'd lifted some hubcaps off a car. Mary had taken her son to see Commissioner Bischof, who famously held 'clinics' every Saturday at his office headquarters at North Quay. There, he set wayward boys and girls onto the straight and narrow, proffering his firm, fatherly advice that would steer the children towards a clean-living and morally correct life.

To the public, the clinic was tangible evidence of Bischof's deep commitment to the youth of Queensland. He would, in 1963, establish the Juvenile Aid Bureau – the first of its kind in Australia – and install Terry Lewis as its founding head. Hundreds of children drifted through Uncle Frank's clinics over the years.

This was the first meeting between the soon-to-be lovers and also how Bischof met Geoff. He would soon meet Geoff's brother Dennis, and in turn their little brother Ross Fels. Mary could not have known what she had drawn herself and her children into.

An affair with Bischof commenced. Was it the excitement, the novelty, for the farmer's wife from Eight Mile Plains? Was it the thrill of a life she could have never dreamt of, being so close to a man with immense power, a celebrity of sorts, a snappy dresser, punter and socialite with seemingly endless rolls of cash at his disposal?

It may have blinded her to Bischof's other target – her children. When the affair with Fels was eventually made public in the 1960s, Bischof wrangled with his lover through the courts, keeping the full story away from the public gaze. In the end, it was settled in court and disappeared. Sub judice had seen to that.

Throughout the court battle, Bischof had ordered police to monitor and harass the Fels family. It was nothing for them to see police cars parked out the front of the farm, watching their every move. Bischof needed to contain them – but why?

While the saga destroyed the Fels', Bischof saw out his commissionership partying at the National Hotel, milling with judges and politicians at the racetrack, throwing his muscle about, and extorting huge sums of graft from SP bookmakers, brothels and anywhere else he could turn a quid.

Then in 1969 Ross Fels, in his late teens, was walking along Adelaide Street in the city when he bumped into old 'Uncle Frank' Bischof. The Commissioner, due to retire within weeks, was walking alone in full regalia.

Fels stood in front of Bischof and blocked his path. 'Do you remember me?' Ross Fels demanded.

Bischof appeared confused. 'You do know you're talking to the Police Commissioner,' he responded arrogantly.

Fels identified himself and Bischof turned pale. According to Ross Fels, in the late 1950s Bischof – his mother's lover – sexually assaulted him. In addition, in the early 1960s, older brother Dennis Fels was instructed to go to one of Bischof's Saturday morning clinics. He'd already been once or twice before. This time he refused.

'He just wasn't going to go, come hell or high water,' remembers Ross Fels. 'When he had to go back this time he disappeared. He was terrified about having to go back into that bloody place.'

Dennis vanished on a Friday night and was found on the family farm on the Sunday evening. He would later allege that he refused to be in the Commissioner's company because Bischof had been 'feeling him up' at the sessions.

Dennis would not escape Bischof's wrath. The police tailed him, harassed and provoked him. In the end and years later, he was forced to leave Queensland.

'Our family was screwed over by the police,' Ross Fels says. 'What happened to me with Bischof when I was six, I thought nothing of it. It meant nothing to me. Well, not nothing. He scratched my genitals. But years later I started talking to my brothers ...'

Then there was the older boy Geoff. Just before his death, decades later, Ross sat with him and they had a long talk. They discussed Bischof.

'When we spoke about it, Geoff just cried,' says Ross Fels. 'A grown, adult man. He cried. I stopped at that point.'

The scandal of the Commissioner and Mary Margaret Fels had never been what it appeared. It was not about a woman who had fallen for the charms of the 'Big Fella', and been scorned by his rejection of her years later.

Was it in fact the story of a man – the most powerful police officer in the State – who had set up these Saturday morning clinics not for the benefit of troubled children and their parents, but as an arrangement to trawl for vulnerable kids and satisfy Bischof's sexual proclivities? How many other children had Bischof laid his hands on, and how many other families were left destroyed in his wake?

It must have weighed heavily on Mary Margaret Fels, that she had unknowingly put her children in such an insidious position. But it was too late. The family had fractured beyond repair.

Throughout the final years of his tenure as Police Commissioner into the late 1960s, Bischof had been in and out of hospital with nervous breakdowns and bouts of poor health. Now, in retirement, he continually failed to find solid ground after life as one of the state's most powerful and famous policemen. After decades of murders and hard criminals, of prostitutes and rapists, and then the privilege of the commissionership which saw him, like a spoiled child, take what he wanted when he wanted it – the lot of the pottering suburban gardener did not suit him.

At one point during his retirement he secured some menial employment, applying for work as a ticket seller with Mater Prize Homes. According to one witness he cajoled senior members of the organisation into taking him on, offering free dinners in some of the city's finer restaurants. He was subsequently hired, but dismissed a few weeks later after being caught stealing money off the ticket sales.

The childless former Queensland Father of the Year had, in fact, been the father of the early incarnation of 'The Joke' – that system of graft and protection payments levelled at the state's SP bookmakers that yielded hundreds of thousands of dollars to Bischof and his bagmen. Under his watch, he had established the culture for systemic police corruption that, by the time of his retirement in 1969, had taken root and flourished. But the Bischof ego found it all too hard to let go.

The humble cactus grower and dog lover of The Gap was becoming the suburb's resident eccentric, and while he irregularly kept in touch with his earlier protégés – Terry Lewis and Tony Murphy, in particular – his crimes as Commissioner became legend within the police force.

What Bischof started in the late 1950s grew into a murderous and ruthless system of greed that ultimately distorted the democratic infrastructure of the state of Queensland. In the detritus, too, were broken families.

As for Alonzo Fels, he always held out hope that one day he would be 'reunited' with his wife Mary. He purchased two grave plots – side by side – in the lawn section of the Mount Gravatt Cemetery. He would die in the winter of 1980, aged just 67 years.

Today, the plot beside him remains vacant.

The Theatrical Constable Moore

He had wanted to be a movie star.

Instead, he ended up in the Queensland Police Force, and despite the blokey culture he found himself immersed in, young Constable David Moore found an unexpected ally in Police Commissioner Ray Whitrod.

By 1976, Moore, a constable for just two years, had done his penance in Mobile Patrols, based out of the old Petrie Terrace barracks. Mobile Patrols was famously the purgatory for recalcitrant officers, for those who bucked, however remotely, the status quo. It was also the final stable for senior mid-ranking officers limping towards retirement.

Despite this, Moore enjoyed the experience. 'You were put with a senior officer, a constable first class or senior constable, and given a designated area,' says an officer who worked with Moore. 'You were largely sent out for an eight-hour shift; you handled everything given to you. You were vigilant. Some police weren't.

'Again, it was a tough thing. Back then it was a lot safer to be a police officer on the road because police were feared.'

There was something different about Moore, too. He was smart, artistic and was heavily involved in amateur theatrics across the city. He spoke well and was always presentable. Just four months into Mobile Patrols he was seconded to the Operations centre in the old Makerston Street headquarters.

Operations was on the first floor and Whitrod was on the third floor. Moore was put on radio. He did switchboard and telex. He did the old microfiche system – car registration numbers. He had multiple tasks; but again, he was surrounded by people who were being punished or old sergeants who didn't want to do anything.

Meanwhile, Moore was performing in a play being staged at Brisbane City Hall. With cheek and confidence, he sent his boss an invitation to attend.

'At that time Whitrod was being quite progressive,' a colleague of Moore says. 'He would do a newsletter. It was an interesting way he would identify different people in the force and compliment them or give praise to people if they'd done good work.

'Moore contacted Whitrod and invited him to the play. He sent him tickets. Would he like to come? To his astonishment Whitrod turned up with his wife, and he brought his next door neighbour, a doctor.

'Moore met with Whitrod after [the show] and his neighbour was ecstatic. Whitrod probably couldn't believe it. Moore subsequently got a little write up in the newsletter.'

Unwittingly, Moore had raised eyebrows among the anti-Whitrod forces. Who was this young constable who had somehow inveigled himself with Coco (as Whitrod was facetiously nicknamed by his detractors)? And via the arts, of all things?

As Whitrod faced down the relentless heat of the Rat Pack and its formidable foot soldiers following the student protest march incident, Moore decided to pursue his dream and head off to London to seek fame and fortune. Movie stars didn't man a police switchboard in a former egg board building on the bend of the Brisbane River.

Moore drafted a report and requested a 12-month leave of absence – unheard of in the Queensland Police Force. He didn't submit it to his inspector first, but sent it straight to Whitrod instead. It caused a furore. Moore was in serious trouble. He had overridden the system.

Whitrod had assistants, who looked at Moore's application, and wrote a letter to tell him the leave was not approved. Whitrod saw it and the Commissioner crossed out 'not' and wrote 'this is recommended'.

All of a sudden the other officers were asking – what power did Moore have that he could convince the Commissioner? 'It was probably where the rot started for Moore in relation to that,' the colleague adds.

Moore duly went to Europe and returned within six months, not famous and homesick. He slotted straight back into his old job in Operations. Within days he was summonsed to Whitrod's office. 'How did it all go?' Whitrod asked.

Moore fibbed. He said it went very well.

'I think you have enormous talent and I think you can do something for us,' said Whitrod. 'I'm going to make a position available at the Police Academy and get you to direct re-enactments of scenes of crime using drama.'

Whitrod had set up a specific crime scene investigation unit. He wanted to modernise it. He wanted to introduce new techniques. Moore would train members of the unit with his dramatic flair.

In the meantime, Moore would have to make up for his lack of hands-on police work while the academy specifics were ironed out. He had to work out of a suburban police station for a while. Where did he want to go?

Moore decided he would like to work at Mitchelton.

Neither Whitrod nor Moore could know that within a few short years Moore would, in a way, get at least part of his lifelong wish. 'Constable Dave' would become one of the most recognisable faces on Australian television. He would also become a lightning rod for trouble that would rock the Queensland Police Force to its foundations.

The Hippies of Cedar Bay

The beginning of the end for Whitrod was in fact sealed on a beautiful stretch of beach 2005 kilometres north-west of Brisbane and a little over 50 kilometres south of Cooktown. The place was called Cedar Bay.

Accessible usually by foot or boat, the bay area had been mined for tin from the late 1870s. By the mid-1970s, there was one former tin miner left – the hermit Bill Evans, or Cedar Bay Bill as he became known.

With his permission, two communes of hippies set up camp, one at the northern end of the beach and another to the south. The northerners were meat-eating and slaughtered pigs for food. The southerners were vegetarians, planted fruit trees and sheltered in well-tended huts. They smoked marihuana, lived naked, played music and reared children. They had 'new moon' parties and bothered nobody.

On the wet and humid morning of Sunday 29 August 1976, Laurel Pallister, with baby Tree on her hip, was enjoying the dawn at the southern end of the beach when she saw men in uniforms down at the water's edge.

Offshore was the patrol boat HMAS *Bayonet*, and the narcotics vessel *Jabiru*. Soon a helicopter was circling overhead, dropping officers down onto the beach. Simultaneously, other police and drug agents arrived at the bay's western flank by four-wheel-drive. A light aircraft criss-crossed overhead.

The pilot of the chartered helicopter – Wayne Knight, who was in his thirties – had at one time worked for the CIA's Air America, flying covert operations in the Vietnam War. As he landed with two Narcotics agents at the northern end of the beach he 'could see the faces of the hippies looking at us through the bush'.

The drug raid, ordered by the relatively newly installed Cairns Police District Inspector Robert Gray, saw 34 male officers and two females storm the communes. They chopped down fruit trees, set fire to huts and terrorised the residents. Many of the hippies were handcuffed. Twelve were taken to Cooktown to face charges of drug possession and vagrancy. In the end, police and Narcotics agents retrieved a glass jar containing 120 Indian hemp seeds, and 120 small Indian hemp plants.

It wasn't until Tuesday 31 August that a small story about the raid appeared in the *Courier-Mail*: HIPPIES WOKE TO BIG DRUG RAID.

'Early on Sunday the commune of 34 people, including several children, arose to find their normally tranquil retreat swarming with police and Federal Narcotics agents.' The story quoted a police spokesman saying there was some resistance as police began to search the huts, but no real violence.

In fact, the story had been broken earlier by Steve Gray, a Cairns correspondent for the alternative 4ZZ radio station, and word had gotten to the impressive young reporter Andrew Olle, a gun on the national television current affairs show, *This Day Tonight*. Olle immediately headed for Cedar Bay.

With a teacher's strike dominating the headlines in Queensland, the hippie raid disappeared from the news until the evening of Tuesday 7 September, when Olle's story was aired on the ABC. In an instant the Cedar Bay raid had gone national.

The next day, Queensland's Opposition police spokesman and the member for Rockhampton, Keith Wright, raised in parliament the allegations of police brutality during the operation, stemming from the television report. He said police had used 'storm-trooper' tactics, and demanded an inquiry.

In addition he had seen photographic evidence that revealed huts had been deliberately torched and children's clothes and food had been piled in a heap and ignited with kerosene. Wright added that water tanks had been 'shot up' by police.

The new Police Minister, Tom Newbery, had a different version of events, the truth behind the Olle report that he considered 'one of the most blatantly biased pieces of so-called objective reporting I have ever seen'.

Newbery said police had seized not 120 small hemp plants, but a virtual crop worth $20,000 on the street. He described the northern Cedar Bay commune as a group of undesirables who lived in complete squalor – 'the stench of excrement was overpowering and the rotting carcasses of two wild pigs lay near a sluggish creek which served as a water supply'.

Newbery added that many residents of the area were armed and fired shots at police when they fled into the jungle. 'There will be no haven in North Queensland where people can disregard the law,' thundered Newbery. 'This obvious campaign to discredit police action only increases my own resolve and that of the Queensland Police Force to attack the drug problem with renewed dedication and vigour. I give my full support to the Queensland Police Force in their efforts to stamp out the presence of this evil in our society.'

Bill Hewitt, who was then the Liberal Party member for Chatsworth, never hid his distaste for Bjelke-Petersen. He had no problem with police carrying out drug investigations, but he couldn't understand why 'they had to be belted, why their homes were burned down'.

'It was an excess use of authority by the police,' Hewitt remembers. 'I made a statement that the police conduct should be inquired into. That made it into the press.

'At a joint party meeting I had no illusions. I knew I was going to get a bit of stick. Joh barely said a word when the subject of Cedar Bay was introduced. Then six or seven fellows, one after the other, stood up and did me over. It was brutal. I was a mess when I came out. I took it very badly.'

The demand for an official investigation into police behaviour grew louder, with members of the communes threatening to lay charges against police. Bjelke-Petersen said he did not personally order the raid. 'The first I knew of it was when I read of it in the *Courier-Mail*,' the Premier said.

Towards the middle of September, ALP Queensland Senator Jim Keeffe tabled in Federal Parliament photographs of the damage done by police to the communes during the raid. The political heat over Cedar Bay further intensified.

To nullify it, local newspapers in Brisbane, particularly the *Sunday Mail*, began running stories week after week about the dangers of drugs to society. In addition, a new method of rating senior police, introduced by Whitrod, was leaked to the press.

'A new system under which it is claimed commissioned officers – ranked at inspector and above – are being secretly assessed by other commissioned officers has sparked off a bitter new row in the Police Force,' it was reported.

The messages of the twin diversion from the Cedar Bay story were obvious – drugs were the bane of a moral, civilised society, and those associated with them were therefore immoral and a danger to the community; and the hapless Queensland Police Commissioner, Ray Whitrod, had lost control of his men.

(Lewis himself underwent two such 'secret' assessments around this time and emerged with almost perfect results. One described him as a 'shrewd, intelligent thinker', whose 'potential should be used and stretched to the utmost while he is still a comparatively young man'. Another concluded: 'Has capacity to carry higher ranks and acquit himself well in those ranks.')

These media distractions, however, managed to halt the march of the story of the Cedar Bay fiasco.

In the middle of all this Whitrod suffered another serious blow from a different quarter. He had lost an ally in his minister, Max Hodges. Then one of his most trusted men and assistant commissioner, Norm Gulbransen, retired on 15 September.

By the end of September – a month after the scandal began – the Liberal Party state executive called for an inquiry into the police actions at Cedar Bay, as did the president of the Young Nationals state council, Peter Slipper. Bjelke-Petersen and his colleagues ignored the pleas.

Then came the bombshell: Janice Lambert and Michael Ballister, both victims of the Cedar Bay raid, filed complaints against police in Cairns.

On Friday 2 October Commissioner Whitrod declared he would decide the following Monday if he would order an investigation into the growing controversy. He was once again between a rock and a hard place – the raid had gone ahead on his watch, though it appeared to be an initiative directly out of Cairns and divorced from decision-making at headquarters in Brisbane.

Did Whitrod stay quiet and take responsibility for it? Or, as in the student protest incident at the William Jolly Bridge just weeks earlier, did he go forward and investigate the poor behaviour of his officers?

Whitrod took the latter option. He was also deliberately provoking the Premier. It would be a final test of Whitrod's authority and that of his office in the face of Bjelke-Petersen. On the Monday of Whitrod's decision – 5 October – state Cabinet was meeting in Cairns, and the Commissioner would be there coincidentally to open the new Cairns police station. A showdown loomed.

Bjelke-Petersen, to be expected, stood firm. He said the government would not abdicate its responsibilities by setting up inquiries. 'Allegations are being thrown at our police force that they are guilty of violation of civil liberties. I reject the claim.'

The next day, in direct defiance of the Premier, Whitrod ordered that his top investigator, Don Becker with a junior officer, immediately travel to Cairns and directly question the complainants from Cedar Bay. They were due up north within 24 hours. It was a direct order in contravention of the Premier's directive.

On Friday 29 October, Whitrod received Becker's 403-page report and forwarded it to the Crown Law office.

The next Monday, 1 November, the new Police Minister Tom Newbery took the report, in his locked attaché case, into a Cabinet meeting.

The press speculated that the report was 'hard-hitting' and that at least two police were expected to be charged with arson as a result of its recommendations. In reality, four were to be charged, including Cairns inspector, Robert Gray.

In the midst of this drama, Lewis in Charleville had a phone call from somebody – was it the member for Merthyr Don Lane or the

Premier's Press Secretary Allen Callaghan? – that he was likely to be Gulbransen's replacement as assistant commissioner.

His old mate Tony Murphy, in Longreach, drew up a typed list for Lewis to contemplate. It was a cheat sheet of who he could trust or not trust down at headquarters: Guests (Bischof); Friends (Sgts. Ron Redmond and Noel Dwyer, Ross Beer, Pat Glancy, Graham Leadbetter); Capable (Insps. Syd Atkinson and Brian Hayes, Sgt Graeme Parker); and Others (Whitrod, Bill Taylor, Jim Voigt, Arthur Pitts, Basil Hicks and Lorelle Saunders).

Lewis extended the ambit of those he couldn't trust. He handwrote at the bottom of the list: 'all present CIU [Crime Intelligence Unit]'.

The timing of Whitrod's show of defiance was spectacularly bad. The Commissioner's lie about the 'kill sheets' was fresh in Bjelke-Petersen's mind, and now the police chief had the temerity to publicly snub his boss's directive. In addition, Whitrod wanted to push four more police through the courts on serious charges, despite the string of failures prosecuted out of his Crime Intelligence Unit.

The last straw came a week after Whitrod received his hefty Cedar Bay report – Jack 'The Bagman' Herbert and his co-accused were acquitted after their epic Southport Betting Case corruption trial. Herbert, who had retired from the force medically unfit prior to the verdict, crowed to the press that the force was in need of an administrative 'shake-up'.

Herbert said he was set to seek new employment. 'It will be hard because I'm not trained for anything except police work,' Herbert said. The Bagman had, indeed, been doing it tough in the limbo of his trial. Out of work, and in and out of court during a case that lasted almost two years, Herbert relied on the charity of his friends.

One was Lewis's old mate Barry Maxwell, proprietor of the Belfast Hotel in Queen Street. Belfast manager Les Hounslow remembers Maxwell taking pity on the Herbert family. 'I always drove Barry Maxwell around because he was always pissed, but I recall one day him saying he had a couple of boxes of food – meat and vegetables – that he had to go somewhere and drop off,' says Hounslow. 'We went to East Brisbane. It was a pretty low-class looking unit. We went in there and it was Jack Herbert and his wife and the kids. I think he was out of work, yeah. That's why he got the food. I [also] saw Maxwell handing him over a wad of money.'

A Monster Comes Calling

Over at the University of Queensland campus in St Lucia, Lewis's friend in academia, the criminologist Paul Wilson, was working in his office when he received a very curious visit from a man called Clarence Osborne.

Osborne, then in his late fifties, had been a chief court reporter in Brisbane before being transferred to Parliament House as a Hansard reporter. He was meticulous, exact, analytical and did not suffer fools gladly.

Osborne was so accomplished at shorthand that experts from the Pitman college in London contacted this diminutive public servant in Brisbane if they had a problem. He was, arguably in the opinion of his colleagues, one of the finest shorthand writers in the world. His obsessiveness not only applied to his professional work but to his hobbies. At one point he was a global expert on the breeding of budgerigars.

Malcolm McMillan, then chief of staff to leader of the Opposition, Tom Burns, remembers Osborne as an affable oddball.

'Osborne was a short man with a very friendly, outgoing person-ality, more often than not with a big smile most of the time,' McMillan recalls. 'He used to wear a chain or a leather band around his neck which had something on it. I'm not sure, but it might have been an elephant. The quality which I vividly recall was that he always used to holiday in Thailand – all the time. He would share that with people, not conceal or hide it.'

Apart from travel, it transpired that Osborne had another more disturbing past-time. Since the mid-1950s he had engaged in sexual relations with over 2000 underage boys. In addition, he had kept meticulous files on each one – the majority of them children – including tape recordings (eight kilometres worth), explicit photographs and data on their genitals kept in an index card system.

A colleague of Osborne's, who worked with him as a trainee in the early 1970s, recalls dealings he had with the public servant: 'He used to take and develop his own photos – eight by tens – of the boys he went with. He would show these photographs around at work. I saw hundreds of them. There were even pictures of babies.

'He was on about it every day in the office, about picking up hitch-hikers and rooting them. He was a little muscular fellow, had plenty of money and was very clever.'

Osborne lived quietly in a single-level weatherboard house at 54 Eyre Street, Mount Gravatt. The southern fence line of the deep block fronted onto Orb Lane. Neighbours found the bachelor a bit eccentric but never had any trouble with him. In the backyard were two self-contained sheds with windows, as well as a garage down the side of the house. He owned a number of weights and other gym equipment and was often seen in the yard conducting health and fitness classes with young boys.

When Osborne travelled to the University of Queensland campus to see Dr Wilson on that day in 1976 however, he was an agitated man. He arrived at Wilson's office door with a bag stuffed with paperwork and other documents.

Wilson, overworked and going through personal relationship problems at the time, agreed to talk with Osborne. The criminologist was wary of the stocky little visitor with 'penetrating eyes'.

As Wilson would later write: 'He was seeing me, it appeared, because I was involved in the Queensland Civil Liberties Council and had a reputation ... for attempting to protect the rights of the individual against the might of the state – particularly that agent of the state called the police force.'

What concerned Osborne was that a pornographic film of men having sex that he had purchased by mail order from Denmark had been seized by Australian Customs.

Osborne, normally superior of air and full of braggadocio, was tense. He told Wilson he wasn't so much concerned about being arrested, but that police might confiscate his 'research' – the unprecedented and lurid documentation of his sexual activities with children that he had amassed over two decades. Some of the children caught in Osborne's net, it would transpire, were by this time leading figures in Brisbane, some having come from privileged backgrounds. They were married, had children and reputations to uphold.

'The significance of all this material was not apparent to Osborne nor indeed to me,' Wilson later wrote. 'It was almost as though Osborne had collected data just for the sake of collecting it without any real objective in mind. He was certainly close to his material and several times called it his "life work" and continually worried about the Commonwealth Police taking it away from him and posterity.

'Over the next two months I met Clarence Osborne on several occasions and each time he brought me new material to look at. Transcripts, tape-recordings and his manuscript documenting his own life were freely given to me and supplemented by face-to-face conversations of how he had met the young men in his life and why he acted as he did.'

Had Osborne lost sight of the fact that his 'life work' also constituted criminal behaviour? It would appear ironic that a deputy-chief Hansard reporter might be so inexact with his private activities.

Wilson says: 'I got the strong impression he felt the end was near and he didn't want this hugely important information to be lost to posterity. I think in his own mind he didn't think it was a crime even though it was clearly a crime. He didn't seem so much afraid of the police. He seemed more afraid about losing what he thought was really important research.'

Did Wilson face a moral dilemma? Did he accept this extraordinary story that had come out of the blue and inform the authorities that a major paedophile was at work in Brisbane?

'I think I did have that, but it was made pretty clear to me that he thought he was going to be arrested and that the police were going to be on it, if they weren't on it already,' reflects Wilson. 'I didn't see what else I could do as the police, as he was indicating, were going to be catching up with him. That was the reason he came to me. He thought he was going to be finished.'

Indeed, in 1973 not one but two secret inquiries were held by the Public Service Board into Osborne. Allegations were gathered from court reporting staff who had seen the photos. As a result, the chief court reporter was moved to the Hansard Bureau at Parliament House where his contact with young people was minimised. Here was a case of paedophilia that, in its magnitude, was unprecedented in not just Australian criminal history, but globally. Yet it would be years before Osborne's atrocities would be exposed, and he labelled a 'monster'.

The Regrets of Kingsley Fancourt

By September 1976, while Inspector Lewis was building his contacts out at Charleville and seeing to the usual array of cattle theft offences and domestic disputes, about 700 kilometres north at Anakie, on the gemfields of western Queensland, a relatively young and talented police officer named Kingsley Winston Fancourt had decided to call it a day, and resign.

Fancourt, born in Sydney, joined the Queensland Police Force in 1966 and immediately took to the job. He had found his life calling.

Tall, powerful and intelligent, he had been stationed in Ayr, Far North Queensland, early in his career before settling in Brisbane. In 1973 he was seconded to the Licensing Branch and its headquarters in Upper Roma Street.

'I was only in there about two weeks and they sat me down near Jack Herbert,' Fancourt recalls. 'He used to dress in a short-sleeved white shirt. Open neck. Spick and span. His way of talking was precise; he was very well spoken.

'I spotted this black thing on his arm. I just had a mate die up in Ayr from a melanoma on his back. I said "Jack, give me a look at that? That's a bloody melanoma." It was like a black wart.'

Fancourt suggested he go see a doctor.

'He went and got it seen to,' he says. 'It had just gone into stage three melanoma, the point of no return. They took a huge piece out of his arm. Not long after that he went on sick leave. He left the police force medically unfit [in October 1974] because of this melanoma. He used to say to me: "Fanny, you've saved my life."'

Soon, Fancourt was working undercover. He grew his hair, a beard, and dressed in jeans and leather jackets. But it wasn't long before he began to see a pattern of vice and gambling in the city, particularly in the sleazy streets and back lanes of Fortitude Valley. Then in late 1974 he stumbled onto something that would change the course of his life.

Fancourt had been hanging around Geraldo Bellino's illegal casino at 142 Wickham Street, the Valley, run by Luciano Scognamiglio. At about 10 p.m. on Saturday 7 December 1974, he trudged up the narrow stairs and into the casino. He left his partner, senior officer Arthur Volz, downstairs in an unmarked car.

'We were driving around Brisbane looking for something to do,' Fancourt recalls. 'We pulled up outside Wickham Street. Arthur said just slip in there and have a look and we can put it on the occurrence sheet that we'd been in there. I'd been in there many times.'

Fancourt was met by Scognamiglio and they had a discussion.

Fancourt:	How has everybody been to you lately, Luci?
Scognamiglio:	Good, but what do you mean?
Fancourt:	Have you been paying anybody lately?
Scognamiglio:	No, what do you mean?
Fancourt:	Have you been paying anybody for tip-offs about raids?
Scognamiglio:	No, but why not?
Fancourt:	Are you offering me money to tip you off?
Scognamiglio:	Yes, why not?
Fancourt:	I don't want any of your money.
Scognamiglio:	Why not? There is nothing wrong. I pay you, I even go off when you say.
Fancourt:	What do you mean 'go off' when I say?
Scognamiglio:	Pinch the game.
Fancourt:	I'll see you again Luci and we'll talk some more.

Fancourt couldn't believe what had just transpired. Even if much of the conversation was in jest, an illegal casino operator had intimated that Fancourt could come onto the books with corrupt payments for information about impending raids by the Licensing Branch. Fancourt had been invited inside the tent.

Understanding the gravity of the situation, he went back downstairs to meet Volz. It was close to 11.30 p.m.

'I got back in the car. I was like a goldfish gulping air. I couldn't believe it,' says Fancourt. 'He put it on me; would I be interested in giving him information and being paid? Fifty dollars a month. I was only earning $119 a fortnight.'

Fancourt asked Volz to take him directly to police headquarters.

'What the bloody hell for?' Volz asked.

'Arthur, I can't tell you, please just trust me.'

At headquarters, Fancourt approached the duty inspector. 'I want to see the Commissioner,' Fancourt said.

'What do you want to see him about?'

'None of your business,' said Fancourt. 'It's extremely important and it's highly confidential.'

Commissioner Ray Whitrod was, as it transpired, out of the country at the time. Bill Taylor was in charge. 'I want to see Bill Taylor, then,' Fancourt insisted.

Taylor, who was at home in bed, came in to see Fancourt. 'We sat there until 1 a.m.,' Fancourt remembers. 'I told him that I was aware of all the corruption in the police force and where it was and my knowledge was they'd been trying to crack it for seven years. He didn't disagree with me.'

Arthur Pitts, the head of Licensing, was confidentially informed, as was senior officer Alec Jeppesen. The latter was appointed supervisor of the Fancourt situation. The imperative was to get hard evidence against Scognamiglio and to go deeper into his connections with corrupt police. It was decided Fancourt would wear a wire.

'I had to be very guarded,' Fancourt says. 'This had come down from the CIU [Whitrod's elite Crime Intelligence Unit]. They took me up to headquarters and fitted me up with this microphone. I had to engage him [Scognamiglio] in a conversation, get the admissions of what I had to do on tape, collect the money.

'I went there on a Sunday during the day. Mick [Cacciola, a fellow Licensing Branch officer] was in the boot of my Fairlane [with the wire's receiving equipment]. I pulled the Fairlane up just down the road from 142 Wickham Street. We did a couple of dry runs; we had to work out where the best reception was. We worked out this thing was good for about half a mile.'

Fancourt managed to tape conversations with Scognamiglio on three separate occasions throughout December. On 22 December, just as Fancourt and the team had hoped, Scognamiglio began revealing information about Herbert and the Rat Pack.

Scognamiglio: Jack [Herbert] was a good man.

Fancourt: You were friendly with Jack, were you?

Scognamiglio: Oh yes, good friends for five years.

Fancourt: Yes, very, very sad, actually Luci, very sad.

Scognamiglio: Yes, I am friendly with … the boss.

Fancourt: My own boss?

Scognamiglio: No, no, no, he still in the police, he no more Licensing Branch … big fellow he was, seven years.

Fancourt: Oh, Kev Foley.

Scognamiglio: No, [Tony] Murphy.

Fancourt: Who?

Scognamiglio: Murphy.

On Sunday 29 December, Fancourt returned to 142 Wickham Street and lured Scognamiglio out of the club and onto the footpath. The Italian was arrested on the spot by Alec Jeppesen.

'We had the hard evidence,' says Fancourt. 'My evidence both visual and audible; the money I'd been paid.'

In the first weeks of 1975 – not long after Scognamiglio's arrest – Fancourt was on night duty in the city when he and his partners decided to take a meal at the Lotus Room restaurant in Elizabeth Street, an eatery much favoured by the police. On this night he noticed a grey Mercedes reverse parking not far from Festival Hall. He thought nothing of it.

The next night, Fancourt again returned to Ray Sue-Tin's restaurant for a late dinner. He went downstairs, following the maitre'd, Sheree, and he and two colleagues sat down at a table and ordered.

It was then that Fancourt noticed Geraldo Bellino and four other men coming down the stairs. Fancourt quickly took his .38 revolver from its holster and hid it under a napkin on the table. The memory of the vehicle from the night before now made sense. It was one of Bellino's cars.

Fancourt only recognised one other member of Bellino's crew – a taxi driver with the nickname 'Cyclone', regularly seen parked outside Bellino's nightclub, Pinocchio's.

The situation, Fancourt understood, was potentially extremely dangerous. What was Bellino doing? Was this a show of force after Scognamiglio's arrest? Was this a threat?

Fancourt didn't wait to find out. 'We stood and pointed our guns at all five of them. I had Bellino and we marched them out into the kitchen. I grabbed Bellino by the throat and backed him up against the freezers. He was telling me that he was a good man … I had the pistol pressed up into his nostrils.'

All the while, as the confrontation unfolded, the Lotus Room's owner and chef Ray Sue-Tin could be heard in the background continuing to chop vegetables.

'I heard the toilet flush,' says Fancourt. His colleague later told him he tipped one of the bastards upside down in the toilet. 'I'd upset the ant's nest. It was a show of intimidation and it backfired on them.'

In the end, Scognamiglio absconded on bail and fled to Italy. Several months later he returned to Brisbane and was arrested on the airport tarmac after officer Cacciola got a tip-off through his Italian contacts.

The case against Scognamiglio went to the Crown Law office and a nolle prosequi was entered. It was incomprehensible to Fancourt that the case fell over.

What he didn't know at the time, however, was that someone had pieced together a fake official police statement from Fancourt over the Scognamiglio incident. The 12-page forgery was impeccably typed and went into some detail about conversations Fancourt had with Scognamiglio on those late-night visits to the illegal casino at 142 Wickham Street.

Not only did the statement present at the very least prima faci evidence that Fancourt had induced the defendant into making certain admissions, but it introduced invented police and civilian witnesses within the casino at the time who could, if needed, be called as witnesses to the inducement and thus a conspiracy at the instigation of Fancourt.

The statement was unsigned.

Fancourt was shattered, it was the end of his attempt to smash Herbert and the Rat Pack. 'I gave them the best shot available that they'd had for years,' Fancourt says. 'It was my career. I was very industrious. I would have made a good cop.'

Defeated, Fancourt, who had always had an avid amateur interest in sapphires, applied for a transfer to the little town of Anakie, the centrepoint of the Queensland gemfields. He was successful, but by September 1976 he realised he had nowhere else to go with his career. He'd aimed high with the Scognamiglio bust but it fell off the corrupt system like water off a duck's back. The dispirited Fancourt resigned, just weeks before massive regime change in the Queensland Police Force, and started prospecting full-time.

For years he would dream the same dream – he would be walking down a dark, poorly lit alleyway in Fortitude Valley, Brisbane's inner-city grid of vice. Out of the shadows, figures would repeatedly lunge at him with sharp knives, although somehow he always managed to avoid them and find, at the end of the long laneway, a small doorway or hatch to escape through. The dream not over, he would find himself inside Pinocchio's – the nightclub, gambling den and massage parlour belonging to the Bellino brothers. In the dream, the men do not acknowledge Fancourt. He then makes his way through the club, out the front door and into the street.

That's when he wakes up in a panic. Fancourt would suffer the same dream for the rest of his life.

No. 1 Has Directed So

In the second week of November, Lewis began hearing firmer talk that he was set to be appointed assistant commissioner. He had telephone discussions with Tony Murphy and Member for Merthyr, Don 'Shady' Lane, and noted in his diary that someone coded 007 had supplied him with a tip: 'Next Monday. No 1 [Bjelke-Petersen] has directed so. One at a time. You next time.'

Lewis wasn't the only one hearing mutterings about his appointment. Whitrod loyalists also got wind of the move and tried to head it off.

One Saturday morning two of 'Whitrod's bloody henchmen' telephoned Ron Edington [former Police Union chief] at home. They wanted to use Edington's press contacts to gain traction for a 'special meeting' they had planned that Monday.

'The Government's going to appoint Lewis as Whitrod's Assistant Commissioner. We're going to let the public know that he's not fit to be appointed. We want you to get the cooperation of the press on Sunday to blow this up,' they told him.

'Bullshit,' Edington replied. 'Fight your own battles. I'm not becoming involved in that.'

Edington immediately got on the phone to Lewis. 'They're going to appoint you Assistant Commissioner?' Edington enquired.

'Oh,' Lewis supposedly said, 'I didn't know anything about that.'

'Don't bullshit. Of course you know,' Edington retorted. 'It's like the old what's-his-name who got you promoted, you know, the bloody wool broker.'

Whitrod, oblivious, put forward to Cabinet the names of several candidates for the Assistant Commissionership, including Vern

MacDonald and Alec McSporran. After the Cabinet meeting, he received a phone call from his new minister, Tom Newbery. Inspector Terence Murray Lewis of Charleville would be the next assistant commissioner. Lewis had vaulted 122 other equal or more senior officers to take the job.

'That's astounding,' Whitrod said. He immediately asked to see Newbery in his office. Whitrod repeated he was flabbergasted.

'Well,' said Newbery, 'that is how it's going to be.'

'That is pretty shattering to me because it is widely known in the force that Lewis was one of Frank Bischof's bagmen,' Whitrod exclaimed.

'Oh,' Newbery replied, 'well that was when he was a detective sergeant – he is now an inspector and wouldn't do that sort of thing.'

'Well, I don't agree with you,' Whitrod went on. 'Can I talk to the Cabinet or the Premier because it's important to me. I've been conducting an anti-corruption program here for seven years, and everybody in the police force knows that Lewis is corrupt.' Whitrod added that Lewis's appointment would nullify all his efforts.

'I will talk to the Premier,' Newbery said. An hour later the Police Minister phoned Whitrod: 'The Premier does not want to see you, nor will he allow you to address Cabinet.'

When asked why senior officers with better qualifications had been overlooked, Newbery replied: 'It was the Premier's decision.'

For almost two years Officer Gregory Early had been the irregular personal assistant to Whitrod, along with Early's friend Ken Hoggett. Early had joined the force in 1956 and as a cadet showed an unusual flair for typing and shorthand, making him a valuable commodity. Through the 1960s he was seconded to the Legal Section, and befriended the commissioner at the time Frank Bischof and Terry Lewis of the Juvenile Aid Bureau.

Early was trusted by Whitrod, but he showed substantial political savvy by remaining on the good side of people like Inspector Lewis. He was also acquainted with Hallahan and Murphy.

Early remembers the final days of Whitrod: 'I recall a day in 1976 ... when several officers in the trusted category were called into the large conference room on the Commissioner's floor. Jim Casey, the departmental secretary, was there, as was Basil Hicks, Jim Voigt, John Dautel, Ken Hoggett and myself. He [Whitrod] indicated that he had put up via a Cabinet submission that a certain officer [probably Superintendent Vern MacDonald] be made an Assistant Commissioner and that Minister Tom Newbery had just called him and indicated that he would be replaced by Inspector Terry Lewis.'

Early says Whitrod declared the situation untenable and that he would be resigning. He asked Jim Casey to find out the particulars of his superannuation entitlements.

'Why would you have to resign over a matter like that?' Early says he asked.

'They would put him in a back room and bypass me for him and that would not work,' Whitrod allegedly replied. As it was, the government was extremely well prepared for whatever indignant reaction might come from Whitrod.

Former Police Union boss Ron Edington confirms the plot to unseat Whitrod. 'Joh had to get rid of him because he bailed up on Joh and told Joh that he wasn't answerable to him,' remembers Edington. 'So he wasn't going to be dictated to by bloody Joh. Then old Whitrod goes down and he objected to it and they said, "Oh well, perhaps we could make him [Lewis] a Chief Commissioner." Whitrod went back and called all his staff together and had a discussion with them all as to what he should do.'

Lewis's new appointment was announced on Monday 15 November 1976. He was deluged with phone calls, cards, letters and telegrams of congratulations. Lewis's diary noted for that day: 'The Premier phoned congratulations on promotion. Numerous other callers. Off duty at 6 p.m. Received 44 telephone calls up until 11.30 p.m.'

One typed letter came from none other than Whitrod staffer and supposed loyalist Greg Early, who divulged some interesting political machinations around the decision.

'Dear Terry,' he wrote, 'congratulations on your promotion. It seems likely that you will go one step further. Two weeks ago I was talking to 'Shady' [Lane]. He said that next week (last week) was to be a very important week. I took from that comment that there would be some movement but I never thought it would be as big as it has turned out to be.'

(If Early is accurate, Don 'Shady' Lane knew about, and was freely discussing, Lewis's elevation to Assistant Commissioner from the week beginning Monday 1 November. It was on that precise day that Newbery took Whitrod's controversial Cedar Bay report to Cabinet for discussion. It was most likely the moment the decision about Lewis was sealed. Five days later, Lewis would have his meeting with National Party president Bob Sparkes in Charleville.)

Lewis also received a telegram from his old mate in Sydney, former detective Ray 'Gunner' Kelly. 'Warmest congratulations. STOP. Your appointment heralds reprieve of wonderful service. STOP. Sincere wishes long successful reign, warmest regards, Ray Kelly.'

And another: 'Congratulations best wishes for future, Glen and Heather Hallahan.'

Also a note on writing paper featuring an illustration of flowers and a teapot, from Lewis's daughter Lanna. 'Dear Dad,' she wrote, 'this is just a short note to say how pleased I am about your new promotion to Assistant Commissioner. I would just like to say that I am very proud of you and love you very much.'

Lewis also says he received a call in Brisbane later that afternoon, concerning Whitrod's objection to his appointment as Assistant Commissioner.

'I'll tell you something ... not to name people but somebody phoned me ... when I got appointed Assistant Commissioner he [Whitrod] said apparently he wouldn't work with me,' claims Lewis. 'And apparently the Premier – again I wasn't there – I was told that the Premier said either to him or to the Minister [Newbery] to tell him if that was going to be his attitude he'd make Lewis a Chief Commissioner and Whitrod could work for him.'

Lewis's diary for 15 November recorded that apart from the Premier ringing with his congratulations on his new appointment, he was also phoned by 'Mr [Ken] Crooke, Press secretary to Min. for Police … Mr N. Turner M.L.A … numerous other callers'.

As for Raymond Wells Whitrod, he immediately offered his resignation, defeated.

The Man with a Light Touch

Whitrod's sudden departure shocked the state.

The press reported the following day that Whitrod personally handed in his typed resignation to Minister Newbery, and it was taken straightaway to Cabinet and approved unanimously. Whitrod cited personal reasons for leaving.

(Lewis says he got a call from Don 'Shady' Lane in Brisbane about the Cabinet vote: 'I assume it was Don Lane – they said when it came up in Cabinet about Mr Whitrod putting in his resignation, [Russ] Hinze said, "Accept it before the bastard changes his mind."')

Speed seemed to have been of the essence. The *Courier-Mail* reported that following the unanimous vote '… a minute was sent immediately to the Governor [Sir Colin Hannah] for his signature, to make it an Executive Council decision.'

The haste wasn't the only insult to Whitrod. The government also announced an inquiry into criminal law enforcement, presentation of evidence and police investigation, interrogation, search and arrest techniques. (It would formally become the 'Committee of Inquiry into the Enforcement of Criminal Law in Queensland', or the Lucas Inquiry, presided over by Justice Geoffrey Lucas.) An investigation into any allegations of police corruption or malpractice was not included in the terms of reference.

This gave a powerful if erroneous impression that the Bjelke-Petersen government wasn't looking into any poor behaviour by the force itself, but was moving in to sort out the mess made by Whitrod's shoddy tenure.

Furthermore, on the day Whitrod resigned, Cabinet announced other police changes, one being that Brisbane Metropolitan Traffic superintendent, Inspector Michael Beattie – the officer charged with beating the female student on the head with his baton during a demonstration just over three months earlier – was given a promotion. It was another clear stab at Whitrod.

When asked about Whitrod's resignation, Bjelke-Petersen answered: 'I did not expect it.'

The former commissioner gave two weeks' notice, and the press speculated that he was set to 'blast' the government before returning to civilian life. His final day would be Friday 26 November. On the following Monday, he planned to give a press conference. The government forthwith called for submissions for a new commissioner, though few doubted Lewis was the prime candidate.

Throughout the rest of the week the press focused on the humble Inspector Lewis, seeking out public opinion in the Charleville police district. He was described as an 'arch-diplomat when he was a judge at the recent local Booga Woongaroo Festival tiny tots competition', and 'a man who has the secret of getting on with people'. He had learned his 'light touch' as head of the JAB. In short, he had the respect of the people of Charleville and beyond.

Days before the Cabinet meeting to formally appoint Lewis as Commissioner, the head of the CIU, Basil 'The Hound' Hicks, was contacted by then Transport Minister Keith Hooper, the Liberal member for Greenslopes.

Hooper surreptitiously approached Hicks seeking information on Lewis. They then met secretly in Hooper's car outside his house on the Sunday night before the Cabinet meeting. In short, Hooper wanted incriminating evidence on Lewis to stop his appointment to Commissioner.

'He [Hooper] said some Liberals didn't want the Premier to make Lewis Commissioner,' Hicks later said. 'They said he [Lewis] was corrupt.

'He [Hooper] wanted something in writing – he wanted copies of files from the CIU. He said the Premier would not do anything until he got something in writing. I told him that if Lewis was made Commissioner, my head would be on the chopping block [if the files were supplied].

'He [Hooper] said that if you can't give me anything in writing, Lewis will be made Commissioner within a few days.'

On Monday 22 November, just six months after Lewis and Bjelke-Petersen had chinwagged at that lonely airstrip out in Cunnamulla, state Cabinet took ten minutes to crown Lewis the new Queensland Police Commissioner. Lewis was the only name submitted to and discussed by Cabinet.

Bjelke-Petersen said: 'He's a straight-shooter.'

Minister Newbery added: 'I am confident he is the right person to take over a very difficult and demanding job.'

Needless to say, the Premier wanted him to step into his new role immediately. The congratulations poured in. Ray 'Gunner' Kelly wrote a note, asking if Terry could help out an old friend who had fallen on hard times. New South Wales Police Commissioner Fred Hanson rang to offer his fullest cooperation. Jack Roberts of the National Hotel wrote in a telegram: 'Best wishes many true words said in jest.' Bob Sparkes also telegrammed: 'Hearty congratulations on your well merited elevation.' Judge Eddie Broad wrote a note out of his District Court chambers: '... best wishes for a successful career as Commissioner.'

And Wally Wright, the former policeman who urged Lewis to move from the Fuel Board and join the ranks in the late 1940s, sent a one-page typed letter. 'Congratulations of the most sincere feelings,' said Wally. 'No one was more enthused than I was of learning of your appointment which can be understood when I claim some involvement in your entering the police and your later appointment to the CIB. Best of luck, but you have no worries.'

Wright's touching letter was an example that some saw Lewis's meteoric elevation to the top position as some sort of Horatio Alger rags-to-riches fable. The poor boy from Ipswich climbs to the top of the mountain. While that was technically a part of the story, what was not understood at the time was the relentless, well-organised and vicious campaign that had been waged to unseat Whitrod since his first weeks as Commissioner.

This was an assault by stealth on several fronts over many years, involving senior police, the powerful Police Union and a network of anonymous informants from within and outside the government. It involved personal harassment, public slanging and the ceaseless shovelling of private harmful chatter. (Drug dealer and Hallahan informant John Edward Milligan would later, in a police interview, describe the campaign against Whitrod as 'a coup' and a 'political overthrow'.)

The eloquent and educated member for South Brisbane, Colin Lamont, had befriended Whitrod and admired his honesty and integrity. Lamont had his own theories about the resignation of Whitrod and the meteoric rise of Lewis.

'He [Whitrod] ... believes he was treated very badly,' Lamont reflected later in an interview. 'He believes that he stood in the way of Joh's ambitions. And he was allowed to go. I mean ... Joh ... out of the blue somebody came up with the name of Terry Lewis. He was an

Inspector in Charleville. I mean, that's nearly as nondescript as being … a chemist in Thargomindah. And I mean, suddenly this inspector is to jump all these ranks and become Deputy Commissioner. Why?'

Lamont initially suspected the member for Merthyr, Don Lane, being a former police officer and 'part of what we think was the Rat Pack', had a hand in Lewis's elevation. '[But] Lane didn't have any influence with Joh at all at the time,' Lamont later said. 'In fact, Lane didn't get on with Joh at the time.

'Lane was [Bill] Knox's man. He … Lane kicked heads to get support for Knox, as Knox had tried to do for Lane. And I … therefore have to conclude that it was Knox who pulled the name Terry Lewis out of the hat and said to Joh, "This bloke will do what you want him to do. This bloke will take instructions."'

When Whitrod did resign, Lamont spoke out in his defence. 'I went on television that night … and suggested that the people of Queensland should demand that they withdraw his resignation,' Lamont reflected years later. 'I said if … Whitrod won't accept this man as his deputy, then you can be sure he's got very, very good reasons, which he's not at liberty to tell us without the privilege of parliament. And I had hoped Whitrod might ring me and tell me, but he never did, because I'd have said it in parliament.'

Lewis had a number of farewells in Charleville before heading home to Brisbane. Lewis says: 'He [Whitrod] left on the Friday or whatever and I got … Hazel, I and [son] John got one of the sergeants there to drive me to Brisbane. I don't know if it was the Saturday or the Sunday and of course I had to go into the office the next day.'

His official diary stated that Lewis and family left Charleville on Saturday 27 November at 6 a.m. 'Petrol at Roma and Toowoomba. Brisbane at 4.30 pm.' The Lewis family was back together in Garfield Drive.

Meanwhile, Whitrod and his wife Mavis were busy packing up their neat, one-level house over at St Lucia, a suburb visible from

Lewis's perch on Garfield Drive in Bardon. On his final day in the job he wrote one last Commissioner's newsletter. The press said there were no farewell functions organised for him. 'Not even his fellow officers had anything planned,' it was reported.

However, he did have some choice words for the press during his final moments in the chair, and prior to his big press conference on the Monday. Whitrod told reporters the force had an 'unsavoury Rat Pack' which he said contained eight police officers. He said 'Rat Pack' had become a common expression around headquarters, and that they were characterised by 'dishonesty'. He refused to go into detail.

Whitrod also had one last clerical job to perform following a meeting with his trusted officer Basil Hicks. Hicks was worried that information gathered from outside informants about the Rat Pack would place them in danger if exposed. The informants on file had believed their identities would never be revealed to the Rat Pack. With Whitrod soon to be replaced by Lewis, Hicks was concerned he would no longer be able to shield his sources. Whitrod gave Hicks written instructions to burn any material that Lewis could view as hostile.

Hicks later recalled the order to destroy any paperwork that might identify informants: 'He particularly mentioned Hallahan, Murphy and Lewis, anything in relation to them, more particularly against Murphy. He wanted anything destroyed that could be used to sue anybody or be used to the detriment of anybody at all. At the time he suggested that the first thing that would happen would be Mr Murphy would try to come into the section to look at the files.'

Hicks took the sackfuls of documents to his home and put a match to them in his backyard incinerator.

Whitrod's much-anticipated and packed final press conference was held at a Brisbane TV station on Mount Coot-tha, one of several hills fringed with gum trees that backdrop the state capital. Whitrod wore a dark grey suit, white shirt and a maroon tie. On seeing the size of the waiting media contingent, he exclaimed: 'I should have charged for admission.'

Brisbane journalist and writer Hugh Lunn was present. He said the press conference was one of the biggest of its type ever held in Queensland.

'It was the first time I had attended a press conference where some reporters had been sent a list of key questions to ask,' Lunn later wrote. 'Many of these questions were met with hesitation and pauses followed by the pointed "I can't answer that" or "my lawyers tell me I can't answer that".'

Whitrod blamed political interference in major policing decisions, including transfers, promotions and politicians demanding favours of police, as the reason for him no longer being able to perform his job effectively. He didn't think Terry Lewis was the most suitable man to fill the vacancy. He thought there were signs that Queensland was developing into a police state.

He believed there was a 'Rat Pack' alive and well in the force, taking bribes from SP bookmakers and prostitutes. He was asked if any members of the Rat Pack were on the last promotion list.

Whitrod refused to answer.

Just prior to Lewis starting the top job, rumours were flying around about who would or wouldn't be demoted depending on their loyalty to Whitrod during his administration. Greg Early – friends to both Lewis and Whitrod – was certain a coup had been mounted against Whitrod.

'Much consternation took place as to what was going to happen, particularly to the pro-Whitrod personnel like John Dautel, Ken Hoggett, myself, Basil Hicks and Jim Voigt,' Early records in his unpublished memoir. 'Ken Hoggett said to me once that Basil Hicks had said that we should form our own little power group like [what] obviously had been done by members of the Union Executive and others. My response to Ken Hoggett was that I was not going to join any group and that I was going to look after myself.

'There is no doubt in my mind that Ron Redmond, as President of the Queensland Police Union of Employees; other members of the Union Executive; Don Lane, former police officer and then a Member of Parliament; Inspector Terry Lewis, District Officer Charleville; Inspector Tony Murphy, District Officer Longreach; and Inspector Les Hogan, officer in charge of the Special Branch, at least were involved in overthrowing Mr Whitrod and replacing him with Terry Lewis.'

Early was also convinced that Detective Sergeant John Herse, who for several years was a member of the Special Branch and a bodyguard to Premier Joh Bjelke-Petersen, was a messenger between the group and Joh. Herse would swiftly be appointed one of Lewis's personal assistants on becoming commissioner.

Early remembers: 'Somehow, during the last few days of Mr Whitrod's time as Commissioner, I was speaking with Les Hogan, probably about an official matter, and he sounded me out about working for Terry Lewis as a personal assistant.

'I said I would be happy to do that because I had always had a good relationship with and regard for him. I told no one of this approach and towards the last week of Mr Whitrod's term as Commissioner I got a message from Les to ring Terry Lewis at his home on the Sunday evening [28 November] on a number he gave me.

'I rang Terry at his home and he asked me if I would like to come and work for him. I said I would and he then asked me how I got on with John Herse and I said fine because I had worked with him in the Legal Section. He said he would be coming in to work with me.'

As for Lewis, he took his place behind the Commissioner's desk at 7.30 a.m. on Monday 29 November. There were no more trams into the city for Lewis. He travelled in the Commissioner's car down from Garfield Drive.

'Commenced duty as Commissioner', his diary noted efficiently. His large desk had a small side table that carried the telephone. His chair was black leather. In the office across the desk were two white leather and wooden armed visitors' seats, and a large pot plant.

Lewis remembers: 'Contrary to what they do at other places and that, I wasn't sworn in. I was sworn in as a Constable in 1949 – that was it. All I got was a little card signed by Mr Newbery saying – this is to identify T.M. Lewis as Commissioner of Police. Boom – that was it.'

The promotion had been so swift he did not even have a proper commissioner's uniform. He had to order a new visor for his old cap. 'When I got the job it was a surprise, I mean there's no two ways about that,' he says. 'But I was very pleased about some aspects. One that I was coming back to Brisbane with the family and secondly that so many of my men, both in the job and people outside of the job, welcomed the appointment if you like, for want of a better way of putting it. But it was a funny feeling to go in there that Monday.'

That morning Lewis questioned Assistant Commissioner Bill Taylor about allegedly slandering Lewis. Taylor said he acted on incorrect information. Lewis suggested Taylor, who was to retire just two months later, leave the office of the Commissioner.

Next was Ken Hoggett: 'Informed Sgt 2/c Hoggett he was to move from personal assistant position immediately.' (Lewis continued to keep a meticulous diary despite the fact that the Commissioner was not required to do so.)

Lewis called in Hicks: 'Insp. Hicks admitted having burnt six sackfuls of files on Mr Whitrod's approval; he said they related to Police, Politicians, Solicitors and Informants.'

Commissioner Lewis retained the services of Greg Early. 'I had a number of people say to me to get rid of everybody who was loyal, if you like, to Whitrod,' says Lewis. 'I said, everybody deserves a second chance. Well, nearly everybody.'

That night, Whitrod was interviewed by Mike Willesee on national television. His cryptic answers just raised more questions about Premier Bjelke-Petersen and corruption in the force.

Allen Callaghan, Joh's press secretary, says Lewis was installed to 'fix up the administrative side' of the police force.

'They weren't close,' Callaghan says of the relationship between the Premier and Lewis. 'Joh did not have a lot of close friends. He was a very private man. He lived for his family. He'd learned very early to be careful who you call your friends. Lewis set out to do what he was sent to do.'

Did Bjelke-Petersen, however, have a special interest in the police force and its use as a political weapon?

'It was the same interest as he would have given to any department with a problem,' recalls Callaghan. 'He had enough to do himself. He would have been keen to see it work. He had an interest in it. In any revolution, you always grab [the] police, Treasury and the television station.'

A revolution or not, state parliament was sitting the next day, and a major storm was gathering.

A House on Fire

If former police commissioner Ray Whitrod thought he could resign, make some parting shots at the government and his successor, then quietly leave Brisbane Town, he was to be sorely mistaken.

As the government and the opposition settled into their seats in Parliament House before Acting Speaker Bill Hewitt, Minister for Police Tom Newbery rose just after 11 a.m. to read out a ministerial statement on police administration and the former commissioner.

It was going to be a long day.

Newbery wanted to defend himself against allegations Whitrod had made in the press conference and address criticisms of the government. 'The previous Commissioner of Police was reluctant to recognise my responsibilities,' Newbery stated. 'I feel that Mr Whitrod wanted to be a power unto himself – responsible to no one. What Mr Whitrod considers to be political interference is, as I see it, only responsible interest and concern by the government.'

Newbery also addressed Whitrod's claims that the minister had shredded the official police reports into the Cedar Bay fiasco and had assisted in the extradition to Western Australia of two people arrested at Cedar Bay who were due to give evidence against police charged over that incident.

Newbery meekly defended himself. He said he acted in the best interests of the people of Queensland.

And with that, parliament drifted back into its usual humdrum ebb and flow. Matters discussed included: improved housing conditions for railway employees in far off Hughenden; the reintroduction of free milk for school children; the speed limits for boats on the Brisbane River; and a plague of phasmatid giant stick insects supposedly afflicting a more than 1000-kilometre spread of gum trees in both Queensland and New South Wales.

Then Acting Speaker Hewitt presented a Motion for Adjournment to the house. He announced he had received that morning a letter from Opposition leader Tom Burns, asking that the house adjourn to discuss a matter of urgent public importance.

The letter outlined the following issues: '... namely the concern felt by wide sections of the community as a result of statements [made] by the State's former Police Commissioner, Mr Ray Whitrod, following his forced resignation after six years in that position, which he clearly indicated was forced as a result of political pressure from the premier, Mr Bjelke-Petersen.'

Burns said the debate was necessary following public statements that pointed towards the belief that there was a desire from the Premier to make Queensland's top law enforcement officer a 'puppet'. He cited numerous further reasons for the adjournment, including the 'Girl Bashing Baton Affair' and the street marches earlier in the year, the Cedar Bay raid, and the truncating of Scotland Yard detectives O'Connell and Fothergill's investigation into corruption in the police force (from 1975).

'I believe the citizens of Queensland expect their Police administration to be impartial and free from political pressure and any doubts to the contrary – voiced as they are on this occasion at such a high level – should be urgently debated by this House,' Burns argued.

Acting Speaker Bill Hewitt, a Liberal but no friend of Bjelke-Petersen and his regime, allowed the debate to progress.

Burns stood again and let fly: 'Ray Whitrod was politically persecuted by the government. He was hounded by the Premier's henchmen on the front benches. He was hounded from office by the Premier. The Minister for Police was placed in his position as a stooge for the Premier. He set out ruthlessly to destroy the Police Commissioner.

'As I say, the Premier has enshrined himself as the political judge and jury not only of the merit of public complaints in police matters but also whether they should be investigated.'

Burns revealed that Minister Newbery had reached a point near the end where he 'censored' Whitrod's newsletters to the troops. 'Where are we going when top professional people appointed by the government must have even their newsletters censored?' Burns queried. 'Senior appointments were made against the Commissioner's recommendations, and Cabinet took control of normal routine transfers. There are grave allegations of copies of official reports, vital to pending investigations, being destroyed – perhaps burned.

'It is a tragic, frightening day for this state when a man such as Ray Whitrod would say publicly that political control of the police force, to even a slight degree, resembles Goering's Gestapo in Nazi Germany.'

A young Bob Katter interjected loudly during Burns' condemnation. 'Why was Lewis sent to Charleville? A vendetta! That's all it was, a vendetta!'

Burns shot back: 'Honourable members opposite are all now going to make statements about people going to Charleville. Why didn't they say this before?'

The Opposition leader again cited Nazi Germany. 'Joh wanted his own Commissioner and his own police,' Burns went on. 'This is the sort of government we are going to have. We will have political police who will not be enforcing the law but will be enforcing political decisions.'

Burns was adamant that Queenslanders did not want 'a squadron of Kingaroy cops, whose operations are dictated by the political objectives of an extremist Premier and an obedient Police Minister'.

Jack Houston, the Labor member for Bulimba since 1957, read an extract from a newspaper article. 'Unfortunately, in recent years, Cabinet Ministers have regarded the Police Force as just another Government Department – something it can never be while it controls the lives, liberty and safety of every person in the State,' he quoted.

Houston said it could have come from a newspaper the day before, but that it was in fact published in the Brisbane *Truth* on 24 January 1965, at the height of the Bischof era.

While Lewis and Murphy were not named, again the issue of remote transfers was mentioned.

'Another thing that has been said is that men were sent to the country because Mr Whitrod was upset with them,' Houston said. 'I think it is understood that normally the transfer of commissioned officers is a matter for Cabinet, not simply an order made by the Police Commissioner. That automatically rules out that Mr Lewis was sent to the country because of some feeling held by Mr Whitrod.'

Newbery stood again to defend himself and then Bjelke-Petersen and his lieutenants wiped the floor with Whitrod.

The Premier repeated that Whitrod wanted to be a law unto himself, that he was loathed by the majority of the police force, that he was a 'figures man' only interested in statistics and his daily 'killer' [kill] sheets. 'I didn't sack him,' Bjelke-Petersen said. 'He sacked himself.'

Lewis's friend Don Lane, the member for Merthyr, used the opportunity to present a glowing crib sheet of Lewis's career. Lane declared: 'He is a man whose academic qualifications are equal to the job, and equal to those of anyone else available; he is a man who has a depth of police experience in the Criminal Investigation Branch, handling juveniles, and in respect of general police work.

'He is an innovator – the man who established the Juvenile Aid Bureau; he is a Churchill Fellow who travelled the world on a scholarship and studied Police Forces throughout the world. He is a man whose courage and bravery was recognised by Her Majesty when he was awarded the George Medal a few years ago for disarming a man at Wynnum. I know the man well, and I know he will handle the job to the satisfaction of all Queenslanders. He is a Queenslander; he understands Queenslanders and he understands Queensland policemen; and he will produce the goods.'

Lane dismissed Whitrod's complaints and reflections offered to the media since his resignation. 'His clumsy attempts to canonise himself as a saint at this particular time make me sick,' Lane added.

In the early evening of that Tuesday, after a fiery day in parliament, the new Commissioner farewelled the old at a modest function in the restaurant and bar of the Metropolitan Motor Inn in Leichhardt Street, Spring Hill. A total of eight people, including Whitrod, attended. Among them were judge Sir Mostyn Hanger and Sir Gordon Chalk.

'I didn't even want to go to that,' remembers Lewis. 'Newbery asked me to come to keep him company. Whitty was all over me like a bloody rash. He would have been very shitty. It would have been a false smile.'

Lewis was photographed at the function with Whitrod and Police Minister Newbery. Lewis wore a dark suit with a floral tie; Whitrod a grey suit with a polka dot tie. In the picture, Whitrod's face is creased with laughter. Lewis, holding a small beer, is also laughing, but his eyes are not. They look weary at the sight of his predecessor.

The farewell was sufficiently brief enough for Lewis to later meet up with Bill Knox and Don Lane to discuss the government's wish to 'suppress SP betting', and still be home at Garfield Drive by 10 p.m.

Flight

After his humiliating farewell drinks hosted by Tom Newbery and Terry Lewis at the Metropolitan, Ray and Mavis Whitrod wasted no time in getting out of town. Between his formal resignation as Commissioner and his farewell press conference, Whitrod had been offered teaching posts at both La Trobe University in Melbourne and the Australian National University in Canberra.

Whitrod selected Canberra. A daughter still lived there, and it was the place where he'd had many happy years with his family while reforming the Commonwealth Police.

So in early December 1976 Ray and Mavis packed up their house in St Lucia (which they expediently sold to a friend who had always admired it) and headed south in the family car – a dark blue Austin 1800. The former Commissioner's furniture and voluminous personal files and documentation would follow in a removal van.

The Whitrods took the fastest route possible – the Newell Highway, via Goondiwindi, Coonabarabran, Gilgandra then on to Yass and the Acton campus of the ANU, close to the Canberra CBD.

'When the removalists' van was a week overdue … I began to phone the company asking about our furniture,' Whitrod said. 'After three weeks, I was told that everything had been burned. On its way to Canberra, the truck had hit the side of a bridge and burst into flames.

'This was distressing enough, but I had strong doubts that the fire was accidental. I thought of having the matter investigated, but this would have involved using the Queensland police, now under the control of Commissioner Terry Lewis. I hadn't the heart to even try.'

The Whitrods, still without a home in the national capital, lived for several months in accommodation provided by the university. Meanwhile, Ray taught criminology within the law faculty.

'He wasn't bitter,' his daughter Ruth remembers of that period. 'People used to ask – "Why isn't your dad more bitter?" I think his [Baptist] faith had a lot to do with it.'

His son Ian says his father only occasionally spoke to him about what went on during those almost seven years in Queensland. 'He thought there were some pretty evil forces at work there,' Ian says. 'There was a time when he was sleeping with a revolver under his pillow and that upset my mother no end. I think he saw his time up there as unfinished business. He thought he had the backing of the Queensland Government. He didn't. It was a tough time for him. He said to me that he was certain that Terry Lewis was very crooked.'

The New Boy

Things couldn't have been better for Lewis. He was back home. He'd seen off Whitrod, his arch rival. And he had the top job.

On the evening of Thursday 2 December, just days after taking up the position of Commissioner of Police, he dropped into the Belfast Hotel to see his old mate Barry Maxwell and have a beer with his friend, Detective Sergeant John Meskell.

'I just walked in there and saw this well-groomed bloody commissioner with all the regalia,' recalls bar manager Les Hounslow. 'It was Lewis. I said, "Shit, what do I call you now?" And he said, "Still Terry".'

Apart from catching up with old mates, Lewis quickly got a taste of the rarefied life of a top public servant. He was a kid in a lolly shop.

On Sunday 5 December, he enjoyed a Christmas function at the Chinese Club. Two nights later he was back at the Belfast, this time for drinks with Bill Glasson, MP, and Inspector Tony Murphy, who regularly visited Brisbane during his time in distant Longreach, and could now celebrate his old friend's extraordinary promotion. The day after that Lewis was up at Government House for a function hosted by the Governor, Air Marshal Sir Colin Hannah.

There were more functions at the Belfast, Tattersalls, the Grosvenor and the Park Royal, dinner with his old media pal Ron Richards, and an invitation from entrepreneur Keith Williams to visit his theme park, Sea World, on the Gold Coast and take an aerial flight over the glitter strip with Premier Bjelke-Petersen.

(Lewis would take up that invitation on Saturday 22 January 1977, when, having been in the job for just seven weeks, his family and that of Bjelke-Petersen and Keith Williams gathered together in the sunshine for happy snaps on board Williams' boat, the MV *Ulysses*. They also took that promised flight in the white, yellow and orange Sea World chopper over the Broadwater and a rapidly expanding Surfers Paradise.)

But despite his delight in being elevated into the top position, Lewis was nervous about how the troops would receive him. He was particularly anxious about the reception he would receive at the regional superintendent's conference that Whitrod had established, one of which was scheduled just weeks after he started. 'One, of some consequence, was the one in December ... and there was a swearing in, an induction ceremony ... [they] were a bit daunting because everybody at that regional superintendent's conference had been senior to me. So I was at the top of the table actually with a couple of the assistant commissioners and all the others were down the other side of it.'

Lewis told the top police officers he would do his best and hopefully they would see that and cooperate with him. 'When I finished the conference that week and thanked them they all stood up and clapped,' Lewis says. 'So I thought that was very decent of them.'

On Christmas Eve in 1976 Lewis sat down in his office with Arthur Pitts, Whitrod's fearless corruption-buster and one of the stars of the

Southport Betting Case trial, and discussed Pitts' future. Lewis advised him point blank that there was 'little likelihood of promotion'. Pitts was assigned the ultimate humiliation – he was put in charge of Stores.

On Tuesday 18 January 1977, Lewis caught up again with Scotland Yard's Commander Terence (Terry) O'Connell. In late 1975, O'Connell and Detective Superintendent Bruce Fothergill had been flown to Brisbane to conduct an inquiry into Queensland police corruption following the public and political clamour that stemmed from Jack Herbert's Southport Betting Case. Their report had been submitted to the Premier, but it had never been tabled in parliament, and word was that it had been shredded. Even so, O'Connell had been asked back to Brisbane to give evidence at the Lucas Inquiry.

O'Connell had been briefed in London on 15 November – coincidentally the day of Lewis's appointment as Assistant Commissioner – by visiting Justice Minister Bill Lickiss. The men met in Queensland House on The Strand to run through O'Connell's investigation the previous year and the evidence he planned to give on administrative matters only.

O'Connell, despite receiving volumes of information from police and prostitutes on corruption in the Queensland Police Force during research for his initial report in 1975–76, and the repeated assertions that figures like Tony Murphy loomed as being seriously corrupt, would compile a further report to assist Justice Lucas. He did not want to be branded 'a whingeing Pom' on his return visit.

While he was in Brisbane, O'Connell dined at Lewis's home in Garfield Drive.

On 20 January, according to Lewis's Commissioner's diary, O'Connell met with Police Minister Newbery and Lewis and they discussed how there would be 'no further inquiries needed'.

They did, however, talk about O'Connell's observations on corruption in the force. 'One particular person that I was concerned with from the information that I had been given was a man called Murphy,' O'Connell later said. 'From what I was told and his name was mentioned more than anyone else by police officers who I saw [during their inter-views with O'Connell in late 1975], he was obviously one they feared, a dominant man and highly intelligent.

'They spoke of him in awe … and you got this sense of fear … you got this sense they were frightened of him.'

Lewis says he later learned that when O'Connell interviewed Basil Hicks and Jim Voigt, of Whitrod's prized Crime Intelligence Unit, for his report, much was mentioned about Tony Murphy. 'O'Connell didn't want to know about Murphy,' Lewis recalls. 'He said he didn't want to know anything about him. It seems that somewhere along the line people don't want to get involved in knowing about Murphy.'

On 24 January, O'Connell called Commissioner Lewis and assured him he had shredded the hundreds of statements he had taken during the initial stages of his investigation in 1975. O'Connell may have felt the need to reassure the new Commissioner in light of their expansive hospitality towards him during his visit to the Queensland capital.

Indeed, O'Connell decided he would not burden the new Commissioner with allegations of corruption and felt Lewis had a right to put his own house 'in order'. O'Connell later said: 'I was not telling lies. I was supporting the new regime.'

Before he returned to London, Lewis and Newbery presented O'Connell with 'albums' and a 'print' of an old etching of Scotland Yard as souvenirs of his return trip to Brisbane.

Old friends checked in. Eric Pratt telephoned for a natter about the Lucas Inquiry. Then on Wednesday 9 March, Lewis headed out to Eagle Farm airport to meet Queen Elizabeth II and Prince Philip, in the city as a part of their 1977 Silver Jubilee tour. The Commissioner escorted the famous couple to City Hall and then on to Government House. Late that afternoon he was formally 'presented' to the Queen and Prince. The Royals were gone by Friday.

On that same day, Lewis met with Tony Murphy 're unsolved murders'.

The following Monday – 14 March 1977 – Commander O'Connell finally issued his sanitised report on corruption to the Queensland Government. It concluded: 'No purpose would be served in pursuing our investigation any further. During the course of our enquiries we did not uncover sufficient evidence to justify a prosecution.'

The report, ring-bound and book-ended in thick, creamy cardboard, was a total of five pages long. It was filed and never made public.

Slacks

Lorelle Saunders was a police officer on the up and up. Not only was she Queensland's first female detective, but she had been excited by former Commissioner Ray Whitrod's reform agenda, particularly in relation to women in the police force.

She had only been in the force a little less than five years by the time Whitrod resigned and Terry Lewis took over the top job. When she had first joined, one of her first postings in late November, 1972, was to the JAB, then run by Senior Sergeant Terry Lewis. She spent only a few months there before being moved over to the Gabba CIB, then the City Police shortly after.

By April 1973 she was back in plain clothes at the JAB. While there, she said that a major disagreement occurred between Lewis and Tony Murphy towards the end of the year. The argument was over the location for the JAB's annual Christmas party. Lewis had arranged for it to be held at the old National Hotel, epicentre of the inquiry into police misconduct in 1963. Murphy indicated they should never set foot in the hotel, owned by the Roberts brothers.

Curious, Saunders had started asking around about the National, and was told the story of Bischof, the Rat Pack – supposedly Lewis, Murphy and Glen Hallahan – and police corruption during the era.

Lewis would later deny that the argument with Murphy ever took place.

Later, Saunders was transferred to Whitrod's new Education Department Liaison Unit (EDLU) – a body established in direct opposition to Lewis's JAB. The EDLU would get tougher on juvenile offenders. In accepting the transfer, Saunders said Lewis went 'crazy' and accused her of disloyalty. If true, Lewis's perception that you were 'pro-Whitrod' would be enough to seed an immovable enmity. From that moment, Saunders' name would have been blacklisted.

Saunders later had a stint at the Inala suburban station west of the city before she was brought back in to the Metropolitan CIB, South Brisbane Area Office, in January 1977. By this stage, following his spectacular ascent, Lewis had been Commissioner for just a few weeks. One of the first notations in his Commissioner's diary, however, would relate to Saunders. Lewis recorded: 'Mr Riley mentioned re P/W Saunders and [P/W Janet] Makepeace soliciting signatures for petition.'

The petition that had become diary-worthy for Lewis was in fact in relation to overturning police regulations and allowing female officers to wear slacks on duty. Saunders contacted virtually every female Queensland officer seeking their signatures. Saunders and Makepeace also compiled a report on the issue.

Lewis believed policewomen should be dressed in the traditional sense – skirts, for example – and said slacks were not common practice in overseas police forces.

Saunders immediately contacted several international police forces, including Japan and the United States, to seek clarification on women wearing slacks while on active duty. The petition and research dossier were presented to Lewis for consideration.

To his credit, Lewis relented and permitted slacks to be introduced as a part of the official wardrobe of Queensland policewomen. Lewis, by and large, did not share Whitrod's more liberated view in relation to women and policing. And he would have taken umbrage at

Saunders not only stirring the pot with the petition, but correcting him on the wearing of slacks in other forces overseas.

Within weeks, reports from senior police expressing their dissatisfaction with the quality of Lorelle Saunders' work were being generated and added to her official police file.

Saunders' odyssey had begun. She could not imagine in her wildest dreams how it would end.

A Small Target

They would have looked like any typical young family over on the Redcliffe peninsula, a suburban outpost of Brisbane, 18 kilometres north-east of the CBD.

To get to it, you had to traverse the rattly 2.68 kilometre Hornibrook Bridge. Once there, it was a great place for families, with Suttons Beach and the Redcliffe Jetty regularly swept with breezes off Moreton Bay. It was also the perfect place to live for someone who did not want to bump into anything or anyone from the past in Brisbane. Redcliffe, in the 1970s, could have been its own small town by the water. In Redcliffe you could disappear.

It was where Mary Anne Brifman settled with her husband 'Graham' after they had married just a few days after Mary Anne's 16th birthday in December 1972, just nine months after her mother's death.

It was Graham who was sleeping over in the apartment in Bonney Avenue the night that Shirley died. It was Graham who witnessed a visitor come to the door close to midnight and hand her a small amber jar of drugs. Later, in the early hours of the morning, he had also seen an anxious Shirley moving about the apartment before standing before him in the dark in her floral nightie with side pockets.

'What's wrong?' he had asked her quietly.

'Nothing,' she replied.

So Mary Anne and Graham had married, and in 1975 had their first child, Christiaan. The next year they had a daughter, Ingrid.

'I was working as a waitress for a while but I was still haunted by all the things that I'd gone through,' Mary Anne says. 'I went back to doing what I hated and what they had trained me to do [in Sydney] when I was 13.

'He [Graham] had been sheltered in a very religious household most of his life, he didn't have much life experience. I couldn't get my husband to do anything. So I had to go to work. It was a repeat of my mother and father's marriage.'

She said she deliberately made herself a small target. 'I tried to keep a very low profile,' she says. 'Nobody knew who I was. I never mentioned my mother. I didn't want to get involved in anything too organised, where the girls were bullied by the men who ran the parlours.

'I was scared stiff of being recognised. I decided I would work as an escort.'

Confidential

Just three months into his commissionership, Lewis wasted no time drafting a confidential memo to Inspector Basil Hicks, head of Whitrod's cherished Crime Intelligence Unit. It was time to let Whitrod's old faithful know who was boss. And to delineate what actual intelligence the unit had on corrupt serving officers. What did they know? How much?

Lewis's memo – dated 10 February 1977 – not only requested details of the machinations of the unit, but accused it of being disruptive to police morale and operating as some sort of unaccounted for rogue body persecuting good policemen and wantonly besmirching reputations.

Hicks strongly refuted the allegations in his memo in reply on 17 February. 'I am deeply concerned at two matters which were inexplicably raised in your memorandum,' Hicks wrote. 'One matter is that the Unit was working contrary to its original charter. The second matter is that there was disquiet in the Police because they were being investigated by the Crime Intelligence Unit. Both statements are incorrect.'

Lewis hit back on 17 March: 'Please supply me with particulars of the field investigations conducted by the Crime Intelligence Unit which resulted in the prosecution of the six police officers mentioned in your report. Your report should include the names of the alleged offenders, the charges and dates preferred. A précis of the circumstances in each case is also required.'

How much was Hicks willing to tell, given his knowledge of Lewis's friendships with men like Jack Herbert, Glen Hallahan and Tony Murphy? Or did he tell all, reminding the new Commissioner that he was aware of a growing network of corruption, and that some of the major players had strong connections to the force's highest office? In short, that he knew what the bad apples were up to.

It was a dangerous game, and one that Hicks must have understood he could not win. His confidential six-page report to Lewis on 23 March laid out the skeletons in the closet. He mentioned – but not by name – the information of deceased prostitute and whistleblower Shirley Margaret Brifman, obtained by the CIU in late 1971, adding that her testimony 'could neither be proved nor disproved'.

An investigation into the extent of prostitution revealed that 'official records did not give any indication of the true position regarding police corruption connected with prostitution', and that field investigations in the early 1970s showed that 'some Police Officers were giving protection to prostitutes'.

His report detailed former officer Glen Hallahan being charged with official corruption over the Dorothy Knight pay-off in New Farm

Park, and the Rat Packer counselling criminal Donald Ross Kelly to rob a bank at Kedron.

According to Hicks, the CIU began to look seriously at SP betting in Queensland and found that the industry was worth in excess of $50 million a year, with more than 20 operators turning over $50,000 each a week.

His report had some choice things to say about the Licensing Branch. 'A number of Police in the Licensing Branch had been receiving protection money for some years, with one member receiving on behalf of himself and others in excess of $1000 a month,' Hicks reported. 'Honest Police Officers in the Licensing Branch were being neutralised or completely dominated by dishonest members.'

Hicks wrote of the Southport Betting Case and the involvement of Jack Herbert.

The report went on that in March 1976 – when Lewis was marooned as a lowly inspector in Charleville – 'investigations were made by the Crime Intelligence Unit into the activities of Detective Sergeant A. [Allen] Bulger and a solicitor, Stuart Thomas Bale and a criminal Jeffrey Colin Jones. In March 1976, Sergeant Bulger was charged with others with conspiring to pervert the course of justice … the evidence was also that Bulger received money from Jones in consideration for giving him [this] protection.'

He told Lewis that it was not possible to 'seriously investigate' police corruption without a 'field force'. Finally he concluded: 'Prior to the commencement of the Crime Intelligence Unit there was no real machinery to deal with the problem of Police corruption, especially where it was connected with organised crime, nor was there any encouragement to do something about it.

'This is evidenced by the fact that the conditions which existed during that time, should have been obvious to both junior and senior officers, yet there is no trace of any such information ever having been recorded or investigated.'

He urged 'better steps' be taken to deal with police corruption. Hicks was wasting his time.

Within weeks – with a masterful touch of spite and irony – Commissioner Lewis would disband and re-badge the CIU, and put his old mate Tony Murphy in charge. Basil Hicks was ordered to head up the new Internal Investigations Unit, where he was given a small office, no equipment, and essentially, no work.

Yet another Whitrod initiative was turned to dust.

Murphy Takes Charge

Constable Jim Slade was working at the Woodridge police station south of the CBD in early 1977 when he was told to report to Inspector Tony Murphy at headquarters.

Since the ousting of Whitrod, and the ascension of Lewis, Murphy had been brought back to Brisbane to command the Consorting Squad and to dismantle and refashion Whitrod's 'police spy' operation, the Crime Intelligence Unit or CIU. For years it had been known sarcastically among anti-Whitrod officers as the 'ICU'. Murphy started duties back in the city on Monday 7 February.

As Lewis noted in his diary: 'Saw Insp. Murphy on arrival on transfer.'

Lewis says he needed Murphy to get the team working again following the departure of Whitrod. 'See the branch was in this disarray,' reflects Lewis. 'I don't know why, because probably they'd had Whitrod's men there. They'd had [Basil] Hicks. I don't know who else.

'But anyhow as soon as I could I brought Murphy back to the Branch and I brought Noel McIntyre back as Assistant Commissioner. Unfortunately he didn't have that long to go before retirement because he was a really great bloke.

'Murphy did get the Branch going I must admit. I wouldn't have thought it was a mistake to bring him back there. It might have been a mistake to make him an Assistant Commissioner in retrospect ...'

Murphy wasted no time throwing out the old furniture. 'The "ICU" was absolutely disbanded, shattered, taken over by Tony Murphy,' says Slade. 'Tony Murphy was the boss.'

When Slade arrived in Murphy's office, both men were surrounded by empty filing cabinets – the skeletal remains of Whitrod's crack investigating force. Slade sat down before the famous detective. 'I've had a look at what you've done in the Commonwealth Police,' Murphy said. 'I'm starting this new team.'

It was a dream come true for Slade. 'Here was me walking into a job that I'd wanted for years,' Slade recalls. 'I must say he was without a doubt the greatest police officer I ever worked under.

'He taught me to be, and I would consider myself to be, a very good investigator. The only reason I'm patting myself on the back and giving myself that tag is because it's something that is measurable and by a very good investigator, someone that puts a number of matters before a magistrate and there's sufficient evidence to send it to a higher court, and the numbers of pleas of guilty and the success rate is the measure of a good investigator.

'I had the most amazing record of pleas of guilty. I learned everything from Tony Murphy.'

Murphy had other protégés – Alan Barnes, Pat Glancy and Barry O'Brien – but for whatever reason Murphy saw great promise in Slade, and gave him 'special treatment'. Could an element of it have been Murphy's own passion for photography in the early days of his police cadetship?

With the unit re-badged the Bureau of Criminal Intelligence, Slade immersed himself in his work. 'When I first went into the job with Tony [Murphy] our job was surveillance and it was my job to start a very, very proficient and efficient photographic section in there, to have equipment that was able to take really good telephoto shots, to be able to produce photographs in all light and really to be able to produce photographs for evidence that were worthy of evidence,' says Slade.

In no time Slade – fortuitously the owner of a face that could blend very quickly into a crowd – was doing undercover work. He had curly hair and grew a beard. Not even his children knew what he did for a living.

'We never did one single thing on the brothels,' he recalls. 'We did do one job on an SP and I reckon it was just to get evidence to get him out of the way. We didn't do anything after that in relation to SPs. But we did a lot of undercover work.

'We had this system of being a squad that detectives could come and use and we would put the whole brief together for the detective. If they had an informant, we would work the informant, we'd go undercover, we'd be with the informant the whole time, we used tapes absolutely continually, listening devices. We were getting warrants for listening devices for every bloody thing.

'We worked on murders, bank robberies, major break and enters, and drugs, they were the main areas.'

It was a far cry from Whitrod's CIU outfit, fighting to bring down the Rat Pack. That, now, was just a memory.

'When I went in there all the files [from Whitrod's unit] were gone but there were still tags on the empty files,' Slade says. 'They didn't mean anything to me for quite some time.'

Miss America

The well-mannered Jack Herbert, now free of the Queensland Police Force, his malignant melanoma, and a custodial sentence following his epic Southport SP betting trial for corruption where he was found not guilty, was at a loose end.

He needed a job, despite the continued generosities of hotelier Barry Maxwell and former police mates like Tony Murphy. Herbert, however, wasn't broke. Before the trial he'd sealed $30,000 in cash inside a number of Besser bricks which he'd waterproofed and cemented over.

By chance, he was paid a visit by friend and local nightclub entrepreneur Tony Robinson Snr. Robinson had been friends with the likes of Terry Lewis and Tony Murphy since the 1950s, when the young consorters kept a constant eye on the city's saloons and wine bars, and shared long dinners and drinks at Sue-Tin's Lotus Room restaurant and cabaret in Elizabeth Street.

Robinson had recently ventured into the gaming machine business. He had an amusement arcade in the city. He was smart enough to know that Herbert had a vast array of contacts and just might be able to help him secure his lucrative ticket machines in clubs and hotels.

The machines became known as Joh's Pokies – given the Premier's staunch opposition to regulation poker machines in Queensland. You inserted a 20 cent piece, received a numbered ticket and potentially won a prize. It was illegal for proprietors to replace the prize with cash, but this is how the machines were used. They quickly became popular in club land. Robinson ran Austral Amusements. Obviously the more machines that were in circulation, the more money could be made.

Also taking advantage of Queensland's pokie deprivation was Sydney businessman and famed yachtsman Jack Rooklyn. The cigar-puffing Rooklyn was the Australian distributor for the American Bally poker machine company.

Indeed, just four years earlier, Bally Australia came under the microscope of the royal commission on organised crime in Sydney clubs, presided over by Justice Athol Moffitt. Moffitt concluded that Bally was a front for organised crime and accused Rooklyn of lying before his commission. Moffitt said it was a risk to have the Bally organisation trading in Australia.

One of Rooklyn's companies, Queensland Automatics, supplied 'in-line' machines to clubs north of the New South Wales border. In-line machines were similar in appearance to flipper-operated pinball machines. Silver balls were sent onto the playing surface which contained grids of numbers and depressions able to accept the balls. The object was to secure four or five numbers in a line with the balls and match the numbers shown electronically on the game's headboard. Getting balls 'in-line' yielded a free game.

From the moment in-line machines were legally permitted in Queensland, however, the free games were illegally replaced with cash prizes and their popularity went through the roof. Dozens of suppliers competed for a slice of the action, but two immediately controlled the market – Robinson's Austral Amusements and Rooklyn's Queensland Automatics, the latter dominating Austral by a factor of four.

Not only were the machines a licence to print money for the suppliers and clubs, but they provided substantial income to the government. A permit for an in-line machine was ten times that for a regular amusement machine. By 1977, each machine, of which there were hundreds, funnelled up to $600 each per year into government coffers.

Robinson suggested Herbert start working for Rooklyn, and the three men met later that year at Lennons Hotel in the city.

Herbert was a handy man to know. When he agreed to work for Rooklyn he immediately got in touch with his old friend Don 'Shady' Lane, MLA. Lane, as it happened, was a member of the Justice Committee reviewing the permit system for in-line machines in Queensland.

Herbert's favourite in-line machine was Miss America – on its illuminated backboard stood two voluptuous blondes. One was wearing a red evening gown. The other, a red bikini.

Committee of Eight

Commissioner Lewis would find very quickly that the residue of Ray Whitrod and his ambitions still lingered within the force he had inherited. Whitrod had his fair share of acolytes, the intelligent, hand-picked officers who agreed with his reform, the 'incorruptibles' who had put their neck on the line to support the boss in a police culture that by and large loathed him.

Word got to Lewis that a handful of them were meeting and talking behind his back, plotting and scheming to undermine his regime. They became known as the Committee of Eight.

'They were a little group that were against me and they were probably I suppose still pushing Mr Whitrod's ideals,' Lewis remembers. 'See, I was told, well a number of people said to me when I was appointed – when you get there, get rid of all Whitrod's supporters. Every bugger was talking to me then. And I said no, no, no I can't ... and anyhow that's easier said than done. But what I did do, I still promoted some of them, which I was probably a little bit ... too lenient in relation to that.'

He said he saved some of the Whitrod faction because he believed they were reasonable police officers. He would come to regret it.

'They [members of the Committee] talked to whoever their friends were in the media,' says Lewis. 'And it was all bullshit, total bullshit.

'My quick promotion, that got a lot of fellows' noses out of joint. One of them was a fellow called [Jim] Voigt of course and a few others. When I became Commissioner ... there was a group of police who called themselves a "Committee of Eight". Now I'm not too sure who they all were, I'm sure I know some of them and they set about to wreck me.

'And they did it through feeding stuff, concocting stuff and feeding it to [the member for Archerfield] Kev Hooper who'd throw it in parliament. One fellow was a fellow called [Bob] Campbell ... he wrote articles. I think from memory it would have to be Voigt and [Basil] Hicks and Campbell and a fellow called Peter Dautel. [Ross] Dickson certainly would be, Huey certainly was … the two Hueys [John and Hilary] probably.'

Walking to a Different Beat

Across the other side of the world, in the West Midlands city of Birmingham in the United Kingdom, Police Constable Nigel Powell, 25, was walking the beat.

While technically not a rookie, Powell had been sworn in on 5 September 1975, and was beginning to find his feet. He patrolled, as part of B-division, everything from the rarefied streets of the suburb of Edgbaston, to the working-class housing commission estates of Quinton.

Powell, who had dabbled in catering, was encouraged by a friend to enlist. Despite the horrific Birmingham pub bombings in November 1974 that killed 21 people and injured a further 182, and the stabbing death of young West Midlands police constable David Green in the summer of 1975, Powell was not deterred from a career in law enforcement.

In fact, he relished the job. Living in a police house at King's Heath with his wife Heather, Powell had found his calling. He could not know that in a little over three years he would be domiciled in far-off Brisbane, joining a very different police force, and culture, from what he was used to.

Powell would leave behind a force that placed enormous emphasis on how officers worked on the streets and how they reacted to, say, incidents of football-crowd hooliganism. Part of his training was spent learning how to march properly and how to resolve violent domestic disputes. He also participated in full-on, in-your-face physical training.

As for Brisbane, he would be heading into a force whose members in their cadet training sat at little wooden desks like schoolchildren and learned aspects of policing and the law by rote. As in Lewis's time, training consisted of a few hours in the exercise yard at the Petrie Terrace depot playing with old rifles, or jumping fully clothed into the nearby Ithaca public pool – just in case their policing saw them in the drink.

He didn't know it at the time but Powell was on his way to a place so languorous and informal that he would not believe his eyes.

A Visit to the Matador Club

On the evening of 3 March 1977, Commissioner Lewis was enjoying a meal out at the Police College on official business after a busy Thursday.

Earlier in the day he had personally seen Superintendent Tony Murphy 're functioning of CIU', and had been briefed on yet another upcoming Royal tour. So by the time he'd gotten home to Garfield Drive in Bardon, he was due for a rest.

Over in South Brisbane, however, his troops were readying themselves for a raid on the notorious Matador Club, owned and run by petty gangster Roland Short. The Matador Club advertised regularly in Brisbane newspapers and promoted as a feature its fortress-like security. It ran games of Manila and blackjack, along with pornographic movies, prostitution and 'all manner of obscenities', in the words of the ALP attack dog from Inala, Kev Hooper.

On Saturday evenings at the Matador you could join in 'Swingers' Night', an event that attracted clients from as far afield as Dalby, Warwick and Toowoomba. Its newspaper advertisement read: 'BIG SWINGERS PARTY NIGHT. Come and meet new faces at our Swingers Party relaxing atmosphere in Spanish style setting. All couples welcome. Single girls invited. All amenities available. Ring Geoff – 446345.'

Geoffrey Luke Crocker was the club manager. He also ran the Key Club and other parlours for Short. He would later describe what went on in the Matador. 'On a Saturday night it was opened as a swingers' party night, you know, couples only ... like wife-swapping and that sort of thing,' said Crocker. 'We used to provide nibbles, you know, sausage rolls, cheerios and sandwiches and they bought their drinks; we supplied movies, blue movies. I used to supply two strippers on a Saturday and they used to pay $20 a couple to come in – and we were getting 50, 60, 70 couples some Saturday nights.

'Well believe it or not none of the wife-swappers hardly ever used the rooms on the premises. It was more or less a meeting place ... then they'd leave and go off to one of their own places. On odd occasions four of them would use one of the rooms.'

Monday night was 'Strip Night', where members had to undress. The club had sunken baths, private bedrooms and two-way mirrors.

Private investigator John Wayne Ryan was hired by Roland Short to fit out the security for the club. His work on the Matador was unparalleled in Brisbane's club scene at the time.

'Halfway up the front stairs of the club was a landing,' recalls Ryan. 'I installed steel gates there, and Short put in closed-circuit TV. I had a PMG technician I knew set a lot of this stuff up.'

On a typical Thursday, gambling was competitive and the house usually brought in thousands of dollars. At least ten prostitutes were rostered on.

During the raid a large contingent of police used force to batter down the wood and steel doors, utilising sledge hammers to penetrate the heavy security. They found little money on the tables and just three girls on the call-girl roster. The raid was led by police officer Kevin Dorries. At one point, Crocker ended up in a headlock as police broke down the steel door and elbowed Dorries in the face, cutting him above the eye. Crocker was handcuffed.

'Dorries kept saying to everyone, "If this prick moves, kick him in the guts, he's an animal",' recalled Crocker. 'He had me handcuffed and slapped me to the desk and he said, "You're wearing everything, smartarse", and I could hear screaming and yelling out the back of the place where the toilets and sauna and showers were, and that was Roland going up through the air conditioning duct – a copper met him going through the other way ...'

Fifty people found on the premises were charged with a total of 71 offences including keeping a common gaming house, using premises for the purposes of prostitution, various drug offences, assaulting police, resisting arrest, illegal sale of liquor and exhibiting obscene movies. Short was arrested, as was Geoff Crocker.

Kev Hooper was suspicious of the raid. 'As no VIP members were in the club at the time of the raid, this leads me to suspect that they had been tipped off,' he later theorised. 'My enquiries show that Roland Short is well known to a senior commissioned police officer. He visited this police officer some days before the raid and after the activities of his club were exposed in [the] *Sunday Sun*.

'I believe that Short had a good idea when the raid would be made.'

Hooper said one of the missing VIPs of the Matador, not sighted during the raid, was a prominent member of the National Party. 'This National Party man is also well known to the night manager of the Matador Club on the night of the raid, Geoff Crocker, who tried to thump one of the policemen who was merely doing his job.

'Crocker is also in the massage game in his own right as the owner of a Valley massage parlour.'

Commissioner Lewis noted in his diary for Friday 4 March: 'Saw Supt. MacDonald re successful raid on Matador Club.'

The club was open for business again a few days later.

The Studious Constable Campbell

With Lewis settling in as Commissioner, and the new post-Whitrod landscape still something of a chimera, 28-year-old Constable Bob Campbell made a decision to enrol in a Bachelor of Arts degree at the University of Queensland.

Campbell had been sworn in on 10 December 1968, and was serving at the Fortitude Valley police station. He had been an enthusiastic advocate of former Commissioner Whitrod's police arts and sciences course, which he had completed, and now wanted to take his education even further. He was interested in psychology and history.

Campbell informed the police department: 'I am undertaking this course in order to improve my knowledge in the field of human relations and I feel that such knowledge would assist me as a police officer.'

Subsequently, he applied for eight hours off each week to attend tutorials and lectures. This was granted under the proviso his lectures were not available outside duty hours, and his attendance in departmental time did not interfere with 'the efficient functioning' of his station.

Campbell had taken the usual path to Mobile Patrols after he was inducted, and uniquely was a 'community police officer' at Jamboree Heights, 14 kilometres south-west of the Brisbane CBD. It was upon his arrival at the Fortitude Valley station, however, that his eyes were opened to another side to policing – graft and corruption.

It was no accident, Campbell theorised, that things had changed dramatically since Whitrod's departure. 'After Mr Whitrod left Queensland, I observed a gradual transition in the Police Force in which those who had been suspected of dishonest practices were no longer being kept from positions of Trust within the Force,' Campbell would later write. 'At the Fortitude Valley Police Station, where I was attached, a few other Police Officers and myself continued to work honestly and diligently. The norm of conduct, however, had changed, and drinking and loafing were at an alarmingly high level.'

Campbell was urged by other officers to 'slow down' so he wouldn't show them up. He continued working at his own pace. This, in turn, led to bullying and harassment. In addition, he was seeing some disturbing police practices on the streets. 'The era of honesty ended with Whitrod,' Campbell wrote in hindsight. 'Any person who had a reasonable intellect or who was honest, like I pride myself on being, was subject to a new form of treatment.

'On one occasion, I heard a detective, who had recently survived a court battle involving a corruption charge relating to the attempted bribery of Inspector A.V. Pitts, attempt to persuade a gentleman involved with the Ugolini Realty gaming parlour, one of the many protected by [Inspector Tony] Murphy, to pay him money, on behalf of Murphy, in return for allowing him to operate without prosecution. I have been well aware … that there are certain massage parlours and gaming centres that weren't to be touched.'

Campbell, like so many before him, had unwittingly wandered into one of the Rat Pack's many whirling pools of graft, and learned things he shouldn't have.

Just months earlier, former Licensing Branch officer Kingsley Fancourt had resigned after finding himself caught in another such whirlpool. He felt he had no future in a police force strangled with corruption.

Campbell, though, was different. He would stand and fight. And he would pay a heavy price.

Old Acquaintances

It didn't take long for Jack Herbert to zero in on his acquaintance with the new Commissioner. Herbert would refer to him as an 'old friend'. Lewis begged to differ. His time in Charleville had obviously put on ice any direct contact they might have had as friends.

Lewis says their social interaction at the best of times was limited. 'I'd never ... to the best of my knowledge, been closely involved with him prior,' Lewis says. 'I would have met him in pubs and some sort of function ... but when I was Commissioner I know I met him again at the home of Barry Maxwell, who had the Belfast Hotel. And it sort of went from there. Oh, he's a good operator there's no two ways about it.'

Lewis remembers Herbert for his sartorial elegance and his manners. 'He was, you know, he was a very presentable bloke,' Lewis recalls. 'He was always cleanly dressed and behaved himself and never swore in front of women and I think you'll find there was a fellow wrote a book about him, which I never bought and never read but I think at the end of that he said, the one thing you can say about him was ... he was a great liar.'

Lewis's wife Hazel liked Herbert, and his wife Peggy. 'Hazel spoke well of him, everybody spoke well of Herbert in that respect,' Lewis says. 'But a couple of times ... he did use me. I thought he was being helpful but he was – how can I put it? – paving the way for himself all the time. And using people and doing it well.

'And of course primarily, as well as seeing me from time to time, keeping in touch with his old workmates in the Licensing Branch, he ... didn't use me as far as I know, to personally protect his interests in the Licensing Branch. He used me to tell them that he was friendly with me.'

Lewis says he has no doubt Herbert abused the fact that he had a form of relationship with the top police officer in the state. 'By Herbert keeping in touch with me and me seeing him from time to time and that, he was able to say to these fellows, "Oh don't you worry, Lewis is on side, I'm giving him money," or whatever ... and yet not in any stage of that game did any one of them, up to and including inspectors or assistants say to me, "Hey, how's our mate Herbert going?" Or, "I understand you're matey with Herbert." Because ... Herbert probably realised that they're not going to go to Lewis and say Herbert told me so and so. That's a bastard of a situation. You sure used me, old fellow!'

Herbert would take away different memories of their friendship. 'Around this time I started seeing Terry Lewis again,' he said in his memoir, *The Bagman*. 'It was quite a few years since the days when we'd both been taking money to protect SP bookmakers. I'd see him socially from time to time but that was all. By now Terry was Commissioner for Police.'

Another friend poking his head through the boss's door was the former police officer and state member for Merthyr, Don Lane. 'I never had much respect for him,' Lewis says. 'I never worked with him ... He was a policeman of course, he was in the CIB at one stage I think, but he was then in the Special Branch for quite a while ... His obvious interest was to get into parliament and he was very good mates with Bill Knox who was quite a pleasant fellow.

'When I came back to Brisbane he used to ring me from time to time and ... I don't think ... I never went to his home and he never came to my home. I might have seen him in a pub somewhere. Joh [Bjelke-Petersen] didn't particularly like him I know that.

'Joh didn't trust him. Unfortunately, I think Joh was right as it turned out and I ... and as a matter of fact at one stage of the game they used to swap [Police] Ministers a bit ... and I know I said to Joh one time, "What about giving Lane, you know, consider giving Lane the police [portfolio]? He'd know it all." And Joh said, "No way in the world."

'I'd have to say Lane was an opportunist.'

Lane's memories would prove a little different. 'In the police, he [Lewis] had occupied the Juvenile Aid Bureau office adjacent to that of the Special Branch where I worked and I saw him most days in passing,' he records in his memoir, *Trial and Error*. 'We had shared a beer after work on a number of occasions with other officers, some-times including Jack Herbert.

'On one occasion I had been to his [Lewis's] home for a barbecue attended by twenty or so police and others, with their wives. I knew him to be an intelligent and courteous man ...'

Enter the Phantom

William Daniel Alexander [Alec] Jeppesen arrived at the Police Depot on Petrie Terrace for his cadet training precisely three days after Lewis had been sworn in way back in mid-January 1949.

By the mid-1950s he was posted to Townsville and Ayr and variously served in the CIB and Licensing Branch when he became embroiled in the Southport SP Betting Case along with Pitts, withdrawing as pros-ecutor in that case after allegations of misconduct were brought against him. He denied any wrongdoing.

Still, the stench from the Southport case lingered, though in terms of Jeppesen – highly regarded as an honest officer – it didn't affect Ray Whitrod who, on 15 October 1976, and just prior to his resignation, proposed to Cabinet that Jeppesen be promoted to Inspector (Grade 4) and be put in charge of the Licensing Branch.

Cabinet approved Jeppesen's promotion on 15 November – the day Lewis was himself promoted to Assistant Commissioner, and the trigger that ended Whitrod's police career. Jeppesen was initially assigned to the Office of the Commissioner of Police (Staff Enquiry and Relieving). Then, on 2 December, just days after Lewis taking the top job, Jeppesen was instructed to head the Licensing Branch from late January, 1977.

Jeppesen was a straight shooter and admired by Whitrod. Why, then, did Lewis agree to him taking over Licensing, a cash cow for corrupt police and still effectively 'managed' by Jack Herbert and Tony Murphy? Did he feel he couldn't block such an important appointment so early in his commissionership? That doing so would draw attention to the branch and raise suspicions?

From the outset Jeppesen conducted Licensing business to the letter of the law. He began cracking down on prostitution and SP betting – hundreds of charges were being laid week after week. Just months into his new appointment he heard within the branch and on the street that Tony Murphy and his consorters were set to take over the policing of prostitution and the massage parlours. He had already heard it from one of the Licensing Branch constables, Brian Marlin.

Marlin was relatively new to the Queensland force, though he had worked in Sydney as a policeman for four years, and prior to that had been a member of the Australian Army. He claimed he had been trained in police work by the legendary Ray 'Gunner' Kelly in Sydney (though Kelly had resigned from the force in 1966, years before Marlin was eligible to enrol). There was talk that Marlin had been removed from the New South Wales force on medical grounds, namely psychological reasons.

He was a tough young cop with a strange obsession – he was addicted to the comic hero The Phantom. Some officers had heard he even built a Phantom 'cave' in his house. Not only that, despite being new to the branch, he seemed to be a limitless font of information.

Licensing Branch officer Bruce Wilby remembers: 'Marlin was with us for 12 months. When he first came he brought with him a wealth of information. It amazed us he knew so much.' Wilby suspected that the anti-Jeppesen forces were feeding him.

'Jeppesen fell for Marlin hook, line and sinker,' Wilby says.

It would be a potentially fatal error of judgement.

A White Uganda

In the early afternoon of Thursday 17 March, Opposition leader Tom Burns readied himself in state parliament for a blistering attack on the

Premier and the National Party. The Liberals also would not escape his ire.

The occasion was a debate on the proposed changes to the *Electoral Districts Act* prior to a state election later in the year. The Act had last been tweaked in 1971. Burns was all for an electoral redistribution, but a fair one. He knew that under the current arrangement, with the weight of votes in Queensland's vast rural hinterland disproportionately skewed in favour of the Nationals, he and his Labor colleagues were looking at not just years but potentially decades in the political wilderness.

The redistribution, if the legislation was passed, would see three Liberal seats – Baroona, Belmont and Clayfield – eliminated, and new seats created on Brisbane's ever-expanding urban fringe, taking into account the growth of places like Redcliffe and in particular the Gold Coast. The new seats gave Joh and his National Party an opportunity to contest for more seats. It was a win–win for the Nationals.

The Liberals, still smarting over the fierce debate with their Coalition partners during the last redistribution in 1971, decided to go down a quieter path this time around. As David Ford, former research officer for the Queensland Liberal Party would later surmise: 'The 1977 redistribution was a reflection of the Liberal Party's weakness within government ... the Liberal Party believed that it would be political folly to embark only months before an election on what would be undoubtedly another acrimonious intra-Coalition struggle.

'Uncertain gains in some seats seemed poor compensation for the public wrangling and the inevitable upheaval in marginal seats which would follow a redistribution.'

As for the Nationals, the prospective redistribution was more than tantalising. It would underline Bjelke-Petersen's growing sense of personal power and indirectly his disdain for Liberal leader Bill Knox. To expose Knox and his party's collective sheepishness and their willingness to bend at will to the Premier could only be good for Bjelke-Petersen and his cronies.

'To the National Party, however,' wrote Ford, 'the prospect of causing considerable disturbance within the Liberal ranks, while, at the same time, assisting marginal National Party members in the south-eastern zone, seemed most appealing.'

At precisely 2.40 p.m. on that Thursday, with Bjelke-Petersen out of the country trying to drum up mining business in the Middle East, Burns let fly.

'Today this parliament is asked to dishonour democracy,' he began dramatically. 'We are asked to remove the last legal obstacle so that the Premier and his 28 per cent National Party can further disfigure – indeed, rape – the parliamentary system of this state.

'Labor acknowledges the urgent need for a full, fair redistribution but will not lend its approval to the predetermined electoral rort that is going to be given to us here today. There is not one person inside or outside this parliament who imagines for a moment that any redistribution manipulated in the secrecy of existing guidelines by the Premier and the back-room busybodies of the National Party will be just.'

Burns quoted extensively from the editorial of that day's issue of the *Courier-Mail*: 'The present system of distributing electorates based on four zones created in the *Electoral Districts Act* of 1971 is totally slanted in favour of the Nationals. The Act is grossly unfair, even iniquitous.

'It may rearrange boundaries and lessen some anomalies in the process, but the root cause of the Queensland gerrymander is to be ignored ... if they follow him [Bjelke-Petersen], the Liberals will make themselves partners in one of the shabbiest deals the State has known – and it has known a fair number.'

Burns drew comparisons to the state of democracy in Queensland with crazed dictator Idi Amin's Uganda. In 1977, *Time* magazine described Amin as a 'killer and clown, big-hearted buffoon and strutting martinet'.

Burns railed: 'This legislation, without accompanying revision of the entire *Electoral Districts Act*, takes Queensland one step nearer to becoming a European Uganda. One could say an Oceanic Uganda – a white Uganda. In jest, the Premier recently likened himself to Idi Amin, a comparison which I fear is much closer than he would concede.'

Burns offered a withering character summation of Liberal leader and Treasurer Bill Knox, describing him as a 'schoolboy obeying his headmaster', and that 'he comes quivering to the parliament with a National Party amendment for a National Party redistribution on National Party lines'.

The National Party's 'political gangsterism', he went on, made a mockery of the Westminster-style of democratic government.

Not to be outdone, Kev Hooper, member for the seat of Archerfield, threw his weight into the debate. Following an interjection by Bob Katter, Hooper quipped: 'The honourable member who just interjected is an expert in figures – but the only figures he is interested in are the ones that he finds available in the Diamond Drill and the World by Night [owned and run by the Bellinos in Fortitude Valley] restaurants.'

That day, as the three parties slugged it out into the evening, Commissioner Terence Lewis went to lunch with several dignitaries, including two knights of the realm – Sir David Muir, former Queensland Agent-General in London and Inaugural Chairman of the Queensland Cultural Centre Trust, and Sir Theodor Bray, former long-time editor of the *Courier-Mail* and founder of the newish Griffith University.

Bray was a fierce Royalist and an early admirer of Premier Bjelke-Petersen. He said in an interview in the early days of Bjelke-Petersen's premiership: 'Mr Bjelke-Petersen, is a man who believes in his own honesty. He believes in his own strength as a man who has made a success of business, he is a business farmer, a man for whom I have great respect and a man who can be quite tough in the party rooms. He has learnt the hard way ...'

Lewis may have been oblivious to the accusations being hurled about the parliamentary chamber regarding the erosion of the Westminster system in Queensland, but he was, unwittingly or not, an unsung part of the debate.

Bjelke-Petersen had learned not just the hard way, as Sir Theodor had suggested, but well, specifically from the Springbok riots of 1971. Combining his leadership with the power of the police force was appealing to Queenslanders. And now the Premier had a police commissioner in place who would do his bidding.

Between 1 January 1977, and the day of the debate in the third week of March, Lewis had had contact with the Premier, or his personal staff, no less than 18 times, or roughly once every four days.

Lewis met with the leader of the Opposition, Tom Burns, just once in the same timeframe.

Learning to Work with Joh

From the moment of their frank and wide-ranging discussion together in the winter sun on the airstrip at Cunnamulla prior to Lewis becoming commissioner, Lewis held the Premier, Joh Bjelke-Petersen, in some form of awe.

While Lewis had no time for the vanquished commissioner Ray Whitrod, after straining under his leadership for years, he had an instant rapport with the church-going Joh.

For Lewis, the equation was simple – as Police Commissioner, he served the Premier with every ounce of his being.

'I never had a cross word with him, and he never had one with me,' Lewis says. 'As I said he was always out and about, he used to either have Allen Callaghan with him or [private secretary] Stan Wilcox or whoever … he had my direct line and he'd ring you and say, "Oh, Joh here".

'Or frequently it would be Allen or Stan ringing and saying, "Look we're up at somewhere … there are no major problems." You know?

He needed this or he needed that or he wanted a transfer. And you'd have a look at it and sometimes you could do it and sometimes you couldn't. And you'd ring back and you'd get back to Joh … "Oh, sorry Premier".

'"Oh, that's a shame Terry," he'd say. "Can't do it? No. Oh well, thanks for trying".

'He wouldn't say, you know, go and get nicked.'

Lewis's working relationship with the Premier was also at times casual and always cordial. 'Joh used to say, "Come and see me from time to time,"' remembers Lewis. 'He'd say, "I get around the state and I'd like you to fill me in if there's anything I should know."

'So I'd go and see him … every time I went to see Joh about anything, the next day or two I would see the Minister … so that I never, ever, ever went behind the Minister's back.'

Lewis says his relationship with the political leader of the day, as far as he saw it, never compromised the doctrine of the separation of powers – the division of the institutions of government into three branches: legislative, executive and judicial, working interdependently.

'No, that didn't matter,' says Lewis. 'How do you not have it? [A strong relationship with government.] If you have a Premier or Minister they're supposed to be the supreme power, okay?

'You have to have a working relationship with your Minister and they can, as I understand it, say to you we're going to give you another hundred men, the government wants you to put 50 of them, say, on traffic work, 50 in the country.

'That's not unreasonable I don't think. They're providing the resources. I would put an application in each year saying, we need this, we need that, we need them here and there – and normally they'd go along with that. But your Minister is entitled to have … he can sack you if he wants to.

'You can't tell the Premier or the Minister that you're not going to take any notice of them.'

Lewis says Bjelke-Petersen's greatest virtue was his singular focus on the job as leader. 'He wasn't interested in getting full of piss or backing it on race horses or chasing sheilas as some of them were,' Lewis says. 'And he devoted his energies to being the bloody Premier and I don't know if anyone could do it now.

'I can't recall him ever having malice in what he did. He never rang me and said, "Look Joe Blow's a shithouse who is … is there anything you can find on him?" I don't think it would be in his nature to do that, I think he'd be more likely to tell the fellow to his face what he thought of him.'

If Lewis had found a father figure in former commissioner Frank Bischof during the 1950s and 1960s, he had another in the former Kingaroy peanut farmer.

Crossing the King

As escort services began cropping up throughout the city, the Vice Squad employed some creative tactics to nab girls and their pimps. One was to take a hotel room and order in a lady. Once she arrived the negotiation for sex would be made, the money paid, and the cash taken by her to her pimp waiting in a vehicle on the street. She would then return to acquit the contract and the police could make an arrest.

One evening, Detective Dennis Koch of the Vice Squad was employing that precise tactic in the city. He and another officer booked a hotel room and phoned an escort service for a girl. Koch's partner, the 'John' or client, waited for the prostitute on this particular night while Koch hid in the closet.

'She came in and we busted her,' recalls Koch. 'We went out to grab the pimp but by the time we got there he was gone.'

A short time later they tracked him down. It turned out it was 'Graham', the husband of Mary Anne Brifman, who had established her own prostitution service – Quality Escorts – following the suspect death of her mother, prostitute and madam Shirley Brifman, in 1972.

Graham seemed unconcerned when he was questioned by Koch and the other officer. 'You can't touch me,' he said confidently. 'Murphy will look after me.'

'Who?' the detective asked.

'Tony Murphy.'

'You mean Superintendent Murphy?'

'Yeah,' Graham said.

'Why would he look after an arsehole like you?' asked the detective.

'I've got letters from Shirley Brifman,' he said. 'She was my mother-in-law.'

He told the stunned officers he could prove through letters – supposedly authored by Murphy – that Brifman had been 'scared' of Murphy prior to her death, and that 'Murphy was out to kill her'. Brifman, on her death in March 1972, was just weeks away from appearing in court as chief witness against Tony Murphy, who had been charged with perjury following allegations Brifman had made on *This Day Tonight* the year before.

Koch, acting by the book, felt compelled to contact Murphy and let him know about Graham's allegations. He had had some minor disagreements with Murphy over past investigations and wanted to keep the peace with his boss.

'This guy says he has all these Brifman letters,' Koch told Murphy. 'I'm just letting you know.'

Murphy had an immediate solution. He sent over to young Koch a sawn-off .22 rifle with instructions that Graham be loaded up and charged with possession of a concealable firearm. It was an age-old Murphy method – the planting of a 'present' on defendants the police believed were good for the charge but may legally slip the net. Graham was also charged with living off the earnings of prostitution.

When the case got to court, Koch was stunned to see that Graham was represented by one of the state's finest lawyers. 'I was surprised to see [the lawyer] in the court,' Koch says. 'I was accused of trying to frame Murphy with the planting of the gun. They accused me of the plant.'

It was alleged in court that the suspect gun supposedly belonging to Graham was on the books of the Queensland Police Force. Koch felt he was being framed. The case against Graham was thrown out.

'My name was mud,' says Koch, who had a reputation as a straight-shooter. 'Murphy was great at getting things on fellows and keeping them in reserve. [The defendant] walked out of there. I'm surprised Murphy didn't have him bumped off. I was told that the attack on me was to get me out of the way.

'Shortly after that I was shuffling papers over at the Fraud Squad.' Not long after, Koch was transferred to western Queensland.

Koch remains in awe at the power and sway of Tony Murphy during his prime. 'Murphy was the head honcho,' Koch recalls. 'He had his fingers in everything. Lewis was at his beck and call – a puppet. Murphy wouldn't dirty his hands. He was too smart for any of those other fellows. All of his instructions, they were all verbal. Nothing was in writing – he was intimidating. He was like a "Godfather".'

The Premature Death of Bob Walker

On the morning of 18 April 1977, Mrs Elaine Walker, having seen her two sons and daughter off to school earlier in the day, made her way up the hill to the wooden house on the 33-acre property she shared with her husband, Bob Walker, at Upper Brookfield, west of the Brisbane CBD.

The bushy property at 435 Upper Brookfield Road – with less than two acres cleared for the house and gardens – had been in the Walker family since the 1920s. Recently, however, Elaine had been living with the children in a caravan some distance from the house. Bob had been drinking heavily – mainly beer – and was violent when he was drunk. She was loyal to her troubled husband, but things had become untenable.

That day, Elaine entered the house and found her husband dead in bed. A post-mortem revealed he had suffered an enlarged heart and the ravages of alcoholism. Robert Thomas Walker was just 48.

Walker had been born in Brisbane and attended Brisbane State High. His father Thomas was a policeman, and while Bob flirted with the idea of settling in Melbourne and training to be a professional dancer, he remained in Brisbane and also entered the force in 1950, just one year after a young Terry Lewis.

In the late 1950s he was working in the Special Branch and made the acquaintance of a teenage Greg Early. 'I always got on well with him but he was a bit different,' Early recalls. 'From recollection he had a rough crew cut. He lived at Upper Brookfield on, I think, acreage. He ran a Morris sedan into the ground and left it there and then bought from me an Austin A40 for $100.'

Walker had a stable career and after a transfer to Townsville with the Special Branch in the early 1960s he had settled back in Brisbane by 1964 – the epitome of a happy family man – enjoying holidays at the beach with Elaine and the children, Tony, Fiona and later young Robert.

In the early 1970s – upon the arrival of Commissioner Ray Whitrod – Walker entered the Licensing Branch. There he came into contact with Jack Herbert and Tony Murphy. An early supporter of Whitrod's reform, Walker was excited by the new boss's commitment to further education. He began studying a part-time course at the University of Queensland.

At work, Walker quickly became aware of the incessant under-mining of Whitrod. He learned that when Whitrod took the top job certain police had conducted a thorough search of his background looking for any skerrick of dirt they could use against him. They found nothing.

If they'd gone all the way back to Whitrod's childhood in Adelaide they would have sourced the man's dedication to honesty and truth. As a boy, Whitrod had once hopped the fence at a local Australian Rules game without paying admission. Later, wracked with guilt, he had returned to the grounds and paid up. He vowed from that moment to lead a clean life.

As for Walker, he was acutely aware of the reputation of the Rat Pack – Lewis, Murphy and Hallahan – and their pursuit to unseat the Commissioner. Near the end of the notorious Springboks tour, the Queensland Police Union held a meeting at Festival Hall in Albert Street, the city, on the night of Thursday 29 July. More than 400 police, including Walker and Whitrod supporter Basil Hicks, attended. The meeting was closed to the press.

Almost immediately, a 'no confidence' motion in Whitrod and his handling of the Springboks state of emergency was put to the floor. The union, led by Ron Edington at the time, later declared that the motion had been carried by at least six to four in favour. It also claimed this was followed by a unanimous vote of confidence in Premier Joh Bjelke-Petersen. (The Premier, days earlier, had promised extra recreation leave for any officers involved in the Springboks fracas.)

At the meeting, which in itself threatened to become riotous, Walker tried to speak against the motion of no confidence in Whitrod. He was told that enough speakers had already been heard.

Lewis remembers: 'They had a mass meeting down at the bloody Festival Hall … of no confidence in him [Whitrod]. I think it was Bob Walker was probably the only fellow that walked over the other side and wouldn't support it … he was quite odd.'

Outside the hall at the end of the meeting, an indignant Detective Sergeant Walker spoke to a reporter from the *Courier-Mail*. He claimed that when the vote was taken a large number of police remained in their seats and 'no attempt was made' to check their attitude to the vote. Walker's opinions were quoted in the newspaper the following morning.

A week later, a still-simmering Walker attended a meeting of the University of Queensland Strike Committee over the Springboks issue and violence against students and civilians. More than 300 people were in attendance, including the press. Walker took to the stage and detailed that the previous week's Police Union meeting had been held in a 'state of anarchy', and that any officers opposing the motion against Whitrod had been shouted down by an angry mob.

'To this day, no one really knows whether the motion was carried or not,' Walker told the meeting. He said the real issue at hand was conflict between a 'larrikin' element in the force and the office of the Commissioner. 'And we cannot have our public image ruined by larrikinism.'

Walker dared to say in public that the force had never been properly trained, which was why Whitrod had been brought in. He added there was no doubt police brutality had been used during the Springboks riots, and questioned its justification. More dangerously, he said the 'doors in the corridors of power' within the police force had been closed to 'a certain clique of policemen' since Whitrod's arrival. It was an oblique, but powerful, reference to the Rat Pack.

Union president, Detective Sergeant Edington, immediately hit back. 'The union feels this matter has been completely resolved and it is distressing to think that Mr Walker is attempting to continue a slanging match for his personal satisfaction to the detriment of the good name of the Queensland Police Force.'

From that moment, Walker was a marked man.

Edington clearly remembers the issue: 'There was a fellow named Bob Walker, he used to be in the Special Squad [Branch] going around looking for Communists and things like that, and Bob was a bit eccentric. But Bob went out to the university and he addressed a team of bloody university students and he told them that the police were corrupt and that the police used to bash people to get confessions out of them. And anyway, somehow or other Whitrod got onto it and ... he took advantage of it to … nominate them [Lewis, Hallahan and Murphy] as being corrupt and he called them the Rat Pack.'

Murphy was apoplectic. He demanded Walker be expelled from the union.

At this time son Robert Walker, who was only six years old when his dad took his dangerous stand, had fond recollections of his father leading up to mid-1971. 'I have really good childhood memories,' he says. 'He would take me into the surf when we went to the beach. I remember catching my first wave. I remember a good man. Then it turned bad. It all just imploded.'

Robert says his father would often mention the members of the Rat Pack in derogatory terms. He would talk about corruption in the force. 'He was by the end a chronic alcoholic,' says Robert. 'That's the legacy of his time in the police force. Our family life was terrible. What he did to our mother was reprehensible; unforgivable. She held us together.'

Greg Early recalls that time: 'I never heard of him using the term [the Rat Pack] and linking it to those three [Lewis, Murphy and Hallahan], but that was the buzz at the time.'

During Walker's decline, his son Robert remembers one particular day. 'He was taken to Wolston Park [mental health facility] at one point,' he says. 'Police officers came to the family property to take him. My sister and I hid in the shed and watched. It was a scary thing for me.'

Union boss Edington, who was legendary in the force for his lack of fear in standing up to senior officers – particularly his memorable stoush with Frank Bischof – or championing something he believed in contrary to popular opinion, felt pity for Walker and his predicament. He explained to Walker that his resignation from the Police Union precluded him from any future pay rises.

'Bob,' Edington told him, 'now you're not entitled to any increase because the government maintains that you had to be a member of a union. Now, any increase given by the Industrial Court, to the union, you're not going to get it. They won't pay you.'

Edington said, as a result Walker lost a lot of money over the years and in a gesture to the ailing police officer he moved that he be reinstated as a union member. 'So he came back and he got reinstated but then he ... something happened, he got crook,' Edington recalls.

Walker retired medically unfit from the force in 1974 and drove taxis in Brisbane for a couple of years. At one point he received in the post a greeting card from Commissioner Ray Whitrod.

On the day of his death, Robert and his siblings – who were attending class at Upper Brookfield State School – began hearing rumours that something was wrong at home. They found their mother waiting for them with the sad news at the front gate of the property.

Years later their father would be disparagingly referred to as 'Crazy' Bob Walker, and wrongly tagged as the author of the phrase 'the Rat Pack.' (The term had been booted around the force since the 1960s.)

Says Early: 'I wouldn't have heard it until the real early 1970s.' Early adds he believed Walker 'took his own life but I never heard by what means'.

Later, Tony Murphy would peddle the standard lies about Bob Walker. 'The Rat Pack expression was never, ever used until a certain police officer, a gentleman called Bob Walker – he used to do ballet as a young constable while he was in the police force – nothing wrong with that, of course,' Murphy said.

'Bob Walker was a member of the art student faculty at the university. The Springboks tour came. There were violent scenes between the police and protestors. Walker got up a few days after the clash at the Tower Mill, got up on campus before about 600 university students, and he denigrated the police force for what he called arrogant behaviour, unruliness, brutality, at the Tower Mill.'

Murphy said the allegations were given widespread coverage in the press. 'I was on the Executive of the Queensland Police Union,' recalled Murphy. 'I received complaints from all over the state, to do something about Walker. I then put a motion through to the executive to call on Walker to show cause why he should not be dealt with.

'Walker resigned rather than appear before the union Executive, and then he was the one that kicked off this Rat Pack term. It had no connection – no relevance to alleged corruption, whatever.'

Ironically, Walker had been destroyed by the Rat Pack, the moniker of which he had supposedly authored. He joined a long queue of honest police and civilians who'd had their lives upended, in many cases destroyed, for trying to tell the truth about corrupt police going all the way back to the National Hotel inquiry in 1963.

Robert Thomas Walker was buried in the Pinnaroo Cemetery at Bridgeman Downs on the city's northside. His wife Elaine remained on the sprawling Upper Brookfield property. She never spoke to her children or anyone about Walker's troubles with the police.

Her son Robert says: 'She was still fearful that something might happen [to her].'

Ride for Democracy

When it came to the National Party gerrymander, Tom Burns and the Labor Party didn't leave well enough alone on the floor of the parliamentary chamber. They wanted to get the message out to all Queenslanders. But how could they spread word of Bjelke-Petersen's disfiguring of the parliamentary system throughout dyed in the wool National Party electorates?

They could take the message by horseback.

In April, the party launched its epic 'Ride for Democracy' campaign. It was the brainchild of the 'Bank on Burns' policy unit, staffed ad hoc with University of Queensland academics and supporters and run by Burns staffer Malcolm McMillan.

A solo horseman, ALP supporter Pat Comben, would ride from Cairns through to Innisfail, Ayr, Mackay, Clermont, Emerald, Bundaberg, Toowoomba, Ipswich and finally onto Brisbane, carrying a 'mammoth petition' in protest at the gerrymander.

A promotional leaflet for the ride said the 'petition protests the gerrymander in Queensland which gives disproportionate representation to small pockets of National Party support within a few hundred kilometres of Brisbane at the expense of the vast part of the Queensland country and the provincial cities'. It intended to 'challenge the Premier to face the Queensland people in honest elections'.

The plan was that Comben would make the 2200 kilometre trek collecting signatures and arrive at Parliament House in George Street, Brisbane, to deliver the petition by late July. Comben himself would later become a Labor parliamentarian, and the legend of his long ride would raise its head to the great delight of the sitting National Party members.

In an Estimates debate on crops and soil management, Agriculture Minister Neil Turner, Lewis's old friend from his days in Charleville, would have this to say about the horse-riding member for Windsor. 'The lack of knowledge of [Comben] about primary industries is perhaps understandable when it is realised that he first ventured off the footpath on his so-called horse ride for democracy some years ago and got lost on the outskirts of Aspley! Riding for democracy would be a difficult task for any ALP horseman, because democracy is completely foreign to Labor philosophy. My advice to the honourable member for Windsor is that next time he goes riding he should wear a bell; it will make him easier to find.'

According to a confidential Cabinet Minute dated 7 April 1977, Premier Bjelke-Petersen, incredibly, given the importance of the issue, gave an oral submission regarding the appointment of Electoral Commissioners who would handle the controversial redistribution.

It was recommended that Sir Douglas Fraser, former chairman of the State Public Service Board, Archie Archer, grazier and senior figure at the

Royal National Agricultural and Industrial Association of Queensland (RNA) and K.W. Redman, Principal Electoral Officer, be appointed.

Tom Burns' private secretary, Malcolm McMillan, recalls: 'A member of the 1977 State Redistribution Commission was an old Country Party type called Archie Archer.

'Tom used to go out to the Ekka [Brisbane's annual agricultural show held in August] each year and put in countless hours as a ring steward in the main arena. Archie, who was Senior Vice President of the RNA, thought Tom was a good bloke for doing this. Apparently, the Nats wanted to do as much damage to Tom's then seat of Lytton as was possible in that redistribution.

'Archie and Tom hardly knew each other, but Archie came up to Tom in the ring [in 1977] and mentioned the issue. He said something along the lines – "That won't be happening". Tom thought nothing more of it.

'When the boundaries came out only two seats in South-east Queensland had absolutely no change to their boundaries. One was Aspley, then held by Industrial Affairs Minister Fred Campbell, and the other was Lytton, held by Tom Burns.'

Milligan and the Corn Farmer

In July 1977, Ian Barron, an assistant manager for Sharp Electronics, based in Sydney, took a flight to Cairns in Far North Queensland. He had a meeting with Charles Du Toit, a sales agent who owned Cairns Aerial Services.

Barron was interested in purchasing two Piper Comanche twin engine light aircraft on behalf of Sharp. The company was opening an office in New Guinea, Barron said, and needed some personnel transporters. Du Toit agreed to let Barron take a test flight to New Guinea hoping to close the sale.

Meanwhile, in Brisbane, John Edward Milligan, one-time informant to former policeman Glen Patrick Hallahan and business associate of gunman and gangster Johnny Regan (shot dead in a laneway in Marrickville, Sydney, in September 1974; three weapons were left at the scene – one supposedly a police-issue revolver), was packing his bags for his own flight to Port Moresby.

Before he left, he put in a call to Hallahan at his home in Obi Obi, in the Sunshine Coast hinterland, where the former famous detective and friend of Milligan was now growing corn on his small acreage. (Hallahan's phone number was Obi Obi 25.)

Milligan arrived in Port Moresby on 13 July and checked into the Papua Hotel. The next day, Barron flew in aboard one of the Piper Comanches and that night the two men shared a drink at the Port Morseby Aero Club.

A couple of days later Barron returned to Cairns, then back to Sydney. On 17 July, Milligan took a commercial flight to Sydney and was back in Brisbane the following day. After settling into his New Farm flat, he phoned his mate Hallahan twice.

Barron and Milligan's activities pointed to one thing – not an aircraft purchase, but a dummy run for heroin trafficking. Milligan – in the years since his arrest for possession of hashish in bolts of cloth at Eagle Farm airport by Federal Narcotics Agent Brian Bennett – had graduated to full-scale heroin importation.

Matters Big and Small

Around the first anniversary of Terry Lewis's private audience with Premier Joh Bjelke-Petersen on the airstrip in Cunnamulla, western Queensland, the boss was dealing with myriad matters in the lead-up to his first overseas Interpol conference as Queensland Commissioner of Police.

That winter, Bjelke-Petersen was a regular telephone caller to Lewis. Indeed, the Commissioner had slotted seamlessly into the rarefied landscape that was government and power. 'To Parliament House re: art exhibition for Mrs Bjelke-Petersen,' he noted in his diary.

Lewis dined with the relatively new Governor of Queensland, Sir James Ramsay, up at Government House, just a quick stroll from his own family home in Garfield Drive. He attended lunches and dinners at the Queensland Club. He met a visiting Governor-General of Australia, Sir John Kerr and his wife at the Terrace Motel on Wickham Street. In Longreach on a fleeting visit, he ate at the table of the legendary cattleman and staunch Royalist, Sir James Walker. Back in Brisbane he met with the president and committee of the prestigious Tattersall's Club. He had lunch with Judge Eddie Broad.

Yet his parallel life as the state's top-ranked policeman, away from knights and private clubs, continued apace. Lewis had reason to talk with Detective Neal Freier, he of the Southport Betting Case corruption trial, 're: alleged comments by him of having direct contact with me'. Lewis saw Inspector Vern MacDonald in relation to the trials stemming out of the Cedar Bay incident the previous year. He had a beer with his good friends Tony Murphy and Barry Maxwell of the Belfast Hotel in Queen Street, in company with journalist Brian 'The Eagle' Bolton. He had discussions with Murphy about police transfers.

And he saw in person a man called Eric Nixon, public relations officer for Queensland Government Railways, regarding some scuttlebutt Nixon had allegedly been spreading, defaming Lewis. '... said he had been told by Messrs Whitrod and Gulbransen that I had been involved in counterfeit money,' Lewis recorded in his diary.

On the same day the member for Merthyr, Don Lane, called his old friend, 're: site for new Clayfield police station'. He also got a call from Murphy about the mysterious theft of a light aircraft in Cairns.

Murphy and the Plane Thieves

In an extraordinary coincidence, at the time Milligan was executing his dummy run for a heroin importation from Papua New Guinea and repeatedly contacting Glen Hallahan, Tony Murphy was alerted to the theft of a plane in far-off Cairns.

At 4.30 a.m. on 22 July 1977, a Beechcroft Baron twin engine aircraft, the property of the New Era Sewing Machine Company of Brisbane, took off for the Solomon Islands. Just half an hour earlier, an explosive device had been detonated behind the Cairns Showgrounds. This unusual event tied up the majority of local police on duty.

Back at the airport, employees witnessed the suspect plane taxi and take flight without lights, then turn and head towards the Pacific Ocean. The control tower was not manned that early in the day.

Police later learned that the plane had been stolen, and the culprits had siphoned fuel from four planes parked near the Beechcroft. Seven hours later, villagers on Mono Island noticed an aircraft preparing to land on the airstrip, built by the Americans in World War II, on the nearby uninhabited Sterling Island.

The villagers paddled over to greet the visitors and were told in no uncertain terms by the plane's occupants to keep away. The locals managed to convince two of the thieves to join them on Mono Island for a tour. In the meantime, another villager paddled to a neighbouring island that had radio communications with the capital, Honiara, to the south, and reported the presence of the strangers.

That afternoon, word reached Tony Murphy in Brisbane that a plane had turned up on Sterling Island, and that it could be the missing aircraft out of Cairns. He arranged with Solomon Islands police to gather more specific identification of the aircraft.

Just hours later, perhaps smelling a rat, the plane thieves attempted yet another night flight in the Beechcraft, but crashed into the jungle at the end of the airstrip. Local police arrived at dawn the next morning and arrested the trio.

On 24 July, Murphy along with Detectives Barry O'Brien and Pat Glancy flew to Honiara, and the following day inspected firsthand the crashed plane on Sterling Island. It was astonishing to think that the theft of a light aircraft in far-off Cairns was deemed so urgent that it delivered the Brisbane-based Murphy to a remote Pacific Island less than 72 hours after it had been committed. The defendants alleged they had taken the plane to airlift a cache of jewels recovered from a shipwreck in the region.

The men were brought back to Brisbane and installed in the city watchhouse. In there they found a scruffy 'bikie' they chatted with. It was in fact a disguised Peter Le Gros from the Bureau of Criminal Intelligence. All three were later convicted and sentenced to prison.

Murphy surmised that the object of the daring heist was to have been $1.4 million in Australian currency held at the time in the Bank of Nauru – the annual phosphate bounty owed to Nauru islanders. The bank itself was described by Murphy as being housed in a structure as something 'similar to a western Queensland galvanised-iron bank structure of 50 years ago'.

It was another triumph for Murphy and his boys. Indeed, years later Murphy would write an expansive two-part feature story on the extraordinary 'Operation Honiara' for the *Police Union Review.*

A few years later, John Edward Milligan would tell Federal Narcotics Agent John Shobbrook: 'Tony Murphy had gone to the Solomon Islands to check out the Solomon Islands – to see how feasible it was to use these places as halfway houses smuggling drugs into Australia. Tony had gone over there on official business ... somebody stole an aeroplane ... and flew it to the Solomon Islands and crashed it ... while Tony was there Tony had a mind to looking at what the set-up was like.

'Tony reported to Glen and Glen advised me that the Solomon Islands were perfect.'

Was this the braggadocio of a veteran criminal and liar? Or had Murphy and Hallahan discussed drugs and the use of light aircraft precisely when Milligan was about to embark on a major and audacious importation?

Milligan Plans the Drop

On 12 August, Commissioner Lewis had a busy day ahead of him – the usual 9 a.m. 'prayers' with his top men discussing police matters from the night before, meetings, a luncheon invitation and a matter of the past to deal with.

He chinwagged with a clutch of his most senior officers, including Superintendent Noel Dwyer and Inspector Tony Murphy, before taking lunch as guest of the Rural Fires Board with National Party Minister and Member for Roma, Ken Tomkins, at the Brothers Leagues Club in Stafford, just north of the CBD.

Back in the office, Lewis accepted the resignation of Ken Hoggett – Ray Whitrod's former personal assistant and the alleged snitch who warned his new boss back in 1970 about Lewis, Murphy, Hallahan and the so-called Rat Pack. The resignation, Lewis noted in his diary, was 'effective immediately'.

On that same day, John Milligan telephoned Hallahan and later transferred $1000 into his bank account. The heroin drop was ready to go.

The next day Milligan took an Alitalia flight to Bangkok with one of his associates, Graham Bridge, while another syndicate member, Bryan Parker, headed for the same city on a Singapore Airlines flight. Parker would buy the heroin and get it to New Guinea.

By the end of the month Parker and Bridge got between one and two kilograms of heroin to Port Morseby in a red tartan suitcase with a false bottom. Everything was going to plan. They secured the suitcase in the Davura Hotel's 'left luggage' room, and both men returned to Sydney.

Milligan took a fortnight's holiday while he was in Thailand.

Still No Letters from Home

Come August, Commissioner Lewis was enjoying the annual ritual of the Brisbane Exhibition or Ekka at the Royal National Agricultural and Industrial Association of Queensland showgrounds in the inner-Brisbane suburb of Bowen Hills. In his younger days he patrolled sideshow alley as a constable during the ten-day event. Now he had more illustrious duties. His diary for Wednesday 17 August recorded: 'To Exhibition Grounds ... inspected Police Mounted Escort, luncheon with RNA council members and wives.'

After looking over the Police Exhibit he then proceeded 'to main Ring and took part in judging of Police Horses. With Hon. Sir Wally Rae ... presented ribbons.' Sir Wallace Rae was always good company. The former jackaroo, rodeo rider and grazier had held the huge seat of Gregory in western Queensland from 1957 to 1974, and was appointed by Bjelke-Petersen as Queensland Agent General in London.

Sir Wally was not averse to controversy. He was one of several Cabinet ministers who in 1970 had accepted Comalco shares from the company for a pittance. In 1975 he also went to Switzerland at the request of Bjelke-Petersen to hunt for documents relating to an alleged loan scam involving former ALP Prime Minister Gough Whitlam.

But Sir Wally loved a good Ekka in Brisbane, was a qualified show-riding judge and had himself in the past won several exhibition ribbons. He and Lewis no doubt discussed Commissioner Lewis's imminent Interpol conference and global study tour that would take in Europe and the United States, and made tentative plans for dinner together in London.

At 7.30 a.m. the following Tuesday, Lewis was conveyed to Eagle Farm airport by his driver Gordon and commenced the long journey to Paris via Singapore, Bahrain, Frankfurt and Vienna.

He arrived at his hotel – the L'Ouest, in the central 8th arrondissement near the Champs-Élysées and the Louvre – at 11 p.m. on Wednesday 24 August. He wrote in his diary: 'An amazing coincidence in being booked into very same room as I had in 1968 [while on his Churchill Fellowship].'

As a solo traveller, he had not improved since those earlier days. He was immediately lonely, and struck dumb by foreign customs that would never pass the grade in prudish Queensland. Walking through Montmartre, he noted the proliferation of 'sex shops'. 'Large photos on display of nude males and females in various sexual intercourse positions and even of women apparently preparing to allow dogs to have intercourse,' Lewis recorded in his diary.

He found Notre Dame cathedral 'very dismal'.

As in his 1968 world tour, he made numerous social observations. 'In Paris there are many petite women, many appear suntanned, dainty feet and generally well proportioned. There are many black men with white girls and a fair number of old men with quite young girls, some quite good-looking. Men and women shake hands every time they meet, even at work each day.'

By 1 September Lewis was ensconced in Stockholm, Sweden, already feeling 'very lonely'. He was deprived of a sidekick, unlike his mentor Frank Bischof when the Big Fella attended the 31st Interpol conference in Madrid in 1962.

But on the first day of the conference he did hook up with New South Wales Police Commissioner Merv Wood, who was approaching his first anniversary in the top job. Wood was ten years older than Lewis and famed as a gold medal–winning Olympic rower. Despite the age difference, they had some common views. In an interview with the *Sydney Morning Herald*, just months before the conference, Wood had declared Sydney was 'a big city and you can't drive everything underground. You're foolish to try. It's better to let a thing exist where you know everything about it. I remember years ago we tried to eradicate prostitution. The next thing we knew they were popping up in the better suburbs. None of these things are felonies. They're what we call social offences, SP betting and so forth.'

Lewis, between conference duties, walked the streets of Stockholm. He declared it a 'swinging' city, and wrote: '... very little business for bra makers'.

He dined with Wood who regularly got drunk. 'A terrible boaster,' Lewis recorded in his diary. At dinner on the last night of the conference, 8 September, Wood and Lewis clashed again. '... I got up Merv re his claim that New South Wales only real police. Left them as soon as I finished dinner. Completed letter home.'

The following morning Lewis was on board a Pan Am Boeing 707 headed for London. After checking into the Bristol Hotel he was picked up by his old acquaintance, detective Terry O'Connell, whom he'd seen and dined with in Brisbane earlier in the year, and they went to New Scotland Yard for talks. Lewis was 'very annoyed' there had been no mail from home waiting for him at the hotel.

He later dined at O'Connell's home in Epsom, outside London. O'Connell's wife, Margaret, prepared a meal of meat, beans, potatoes, marrow and rhubarb, which Lewis considered 'quite nice'.

During the rest of his London leg, he caught up with Sir Wally Rae at Australia House on The Strand and repeatedly socialised with O'Connell, taking in a meal and a show at The Cockney on Charing Cross Road.

Lewis flew out to Toronto on Saturday 17 September, suffering neck pain and homesickness. 'Feel quite insignificant on world scene,' he wrote in his diary. 'Still no mail from home. Really fed up.'

He went on to Baltimore. 'STILL NO MAIL FROM HOME,' he diarised with emphasis. 'More blacks in streets than whites. Extremely lonely.'

A week later in Los Angeles, he discussed the policing of prostitution and pornography laws with Captain J.R. Wilson, officer in charge of the Administrative Vice Division for the LAPD. 'Cannot have nudity where liquor sold. Viewed "Hustler", "Cum Licker" ... nudity not illegal. Only bestiality, children urinating or sadistic torture is unlawful. Movies of all types including women masturbating stallion; oral sex with hog etc. Have Fist Fuckers America book. $12.50. Unbelievable.'

Back at his hotel, he checked on the number of Lewises in the local phone book and found four with the Christian name 'Hazel'.

On the morning of Friday 30 September, Lewis attended the International Symposium of Chiefs of Police, addressed by LA Mayor Tom Bradley and others, before flying to San Francisco and on to Australia. He was back in Brisbane on the Sunday morning, met by Vern MacDonald and his assistant Greg Early. They welcomed him home with a few beers at the Hamilton Hotel.

Lewis was back at his desk and in control the next morning.

That week, Premier Joh Bjelke-Petersen phoned him with concerns about the rash of protest marches in the city. It was as if Commissioner Lewis had never been away.

Tales of Roland and Ron the Maori

If the people of Brisbane were in need of stories of sex and sleaze and the sordidness of the city's underworld, they need only have gone into the public gallery of the chambers in Parliament House, that splendid Classical Revival pile on the corner of George and Alice streets, facing the Botanical Gardens.

In the cool of the lofty gallery on Tuesday 30 August, the tireless ALP firebrand Kev Hooper pressed on with piecing together his mosaic of Queensland's unsavoury criminal present, dragging in what he saw as a puerile Police Minister (Tom Newbery), a blinkered National

Party government and corrupt police. Week after week, month after month, he built his picture.

On that Tuesday, he gave the public a glimpse into the dangerous world of massage parlours and gambling dens in Brisbane and on the Gold Coast. Always colourful, always biting, Hooper told the House he had recently driven a massage parlour out of his home suburb of working-class Inala with the help of the police and the media. Thanks to big Kev, 'The Seventh Heaven' of Begonia Street was no more. He now had bigger prey in mind.

'One could almost call the massage racket in this city a cottage industry,' Hooper said. 'Unfortunately it is in the hands of some of the nastiest criminal elements at large in this state.

'Undoubtedly the best known frontman is Roland John Short, who has managed to establish some friends in high places as well as indulge in his brutal tendencies. He is nothing but a standover thug.

'Short is well known to the police, and has a very heavy grip on massage parlours and vice dens in Brisbane and on the Gold Coast.'

Roland Short was part-Burmese, tall and powerfully built. He often worked out in gyms across the city. He dressed sharp and had a fervent interest in the latest technical equipment that he utilised in his clubs and parlours. He was one of the first in the Brisbane club scene to install sophisticated closed-circuit television cameras. He was also obsessed with security, and spent small fortunes barricading his enterprises against police intervention or that from his professional rivals.

Hooper listed Short's businesses: the Matador in South Brisbane, a one-stop shop of gambling, pornography and prostitution; the Koala Court gambling joint in Surfers Paradise; the Penthouse Massage Parlour in Fortitude Valley; the Oriental Bath Massage Parlour in Logan Road, Mt Gravatt; and an out-call prostitute service called Charlie's Angels.

Short's most 'despicable accomplice', Hooper went on, was 'a Maori with bullet marks across his shoulders known as Ron. He was formerly employed as a bouncer at the Sunnybank Hotel, where he was known for the merciless thrashings he dealt out to hotel patrons.'

Ron now stood over Short's parlour girls. 'He forces them to perform sexual acts with him whenever the desire takes him, and metes out brutal thrashings to those who protest,' said Hooper. 'He is the lowest of men and should be deported immediately to where he came from.'

Hooper in part blamed the state government for 'sick minds reaping fortunes from organised vice in this city'.

While the government banned numerous classifications of pornography, Hooper opined, it allowed explicit advertisements for vice dens in local newspapers. He described some of the ads as 'disgusting' and said the government 'had ample scope … to act in this area'.

'It is vital the government provide the law enforcement agencies with adequate means to clean up the streets of our cities,' Hooper declared. 'The terms "massage parlours", "health clubs", or whatever they are called, are nothing but euphemisms for brothels.'

And he closed with a classic Hooper line: 'Some honourable members, because of their cloistered upbringing, think that brothel is the name of the soup of the day in the Parliamentary Refreshment Room.'

It may have drawn some laughs, but Hooper was making a serious point.

Just as the new Country Party, elected after decades in the wilderness in the late 1950s, had moral dilemmas when it came to the city's then six tolerated brothels and the dark whispers concerning corrupt commissioner Frank Bischof, Hooper had identified the hypocrisy in a National Party government that banked on its perception as Christian and proper and tough on law and order. Why did they do nothing?

Hooper further observed that the Matador Club was open just days after the March raid.

'This reminds me of the old days of the SP bookmakers,' he reflected. 'They were raided one day, later paid their fine and were open for business again the next day. They were virtually paying a licence fee, and the same thing is happening in connection with the Matador Club.'

The next day, a frustrated Police Minister, Tom Newbery, berated Hooper. Newbery defended the police raid on the Matador by pointing out that, '[Roland] Short had received such advanced notice of the raid from his "senior police contacts" that he was apprehended attempting to escape through the roof of a toilet on the premises.'

He added that during a subsequent raid on the club on 22 June, 41 people were arrested on a total of 59 charges, and that as a result of this attention Short 'moved his activities to the Gold Coast, setting up a new gaming establishment at Koala Court, Broadbeach', which was also raided on 4 July. Newbery claimed that according to police information Short had been unable to pay his phone bill, was behind in his rent and was in arrears in payments for the lease of his luxury motor vehicle.

The Nationals didn't let up on Hooper, and on 1 September, in parliament, showed that in an effort to disparage someone's reputation they were capable of digging up personal dirt with the same dexterity as the Rat Pack. The verbose independent for Townsville South, the burley and loud Thomas 'Tory Tom' Aikens, asked Newbery a series of Questions on Notice.

The questions were:

1. Is he aware of a woman named Kathleen Mary Hooper, aged 20, of Brisbane?

2. Does he know if this woman is a relation of the ALP member for Archerfield?

3. Has this woman three convictions for prostitution?

4. If so, did these convictions result in fines ranging from $150 to $400?

5. Is this woman the source of the honourable member for Archerfield's intimate and detailed knowledge of prostitution, massage parlours and standover criminals in Brisbane which he used yesterday in this House to smear unnamed senior police officers and members of this parliament?

Newbery responded with relish: 'I have no desire to score points off any family problems the honourable member for Archerfield may have. It is unfortunate that his recent irresponsible and provocative actions have precipitated this question, but he can only blame himself for it.'

Newbery confirmed that Kathleen Mary Hooper had indeed collected three convictions for prostitution. 'From recent utterances in this House by the honourable member for Archerfield, it seems evident that he has close contact in the massage parlour business,' he added.

For Hooper, it was grist to the mill.

That's Government Policy Now

As Commissioner Lewis was taking in the sights of Stockholm in early September, walking to the Royal Palace with New South Wales Police Commissioner Merv Wood, enjoying a show at the sumptuous centuries-old Drottningholm Court Theatre and admiring a female in the foyer of his hotel, the Continental – 'saw most beautiful black woman … had glorious hair, chest and legs' – Premier Joh Bjelke-Petersen and his Cabinet were thrashing out some important upcoming legislation ahead of the election later in the year.

The National Party would ban protest marches on the streets of Queensland.

The Premier told a reporter for the Brisbane *Sunday Mail* on Saturday 3 September, of the impending ban, linking the decision to the Federal Government's recent proclamation that uranium mining would be permitted in Australia, and the street protests that would inevitably follow.

'Protest marches are a thing of the past,' Bjelke-Petersen said. 'Nobody including the Communist Party or anyone else is going to turn the streets of Brisbane into a forum. Protest groups need not bother applying for permits to stage marches – because they won't be granted.'

Incredibly, the Premier also denied that 'files' were kept on demonstrators – only on people who committed offences. 'Files are not kept for the fun of it,' he said.

The following day Bjelke-Petersen qualified this new policy. 'Recognised non-political processions' such as Anzac Day, Australia Day, Labor Day and Warana, the annual cultural street parade, would be exempt from the ban.

'Anybody who holds a street march, spontaneous or otherwise, will know they're acting illegally,' the Premier added. 'Police will be fair, but firm. Don't bother applying for a march permit. You won't get one. That's government policy now.'

The amended *Traffic Act* legislation would remove any appeal for a permit to a Stipendiary Magistrate. Anyone who wanted to argue for a street-march permit now had to deal directly with Police Commissioner Terry Lewis.

Bjelke-Petersen had learned a lot since the famous Springboks demonstrations of 1971. That tense winter had in many ways set the course for his premiership – the police force could be an extension of his political power, and the greater Queensland electorate seemed to like a firm leader who shared their conservative values.

One member of the National/Liberal Coalition, however, was far from happy with the course the government was taking. Colin Lamont was the member for South Brisbane, a first-term parliamentarian who had lived an extraordinarily colourful and full life prior to entering politics.

Lamont was born Colin Bird in Brisbane in 1941. He would go on to change his surname by deed poll to Lamont. 'He fancied himself as a writer,' remembers Malcolm McMillan. 'He thought C.C. Bird didn't have as good a ring to it as C.C. Lamont.'

Lamont studied at Brisbane Teachers College, then immersed himself in a degree in political science, history and government at the University of Queensland. As a student, he was the arts representative on the student council, and was the Queensland education officer of the National Union of Australian University Students in 1963. He was also the editor of the student magazine *Semper Floreat*.

Lamont then tried his luck in London where he committed to further studies, before heading to Hong Kong where he was a detective-inspector with the Royal Hong Kong Police. For a time he worked in the special intelligence branch of Britain's MI6. Returning to Australia in the early 1970s, Lamont went back to teaching, holding the position of senior history master at Brisbane Grammar School until trying his hand at politics.

Wanting a shot at Federal Parliament, Lamont contested the state seat of South Brisbane as a Liberal candidate in the 1974 election as a sort of dry run for higher ambitions. The strong ALP seat was once held by the crime fighter Colin Bennett. Most said Lamont had little hope. He, however, was confident. He needed an 11 per cent swing.

In the end he got 17 per cent, comfortably taking the seat and his place in Parliament House on George Street. It may have been something in the South Brisbane electorate waters, but Lamont was a feisty, passionate politician from day one, and believed with vehemence in the accountability and transparency of government. He was outspoken against the Cedar Bay raid that had contributed to the unseating of Police Commissioner Ray Whitrod, and he was publicly opposed to the street-march legislation and its strangulation on civil liberties.

Lamont got to know and like Whitrod, particularly following the latter's resignation in November 1976. Both men were well educated. Lamont, on his election to parliament, chafed at the intellectual paucity in the House. 'I remember Don Neal [National Party politician and farmer from western Queensland] half laughing at me and saying, "You've got a Bachelor of Arts ... what do you paint?"' Lamont remembered in an interview. 'They weren't very sophisticated people, some of them.'

At midday on 7 September 1977, Lamont rose and relayed an extra-ordinary story to the House. He was familiar with his old alma mater, and he was also familiar with street violence, experienced during his years as a police officer in Hong Kong. A pro-active politician who did what he said, he had gone out to the University of Queensland that morning hoping to prevent a student protest planned for later that day.

Lamont implored the students to desist in a soapbox address with logic and compassion. 'I went out there in the hope that I could address the students because I knew that they were contemplating an illegal march,' Lamont said. 'When I arrived I found a couple of hundred students listening to a student leader who was reading out the rules of the march.

'Mr [Derek] Fielding, the President of the Queensland Council for Civil Liberties, came across to me and said, "I think we are here in the same capacity today. We are trying to talk them out of it."'

Lamont was permitted to speak to the students. He later addressed parliament:

> I told the students that I have a great concern, as do, I think, other members of this Assembly, for the right to freedom of assembly and the right to freedom of expression. I also told them that I felt that the decision to march in protest was made in ignorance of the decision made by government members yesterday afternoon. We made the decision yesterday afternoon as government members that permits should not be issued for street marches where it clearly appeared that such marches would be provocative and therefore probably result in violence.
>
> You know as well as I do, Mr Speaker, that some marches are deliberately provocative. And we said that where violence was

likely or probable we felt the permit should not be given. That was not directing the Commissioner of Police; this was supporting what the police themselves wanted.'

Lamont had explained to the students that if they continued to march they 'would be marching deliberately to come into conflict with the police.' The students accepted the logic and voted not to march.

Lamont gave the House an insight into the responsible attitude of the students to street protests by reading a document circulated by student leaders that morning. By exposing the extent to which students were prepared to abide by new draconian laws to curtail their civil rights, Lamont also highlighted the ridiculousness of the legislation itself.

The point–by–point protest march guideline stated:

1. The march must disband immediately when the marshalls give the direction to do so. Disbanding will take place at least 50 metres from any police lines.
2. Once the marshalls have directed the march to disband people should do so in the following manner:
   i. Move away from the police and keep moving away.
   ii. Move on to the footpath and form into twos and threes.
   iii. Move quickly but do not run.
   iv. Disperse over a wide area.
   v. Cease chanting the moment the marshalls give the order to disband. Remain quiet and especially do not swear.
   vi. Fold up all placards and banners.
   vii. Observe all 'Don't Walk' signs; when crossing the road do not obstruct traffic – cross in twos and threes.
   viii. If you are close to the University grounds move back there.
   ix. Make your way to Roma St. Forum Area.

'I can see members of the Opposition looking terribly glum at this turn of events,' Lamont concluded. 'I hope that we can look forward to police not having to put their own selves in danger in the future. The smiles today are on the faces of the police officers who were at the site and were happy to be able to go back to a normal day's work. I hope this augurs well for the future.'

According to Lamont, two hours after his address to parliament, an incensed Premier Bjelke-Petersen 'lunged at me across the floor of parliament, waving a tape recorder and spluttered, "I've heard every word. You are a traitor to this government!"'

'I went out and spoke on a soapbox the morning that the students were ready to march for the second time. And I managed to persuade them to disburse,' Lamont remembered. 'And Joh had the police down the bottom end of Sir Fred Schonell Drive ready to beat the living daylights out of them and throw them into the clink, and say, "Righto, there you are, law and order issue, bang, let's go to the polls."'

'He ... had a tape, or he had a ... well, he said he'd heard, so I assume he had a tape recording of everything I'd said to the students. And the frightening thing was that it had got to his hands as quickly as I'd got back to parliament. So it was ... you know, it would lead to the reasonable assumption that the police had ... the Special Branch had reported direct to the Premier.'

In a couple of months, at the 1977 state election, the Premier would have a very special surprise for the prickly and unpredictable Colin Lamont.

But This Was Not Peace

Outside the south-east corner of the state, the street-march question was not one that engaged cane farmers in Ingham or cattle barons in western Queensland. It was a Brisbane problem, seen if at all through a telescope.

In Joh's heartland, this was their Premier taking an iron fist to urban ratbags whose nebulous ideals and actions did nothing more than disrupt the social harmony of the capital. If the streets are clogged with demonstrators, how would the children get picked up from school? How would workers get home to their families after a long day in the office? And why should massive police resources be utilised to control university students and ill-kempt socialists determined to thwart the progress of the great economic juggernaut that was Queensland?

The bill to amend the *Traffic Act* was introduced to parliament on Wednesday 14 September at 2.15 p.m. The bill was passed, with the necessary amendments, at the adjournment of the House at 8.25 p.m.

Lamont remembered the passing of the legislation. '… I stepped out for a short time to attend to some business,' he recalled. 'When I came back I was astounded to hear that the bill had been read. "What, the first reading?" I asked. "No," I was told, "all three readings."

'A bill had been discussed on a Tuesday, read on Wednesday, and made law on Thursday. People ask me how, as a member of the government, I let this legislation pass. I wasn't a member of the government. In Queensland the Cabinet is the government.'

Liberal MP Brian Lindsay said of the bill: 'The lunatic fringe now seek to dominate society and society rightly expects us, the democratically elected representatives, to do something about it.'

Don Lane linked street marches to an international socialist plot to prevent the Western world developing its uranium capacities.

Local writer Bruce Dawe penned a poem – 'News From Judea' – in response to the government's latest infringement on civil liberties.

And went out to meet them about six hundred
Officers of the law who had been told
By Herod himself There will be no more
Political marches. Clear the streets
of all whose ideas are not those

of the governing party. And they did
just that and the keepers of the public
purse
looked down on the streets packed with
chariots
and said It is good. Now there is law and
order
in the land.

And many more were brought before the
Courts than heretofore
And Herod said again There will be peace
In all my land ...
And the land became exceedingly quiet;
But this was not peace.

Meanwhile up in Bundaberg, 365 kilometres north of Brisbane, Dr Harry Akers, a likeable and popular dentist in his late twenties, read of the ban on street marches in the local newspaper with incredulity.

Akers had graduated with a Bachelor of Dental Science from the University of Queensland in 1971. A few years earlier, aged 18, he had marched on the streets of Brisbane as a conscientious objector to conscription for the war in Vietnam, but considered himself without political allegiance.

After moving to Bundaberg and establishing a dental practice with a partner after his graduation, he had settled nicely into the sugar town. While still not considered a 'local' despite having been there for almost seven years, he had a superb reputation as a dentist.

By the spring of 1977 Akers was married with a young family, and they lived, with their pet cattle dog Jaffa, not far from Bundaberg's pre-eminent geographical landmark – The Hummock – a dormant volcano at 96 metres above sea level between the township of

Bundaberg and the neighbouring beaches of Bargara. Before public access was available in 1931, it had remained marooned in fields of sugar cane. The local Indigenous Taribelang people always referred to it as 'Burning Mountain'.

Akers believed the forthcoming ban on street marches was unconscionable. He might have been domiciled in a small country town on the coast and a long way from the Big Smoke, but he was going to take a stand that people would remember for a long time.

Into Thin Air

Simone Vogel, aka Norma June Beniston, moved to Queensland from Sydney in 1970 with her husband Raymond Eugene Baptiste after a successful career as a prostitute and brothel madam.

Vogel, born in 1935, worked the streets of Kings Cross in her early twenties before hooking up with vice king Joe Borg, who owned and ran numerous brothels in East Sydney. Borg's de facto, before her death of a suspicious drug overdose, was Ada, former wife to Brisbane gunman Gunther Bahnemann who had been famously disarmed by Lewis and Hallahan in the late 1950s – an action that delivered both young men the force's highest honour, the George Medal for Bravery.

Borg himself was killed by a car bomb in North Bondi in May 1968. By then, Vogel was an astute business partner to Borg, and on his death she and Baptiste briefly set up a 'massage parlour' in Newport, Sydney, before settling in Queensland.

Whether she felt it too dangerous to branch out on her own in Sydney after Borg's murder, or wanted to start business afresh in a new town, nobody knows. But the diminutive Vogel – 160 centimetres tall and, like Shirley Brifman, fond of wearing wigs – flourished in Brisbane and on the Gold Coast.

Her innovation was the 'massage parlour' – a brothel disguised as a health studio. She quickly established the Costa Brava in South Brisbane. This was followed by Golden Hands at Moorooka, The Executive Suite at Stones Corner, Napoleon's Retreat at Lutwyche, Saunette in Adelaide Street, Beau Brummel at Zillmere and Kontiki at Kedron. (She had purchased the salubrious Kontiki off prostitute and parlour owner Katherine James in early 1976 for $125,000. James was having difficulty with a heroin addiction, but she stayed on for a short time after the sale to help Vogel run the health studio.)

By the mid-1970s Vogel's net profit from her businesses exceeded $4000 per week. Around this time Vogel was interviewed on several occasions by Licensing Branch officer Kingsley Fancourt. She was anxious about her businesses, and he was starting to get some information out of her.

'I got her in the office there at one stage,' Fancourt recalls. 'She was a very, very attractive woman. A $2000 a night job.

'She was a well-spoken woman. She conducted herself in a very stately manner. I'd actually got two statements out of her.'

During their last talk, Arthur Pitts stuck his head into the interview room and asked to see Fancourt. Don Becker had telephoned and asked that Vogel be locked up. Fancourt protested – she knew all about police corruption and he had promised her she wasn't going inside.

'Pittsy and I had an outrageous blue over that,' Fancourt says. 'I was starting to ... get information. That's what we were supposed to do. I had to go back on my word. It was well known she was going to start name dropping and all the rest of it.'

A couple of years after this incident, in 1977, Vogel was living in a well-appointed canal-front home at 13 Alma Street, Coral Gables, Broadbeach Waters, with her new husband Steven Pavich, a plasterer and builder.

On the morning of Friday 16 September, she drove her white Mercedes SLC convertible to Brisbane, firstly stopping at a Mercedes dealership in Fortitude Valley to arrange for a broken tail-light to be repaired, before heading to The Executive Suite at Stones Corner, just south of the Brisbane CBD. She arrived there about noon.

At 12.15 p.m. she received a phone call from her only son, Mark Baptiste, who was then living in Sydney. Immediately after that she got another telephone call. Vogel's assistant, Marcia Barnard, heard her boss say to the caller: 'You name the place and I'll meet you there.' She soon left the parlour and didn't discuss her movements with Barnard.

Vogel was back in the office at 3.30 p.m. and received another call. She responded: 'I'll meet you in the same parking spot that I met you at before, about half past six.' She asked Barnard for a loan of $3000 from the business account. A cheque was written and cashed by Vogel at a nearby bank.

The brothel owner then drove over to Kontiki at Kedron and borrowed a further $3000, drawn in cash earlier in the day at Vogel's behest from the parlour's account. She left Kontiki at 6.15 p.m.

Pavich expected his wife at home on the Gold Coast at her usual time – 6 p.m. When she didn't arrive he phoned Barnard, who told him what had transpired that afternoon. Pavich then phoned all the other parlours without any luck. At 9 p.m. he called the Surfers Paradise police with his concerns.

They knew Pavich as an associate of criminals and did not give his report a high priority. No official police enquiries into Vogel's whereabouts were made that night. The following day, Pavich called a friend, former Gold Coast detective Greg Bignall, and asked him to make some enquiries.

On Sunday 18 September, Bignall found Vogel's unlocked car at Brisbane Airport. She had vanished into thin air.

Simone Vogel's disappearance soon became a murder investigation. Two detectives from the Homocide Squad were assigned to the case and they began by interviewing Pavich and employees of Vogel's brothels.

One of the detectives, Keith Smith, recalls: 'Our early investigations naturally included an interview with Pavich. This interview took place at the home at Coral Gables on a Gold Coast canal. Theirs was a luxurious house, probably at that time worth at least $750,000.

'We found out very early in the piece that Pavich was an extremely heavy spirits drinker. He was drunk when we first spoke with him and despite his condition he did show emotion which on the surface seemed genuine and reflected concern for his missing wife.

'The interview was not satisfactory and we decided to revisit him very early the next day hoping to find him sober. Our early interviews with Pavich disclosed nothing that was inconsistent with the conduct of a husband whose wife had gone missing. He had enquired around all of their immediate friends and acquaintances. He had also contacted a private investigator who he knew on the Gold Coast to make enquiries in Brisbane at the health studios to see what he could find out.

'Of course Pavich was well aware of the nature of Simone's business affairs and no doubt had benefitted financially from her business.'

Smith also managed to interview Vogel's full-time Filipino housekeeper, Lina. 'She came across as an honest hard-working woman who had grown attached to Simone and like others she was very worried about her,' the detective remembers. 'We asked her to discreetly observe Pavich's conduct while she was in the house with him. She did tell us that since Simone had failed to come home, from what she had seen, Pavich had been genuinely worried about Simone and had been drinking heavily and phoning a lot of people asking about Simone.'

The detectives, during the course of the investigation, found power of attorney documents signed by Vogel. They gave Steve Pavich power of attorney. The signatures proved to be forged, which Pavich later admitted to. He was subsequently charged.

Vogel's assistant, Marcia Barnard, told them that she was regularly visited by members of the Licensing Branch – in fact, she knew most of them by their first names. Vogel was paying large sums of protection money to the Licensing Branch, which reported directly to

Commissioner Terry Lewis. (At this stage the Licensing Branch was still headed by Jeppesen, although he was not in on The Joke.)

The Licensing squad had an additional advantage when it came to corruption in the mid- to late 1970s. Its members had carte blanche on policing massage parlours and brothels. The Consorting Squad, against traditional practice, was excluded.

As for Vogel, her husband, Pavich, seemed genuinely puzzled and distressed at her disappearance, and friends and associates were incredulous. There was no way she would deliberately run out on her family, given her beloved son, Mark's, twenty-first birthday was just a few weeks away. She had discussed the milestone event with him many times, and a big party was planned. Besides, detectives found no evidence that she had flown out of Brisbane, despite her car being found at the airport.

So what happened to the petite madam who famously had a passionate dislike of drugs and banned any drug use in her health studios? And why had she hastily got together $6000 in cash on that Friday?

As the two homicide detectives patiently and expertly exhausted any leads, they came to an extraordinary theory. Had Vogel, who had intimate knowledge of The Joke, finally decided to leave the parlour trade behind and, using her business acumen, legitimately start afresh?

If so, was the $6000 cash a final corrupt payment to the Licensing Branch, or the price of getting out of The Joke?

With her intricate knowledge of the corrupt police network, though, what if Simone Vogel, at some point, decided to blow the whistle, as Fancourt had believed she would do a few years earlier? An unchecked brothel operator like Vogel could be extremely dangerous to high-ranking police.

If this theory was in any way close to the truth, it naturally followed that police might have been involved in the disappearance.

'Simone, over many years, had become a central part of this corrupt system even if as a willing participant in what was described as victimless crime,' Keith Smith says. 'She had become quite friendly with the senior officers of the Licensing Branch. Her knowledge of what was later to become known as The Joke was vast and if she ever decided to blow the whistle for whatever reason, she could bring down the whole Licensing Branch with serious repercussions through to the very top police officers in the state.'

It was a notion investigating officers couldn't shake. Who better to make someone vanish than corrupt and experienced police officers?

Smith recalls: 'In what I believed to be a confidential conversation, I expressed my concerns of possible police involvement to my immediate superior officer ... he gave me a good hearing but I could tell that he was somewhat disturbed by what I had related to him and virtually told me that I was on the wrong track and that I should forget about any such conspiracy theories.

'I later recognised that what I had done had not remained confidential and I noticed that I was being shunned by some who I had previously regarded as mates.

'On one occasion during an after-work drinking session, one of these detectives accused me in front of others of having become a mate of Steven Pavich and of receiving money from him. He suggested that this was the reason I had never pursued Pavich as the most likely suspect in Simone's disappearance.'

Still, the homicide detective went ahead and committed his theory of police involvement to paper, typing a confidential report and handing it to a superior, head of the CIB. 'I put my "theory" on paper and against all recognised chain-of-command protocol I confidentially forwarded my report to the Detective Superintendent in charge of the CIU,' the detective recalls. 'I knew this man and felt that I could trust him. He assured me that my report would be kept in his safe and would remain confidential.

'Within weeks after I did this [Tony] Murphy summoned me and my partner to his office. He told us that we "could not see the woods for the trees" and that we had never really sufficiently directed and concentrated our investigations on Pavich who he and many others believed was Simone's killer.

'He told us that he was taking us off the investigation and that all associated material was to be handed over to two detectives who were being seconded to the Homicide Squad especially to have a fresh look at the investigation. Whether by coincidence or otherwise, it was one of these Detectives who had accused me of being in Pavich's pocket. Naturally, I thought this was more than coincidence,' Smith remembers.

The detective later made 'discreet enquiries' within the Bureau of Criminal Intelligence about his 'confidential report'.

'Much to my dismay he told me that after due consideration, my report had been disregarded and shredded,' Smith says.

Simone Vogel's body was never found.

Cleaning Out the House

Around September 1977, Gerry Bellino's illegal casino upstairs at 142 Wickham Street, Fortitude Valley, was doing good business when a famous local identity graced its gambling tables.

It was Luciano 'Lou' Merlo, the Brisbane restaurateur and owner of the extremely popular Merlo's. The New Farm restaurant – one of the first fine-dining eateries in the Brisbane suburbs – was opened in 1974 and frequented by many of the city's notables, including public servant Sir David Longland, politicians Russ Hinze and Llew Edwards, and popular ABC radio announcer Bill Hurrey. Merlo was also hard to miss around town in his 1974 Maserati V6 Merak SS.

On this particular night, private investigator and hardman John Wayne Ryan was pacing the footpath outside 142 keeping an eye out for drunks wanting to get into the casino.

Since being employed by Gerry Bellino to be on the lookout for trouble, the karate expert and well-known figure in Brisbane's underworld made it a point of not working on the actual premises. He would not be knicked by police for being in an illegal casino.

Ryan knew Merlo by sight. He had seen the restaurateur enjoy the hospitality of 142 Wickham a few times. In the early hours of the morning, Merlo made a fairly slow start but then began winning a succession of hands of blackjack. Word got to Ryan that Merlo was on a lucky streak and it was worth seeing.

'Bellino was actually standing behind the dealer, and that was something he rarely did, he usually just socialised with the patrons,' says Ryan. 'Merlo asked Bellino if he'd up the ante – from $1000 to $3000, $5000, then $10,000 a hand.

'Merlo cleaned them out. He won big.'

During this sensational streak of luck, phones started ringing and people started turning up at 142 to try and catch a look at Merlo in action. 'Word got around,' says Ryan. 'There were people everywhere. They wanted to see this big game. It was said he won $50,000, but I understand it was closer to $100,000, in cash. That was a lot of money in those days.

'I walked Merlo back to his car in nearby Duncan Street.'

Merlo's good fortune had a disastrous knock-on effect for Bellino.

While the restaurateur went home with a big bag of cash after a great night out, the Bellinos had a serious problem. Their monthly kickback of around $10,000 to police had to be found. The safe at 142 Wickham had been emptied. Cash had to be brought over from Pinocchio's and other joints owned by the Bellinos to facilitate Merlo's windfall. Where would they get the cash to pay the cops on time?

According to Ryan, gamblers and associates of the Bellinos urged them to pay on time. But they fell behind.

Then in October 1977, just a few weeks after Merlo's miraculous winning streak, a punter walked past John Wayne Ryan and into the gambling joint. He talked to Tony the Yugoslav, the bouncer on the door, went inside for a while, then left.

Soon after, the stranger came back. It was Constable Brian Marlin of the Licensing Branch.

'I'll never forget it,' says Ryan. 'I never used to turn up there until late, after 11 p.m. when the pubs were emptying out and the night-clubs were going. There was a bit of traffic. There were a few cops up and down the street but I didn't take too much notice of that. I saw Phil the Gambler approaching the club with a couple of good-looking girls – he was a professional gambler.

'Then this guys walks in, slips into the club, and the next minute he's king hit Tony the Yugoslav. It was Brian Marlin.

'The next thing there are cops everywhere, at least 20 of them, and I'm bundled back inside the door of 142 and they produce an oxyacetylene torch. They told me if I didn't go inside with them they'd turn it on and use it on me.

'I saw Marlin on top of Tony and he raised himself up and said, "We've got a gun here!" I saw Marlin wipe blood off the gun onto his own shirt and face, as if he'd suffered an injury in the fight with Tony.

'I knew these cops gave people "presents" from time to time, but that was the first time I'd seen it with my own eyes.'

About 30 patrons of the club were rounded up as well as the staff. They were then marched down into the street and into a 'Black Maria' for transportation to the city watchhouse. 'There were boys and girls all in there together,' says Ryan. 'All the way to the watchhouse they sped up and braked, sped up and braked, so we'd all be thrown forward. We were put in the drunk tanks. Bellino was brought to the watch-house in a separate vehicle and placed in a separate cell. The cops then processed us.'

As a result, Bellino was ultimately charged and convicted of keeping a common gaming house at 142 Wickham Street and fined $350. It was his first and last such conviction.

Why did it happen?

'The Bellinos had missed their monthly payment to the cops thanks to the big win by Lou Merlo,' says Ryan. 'That was the lesson. That was what would happen if you didn't pay up on time.'

Milligan, the Reluctant Bushman

John Edward Milligan returned to Brisbane from his Thai holiday on 15 September, rested and refreshed. He called Glen Hallahan in Obi Obi as soon as he got home.

Associate Bryan Parker, meanwhile, returned to Port Moresby and prepared the heroin for the final leg of the mission, taping it up into two packages. He then journeyed to the nearby island of Daru with the drugs and waited, while Milligan and his co-conspirators Graham Bridge and Ian Barron all reconvened in Cairns.

Barron pulled the same scam that he had used two months earlier. He took a test flight in the other Piper Comanche up for sale, and flew into Daru to pick up the heroin. He was back in the air on 19 September. Before landing in Cairns, he took a sweep over Princess Charlotte Bay – 350 kilometres north-north-west of Cairns – and the nearby Jane Table Mountain (or Jane Table Hill, as it was also known). The mountain was Barron's target. The syndicate had done its homework, to a degree.

Jane Table, a sandstone plateau, was spectacularly remote and stood out like a sore thumb. It was surrounded by 200,000 hectares of rich floodplain formed by the confluence of four major rivers meeting to the south of Princess Charlotte Bay. But it was a difficult place to access on the ground.

Barron made the drop as planned, and Milligan and Bridge headed to the mountain out of Cairns in a hired Toyota LandCruiser. The two Sydney-based bisexuals passed themselves off as keen fishermen.

On their first night they stayed in the tiny town of Laura in the Cook Shire. They chatted to locals in the only pub, owned by regional legend Percy Trezise – a pilot, painter, writer, explorer and passionate advocate for protection of the abundance of local Aboriginal rock art.

'Talking to the locals at [the] Laura Hotel where they said they were on a fishing trip, they soon realised that their problems were getting worse for they had no ability to cross the many rivers crisscrossing Princess Charlotte Bay,' said Narcotics Agent John Shobbrook. 'Their first attempt to reach Jane Table Mountain was a failure but they did learn the best way to reach their destination ...'

Milligan returned to Brisbane, again phoning Hallahan.

On 28 September, the men returned to Cape York, this time borrowing a dinghy and making it across Princess Charlotte Bay to the base of the mountain where they pitched camp. Their search for the small packages of heroin in this vast territory failed again.

By chance, they encountered in the region a local fisherman called David Ward. He caught barramundi illegally. Milligan and his crew recruited him, with the offer of money, to help look for two packages of 'jewellery' that had been dropped from a plane.

'Ward was wary of strangers, as his occupation was illegally netting barramundi from the river,' said Shobbrook. However, he soon realised that these weren't Queensland coppers or government snoopers and before too long Milligan felt confident enough to explain to Ward that they had had a couple of parcels of jewellery dropped from a light aircraft and they were looking for them. Ward truthfully admitted that he hadn't seen any packages but if they'd pay him then he would help them search.

Once again nothing was found, and Milligan gave Ward his name and telephone number on a piece of paper, telling him to call if he found anything. The note said: 'Phone me if you ever find the parcels, but don't open them.'

Again, Milligan returned to Brisbane. He rang to break the bad news once more to Hallahan. The former detective was furious. 'Get your backside up to Cairns and find the bloody heroin,' he yelled at Milligan.

Milligan returned for yet another search shortly after, and found one of the parcels. So did David Ward, but he didn't tell Milligan. He figured it was worth more than the reward money offered, and took it back to Cairns where he tried to sell it to a fisherman and petty criminal in a pub, who handed over a huge sample of the drug to a local Customs officer. The fisherman happened to be the officer's informant.

The sample was sent to the Federal Narcotics Bureau office in Edward Street, Brisbane, and on confirmation that it was high-quality heroin, a major investigation was initiated. It was headed by an officer called Greg Rainbow.

Meanwhile, Milligan, with only half his prize, settled back into his New Farm flat, and proceeded to make money transfers totalling $3000 into Hallahan's bank account.

Pincer

The week after massage parlour madam Simone Vogel disappeared, Kevin Hooper, acting on information from confidential informants, stood in Parliament House and asked questions of Police Minister Newbery. Hooper was agitating for a full inquiry into the massage parlour industry. The Vogel case gave him the opportunity for a pincer movement.

He asked if Newbery had been made aware of Vogel's case, and further asked: 'As this disappearance seems to have sinister overtones, will he [Newbery] now reconsider his opposition to holding a full inquiry into massage parlour operations?'

Newbery said he had noted the newspaper articles on Vogel, and had read 'more recent newspaper articles concerning this matter wherein the honourable member for Archerfield has claimed that he has been given information by massage parlour girls that strongly indicates that the woman known as Simone Vogel has been murdered.

'While he is ever ready to pass his information on to the media, he has shown a marked reluctance, despite repeated requests by me, to pass the information on to police to assist them with their investigations,' Newbery continued.

Incredibly, Newbery told the House – possibly on instruction from Acting Commissioner Vern MacDonald, as Lewis was still on his Interpol tour of Europe – that there was no evidence yet to suggest the disappearance had 'sinister overtones'.

Newbery, an ineffectual parliamentary performer, even with prepared speeches, decided no commission of inquiry into massage parlours was necessary. 'While I cannot recall having previously opposed such an inquiry, I do so now,' he said in response to Hooper. 'The operations of massage parlours are under daily scrutiny by the police department. Statistics recently tabled in this House prove the success of police activities in this area.'

Newbery concluded with a flat flourish: 'I can assure all members of this House that police attention will continue to be given to the curtailment, with the aim of elimination, of massage parlours operating for the purpose of prostitution.'

The reality, in the streets of Fortitude Valley and on the byways of far-flung suburban Brisbane, was that the parlour business was expanding at a rapid rate and that men like the entrepreneurial Jack Herbert were beginning to see its potential as a massive source of income.

Certain police, too, were beginning to avail themselves of free alcohol kept on many premises in anticipation of their visits, and some free 'massages' to boot. Despite Newbery's pledges, the industry was as true and constant as the red beacon atop the Brisbane City Hall clock tower.

Taking to the Streets

Justice Lucas's report, following the Inquiry into the Enforcement of Criminal Law in Queensland, compiled with the assistance of legal eagle Des Sturgess and retired Whitrod man, Don Becker, was delivered to the government in April.

At its heart it intuited that the police practice of 'verballing' could be removed with the mandatory audio tape or video recording of criminal confessions. It also saw a benefit in turning over staff more regularly within the Licensing Branch to avoid entrenched corruption.

The report was quickly forgotten. Instead, the end of Lewis's first year as Commissioner was by and large preoccupied with forging a strong relationship with Premier Joh Bjelke-Petersen. And it was the street-march legislation that perfectly aided and abetted this.

Around the time drug dealer John Milligan was wading through marshlands on Cape York looking for packages of heroin in September 1977, student marchers took to Brisbane streets over the dissolving of their right to march and the brutality and arrests began. Out of these clashes emerged a group calling itself The Right to March.

With the election set for November, Lewis pitted hundreds of officers against protestors in a protracted civil arm wrestle that extended over months. Hundreds of arrests were made. Civil liberty groups and members of the public complained about the show of police strength. Television footage of the clashes was broadcast across Australia.

As former commissioner Ray Whitrod had predicted on his resignation, Queensland was showing more than just signs of becoming a police state. That status had arrived.

'They say Joh was against people and no, they couldn't march,' says Lewis. 'But it wasn't like that. They could march any day of the week after 6 p.m. Any time Saturday after midday and any time Sunday. You've got no idea how many people got in touch with us saying their kids [at All Hallows, Terrace and Brisbane Boys and Girls Grammar schools] have to go through the city to get home from school and we don't want people marching … it would have disrupted tens of thousands of people and many of them young people.'

Lewis had other distractions during the turmoil.

There were matters of politicians calling about speeding tickets issued to them and their children; of having to provide 'discreet security' for mining magnate Lang Hancock when he paid a visit to Mount Isa; talking to the Premier about possibly installing a police radio in his official car.

Lewis was in constant touch with Bjelke-Petersen over the street-march problem. 'Premier phoned re his views on Protest marches.' 'Premier phoned re no marches on road.' 'To Executive Bldg., and saw Premier re street marches.'

In the midst of all this, on 20 October his diary records that he saw Deputy Commissioner Vern MacDonald about a raid on an illegal gambling club run by a man called 'Bellino'.

By the end of the year Lewis had time again to catch up with old friends. On Sunday, 18 December at 12.30 p.m., he joined Barry Maxwell and his wife Sheilagh at their Kangaroo Point home for a Christmas function.

He left at 3.45 p.m. and headed over to a three-level block of cream-brick flats at 49 Laidlaw Parade in East Brisbane. There he celebrated with 'Jack and John [his son] Herbert's birthday until 5 p.m.'

A Quiet Word

Around this time, the affable Jack Herbert had Geraldo Bellino – local illegal casino entrepreneur, one-time adagio dancer and songwriter (in August 1963 he had officially copyrighted a musical he called *Sharon, Oh Sharon*) – over to his house for a drink.

Bellino had a query. Would it be possible, he asked the former Licensing Branch officer of more than 15 years, to set up an illegal game without breaking the *Gaming and Vagrancy Act*? Was there a loophole that could be exploited?

Herbert claimed he sat down and poured over the Act.

'He didn't ask me to do anything illegal but in any case I couldn't help him,' Herbert said. 'Since taking over at the Licensing Branch, Alec Jeppesen had instigated a purge of illegal casinos.

'He was also coming down hard on SP bookmaking and prostitution. I told Gerry Bellino there would be no protection while Jeppesen was running things.'

It was becoming apparent that Jeppesen was proving an obstacle to lucrative channels of vice. Money should have been falling out of the sky for Herbert.

He made a mental note and wondered – what if we could have Jeppesen removed from the Licensing Branch?

The Premier Phoned

With Lewis in the top job for just 11 months, Premier Joh Bjelke-Petersen wasted no time in utilising the police force in whatever way he saw fit to exercise his will. If he needed to call on the boys in blue to silence a growing nuisance and critic of his government, then he had zero compunction in doing it.

Such was the case of Brisbane businessman Mervyn Carey. In late 1977 Carey was a senior executive with BP Australia. The company's Brisbane offices were a stone's throw from the police department in Herschel Street, in the city.

The unassuming Carey, married with children, began showing an interest in corporate crime following the collapse of several major Queensland construction companies and credit unions in late 1974 and early 1975, and was elected national president of the Australian Institute of Credit Management.

In late 1976 the *Courier-Mail* ran a profile on Carey, describing him as 'Queensland's most ardent fighter against corporate crime for the past two years'. Carey, BP's credit manager for years, told journalist Mark Williams: 'I don't want to be a Ralph Nader [the American political activist], but if I'm getting a Nader image and it will get some of his results with honesty being returned to the corporate area, then I don't mind.'

Then Carey unwittingly made a big mistake. On Wednesday 12 October 1977, he was a guest speaker at a seminar hosted by the Australian Institute of Management in Brisbane. He gave the keynote address.

Carey had watched with increasing alarm the recent collapse of the Queensland Permanent Building Society (QPBS), and was questioning what had happened to missing society funds. In his speech, he slammed the Bjelke-Petersen government, accusing them of 'pussy-footing around' the company collapse. He called for a full inquiry into the matter and requested statements of missing funds from the society.

'An inquiry would bring out the facts,' he told more than 140 people at the seminar. 'There are too many traumas and dramas within the building society industry. The public's confidence will never be restored until the truth is ascertained.'

Carey went on to directly accuse government ministers of not just falling asleep at the wheel, but deliberately obfuscating the facts behind the fraud. He said: 'The industry has reached rock bottom and the State Housing Minister [Norm Lee, the MP who encouraged then Inspector Terry Lewis to give Police Minister Max Hodges an earful at the country Cabinet meeting in Cunnamulla in mid-1976] must bear full responsibility.

'The Deputy Premier [Bill Knox] and Mr Lee have tried to throw a smokescreen around their own failures and inadequacies to handle the situation in a business-like manner. Now $3.8 million is unaccounted for in the latest collapse and Mr Lee still rejects an inquiry.'

Carey directly accused the Bjelke-Petersen government of ignoring major white collar crime. His inflammatory comments were published on page three of the *Courier-Mail* the following morning. The Carey story sat beneath a picture story on Premier Bjelke-Petersen, rehearsing for his election policy speech to be given in City Hall that night. The state election was set for 12 November.

The day the story was published, life became hell for Merv Carey. 'I got called in by my boss,' Carey remembers. 'He said the Premier had just phoned him and told him to sack me. I was raked over the coals.'

Later that day he received a call at his desk from an old friend, Assistant Police Commissioner Don Becker, the trusted and incorruptible former Whitrod confidant. Becker made the call from a phone box. 'Don told me to shut my mouth and that Lewis had been in touch with the Special Branch and they were investigating me,' Carey says. 'He said the boys involved were bad boys, they had a bad record and that people had been killed as a result of the activities of these men.'

Shortly after, Carey received another phone call. This time it was anonymous. 'He said, "If you open your mouth again, it'll be for the last time,"' says Carey. 'I felt dead scared. I was frightened, not so much for myself but for my family. That's the way Joh used to work. I never spoke again after that.'

The anonymous threat bore all the hallmarks, going back decades, of Detective Inspector Tony Murphy, head of the CIB.

'About that time I was walking down George Street,' Carey says, 'and I saw Tony Murphy walking towards me. I knew who he was. He gave me a good looking over.'

The afternoon Carey received his death threat, Bjelke-Petersen's Cabinet held an emergency meeting into the QPBS collapse. The government resolved that the society would be propped up financially and merge with the State Government Insurance Office (SGIO) and that none of the 140,000 QPBS investors would lose any interest.

The merger immediately showed the public – in the run-up to a state election – that the Bjelke-Petersen government cared about Mum and Dad investors in the community. The missing $3.8 million would, according to the new *Queensland Permanent Building Society Act 1977*, be replaced from the government's Contingency Fund.

Conversely, the bail-out masked the corporate fraud behind the missing millions. They were never accounted for.

Angels Fear to Tread

There was no stopping the Member for Archerfield, Kevin Hooper, when he got on a roll on the floor of the chamber in Parliament House, and Thursday 6 October 1977 was no exception. It was the last state parliament sitting for the year.

On that day he was prepared to take the Bjelke-Petersen government to task over its financial record, and in particular the building society crisis.

He would describe Treasurer Llew Edwards as 'a reasonable man – colourless, perhaps, a puppet of the Premier, perhaps', and Police Minister Tom Newbery as 'inept'.

But that would come later in his florid address. First, he wanted to put on record some facts about the mysterious disappearance of brothel madam Simone Vogel.

Hooper was in his element. He railed that Minister Newbery and the government had done nothing to control massage parlours in Brisbane, despite an explosive growth in the trade. He further accused the government of 'turning a blind eye to the ways and means available to any state government that wishes to stamp out this brand of vice. It can be stamped out.'

On prostitution, he slotted in a reference to the Vogel case: 'It is a type of undesirable underworld activity which, under the Queensland Government's inept administration, has allowed a prominent massage parlour owner to disappear without a trace after she borrowed $6000.'

Hooper continued belting Minister Newbery: 'I would have thought that he [Newbery] would tell the House that in the matter of the disappearance of Simone Vogel, where there is a possibility that a life is at stake, I have made every endeavour to assist the police.

'In view of earlier information I have provided in this House I would have expected him to tell honourable members that, on the day of her disappearance, armed with $6000, Simone Vogel set out for a hotel car park to keep an appointment with the notorious Roland Short. This gentleman's attributes I have previously described to the House.'

He revealed further details. Vogel was to meet Short in the car park of the legendary Breakfast Creek Hotel, the French Renaissance-influenced pub at 2 Kingsford Smith Drive and within sight of its namesake. Here, in 1824, the founder of Brisbane, John Oxley, and explorer Allan Cunningham, met local Indigenous clans for breakfast. A minor skirmish had occurred when one of the clansmen grabbed Oxley's hat.

'Where is Roland Short now? Where is his associate Ron the Maori? Who is running his [Short's] call-girl and massage parlour operations? Who is collecting the money?' Hooper queried. 'It is sad to have to report that the underworld has moved into a state in which, if we are to believe the Premier, angels fear to tread. Perhaps the Minister for Police is afraid to attempt to clean up the criminal elements in this state. When his predecessor [Max Hodges] tried to do this, the Premier moved in and took the portfolio from him. Let government members deny that.'

As his police force was being publicly picked apart by Kev Hooper, Lewis received a peculiar visit in his office. A Susan Antonieff, 20, of Kelvin Grove, saw the Commissioner about whether or not he was actually her father. Lewis noted in his diary: '... Has taken every drug and being treated at R.B.H. [Royal Brisbane Hospital].'

Later in the day, Lewis and his wife, Hazel, were then driven to Eagle Farm airport by Greg Early, where they met Minister Newbery and his wife, before they all departed on TAA Flight 458 for Mackay. That night they all settled into their rooms at Gorries Motel on Nebo Road in West Mackay. The Commissioner was doing what he loved best – conducting, with full entourage, a short tour of regional police stations. This time he went along with royalty – a government minister.

Hooper's attacks were, as usual, disregarded.

Permission to Speak to the Media, Please

Senior Constable Bob Campbell, still being harassed by other officers at the Fortitude Valley station and studying for his degree at the University of Queensland, had decided to get out of the police force.

With a wife and two young sons, he saw a better future for himself free from the mire of corruption that he'd found himself in, and tried a number of ways to extricate himself from his job. On 19 October 1977, he informed the department that it was vital he complete his degree and additional doctorate 'so that I may terminate my employment'.

Two days later he wrote to Police Minister Tom Newbery under-lining his intentions and seeking permission to talk to the media about crime and corruption in the police force. If it was a tactical move to poke a stick at the hierarchy, it worked, but perhaps not in the way he intended. Campbell may have thought they would eject him immediately. Instead, the prickly and outspoken Campbell was in for an all-too-familiar form of workplace misery.

Newbery replied to Campbell: 'You will no doubt appreciate that I have no direct jurisdiction over you as a member of the Police Force. Therefore, it is not possible for me to grant you permission to communicate with the media.

'The Police Rules provide for members of the Police Force to air grievances through their District Officer or Commissioner. The Rules also place certain obligations on members who have knowledge of misconduct on the part of other members.'

The Minister concluded that if Campbell remained dissatisfied with his working conditions having 'explored the Departmental avenues open to you', he could write to the Police Minister once again.

Two days later Campbell tried another tack. He authored yet another report, this time alerting his superiors that he had injured his ankle earlier in the month on campus at the University of Queensland. In a desperate plea, he wrote: 'In view of this, I have requested that I be placed before the Medical Examination Board as I feel that I should be discharged on the Police pension. My work in the Police Force has been criticised in recent times and this injury will by no means improve my work. I do not appear to fit in well with the Police Force and it may be practical for the Department to discharge me ...'

Campbell's action to go before the medical board was refused. Instead, a timeworn trapdoor for recalcitrant officers, for those who didn't toe the line or keep their mouths shut, opened up under the young Fortitude Valley officer. He was transferred to Police Stores, home to the banished, the drunk and the indolent.

The department said it was to assist in Bob Campbell's health and in the progress of his studies.

Three Corners

By 1977, a year in which parliament sat for just 38 days, Bjelke-Petersen was sitting high in the saddle, particularly with a strong police force at his beck and call to deal with the socialist radicals that wanted to bring the city to a standstill with their protests. He was tiring, too, of his Liberal coalition partners.

So for the state election of 12 November 1977, a vindictive Bjelke-Petersen decided to make it hard for them as well as the ALP. In a childish pique, his all-powerful National Party changed the rules of the game and challenged their Liberal colleagues in seats that had had their names changed following the redistribution. If the seat held the same name as it did prior to redistribution, no challenge was offered. The redistribution effectively vanished three Liberal-held seats.

In addition, the Nationals contested for the first time seats on the outer edge of the Brisbane metropolis. Three-cornered contests abounded. The ALP wrested back some of its heartland voters following the 1974 election fiasco, but still lost on preferences, as was to be expected. For the first time the National Party out-polled the Liberals by 27 per cent. It was the first shot in a long war.

Liberal Colin Lamont's seat had been redistributed before the election and he lost. 'I remember when I ran for re-election in 1977, [the former Police Commissioner Ray] Whitrod sent me a card with Snoopy on it,' Lamont recalled in an interview years later. 'He [Snoopy] had a tennis racket in his hand, and it had a $10 tag on it. And he'd written, "Snoopy's boss is well named Peanuts if he thinks you can get a racket in Queensland for $10".'

He said Bjelke-Petersen never understood political principles. 'He was a very simple man,' said Lamont. 'He slept with a bloody goat in his farm before he met Florence. A very simple man. He didn't understand the underlying principles of government. He didn't understand the Westminster system. He didn't understand anything about political philosophy.

'And his view was – we are the government, the National Party is we, and I am the National Party, so I'm it. You know, I've got this job by dint of the will of the people, and you know, I can do what I like.

'The suggestion that there were any constraints ... I mean, you know, I don't mean go out and commit a crime, but I mean, the suggestion that there were any constraints within, you know, normal bounds of power, just didn't occur to him.'

What Wilby Saw

Everyone in the Licensing Branch was aware of the rumours of corruption, the so-called Rat Pack, and the involvement of former branch member Jack Herbert. They heard that huge sums of money were being passed over in corrupt payments. And intelligence was coming in that this wasn't just a local operation, but a vast network that covered most of Queensland. In short, it was supremely organised.

Whenever Bruce Wilby and his fellow officers tried to execute raids on massage parlours and SP betting joints on the Gold Coast, for example, they'd arrive to barred doors and empty houses – Superintendent Syd Atkinson was in charge of the Gold Coast district.

'A memorandum came through from Commissioner Lewis – if you do anything on the Gold Coast you had to let Atkinson know first,' says Wilby.

'[So] when you got down there, everything was shut up. There was nothing going on. We'd find out what was operating and get our warrants. All hell would break loose on Monday morning, with Atkinson screaming at the end of the phone.'

So if Lewis, Murphy, Atkinson, Hayes and others were supposedly benefitting from the largesse of illegal bookmakers through Jack Herbert, where was the money? How was it transacted?

Wilby decided to find out for himself. Acting on a tip-off from an extremely reliable informant, he went undercover and scoped the Belfast Hotel in Queen Street – owned and run by Murphy and Lewis's good friend Barry Maxwell.

Here was Murphy's favourite watering hole. Here Lewis had come on his arrival back in Brisbane following his promotion to Commissioner to show off his epaulettes and see his dear friend Maxwell after a brief exile in Charleville. Here Maxwell gathered a roll of cash for his mate Jack Herbert who did it tough during the Southport Betting Case and drove it, and a case of meat and vegetables, to the Herbert flat in East Brisbane.

If these men were to meet anywhere and supposedly divide ill-gotten gains, it would be in a place where all of them felt comfortable, indeed, felt at home.

Wilby was told to turn up at a certain time on a Thursday.

'I saw it,' says Wilby. 'I wanted to see it for myself. Every Thursday, it was Murphy's table where they used to go and sit. Towards the back. It wasn't well lit.

'Every Thursday. Always Murphy. Atkinson now and then. Definitely Lewis. Herbert was always there of course. That's where they split the money.'

Innocent

In a stifling Boggo Road prison on Saturday 26 November 1977, convicted murderer John Andrew Stuart of the Whiskey Au Go Go bombing fame along with James Finch, had been granted a pass to the reception store of the gaol. He had complained that some of his property had gone missing, and gained the pass. It was around 8.20 a.m. Stuart was not under escort.

On the way back to his section of the prison he climbed a partly demolished brick wall onto an awning, then scaled a downpipe to the roof of A-wing, empty and set to be demolished. Once on the roof, Stuart separated the bars that held entanglements of barbed wire and proceeded to pierce holes in every sheet of corrugated roof iron. He removed some of the sheets and then dislodged dozens of bricks. Stuart had a message he wanted to pass on to the world.

The Comptroller-General of Prisons, Allen Whitney, when he discovered Stuart's protest, told the press: 'He can stop there as far as I'm concerned. He got up there by himself. He can get down that way too.'

Stuart perched on the sloped roof bare-chested and in long trousers. Initially, his act attracted little interest from the Dutton Park residents in the vicinity of the gaol.

He started throwing roof iron and bricks into the gaol yard. By Saturday evening, Stuart had still not come down.

On Sunday, he began constructing his message out of bricks. INNOCENT, VICTIMS OF POLICE VERBAL, F & S [Finch and Stuart].

Stuart paraded along the top of the roof. Sightseers dropped by to witness the spectacle. Police waited. The Prisons Minister, John Herbert, ordered prison warders to leave Stuart on the roof until he came down of his own volition.

At 12.45 p.m. on Monday, after more than 52 hours on the roof, Stuart was having a rest close to a hole in the roof when he was seized by two warders. As the *Courier-Mail* reported: 'After a brief, violent struggle, he was brought to the ground as fellow prisoners cheered.'

Shortly afterwards, Works Department staff climbed up onto the roof and dismantled his protest message made of bricks. It was an irony that probably escaped most, but perhaps not Stuart, that a colloquial word for verballing, or the police fabrication of a criminal confession, is 'bricking'.

The paper speculated that Stuart would lose some privileges and suffer a spell in solitary confinement. The convicted killer was just 36. He had just over two years left to live.

Campbell and the Boss

At some point over the Christmas and New Year period of 1977–78, word of the belligerent Senior Constable Bob Campbell, down in the Stores at the old Petrie Terrace barracks, had made it inside the Commissioner's office.

Lewis, busy as ever during the festive whirl and into the New Year, made queries in March regarding the validity of Campbell's eight-hour study leave. Campbell's course, and university degrees undertaken by any other officers, had to be approved under the Police Department Study Assistance Scheme.

Lewis repeatedly approached the Department of the Public Service Board querying whether an officer who had expressed an intention to resign from the force upon the completion of a degree, might have the course disapproved by the police department.

Why would Lewis take such intense interest in the lowly Campbell? What rumours about Campbell had been circulating through the department that would see him as a threat within an office as high as the Commissioner's?

It was known that Campbell had been a 'Whitrod man', but could Lewis's venom towards his predecessor and his desire to rid anything even resembling a Whitrod influence within a country mile of his administration have included this studious young tennis-playing suburban constable?

Or did Lewis know nothing about Campbell, the scrutiny being applied by people like Deputy Commissioner Vern MacDonald? Whoever it was, and for whatever reason, Campbell was about to be forced onto the transfer roundabout again. This time he would be heading to the Woolloongabba CIB.

A System Set in Stone

By 1978 the barrister Tony Fitzgerald, with more work than he could handle, decided to move offices.

He had, as had legions of lawyers since 1960, been labouring away in the cramped confines of the Inns of Court – the former Johnson and Sons boot factory at 107 North Quay. In its heyday, the factory produced Queensland's finest footwear, from the Imperial, Pall Mall and Piccadilly brands through to the Maranoa, a sturdy buckled boot favoured by stockmen.

The Inns, by the late 1970s, was tired, and Fitzgerald and a few colleagues shifted to the more modern surrounds of the new MLC building with its distinctive weather beacon up at 239 George Street. Two groups of lawyers, including Fitzgerald, Bill Pincus and others, put out their shingles on the 17th floor. From that rarefied loft, far from the boot factory and the river and the city's squalid back lanes, the city's best legal minds went about their work, their briefs taking them interstate, the milestones of their young children's lives – the end-of-year concert, the sports final – often sacrificed to the millstone of law.

Many of them still held similarly lofty beliefs that the civil legal system was pure and unblemished. Yet in their hearts, men like Fitzgerald, and many other Queenslanders, knew there was a gathering stain at the core. By the late 1970s Queenslanders had become immured to the one party state system. As for the civil area of legal practice, there were some players allied with political parties. Those who hitched their star to the establishment wagon did well. Many who didn't often failed to get anywhere.

Fitzgerald, meanwhile, hoed his own field without detriment. He and his colleagues knew, as if by osmosis, that toeing the National Party line had its immense benefits. But there were alternative paths to follow. As for politics, Fitzgerald simply had no interest in it. More accurately, he wasn't disinterested but a busy practice and a family of small children took up the bulk of his time.

The Crown at one point sent over to Fitzgerald a large brief seeking his advice on evidence along with the fee he was expected to accept. Fitzgerald agreed that it was the sort of work that he specialised in, but he rejected the fee. They never briefed him again.

What was common knowledge throughout the old Inns of Court, the MLC chambers and others in the Ansett Building on Turbot Street, however, was the endemic police verballing that had become a virtual fixture of the Queensland courts system. The constant scuttlebutt that began in the era of Police Commissioner Frank Bischof continued apace with Terence Lewis in the big chair. There was verballing and police misconduct, and for whatever reason it was understood by the city's legal practitioners that this behaviour was to some extent condoned by the courts.

The judges, as everyone knew, were pillars of the establishment. They were members of the Queensland Club.

It was how Queensland worked.

The Boxer

Little red-headed Ian Thomas (Tommy) Hamilton grew up in a Housing Commission home in Nielson Street, Chermside, and was a likeable, rouseabout sort of kid who loved to talk. Tommy could talk all day long.

He went to Wavell Heights Primary School with his mate Peter Hall. Two classes up from him was a boy called John Wayne Ryan. Ryan's family lived a block and a half away from the Hamiltons, at 43 Unmack Street. 'Tommy was a real nice kid,' remembers Ryan.

Ryan used to train for judo at the Railway Institute in the city, and soon Tommy was in there. He'd taken an interest in boxing. 'He'd be training five or six days a week, he was fanatical,' remembers Ryan. 'And he was a pretty good fighter. He was just a little naive.'

As children in late 1950s Brisbane, both Ryan and Hamilton were acquainted with an older teenager, John Andrew Stuart. He in turn knew a man called William (Billy) Stokes from their days in the Westbrook Home for Boys up on the Darling Downs.

By the early 1970s, Hamilton, who had been involved in petty crime as a juvenile, decided to turn his life around. He wanted to go straight, and he saw boxing as a means to that end. So he devised a punishing fitness and traning regime. 'He would get up early and go for a five-mile run, from Kedron to Aspley and back,' recalls his sister, Carolyn Scully. 'He had a job as a builder's labourer, mainly working as a plasterer, and he'd go to that all day. Then he'd head over to Jack Kelso's gym and train. He had to train. He had to get fit. He didn't even smoke, though he might have had some pot on occasion.'

He boxed under the name Ian Thomas, though professionally he was making little headway.

It was Hamilton who had torched the Torino nightclub in the Valley in February 1973 on the orders of Billy 'The Mouse' McCulkin. The latter – who had the image of a mouse tattooed on his penis and was an informer to former corrupt detective Glen Hallahan – promised all the perpetrators $1000 for the job. The gang apparently only got half of what was pledged.

'Tommy boasted to me that he'd done Torino's,' says John Wayne Ryan. 'He told me straight to my face in Kelso's gym. He wouldn't shut up about it. I don't know what he was doing hanging out with a lot of those guys. He was out of his depth. He was smoking a bit of dope and might have been introduced to a bit of heroin.'

Carolyn Scully admits her brother, along with Peter Hall, Gary Dubois and Keith Meredith, did bomb the Torino nightclub at the behest of Billy McCulkin. It was an insurance job, she said.

'Tommy did blow up Torino's,' she says. 'I bought the gelignite that they used on Torino's. I walked into Compression Hire Service in Geebung and bought it – four or five sticks. It was done from the inside. They also turned a gas tap on. They knew there would be nobody inside at the time.

'They got the idea from the movie *The Mechanic* (the action thriller about a professional hitman starring Charles Bronson and released in 1972. The film's publicity went: 'In this box are the tools of his trade. He has more than a dozen ways to kill and they all work. They call him the mechanic.')

'The boys got carried away. But they all knew each other – John Andrew Stuart, Billy Stokes, Billy McCulkin.'

John Wayne Ryan says Hamilton's boxing career suddenly improved. 'After Torino's his career started to take off, if you know what I mean,' says Ryan. 'The fights were done, fixed. He was winning them clean but they were fixed. I think it was done to divert his attention, to get him to stop talking about bloody Torino's. That's what went on down at Festival Hall.'

Hamilton's boxing statistics only partially bear this out. He had two bouts prior to the Torino bombing in February 1973. On 26 March of that year, less than two months after Torino's went up and just 18 days after the tragedy at the Whiskey Au Go Go, he won by technical knockout against Glen Mackay at Festival Hall. Tommy went on to win four of his next six fights, the last being his Queensland Welterweight championship against the talented, hyper-kinetic boxer Ian Looker on 25 October 1974. He stopped Looker in the fifth round. It would be Tommy's last fight.

A month earlier, Hamilton's house at 210 Turner Road, Kedron, directly opposite the Lutwyche Cemetery, had been blasted with a shotgun and the bullet had narrowly missed the boxer. He was showered with timber debris and glass when the shot was fired at his bedroom window.

Police believe the shooting was linked to Hamilton refusing to throw a fight. A syndicate lost $1800 in bets on the fight that Hamilton refused to throw. Tommy had last won against Lyle Law by knockout three months earlier on 14 June.

Then around 10 p.m. on Friday 10 January 1975, Hamilton was drinking with a new girlfriend in a house at Hamilton, not far from the CBD, when an armed intruder marched him outside and drove off.

The man, with a stocking over his head, burst into the lounge room at Hamilton as Tommy and his 17-year-old girlfriend sat listening to records. The couple had dined at the nearby Coral Trout Restaurant before buying a bottle of tequila at the Breakfast Creek Hotel and returning to the house in Atkinson Street. They sat at the dining room table, cut up lemons and drank the tequila. 'We were both expecting Tommy's friend [Gary Dubois] to come and pick him up,' the girl later said. 'I saw a person walk into the lounge room and that's who I thought it was. As the figure got closer I realised it wasn't Gary Dubois. It was someone else.

'Tommy turned around to see what I was looking at. At that point this person told Tommy to stand up and Tommy did.' Hamilton dropped the knife he'd been using to cut up the lemons.

The girlfriend later said the man was wearing a flesh-coloured stocking pulled tight over his head and had a pistol strapped with plaster to his right hand and a rifle in his left. 'I recognised the man as Billy Stokes,' she said. 'Stokes whispered to Hamilton and they walked outside to a blue car.'

She followed them out and saw them standing beside the car. 'Stay out of it. This has nothing to do with you,' Hamilton supposedly shouted to her. She identified Stokes by his voice, facial features and build.

When the abduction hit the press, Tommy's mother, Mrs Margaret Hamilton, warned the perpetrators: 'Unless you tell us what you have done with Tommy it will be an eye for an eye and a tooth for a tooth.' She said there would be 'war' if the abductor didn't show his hand. 'He'd better give some indication soon as to what he has done with Tommy. If he doesn't I will see that he remembers us. You won't have to print any more. He'll get the message. And to show just how much I mean it, tell him this: I drove around in a car for five hours on Friday night just looking for one house. He'll figure it out from there.

'I am challenging him to come out in the open. If he doesn't, let him know I mean business.'

Mrs Hamilton and her daughter Carolyn both believed Tommy had been murdered. They and the police also believed they knew who had abducted Hamilton.

After Hamilton vanished, Stokes, who was editor of the *Port News* magazine, started writing about Hamilton and his friends as being part of something dubbed the Clockwork Orange Gang, after the popular and shocking Stanley Kubrick film of 1971 – *A Clockwork Orange*.

Hamilton allegedly walked around wearing a bowler hat and swinging a cane, fashioning himself after the film's ruthless main protagonist, the teenager Alex. His sister Carolyn Scully denies this was Hamilton's regular garb. She said he returned from a trip to Sydney and dressed up in black jeans, a grey, purple and green tank top, and a bowler hat. 'He liked to dress up,' she says.

Stokes wrote in *Port News* about Hamilton:

As a youth, well before the LSD scene, he was attracted by the bizzare, and the unusual. He was in fact once caught by Brisbane police in the act of driving stolen property away from a break and enter offence by using an ambulance.

Some years ago Clockwork Orange entered the boxing ring, initially as a means of keeping fit – he wasn't a good fighter but he was always a trier. However, in the past year, in Brisbane's Festival Hall, Clockwork Orange has surprised all by winning fight after fight.

At present, Clockwork Orange is reported missing, is said to have been abducted at gunpoint from a residence at Breakfast Creek recently. The matter is being treated by Brisbane police as a suspected murder.

In a subsequent issue, Stokes wrote that the most interesting 'effect' of his series of stories in *Port News* about the Clockwork Orange Gang and who really bombed the Whiskey Au Go Go nightclub was that police made it known to the media they wanted to interview him about Hamilton's disappearance.

'Earlier, in Sydney, police had arrested me on a charge of vagrancy regardless of the fact that I was staying at a motel, had $250 in my pocket, was neatly dressed, and had been in full employment for years,'

Stokes wrote. 'Later, when the charge of vagrancy came up for hearing before a magistrate the police simply withdrew prosecution.

'Meanwhile, in Brisbane the local police had contacted my landlady and told her that they wanted to search my residence. A search warrant wasn't necessary. The voice of authority was sufficient and she let them do so when I wasn't there.'

The coronial inquest into Hamilton's disappearance and presumed murder was held in Brisbane on 22 January 1978, before Coroner W.J. McKay. At the inquest, a Sydney builder, Thomas 'Con' Tziolos, 34, of Coogee, said not long after Hamilton's disappearance his friend Billy Stokes had turned up in Sydney and asked him if he knew anyone who could repair his car.

Stokes had told him vandals had damaged the vehicle. The car's front seat had been slashed and according to Tziolos, smelled of human excrement. He noticed the front floor mats had been removed. The court heard Stokes told him he had just cleaned the car.

Tziolos approached his neighbour, motor mechanic John Smith, and said to him: 'Billy's got a bit of trouble with his car. Someone's got in and ripped it up a bit.' He asked Smith if he knew a good trimmer. 'It smelled as if someone had been to the toilet in it,' Smith told the court. 'It was all hosed out but there seemed to be that smell in the air. Inside, the floor had nothing on it. Even the underfelt was ripped out.'

The inquest was adjourned shortly after it began because major witness William Anthony Stokes had not had a chance to organise legal representation.

Mrs Margaret Hamilton told the court she went looking for her son night after night following his disappearance. She said after her son went missing she received a phone call from a female: 'Billy Stokes has done to your son what they did in the film *A Clockwork Orange*.'

Stokes had been friends with Hamilton and members of the so-called Clockwork Orange Gang until an incident in 1973. Hamilton and some of his mates had been charged over cannabis possession in

Caboolture, and Stokes had allegedly refused to help Hamilton with the bail and fines in excess of $2000.

'A week after that Billy came around to talk to Tommy,' says Scully, who lived with her brother in the Turner Road house. 'They had a fight. Tommy told him to leave.'

Stokes had a telelphone answering machine and recording equipment rigged up in his flat in New Farm. Hamilton and others decided to harass him, leaving obscene messages. 'Tommy was trying to get him to admit something; I don't know what that was,' says Scully. 'It would have been annoying. It was a bit stupid of Tommy to do it.'

One message said: '… listen, Bill. The boys are after you for a while. You are nothing but a common 20 cent slut.' And another: 'Hello, could I speak to Bill? This is a recording. You mongrel … I'll cut your throat and tear your rotten arms out. You bastard. You mongrel.'

Mrs Hamilton supposedly wore her son's bowler hat to the home of Meredith and Peter Hall at 1 a.m. on the day after Tommy disappeared. She said her former husband had always treated Tommy badly, and had once hit him on the head with a hammer. (His sister confirms that Tommy was treated poorly by his father.)

Mrs Hamilton told the coroner's court she wrote over 40 poems and sketches concerning her son's murder and sent them to Stokes who was the editor of *Port News*. Many were published.

Another witness, the mother of Gary Dubois, Mrs Hilma Noonan, said Stokes had made false allegations about her son Gary, Tommy Hamilton, Peter Hall and a man called Keith Meredith having formed this Clockwork Orange Gang.

Stokes had written stories about the gang in the *Port News*. She said a man called Vince O'Dempsey actually used to call Hamilton 'Clockwork Orange' because of his ginger hair and tendency to wear a bowler hat.

Detective Pat Glancy, one of Murphy's protégés, then appeared at the inquest. He said Stokes had told him in 1977, in the District Court where Stokes was appealing a six month prison sentence for possession of a concealable firearm, that he believed John Andrew Stuart, James Finch and the Clockwork Orange Gang had committed the Whiskey Au Go Go fire. (Stuart and Finch had been charged for the Whiskey bombing and were serving life sentences in Boggo Road – Stuart insisted he was innocent.) Glancy said Stokes had not accused the gang of involvement in the fire until after Hamilton went missing. Stokes initially thought Stuart and Finch were innocent, but told Glancy he was wrong to believe that.

Stokes and Glancy had a bit of history.

'Billy McCulkin introduced me to Glancy at the Lands Office Hotel a couple of months before the Whiskey firebombing [in early 1973],' says Stokes. 'On the following Saturday at the races I again saw Glancy and he told me I had an old fine outstanding for a traffic offence and he asked me to accompany him to the police station to pay this fine.' As it turned out, he allowed him to stay at the races for the next two events where he happened to back the two winners.

'In 1977 Glancy led a police raid at my Broadbeach flat and charged me with having a gun. While I was in prison over this matter, Glancy organised witnesses to testify at a Coroner's Court Inquiry into the disappearance of Tom Hamilton.'

Then a Brisbane real estate agent, Elva Ryan, told the court Stokes had told her he had abducted and killed a man when she rented a unit to Stokes at Toorak Road, Hamilton, in April 1975.

Stokes allegedly told her the reason he wanted that specific unit was because it overlooked a property where he took a man at gunpoint and killed him. She claimed Stokes told her Hamilton's body was buried beside Barbara McCulkin. (Barbara was the estranged wife of Billy 'The Mouse' McCulkin, who had disappeared with her two young daughters not long after the Whiskey bombings.)

The real estate agent said she hadn't believed Stokes, and that she'd thought it had been a boast. (Stokes would claim in an article in the June issue of *Port News* that he had been evicted from his rented home – Flat 7, York Flats, 66 Merthyr Road, New Farm – by his landlady 13 days after Hamilton was abducted.)

The court also heard allegations that Hamilton had played a part in Stokes's wife leaving him and that Hamilton had made phone calls to Stokes taunting him with sexual allegations against his wife.

Stokes was committed for trial, despite the fact that there had been no evidence retrieved from the suspect vehicle and no evidence of threats made by Stokes to Hamilton. There was a lot of circumstantial evidence, but no body. There was also insufficient evidence to conclude how Hamilton met his death.

Despite this, Stokes was charged with having murdered Hamilton and awaited his trial in the Supreme Court.

Bombs and Knights

In the wake of the shocking Hilton Hotel bombing in Sydney on 13 February 1978, which killed two garbage collectors and an on-duty police officer, two legendary British police officers were flown to Australia to offer advice to local forces, Federal and state, on counter-terrorism. They were Sir Robert Mark and Sir James Haughton.

Sir Robert had had a stellar career. He was noted for the establishment in the early 1970s of an anti-corruption unit called A10. It uncovered police corruption on an unprecedented scale, leading to the arrest and imprisonment of top-ranking officers including Commander Kenneth Drury, head of the Flying Squad. Several more police were imprisoned, and nearly 500 more were sacked or forced to resign.

He was also knowledgeable regarding the IRA threat. He took command of the Knightsbridge Spaghetti House Siege in September 1975 and the Balcombe Street Siege just three months later in

December. He would feel at home in Queensland under Premier Joh Bjelke-Petersen as he loathed anti-establishment demonstrators and groups like the National Council for Civil Liberties. His Special Patrol Group was in the same family as Queensland's Special Branch.

Sir James 'Sunny Jim' Haughton was a crack detective and fiercely anti police corruption. In January 1976 he was appointed Her Majesty's Chief Inspector of Constabulary.

Both men were due in Brisbane on Monday 13 March. They were booked into the Gazebo Terrace Hotel.

Lewis and Deputy Commissioner Vern MacDonald were at Eagle Farm airport at 9 p.m. to greet Sir Robert and Sir James and 'discussed purpose of their visit to Australia until 10 p.m.', according to his diary.

The next day, the two esteemed officers were available to talk to senior Queensland police from 9 a.m. until 4 p.m. at police head-quarters. Lewis was at the office at 7.45 a.m. and helped MacDonald and his personal assistant Greg Early complete arrangements for the day's talks. Then, curiously, Commissioner Lewis left them to it. He was off on a regional tour of police stations, including Beaudesert, Stanthorpe, Texas and Goondiwindi.

Back at headquarters, Sir Robert was late. When he arrived he was introduced to the officers present by Deputy Commissioner Vern MacDonald. They included Tom Pointing from the CIB; Alan Lobegeiger, deputy head of the Emergency Squad; Superintendent Tony Murphy, head of the Criminal Investigation Branch; Ian Hatcher of the Press Unit; and of course Early.

It was, from the outset, a blokey affair. Sir Robert talked at length about counter-terrorism arrangements in the UK. He used expressions like 'jolly good'. He discussed the press and its relationship with the police. '... we have one paper which always gives us a run, the *Sunday Sun*,' piped up Vern MacDonald, 'but we don't worry too much about them anymore'.

MacDonald and others used every opportunity to blame the Labor Party for any perceived misgivings about the police force and its public perception.

Sir Robert admitted he was confused by Australian attitudes to police units like the Special Branch, and how they seemed to have 'a sinister connotation' among the general public.

'Its purpose is to defend the state from subversion from within and if you want a loose definition given off-the-cuff, any organisation which seeks to undermine democracy by the achievement of a corporate state by unlawful means, so far as we're concerned, is a fit objective for the attention of Special Branch,' Sir Robert said stirringly. 'And I don't give a damn if the Australian press print that in letters six feet tall as far as I'm concerned.

'A democracy which doesn't protect itself from subversion from within as distinct from the possibility of an attack from without, really hardly deserves to continue to exist.'

Detective Tony Murphy offered wise local counsel: 'I feel the real problem throughout is the fact that there is this state suspicion that the government today is getting mileage by reason of the access of the government to Special Branch. There is the existence of suspicion all the time that the government today is using the Special Branch facilities to spy on the Opposition.'

During their talk on X-ray machines, Vern MacDonald couldn't resist telling an anecdote about former police commissioner Ray Whitrod, and how the Queensland Police had an excellent scanning machine that was situated directly under Whitrod's chair on the floor below him.

When Whitrod found out about sensitive and potentially suspect packages and bags being X-rayed beneath his seat, according to MacDonald, he arranged for the machine to be moved. 'But he didn't trust everybody, Mr Whitrod, after that at all; he reckoned they may have been trying to get rid of him,' MacDonald told the meeting.

In discussing complaints about police, Sir Robert produced statistics that less than one per cent were ever made against policewomen. 'Because you see the police function is naturally abrasive and yet the ordinary male feels a kind of aversion from complaining about a woman,' philosophised Sir Robert. 'So even if you have got men doing the job with a woman there, they still won't complain.

'They [women] are expensive, they will get married and go after three and a half years and so on. But nevertheless, they do have their uses though one doesn't like to admit it too loudly.'

At the end of the meeting Vern MacDonald stood and declared the session 'one of the most interesting periods I've had I feel in my police career'.

In a telex message about the police and civilian careers of the two great knights sent to the Premier's Department from Canberra prior to their arrival in Brisbane, Lewis underlined with a ruler and black felt pen just two sentences.

'Sir Robert was awarded a Queens Police Medal in 1965, and in 1973 he was made a Knight bachelor. In the 1977 New Year's Honours List he was made Knight Grand Cross of the order of the British Empire.'

After just 16 months in the top job, was Commissioner Lewis already thinking of such honours for himself?

On Burning Mountain

The pacifist dentist from Bundaberg, Dr Harry Akers, continued to smoulder over the National Party's dictatorial street-march legislation and decided to act.

He needed to come up with an ingenious way of exposing the nonsense of the new laws. 'I decided that something had to be done about this,' Dr Akers recalls. 'It was really bad legislation for a whole range of reasons. So I called a public meeting.'

Akers set a time and place – a hall in downtown Bundaberg – and was stunned when more than 50 people turned up, including supporter Philip Barnsley, the young station master from the nearby farming town of Avondale, 24 kilometres north-west of Bundaberg on the Kolan River.

Akers would discover later that the bulk of the crowd were men and women from the National Civic Council – the Catholic political movement originally founded by B.A. Santamaria. Everything proposed at the meeting that night was continually voted down by the interlopers. In the end, Akers proposed that the group apply for a legal street-march permit. The motion was opposed 40 to three. Only Barnsley and one other stood behind him.

'I couldn't understand this,' Akers remembers. 'I decided to march and needed a fairly clever strategy. April Fool's Day was coming up. So I applied for a permit.'

Akers lodged his request for a permit to march with the Bundaberg police on 10 March 1978, where it was received by local Traffic Superintendent K. Seaniger. Akers said he planned to march with his dog Jaffa (a cattle dog covered in spots of red, like the jaffa confectionary) at 2.45 a.m. on 1 April, for a distance of 100 metres on a No Through Road not far from The Hummock. He would be holding a placard.

The application, which stressed that the march would be peaceful, was rejected on the grounds that it was a protest march.

Superintendent Seaniger told Akers: 'If you do this we're probably going to leave you alone. But if anyone else sets foot on that road with you, you'll be arrested.'

A number of quandaries presented themselves to Akers. He could march illegally and get away with it. He could forget about the whole enterprise. Or he could march in company with another person and get himself arrested.

The presence of Jaffa, too, proved a small quandary for police. Was

Akers protesting in defiance of the new legislation? Or was he just a man out walking his dog in the dark?

Akers' rejection attracted an initial smattering of local press. On 16 March the *Courier-Mail* reported that Akers' protest would be against the street march legislation and 'the forces of apathy'.

The dentist decided to go ahead with his plan anyway. 'I was really frightened, to be truthful,' Akers says. 'I'd dug a hole for myself and I had to go ahead and do it.

'On one side of the road there was a vertical embankment about 10 to 15 feet high, and on the other side it was a vertical embankment down. Police couldn't direct you onto the footpath. It was only a couple of feet wide and you'd fall down the embankment.'

On the night of the march he took Jaffa on a heavy chain. Akers wasn't sure what he'd encounter. It was raining heavily. Barnsley turned up to witness the event, as did a *Bundaberg News-Mail* reporter and photographer, and young supporter Peter Leonard.

Akers, dressed in a short-sleeved shirt, shorts and thongs, carried a small sign that read: 'The majority is not omnipotent. The majority can be wrong and it is capable of tyranny.'

'The Special Branch was there,' he says. 'I know because I saw a number of cars go up beforehand. There were police there, too. I had a speech I yelled out in the middle of the night. It was raining. A lot of people disagreed with me and others admired my guts.

'I had no political leanings or aspirations whatsoever. I stand back and I dissect issues and what politicians do, then I decide what I'm not going to be a party to. I saw the police force under Lewis as just another extension of the National Party. A lot of provincial people in Queensland couldn't see that.'

Philip Barnsley says Akers' protest was an attempt to cut through the rural messianic worship of Premier Joh Bjelke-Petersen to show people what was really going on in the corridors of power in George Street. 'As Harry always pointed out, if you make a fool of a certain law you help your cause rather than just fighting against it, if you can point out how silly it was,' he says.

'That helped them down in Brisbane, where they were having the big protest marches and coming up against a lot of police. When do you make the stand and say enough is enough?'

Akers' bold move received a battery of publicity across the country and provoked debate and editorials throughout the Australian press. He had made his point in spectacular fashion – the new street-march laws were petty and puerile.

Akers told the *Courier-Mail* he had marched as 'a protest against the erosion of civil liberties in Queensland'. The newspaper further reported: 'With placard in hand and heavy rain falling, he collected his cattle dog Jaffa and began his 100 metre walk.

'During his speech addressed to the flora and fauna, the rain-soaked Mr Akers said he represented the minority in the community which "must have its rights recognised".'

Some years later Jaffa was struck by a car and the vet determined he'd have to amputate his front right leg and back left leg. The decision was made to put the dog down.

No matter how heroic, you can't have a dog with just one leg at either end.

Hunting the Hound

If anything raised the usually laconic Commissioner Terry Lewis's ire, it was being talked about behind his back, especially if those rumours impugned his image and reputation in the eyes of the one person he wanted to please the most – Premier Joh Bjelke-Petersen.

A close second to that was criticism of his police allies and friends, such as Tony Murphy.

So on Tuesday 4 April, when the Premier's press secretary, Allen

Callaghan, rang Lewis to discuss complaints about Murphy and corruption, it reflected poorly on Lewis himself and his stewardship of the police force. He did what he had always done. He contacted his trusted lieutenants and at some time over the next two and a half weeks, it was decided that the person who had been spreading the rumours that had reached the ears of the Premier had to be Basil Hicks.

Hicks had a history with the Rat Pack that went back to the 1950s. He believed both Murphy and Glen Hallahan were 'on the take' from the 1960s. In the early 1970s he had also met and befriended Jack Herbert at a training course. They jogged together most mornings and it had left no doubt in Hicks's mind that the detectives were corrupt.

Hicks had talked to Herbert about how he'd tried to effect the arrest of prostitutes at the Interlude Club, run by Sydney gangster and standover man Donnie 'The Glove' Smith, supposedly sent to Brisbane by corrupt cop Fred Krahe to operate the bar in Queen Street. Hicks, working out of the Valley CIB at the time, understood that both Murphy and Hallahan were protecting the club in exchange for payments.

Following the Interlude incident Hicks had been told by two informants that Hallahan had told them that he would be 'put in his place with the kids'. Soon after, Hicks was sent to the Children's Court where he worked as a prosecutor.

On hearing Hicks's theories in the early 1970s, Herbert told Hicks: 'Well, everyone will get a quid … everyone will take a quid.'

As Hicks later remembered, 'I wanted to know at one stage who had actually had me shifted from the Valley, whether it was Murphy or Hallahan, and he said it didn't matter whether it was Murphy, Hallahan or Lewis, they are all the one, they are all the same.'

Herbert, clearly trusting Hicks, explained The Joke to him. He confided in Hicks about SP bookmakers and how they were protected by certain members of the Licensing Branch. Herbert explained that

The Joke had been a little disorganised until Murphy had joined the branch in 1966.

Hicks recalled: 'He [Herbert] said there had been a lot of squabbling among those in The Joke and that they had busted each other's bookies, but when Tony Murphy joined Licensing, he organised them and the system now worked well.'

It was Hicks, as part of Whitrod's CIU, who had gone on and arrested Tony Murphy on perjury charges in 1971 over the allegations of prostitute Shirley Brifman. It was Hicks's CIU that had trapped Hallahan in New Farm Park receiving kickbacks from a prostitute, resulting in corruption charges against him and ultimately leading to his resignation from the force. And it was Hicks who had hidden under Arthur Pitts' house with a recording device and recorded Jack Herbert offering a bribe that led to the Southport Betting Case and indirectly led to Herbert's resignation from the force.

In terms of Herbert and the Rat Pack, Hicks had used up all of his credit.

Then someone found out about the prostitute called Katherine James, who by now, in 1978, was serving three years in prison on drugs charges. It was established that James, former owner of Kontiki, had also worked briefly as a prostitute at the notorious Matador Club in South Brisbane, then owned by Roland Short. During this time there were photographs taken of her having sex with a client.

John Wayne Ryan, who helped install the Matador Club's extensive security system, had seen the photographs. They were eight by ten inch black-and-white glossies. 'The guy in the pictures did bear a resemblance to Hicks, even though it definitely wasn't Basil Hicks,' remembers Ryan. 'Those photographs were taken in the Matador Club.'

A plot was hatched.

A rumour would circulate that photographs had been obtained of the supposedly incorruptible Basil Hicks having sex with prostitute Katherine James. While Hicks was acquainted with James as part of his investigative work, the story would be that Hicks was obsessed with James, and that she had arranged the secret photos to be taken to get him off her back and leave her alone.

Was Lewis in on the scam? Or was this the handiwork of Tony Murphy, who had used this modus operandi – the deliberate assassination of a person's moral character – since the National Hotel inquiry in the early 1960s, and before?

On 24 April 1978, Lewis notated in his diary: 'Phoned M. Lewis [then Comptroller of Prisons] re interviewing … James at HM Prison.'

Then on 27 April, something unprecedented occurred – Katherine James was brought from Brisbane Prison to the office of Deputy Commissioner Vern MacDonald to give a statement saying she had indeed had an affair with Basil Hicks in 1973 and that there were photographs to prove it.

Lewis's personal assistant, Greg Early, took the statement down in shorthand. At the close of business that day, Lewis wrote in his diary: 'Deputy Commissioner MacDonald handed me statement by Mrs …, 25 years, re allegedly having sexual intercourse with Hicks. Off 6.30 pm.'

Around this time Hicks was given a friendly warning from colleague Noel Creevey, who claimed to have seen a memo from policeman Graham Leadbetter that Hicks had had sexual relations with Katherine James. It wasn't the only bullet against Hicks that the Rat Pack was loading into the gun.

A Nambour police colleague Merv Roberts told him that Commissioner Lewis had asked Roberts to sign a statement that Hicks, while stationed on the Sunshine Coast prior to being transferred to the Valley CIB in late 1969, had accepted graft from SP bookies, and that he had gotten pregnant a girl, 15, and induced her to abort the child.

In the false statement, Roberts says that on the very first day Hicks started work at the Nambour CIB in the late 1950s, Hicks called him aside and asked him for the names and addresses of local SP bookies.

'I showed little interest and attempted to change the subject,' Roberts was supposed to have said. 'He then said something along these lines, "Come on Merv, you have been here a long time. You know them all. We can arrange with them and organise something on a fifty/fifty basis." '

Roberts declined to sign the statement, though his signature did turn up on the bottom of the two-sheet statement on an attached slip of plain paper and not police stationery. It was allegedly witnessed by T.M. Lewis.

It was a dirty game, Rat Pack-style.

Plenty of Kills

While Basil Hicks might have been seen as a potential threat that needed to be dealt with, Licensing Branch chief Alec Jeppesen's surreptitious accumulation of evidence of police corruption was starting to gain weight. He, too, was becoming a rising distraction.

Jeppesen's findings revealed the city's illegal casinos and massage parlours were primarily run by the Bellino family, and were centred largely in Fortitude Valley. There were other operators of significance – Roland Short's clubs and brothels, and the parlours of Geoff Crocker and Allan Holloway.

In addition, rumours were circulating that police, particularly CIB members under the leadership of Superintendent Tony Murphy, were out of control and running rampant in the massage parlours. Out of the blue, the Licensing Branch was suddenly hitting a number of hurdles in its dealings with prostitutes. The former workable system was that prostitutes were 'written up', then reported for prostitution offences via a summons.

Suddenly, prostitutes and madams were refusing to answer questions and producing legal counsel. Solicitors T.J. Mellifont and Co., represented many of the women and produced a form letter, addressed to the Commissioner of Police, which ended: '… she will not answer any questions relating to any matter concerning any offence alleged against her, nor will she voluntarily accompany any Police Officer to any Police Station'.

It stated if 'she' were to be charged, she would have to be 'arrested and forthwith taken to the nearest watchhouse and formally charged'. Some parlours also installed security gates, barring police entry.

In addition to this, CIB officers were seen drunk and in the presence of known prostitutes in local nightclubs, and others were located in the actual health studios, demanding free sex.

A feared senior officer, drunk in a club, was also overheard to say it wouldn't be long before the CIB took over the control of parlours from Licensing, and that a graft network similar to that in Sydney would be installed.

Someone was deliberately sabotaging and frustrating Jeppesen.

A Call from Across Town

Federal Narcotics Agent John Shobbrook was sitting in his office in Eagle Street in the city when the phone rang. To his surprise, it was Superintendent Tony Murphy of the Queensland Police on the other end of the line.

Shobbrook had heard of, but never met, Murphy. 'He said he had an informant who had some very substantial information about heroin coming into Queensland and could I come up and see him?' Shobbrook recalls.

Douglas John Shobbrook had been born in Brisbane and adopted out to truck driver Alfred Shobbrook – he worked for carriers W. Love and Sons, 'Love Will Move It!' – and his wife Sadie who lived at Kangaroo Point. It was a strict Catholic household.

After a variety of jobs as a youth he noticed an advertisement in the *Courier-Mail* for vacant positions with the Customs Prevention Section within the Department of Customs and Excise and secured a job working out of the navy's shore facility the HMAS *Moreton* on the Brisbane River in New Farm. Shobbrook acquitted himself well for a few years but soon needed more of a challenge.

In early 1971 the Federal Bureau of Narcotics opened a Brisbane office in the old but splendid Coronation House at 133 Edward Street. Initially it had just three staff – Acting Chief Narcotics Agent Vince Dainer, Narcotics Agent Brian Bennett and a secretary, Janette Hollands.

The following year Shobbrook applied for a job as a full-time narc and was successful. He moved to Sydney and began his training. In 1974 he married Jan – of the Brisbane office – and after engaging in several serious drug investigations over the years the couple returned to Brisbane in early 1978 on the death of Alf.

By this time the Brisbane office had moved around the corner to more salubrious digs in Eagle Street. Shobbrook was soon promoted to Supervising Narcotics Agent.

When the famous Tony Murphy of the CIB called him that day, Shobbrook, out of courtesy, walked up past City Hall to police head-quarters in North Quay.

'When I got there, he [Murphy] said: "Mr Shobbrook, I've got this informant, and this is a Narcotics Bureau matter and not a state matter ... the only problem is my informant is going to want a few thousand dollars for the information. If you come up with an envelope with a few thousand dollars, give it to me and I'll give it to the informant."'

Shobbrook said he was stunned. 'How stupid did he think I was? I told Canberra and they laughed their heads off.'

It might have been funny at the time, but Murphy's little scheme and the character of the man stayed with Shobbrook.

Within months the names Murphy and Hallahan would come across his desk in a very different and darker context.

Jeppesen Smells a Rat

From the outset, Brian Marlin was demonstrably supportive of his boss Jeppesen. He was eager to please, sometimes a little too eager. The young constable, on hearing of a plot by Tony Murphy and the CIB to take control of the policing of the massage parlours across the city from the Licensing boys, wanted to take it to the highest level.

He insisted Jeppesen and he go to his friend John Goleby, the member for Redlands, and even the Premier himself. Jeppesen didn't think Marlin had the evidence of a CIB takeover and initially stayed out of it.

Lewis got wind of the shenanigans.

How could junior police secure a secret audience with the Premier without his knowledge? Lewis learned there was unrest building between Licensing and the CIB over control of the massage parlours. Murphy was flexing his muscle and his opponents saw it as an opportunity to destabilise him and his power base. The power play over the parlours was, however, a ruse.

What was at the heart of the unrest was Jeppesen's relentless attack on SP bookmakers. They were paying Herbert and The Joke enormous sums of money for protection, and were not getting value for money – either the bookmakers would stop the payments, or the troublemakers in Licensing needed to be removed.

'When we started to really get into the SP bookmakers is when we stirred up a hornet's nest,' remembers Bruce Wilby of the Licensing Branch. 'There were your pub SPs – you'd go out on a Saturday with a fistful of dollars, and if you could get a bet on you'd pinch them. But it was Jeppesen who had the information coming in. We started to work out it was highly organised, not just blokes sitting in pubs taking a few bets. We were getting bigger and bigger fellows.'

One of Wilby's biggest catches was bookmaker Bob Bax. He arrested Bax twice in a short period of time.

'You won't get me again,' Bax told him after the second arrest.

'You going to give it away, Bob?' Wilby supposedly asked.

'No, you are,' Bax replied.

On Wednesday 5 April, Lewis's diary noted: 'Det. Sgt. Freier phoned re comments … Hicks and recently promoted Inspector "knocking" me.' The latter could only have been Jeppesen.

The next day, hearing of the protagonists in the unfolding campaign of Chinese whispers, Lewis contacted Goleby: 'Phoned J. Goleby, MLA, re policing in his electorate.'

Come Monday 17 April Lewis decided to confront Jeppesen in his office. 'With Dep. Comm. to Licensing Branch and told Insp. Jeppesen what is expected of him re any complaints re Police.'

Jeppesen said to his boss he would police the Licensing staff as he saw fit. He took Lewis's visit as a veiled threat.

On top of that, Jeppesen had recognised a constable driving slowly past his family home in Brighton, on Bramble Bay north-east of the CBD. Jeppesen himself was under surveillance.

As a consequence, he began tape recording information from informants and prostitutes. They began painting a picture of widespread corruption and the intrinsic involvement of Jack 'The Bagman' Herbert.

It was a road other honest officers had been down many times before. But in the late 1970s, with Herbert controlling a corrupt annual income of many millions of dollars, the stakes were high.

Jeppesen sat on his secret tapes, and as they liked to say in the office, kept 'poking a big stick' at the top brass.

Sweet

Hector Hapeta was bored.

In Sydney in the late 1970s, Hapeta had spent a good decade of his life selling pet meat out of two wholesale outlets in the western suburbs of Bankstown and Yagoona. He trained greyhounds on occasion, and was a co-proprietor of some pet stores. But as Hector, an illiterate who simultaneously had a brain for hatching business schemes, would later say, he was at that point 'sick of sitting in a shop and selling pet food'.

Serendipitously, Hapeta's de facto wife, Anne Marie Tilley, happened upon a newspaper advertisement for the vacant lease on a health studio in Brisbane's notorious Fortitude Valley.

The studio was called the Top Hat, and was situated next to the Shamrock Hotel on the corner of Brunswick Street and St Paul's Terrace, a stone's throw from the ill-fated former nightclub the Whiskey Au Go Go. The Top Hat was also just across the road from the Top of the Valley building.

Meanwhile, Tilley had heard good things about the Sunshine State. It seemed a comparative paradise for those in the skin trade compared to the hard streets of Sydney's Kings Cross and Darlinghurst.

The Top Hat was being leased by Brisbane's then King of the Parlours, Geoff Crocker. Tilley phoned him from Sydney about the Top Hat. She used the name 'Diane'.

'I hear you have a place,' she said to Crocker. 'How much do you want for it?'

'I want $1200 a month for it,' he said.

'Can I come and have a look at it?'

'Yeah, sure.'

Tilley flew up the next day. Crocker picked her up from the airport and drove her into the Valley where she inspected the property.

'It's quite good,' Tilley said. 'I'll take it.'

She handed Crocker $1200 cash in advance and promised to pay rent at the beginning of each month. Crocker knew his new tenant as Diane Tilley. She returned to Sydney that same night.

Two days later Crocker got a phone call from Hector Hapeta to let him know he and his wife were driving up to Brisbane straightaway. They had a GT Falcon. Crocker recalled: 'They had an old Falcon, one of those shaker ones … two days after that I got a phone call and it was Hector on the phone and he was stuck in Lismore … this bloody car, it nearly killed him and his wife, the exhaust pipe had come off it and they had no money to fix it so I had to telegram, get some money to Lismore to fix this bloody car up so they could get to Brisbane.'

Hapeta and Tilley met Crocker at his home in Everton Park for a discussion about the Top Hat, then booked into a city motel. While Tilley was setting up the massage parlour Hapeta used to wander over to Crocker's place and play pool during the day. He started to open up about his past. He told Crocker he was chased out of Sydney by criminals.

'I said to him, what were you doing wrong that they chased you out of Sydney?' Crocker related the conversation. 'He said to me that he had sold some drugs in Sydney, right, and he undercut the big boys' price and they found out about it … he lived in a little terrace house … he told me he was sitting there one day about lunchtime watching television, two guys ran in, broke his kneecaps with iron bars and told him to get out of Sydney in 24 hours or he would be dead. That was the story he told me.

'I believed it to be true,' Crocker said, 'because he was a big guy and he walked funny you know.'

The Top Hat went well under the guidance of the astute Tilley. 'We were told there was no corruption, and you just opened up places and it was all sweet,' remembers Tilley. 'We came up and bought this parlour off someone else. We opened it up. That night the police turned up.'

One of Tilley and Hapeta's earliest visitors was Harry Burgess of the Licensing Branch. 'Harry was around in the beginning there,' Tilley says. 'He just started talking to me one night. He said not to bring underaged kids in here. I said I wouldn't be doing that.

'He said if the girls get pinched every three weeks, sorry, then they'd leave us alone. "As long as we know who they are and there are no underages, then we'll leave you alone," Harry said. There was no money [for protection] in those days. It was controlled by the police. They'd come in and have a Scotch or something, and that was about it.'

Tilley discovered in herself a talent for organisation. She had a natural business brain that was not, at the time, impeded by her heavy drinking and the occasional abuse of hash.

The first girl employed at the Top Hat under new management was an overweight girl, about 20, with 'a very pretty face and long red hair'.

'She was such a big girl,' Tilley remembers. 'I told her to be careful hopping in the spa. I was worried it'd overflow. She ended up as a receptionist after a couple of weeks.'

Across Brunswick Street, the Bellinos were running an illegal game upstairs in the Top of the Valley building. Tilley and Hapeta soon heard about their neighbours, but they were kept busy getting their foot in the door of Brisbane's fledgling vice industry. To boot, there was no sign of them having to pay a cent of 'funny money' to corrupt police.

Eventually, both would be surprised at how fast their business interests grew. And how lucrative it would become.

Marlin Goes Fishing

The industrious Licensing Branch Constable Brian Marlin, teeming with interesting information for his boss, Alec Jeppesen, and an enigma to his colleagues, gave himself a confidential assignment. Marlin decided he would immerse himself in Brisbane's gay culture and produce a comprehensive and up-to-date report on the city's homosexuals.

In short, Marlin would compile what would effectively be a directory of gay beats, the covert language used by gay men looking for sex, the city's gay hotels and a list of 'suspected persons'.

Had this unusual mission been requested by Police Commissioner Lewis? On Friday 10 March 1978, Lewis had personally seen Marlin in his office regarding 'his duties generally', and Tony Murphy had met with Lewis in the winter of that year to talk about, of all things, lesbian policewomen in the force. But gay men had not received such special attention to date, until the indefatigable Marlin came along.

'He was a weird person,' says one officer who went through a detective training course with him. 'He was just downright weird. He would make out he knew all these top influential people. Word got around and no one would have anything to do with him. He would walk in and people would just leave.

'He would dob other police in. Anyone who was a dog – that was the biggest fear for any copper.'

Marlin completed his detailed dossier.

'I've seen it, it was shown to me. I was horrified,' says the officer. 'He went undercover on his own volition and did this thing on the homosexual underground scene and he gave reports on gay cruising in public parks, listed all the toilets, the Hacienda [Hotel at 394 Brunswick Street, Fortitude Valley], all the venues, the whole lot, terminologies, suspected persons, and all of that. Lewis would have got that.'

The task was a world away from young Marlin's usual duties in the Licensing Branch, though he had already shown a taste for prowling Brisbane's seedy gambling dens, and he wasn't averse to using his fists, or the butt of a firearm, to get his point across.

Jim Slade, the CIB's undercover young gun and intelligence expert, says he worked on the Marlin operation with his partner Norm Sprenger.

'I remember we did a job ... why did we suddenly have this big interest in paedophilia and gays?' Slade recalls. 'It was a massive job, it went on and on and on.

'It had something to do with Rose's Café in the Valley. We ended up identifying teachers that took kids from their classes in there. That was my first association with paedophilia. Brian Marlin was the one who instigated this whole bloody thing through Tony Murphy.

'Norm Sprenger and I did the whole thing. Marlin would steer us in a certain direction and we would get the evidence or we would establish whether there was anything there. I can't remember if there were any arrests out of that bloody thing, but the intelligence was incredible.

'Looking back on it now, I think it was to identify all of the major players and use that information at a later date. It had nothing to do with crime. It had nothing to do with children's safety. It was to identify major players.'

Some of those players also happened to be working as Queensland police officers. Out of Marlin's investigation came a separate one – an intense look at the sexuality of the force's female officers. This became known as the Lesbian Investigation, and was dictated by Tony Murphy.

One of the female officers interrogated was 'incensed'. 'The matters canvassed with these female officers were their own business and no one else's. No allegations were made about policewomen not working, that they were corrupt or that their work was substandard ... As far as I am aware those, the subjects of the investigation, had contempt for [Tony] Murphy as a result of his questioning.'

A gay male officer at the time said it was a fearful workplace for homosexuals. 'There was this really homophobic element in the police and it was just very oppressive,' he says. 'We had police living in absolute fear like it was the Nazis. I was aware there were other gay officers. I was aware there were relationships happening. Senior police having relationships and all that.

'It was hugely prolific with the female officers. But you couldn't be homosexual … it was illegal.'

Mr Asia Books a Room

On the morning of Friday 9 June, staff at the Terrace Motel on Wickham Terrace had grown suspicious of the behaviour of two guests – a man who had booked himself in under the name J. Petersen, occupation M.P. (a joke at the expense of the Queensland Premier) and another man registered as Wilson. They had also racked up a substantial room service bill that included French champagne. Staff called the police.

Four detectives – Melloy, Chantler, Pickering and O'Brien – headed up to the relatively new brick hotel with commanding views over Albert Park and Roma Street, not far from police headquarters.

They located Wilson and took him back to the CIB for questioning. His real identity was drug runner James William Shepherd. He was charged with being in possession of a large sum of money that was suspected of being illegally obtained.

With Shepherd in custody, a phone call was intercepted in his motel room. This led police to the Coronation Motel on Coronation Drive at Milton. There police found Douglas Robert Wilson and his wife Isabel Martha Wilson. They too were taken in for questioning.

The couple chatted convivially until Detective Sergeant Barry O'Brien brought up the fact that a dog bowl had been located in the Jaguar they had been driving. 'Where's the pup?' he asked.

The couple suddenly went quiet.

The Wilsons, just the month before, had been drying out in a Sydney hospital – both were heroin addicts – when 'Petersen' visited them and suggested a holiday 'in the sun' in Queensland once they were discharged. Nothing like the sun to beat a Sydney winter, he told them.

So they headed north – Petersen, the Wilsons, and their pet dog – in Petersen's hugely powerful E-type Jaguar. At this stage, police were not yet aware of the magnitude of what they had stumbled across, but it involved drugs and large sums of cash and they followed through.

The CIB then immediately staked out the Terrace Motel for J. Petersen. They believed that a blue Jaguar sedan with New South Wales plates JSG-693 was owned by the suspicious Petersen.

Later that morning, a male was observed getting into the vehicle and driving it away. The Jaguar was followed to a motor repair workshop at 6 Dorsey Street, Milton. They soon discovered that the business was run by New Zealand criminal Ian Richard Henry. The man who had driven the vehicle from the motel was one of Henry's mechanics, Stephen Thomas Harrison.

After a short time, a man called Stephen Brian Johnstone and J. Petersen left the workshop and were approached by Detective Sergeant Ron Pickering and Detective Senior Constable Barry O'Brien. Both men, along with Harrison, were arrested and taken in to headquarters.

Detective Jim Slade, Murphy's hand-picked officer in the CIB, did not take part in the apprehension of J. Petersen but he did observe what happened. Slade remembers Pat Glancy and Barry O'Brien driving 'this bloody massive E-type Jaguar' back to headquarters. 'It had all these pistons. They drove it back and we followed them.'

J. Petersen, it transpired, was the notorious international drug dealer Terrance (Terry) John Clark, a New Zealand criminal wanted on charges there. Later, Henry and another man, Kevin Walter Gower, were arrested at the Milton workshop.

It was decided that Constables Robson and Le Gros be placed in the cell with Clark, and later Shepherd. Robson went in at 10.50 a.m. that Friday, followed by Le Gros at 11.20 a.m. Robson told Clark he was in 'for a bust'. Le Gros said he'd been pinched with 'some grass'.

Clark told them he was wanted in New Zealand on heroin importation charges and for possession of a .357 Magnum. (Police found in

Clark's hotel room a Colt Python .357 Magnum revolver, known in firearms circles as the 'Rolls-Royce' of handguns.)

'You're a long way from home if you're wanted in New Zealand,' Le Gros quipped.

'Yes,' Clark said. 'I'm up for 14 years back home.'

When Shepherd was put in the same cell, he and Clark immediately moved to one corner and spoke in low tones. Shepherd informed Clark that he had told police he was in Brisbane on a 'punting trip on the horses', and the others had said they were on a 'sailing trip'. Both men laughed.

Clark then told Shepherd he had $3 million worth of heroin in Sydney and that Shepherd, when released, needed to go to Sydney and contact Clark's de facto partner, Maria Muhary. She in turn would contact her brother Stephen who would show Shepherd where the drugs were buried in bushland around Sydney. He needed to hide the heroin and await further instructions.

Henry was then placed in an adjoining cell. 'What are you in for?' Henry asked Shepherd.

'They got me for that money I had.'

'How did they get onto you?'

'You wouldn't believe it but it was because we used the name Petersen,' Shepherd said. 'Apparently this Petersen, the Premier up here, has got a Jag the same as ours and they thought we were impersonating him.

'They got me at the motel. I never liked motels. They always … mean trouble.'

Henry and Shepherd asked Clark what he expected to happen to him.

'I'll probably do two or three months here and then they'll take me back to New Zealand to face the big one there,' he said. 'I don't mind spending some time here. In fact, the longer I can spend here the better.'

In another part of the building Doug and Isabel Wilson were being interviewed separately. A story was beginning to emerge – the Wilsons were couriers for Terrance Clark and his huge international heroin trade. Police were incredulous to the point of disbelief.

Young Cliff Crawford of the Drug Squad was off duty that night but was called in after the importance of the arrests was understood. 'We got the drum about Terry Clark on a number of occasions previously but whenever we arrived it was too late, he was gone,' Crawford recalls. 'At one stage he was supposed to be staying at a high-rise unit at Ascot, corner of Junction Road and Zillmere Road. It was a brick block of flats.

'We arrived there one day and he'd left two weeks before. The drum was right but it was too late. All we knew was that this guy Terrance Clark was a big importer from New Zealand.'

It was decided that the Wilsons needed to be interviewed at length and that the interviews had to be recorded on tape.

Detective Sergeant Sprenger also contacted Commander Max Rogers of the Federal Narcotics Bureau, Queensland chapter, who was in Sydney at the time.

Meanwhile, the name of the panel shop owner, Ian Richard Henry, rang a bell with Detective Sergeant O'Brien. He later recorded in a statement: 'In about 1976, while attached to the Drug Squad, I participated in making inquiries on behalf of New Zealand Police to locate a notorious drug runner Terrance John Clarke [sic]. While Clarke was not located, inquiries showed that while in Brisbane he associated with an Ian Richard Henry, and this information was inserted in the Drug Squad collating system.

'In 1978 I assisted in inquiries [relating to] an active criminal named William Anthony [Billy] Stokes for the murder of Thomas Ian Hamilton. During the investigation, Stokes' residence at Broadbeach on the Gold Coast had been kept under surveillance and visitors photographed.

'One male person visited the premises driving a vehicle which was registered to Ian Richard Henry of Dorsey Street, Milton.'

On Saturday 10 June, both Henry and Shepherd were released on bail. They caught a taxi to Henry's workshop in Dorsey Street, then to his flat in Gregory Terrace. Shepherd made his way to the TAA terminal at Eagle Farm and caught Flight 406 to Sydney. He travelled First Class. In the rear stalls was Detective Norm Sprenger, keeping an eye on him.

It was decided that the Wilsons would be re-interviewed together on Monday 12 June. They specifically asked that the interview not be taped. It took place in the office of Detective Sergeant Terry Ferguson, the Officer in Charge of the Queensland Drug Squad. Prior to the 10.30 a.m. start, Norm Sprenger had set up two recording devices, the microphone installed behind Ferguson's desk.

'Tony Murphy would have had a hand in the interview from the early stages,' says Cliff Crawford. 'When these people started talking about all these murders, the detectives started wondering – is this fair dinkum? It was bizarre. You didn't get that sort of thing in Queensland.'

Present were Detective Sergeants Syd Churchill and Fred Maynard. They were joined soon after the start of the interview by Narcotics Bureau Investigator Robert Turner.

During the next three hours and 27 minutes, the Wilsons revealed that they were part of a major global drug smuggling ring headed by Clark. The couple told the police that in May 1978 – just a month earlier – Clark had mentioned to them that he had shot a lot of people including a man called Harry 'Pommie' Lewis who had had a falling out with Clark.

They said the shooting took place when Clark was travelling down from Brisbane. They didn't know the location of the body, but said it had happened some distance from Brisbane in bushland.

The Wilsons said they collected money for Clark. Clark would have the heroin delivered and the Wilsons, pretending to be jewellery sales consultants, picked up the gear. Money for drugs was always paid into the so-called Sydney importing agency, Cross and Mercer.

They told detectives they collected at least $100,000 a week for Clark. Alarmingly, the police learned that Clark had a top-level informant in the Federal Customs Narcotics Squad who gathered information for Clark and gave him tip-offs. The officer was paid an annual stipend of $25,000, and additional money for new information.

Wilson indicated he was terrified that Clark would find out that he and his wife had squealed on him. '... I'm quite fucking frightened, serious, about it, you know. I know if he thinks for one moment that I've given him up, you know, if he can possibly organise it, he'll have me shot, without any compunction ...' Doug Wilson said.

Seven tapes were made during the course of the interview. Detective Sergeant Sprenger immediately set up transcription equipment for typist Mrs Robyn Whipps and Homicide/Consorting Squad typist Miss Neroli Taylor.

Queensland police only made available transcripts of the first five tapes to the Federal Narcotics Bureau. As Assistant Commissioner, Crimes and Services, L.R. Duffy reported later in a confidential statement to Commissioner Terry Lewis: 'Although there were seven tapes, it was decided by Detective Sergeant Churchill and Detective Sergeant Maynard, that in view of phone numbers of persons being mentioned in the final two tapes as associates of the Wilsons and also because there had been an allegation made against a senior narcotics officer, that the transcript of the last two tapes be not made available to the Narcotics Bureau at that juncture.'

Slade remembers the day the Wilsons talked. 'We were the first police force in Australia to start on the Wilsons,' Slade says. 'We came straight out [of the recorded interviews] and gave a copy of the tape to Tony Murphy.'

Murphy had in his hands an extraordinary tale of drugs, greed and murder. It was dynamite. But was it true? It was not every day that Brisbane's drug squad was regaled with tales of murder and international heroin trafficking worth millions of dollars. Were the Wilsons legitimate, or just addled junkies?

Just seven years earlier, Queensland police had been told wild tales of crime and corruption by a prostitute by the name of Shirley Margaret Brifman. She too put on the table a complicated tale of corrupt police and the underworld that also stretched credulity.

But $100,000 a week? More than $5 million a year? And a man called 'Pommie' Lewis with half his head blown off and his hands amputated somewhere south of Brisbane?

Terrance Clark was extradited back to New Zealand. Meanwhile, a souvenir of Clark's time in Brisbane was left behind. 'Clark had this crocodile-skin briefcase,' says Jim Slade. 'This briefcase, they [the police] knew where it was. A senior officer got it and it was full of money. He had that briefcase for years.'

Top of the Valley, Top of the World

Not long after leasing the Top Hat off parlour entrepreneur Geoff Crocker, Hapeta and Tilley expanded.

It was surprising to Crocker. Here was the physically huge Hector Hapeta, walking with difficulty and a man who couldn't read or write, spreading his wings having only been in Brisbane for five minutes. Crocker would later notice that Hapeta had considerable organisational skills.

Around this time, friends of Crocker and his wife, Julie, were talking of getting engaged in Sydney. They decided to take a few days off and drive down to the Emerald City. Just two days into the trip Crocker's friend Billy Hayes phoned.

'Everything alright?' Crocker asked.

'I went past the Top Hat the other night – it's closed,' Billy replied. 'There's a note on the door – any customers wishing to see girls from these premises should now go across the road. That old Fantasia place where they used to gamble upstairs. Hector and his missus have moved in there and closed your joint up.'

The newcomers had moved lock, stock and barrel into the Top of the Valley at 187 Barry Parade. Fantasia had been run successfully by Katherine James before she was imprisoned on drug charges. She paid rent to Luciano Scognamiglio and her business co-existed with Scognamiglio's game at the Top of the Valley during the mid-1970s.

'I never worked there [at the illegal casino], but I used to go down there often enough because I worked down the hallway at the parlour,' recalled James. 'Gerry and Tony Bellino would come there at least once a week to collect the money. Either one of them would attend each week. It was usually Gerry, but Tony would also attend. They very rarely came together. While one or the other of them was there, from time to time I would hear them give directions to Scognamiglio about the running of the place.

'I should also add that at about this time I was having a sexual relationship with Gerry Bellino. I would discuss business with him, but he never sought to take over my business nor to direct me in any way. The relationship with Gerry Bellino ended in about July 1975. It could have been as late as the end of 1975.

'From his discussions with me I can say that the only business interests that Gerry Bellino had at that stage was Pinocchio's and the other gambling place at Top of the Valley. He had no interest in massage parlours that I knew of. He showed no interest in that kind of work either.'

Crocker was incredulous at the move from Top Hat to the Top of the Valley. Hapeta and Tilley had promised they'd be renting his place for at least a year. Had they done a runner? What was going on?

He hopped on the next plane back to Brisbane. 'I went around to Hector's,' he said. 'I went around there and blew up. I said, "What the fuck do you think you're doing? You told me you'd lease the place for a year".'

'Yeah, I am,' Hapeta supposedly replied. 'Here's a cheque.' Hapeta handed over the rest of the year's due rent.

Hapeta and Tilley had set the cat among the pigeons in the Brisbane vice scene by agreeing to split takings fifty/fifty with their parlour girls. The workers' wages had never been that high. Other parlours were complaining.

The Penthouse, not far from the Top Hat, was particularly vociferous. 'She [the Penthouse leasee] complained like shit because once [Tilley] got going that's when we found out about [Tilley] giving the girls 50 per cent of whatever money they earned,' Crocker said. 'I said to [her], you're going to have to do it too.'

Hapeta and Tilley were already making an impact. Astute observers would have seen – even in the earliest months of their empire-building – that they would be a duo to be reckoned with.

The Elusive John Edward Milligan

Narcotics Agent John Shobbrook was settling back nicely into Brisbane life by the end of winter in 1978. As Supervising Narcotics Agent for the Brisbane bureau one of his jobs was to approve of the destruction of any redundant drug seizures.

In August, senior agent Greg Rainbow dropped a case file onto Shobbrook's desk and asked for permission to destroy the heroin linked to the case. Rainbow requested that the file be marked 'No Further Action'.

Naturally curious, Shobbrook reviewed the file and couldn't believe his eyes. 'I was surprised to see that apart from the actual seizure of the drug from a fisherman named David Ward, little investigation had been carried out in relation to this matter,' says Shobbrook.

'Rainbow informed me that he had received little encouragement or support to continue the investigation and that follow-up proposals that Rainbow had put forward had been rejected.

'The fact that this was a sizeable seizure of heroin was of note, but equally as important as the heroin, was a small piece of paper attached to the file that had a telephone number and the name "John Milligan" written on it.'

Here he was again – John Edward Milligan, former drug dealer and Hallahan informant.

Milligan was well known to the Narcotics Bureau, particularly to Brian Bennett, who had arrested Milligan leaving the Tran Australian Airlines bond store at Brisbane Airport in possession of two rugs containing more than 30 kilograms of secreted hashish and Buddha sticks in the early 1970s. Bennett had also had an unforgettable meeting in a back alley at Petrie Terrace, near the police barracks, with Milligan's associate, the notorious Sydney gangster John Stewart Regan, over Milligan.

It transpired that in the course of his investigation some months earlier Rainbow had headed to Cairns with two junior officers on a tip-off about a 380 gram package of heroin in the possession of the fisherman David Ward.

Ward had tried to offload the high-grade heroin in a few pubs on the Cairns waterfront, and word got back to the local Customs sub-collector. Rainbow and his men immediately put Ward under surveillance. Shortly after, Ward twigged and confronted the team.

'We're from the Narcotics Bureau,' they said. 'You're in a lot of trouble.'

'I don't want trouble,' Ward replied, and accompanied the men on a Customs launch up the Normanton River to his camp where he produced the parcel of heroin. Rainbow learned that it had been dropped from a light aircraft that had flown out of Papua New Guinea.

Later, Ward asked Rainbow: 'Would you like to take some barramundi fillets back for the missus?'

Shobbrook recalls: 'They're all drinking Fourex, loading up with barramundi. These three stooges fly back to Brisbane with their barramundi.

'Rainbow wrote an indemnity for Ward at the camp. He had no authority to do that. It compromised the investigation.'

Shobbrook asked Max Rogers, the Regional Commander for Brisbane at the time, if he could reignite the case. 'I realised nothing had been done on it,' says Shobbrook. 'I thought it could be followed up.'

He was told that if he wanted to do something about it he had to get in touch with Canberra and sort it out himself. He telephoned Narcotics Bureau National Enforcement Chief Inspector David Schramm for approval. We're up to the 'J's' in our investigations, Schramm told him. 'Call it Operation Jungle.'

Shobbrook wanted to employ United States techniques on this case: a specialist team of his choosing; his own office space with a key to the door; and he didn't want to be encumbered with any other investigations.

Shobbrook soon learned that John Edward Milligan had been one of Rogers' prize informants. His informant number was 138. Within weeks of the operation kicking off, Rogers resigned.

'Everyone was shocked,' says Shobbrook. 'There had been no pre-warning, no office rumours, it came out of the blue; no explanation was offered.'

Rogers' abrupt resignation however had nothing to do with Milligan, Shobbrook or anything else. He simply felt, after long deliberation, that it was time to move on with his life.

Shobbrook and his hand-picked team, including John Moller, headed north to Cairns and began retracing the route of Milligan and his gang. They met up with Percy Trezise, owner of the Laura pub. Percy offered to fly the Narcs to remote locations in his single engine Cessna. The team tracked down fishermen on the Normanby River, and travelled in an aluminium dinghy up and down the Annie and North Kennedy rivers as well as crossing Princess Charlotte Bay.

Shobbrook was curious why their dinghy carried an axe.

'[That's] to kill any bloody crocodiles that get too friendly,' the skipper replied. It was enough to stop him trailing his hand in the warm waters out the side of the boat.

The Operation Jungle team was meticulous. They took witness statements, gathered evidence, painstakingly put together a timeline of Milligan's movements, and began assembling a picture not just of drug importation but a corrupt network that perhaps went to the very top of the Queensland Police Force.

A Private Dinner

By July 1978, select police officers were attempting to contact Premier Joh Bjelke-Petersen directly with information about trouble in the ranks.

It should have spelled out two things very clearly to the Premier – that after less than two years as Commissioner of Police, Terry Lewis and his reign were proving a unique sort of problem, one that was quite the opposite to Ray Whitrod.

Whereas Whitrod and his reforms were slammed for their progressiveness, for their transparency, for their attempt to look forward and join the modern age, Lewis's regime appeared to be looking back to the Bischof era, where power was all and graft just a supplement to a policeman's average income.

The former long-term member for Greenslopes, Bill Hewitt, remembers an incident that tends to underline this. He recalls that Eddie Liu, the prominent Chinatown identity, had an organisation that used to meet in the Valley for a meal on a Sunday night every few months or so.

Hewitt says he felt obliged to go and at one of the meetings got talking to Commissioner Terry Lewis. 'He wasn't discreet, he was vehement about the fact that he didn't get paid as much as commissioners in other states,' recalls Hewitt. 'He was beside himself. It was a really big thing with him.

'I often wondered if he thought – well, if they're not going to give me what I'm entitled to, I'll get it my own way.'

The other thing the Premier should have been cognisant of was that these disgruntled police officers, by going to him, could obviously not air their grievances with their own boss or superiors. Why not?

On one occasion, Redlands MP John Goleby and Constable Brian Marlin arranged a secret dinner at Lennons Hotel in the city with Licensing Branch chief Alec Jeppesen and the Premier. Also present at the dinner was the new Police Minister Ron Camm. During the course of the dinner, Bjelke-Petersen was alerted to police corruption courtesy of the taped interviews with informants Jeppesen had been privately compiling. He also had statutory declarations from SP bookmakers and working prostitutes. Jeppesen told Bjelke-Peteresen the names of senior police he believed were corrupt.

According to Jeppesen, Goleby, on hearing stories of corruption within the police ranks, quipped: 'You have to be careful with those informants otherwise they'll end up with cement boots.'

Jeppesen said he told Bjelke-Petersen at the 1978 dinner that he had been informed that Tony Murphy collected '$10,000 a time' from SP bookies for the legal defence of Jack Herbert during the famous Southport Betting Case.

Brian Marlin then told the guests at the dinner that the consorting squad – on the instructions of Murphy – intended to take over the massage parlours. Marlin, who was supposedly from New South Wales though his past remained a bit of a mystery, believed the scene would become 'as corrupt as Sydney'.

Jeppesen reportedly said: 'Marlin told them the Consorting Squad was taking over the massage parlour scene. He singled out Murphy as the one organising it.'

Jeppesen wanted two former senior members of the Crime Intelligence Unit, set up by Whitrod, to investigate the claims. 'I suggested Voigt and Hicks investigate it and Camm said, "Voigt was a Whitrod man",' Jeppesen reportedly said. 'Camm lost interest in it then.

'The Premier asked me if I would stay in the Licensing Branch for some months but with Camm's attitude, I could see myself in some jeopardy.'

Four Photographs

When Murphy and his crew went in pursuit of Basil 'The Hound' Hicks throughout 1978, they did so with professionalism and vigour.

Their timing was impeccable. Just as they faced yet another hurdle, an incriminating piece of paper emerged from nowhere to shore up the case against Hicks. Now Hicks would feel what it was like to be investigated by Tony Murphy.

'You would never, ever want Tony Murphy on your tail,' says Jim Slade. 'He had the most incredible memory. There were some crims who used to really hold him in awe.

'He was the greatest thing to happen to me regarding doing the job properly. He was a very, very smart man ... I learned how you position informants, how you put in your undercovers, figure out your plan, if you're going to interdict at this point here, think back six months, establish tactics; he was absolutely brilliant. I have seen Murphy convince people to do a thing when no other human being could convince them to do it.'

So it was that at police headquarters in Brisbane on 24 July 1978, police officer Reginald Neal Freier gave a statement witnessed by

Deputy Commissioner Vern MacDonald about Hicks and the prostitute Katherine James.

As it turns out, it was Freier who allegedly became aware of the existence of the compromising pictures of Hicks and James way back in 1974, during the time Freier was suspended from the force over the Southport Betting Case corruption fiasco. Now the reinstated policeman had something to offer against Hicks. Freier, in his statement, said he located James at the Kontiki massage parlour and sent in an informant to talk with her. The informant then gave her a message, asking her to meet Freier 'up the road', in fact at the corner of Gympie and Rode Roads, south of Chermside.

James agreed. Freier says he 'had taken the precaution of having my solicitor … nearby'.

'I introduced myself to her and I told her that I was a Detective under suspension and that I had received information that she was in possession of a number of photographs of her and Hicks in bed,' the statement went on. 'She asked me what my interest in the matter was and I told her that I was no friend of Hicks and that they could possibly be put to some use during my trial.'

James allegedly told Freier that she had been having an affair with Hicks for years and that he was harassing her for sex and she wanted to get him off her back.

'She told me that there were a total of four photographs taken – that she in fact had given Hicks one of the photographs and warned him that if he continued to come and see her she would send the remainder to his wife,' Freier stated. 'I offered to buy the photographs of her and Hicks from her for $500. She laughed and said she would make that much money in a massage parlour in one day.'

Freier revealed how he had given her his personal details and that she had contacted him on a few occasions but never relinquished the incriminating pictures. He concluded: 'Whilst I have never seen the alleged photographs, I have no doubt, from my conversations with

[James], that there are photographs of her and Hicks in bed together in existence.'

The statement was typed not on department stationery but on plain paper. It was a small but nevertheless timely piece of further evidence in the mosaic being compiled against Basil Hicks. It gave the so-called photograph scandal involving a supposedly squeaky clean officer who had once been one of Ray Whitrod's most trusted and loyal sidekicks some history – the saga went right back to 1974, when Hicks was a powerful figure in the force and heading its anti-corruption body, the Crime Intelligence Unit. By backdating the story to that period, it showed Hicks as a hypocrite and a man of dubious character.

'The only way to get Hicks was to besmirch his character,' says private investigator John Wayne Ryan, who knew James and also Roland Short, the owner of the Matador, the swingers club in South Brisbane. 'Roland Short set it all up. They got a guy that looked a bit like Hicks and the photographs were taken in the Matador.

'James would later say on oath that I was there, hiding in the bath-room or the closet. She had a couple of conflicting locations in her statements that the photographs were taken in her bedroom at home. They weren't.'

Ryan claims that at one point Roland Short called him into his office and showed him the photographs. He told Ryan the photos were of Hicks

'I told him no way, not under any circumstances did that guy in the photographs look like Basil Hicks,' recalls Ryan. 'He tried to get me involved in it. I think they were hoping to kill two birds with one stone – to get both me and Hicks. It was a complete set-up, and Murphy was organising it into 1978.'

Set-up or not, somewhere along the line some of the mud hurled at Basil Hicks was bound to stick.

Circumstantial Evidence

William Anthony (Billy) Stokes went to trial for the murder of Tommy Hamilton on Monday 21 August 1978. Stokes pleaded 'not guilty' to charges of murder and deprivation of liberty.

The Crown's case was that a man identified as Billy Stokes wore a mask and armed with two pistols entered a house in Atkinson Street, Hamilton, on 10 January 1975. He then held a gun to Hamilton's head and forced him out of the house and into a blue car.

As the *Telegraph* reported: 'The Crown case was that Stokes and Hamilton had been good friends until Stokes refused to pay a fine for Hamilton and some of his companions who had been convicted on a drug charge at Caboolture in 1973.

'Justice Connolly said it was common ground that Hamilton bore a grudge against Stokes and he received numerous telephone calls from Hamilton and his companions mocking him, threatening and making obscene suggestions about Stokes' estranged wife.

'He said Hamilton had told his companions that he was trying to "crack the chicken".'

Stokes, defending himself, said the Crown had not proved its case. He did not call witnesses or give evidence. He addressed the jury for a few minutes.

At 3.40 p.m. on Thursday the jury retired to consider its verdict but had not reached a decision by 9.15 p.m. The jury was locked up overnight.

The next day, at 10.15 a.m. their verdict was delivered – guilty.

Stokes, in the dock, shook his head and reportedly said: 'How could you?'

Detectives at the back of the court room shook hands in congratulations. Stokes was jailed for life.

The case didn't warrant a mention in the Commissioner's diary. On that Friday he fielded a call from reporter Pat Lloyd of the *Telegraph* regarding a 'civic parade' for Tracey Wickham. (The 16-year-old Brisbane schoolgirl had just won gold medals in the 400-metre and 800-metre freestyle events at the Commonwealth Games being held in Edmonton, Canada.) Superintendent Tony Murphy called about meeting Police Minister Ron Camm. The Commissioner later addressed the Queensland Press Club on 'Juveniles, Crime and Demonstrations' at the Crest Hotel down by City Hall.

Meanwhile, Stokes was transferred to his cell.

Five years after the Whiskey Au Go Go tragedy and the arrest and conviction of John Andrew Stuart and James Finch, aspects of the story were still bobbing up in various court cases and missing persons investigations. So too the mysterious case of Barbara McCulkin and her missing daughters – it, like the supposed drug overdose of the prostitute and whistleblower Shirley Margaret Brifman in a small bedroom in a flat in Clayfield in March 1972, wouldn't go away.

Barbara McCulkin had been married to petty gangster Billy 'The Mouse' McCulkin until late 1973 when he left the family home in Dorchester Street, Highgate Hill, and took up with another woman. Barbara and Billy had two daughters, Vicky Maree, almost thirteen, and Barbara Leanne, eleven.

Following the bombing of the Torino nightclub in the Valley and the Whiskey Au Go Go nightclub in March 1973 that claimed 15 lives – Barbara McCulkin heard innumerable stories about Billy and the involvement of other criminals, such as John Andrew Stuart and Tommy Hamilton of the Clockwork Orange Gang and a host of other suspects. Stuart had supposedly had an affair with Barbara McCulkin before the fire at the Whiskey.

Upset by her marriage breakdown, Barbara was making noises to blow the whistle on her husband and his associates. Then, in January 1974, she and her two daughters vanished from their Highgate Hill home without a trace.

In prison, Stokes would be reunited with John Andrew Stuart. Gossamer webs seemed to connect many people and crimes in the 1970s. There were many tiles in the mosaic. But what was the big picture?

In Queen Street

Fred Collins, a former Queensland police officer, was in Queen Street in the Brisbane CBD around this time when he bumped into an old friend – Jack Herbert.

Collins had known Herbert since the late 1950s, when Herbert sold him a motor vehicle. He also saw him socially at various functions over the years. Collins had left the force in 1971, having worked for five years with Terry Lewis in the Juvenile Aid Bureau.

Collins and Herbert had a chinwag, particularly about Herbert's cancer scare. Collins had noticed Herbert had lost a lot of weight.

Herbert also went on about how the Southport Betting Case and its prohibitive legal fees had cleaned him out. He had had to sell his home. The whole thing had left him broke, he told Fred. 'He then went on to say that he was then engaged in the pinball machine business and was placing them in clubs,' Collins later attested in a statement. 'He then told me he had been to the United States and had visited Las Vegas as a guest of the Mafia.

'He said that the reason for this was that because he was an ex-policeman and said that he knew Terry Lewis, who was then the Commissioner of Police, they assumed that he would have the right connections in having the pinball machines placed in the most profitable places.

'He said that this assumption about Terry Lewis was bullshit but he let them believe it and that he was in a position to assist them.'

It was a curious exchange. Could Herbert have been throwing

around the Commissioner's name to line his own pockets? But what of their friendship? The dinners? The family occasions?

Lewis says he was used by numerous people who he thought were loyal.

'They could abuse me very easily,' he reflects. 'They could have said, "Oh I'm seeing Terry down at the Crest Hotel tonight" or whatever, and we'll have a couple of drinks so you can see that we're mates. I've no hesitation in saying Herbert in particular [did that] and maybe [Tony] Murphy and maybe [Glen] Hallahan, I don't know, I don't know if I can think of any others at the moment but there was probably others.'

As for the friendship between Lewis and Herbert, what was the truth?

The Zebra

In late August the likeable John Goleby, National Party member for Redlands, south-west of the city and in the heart of Brisbane's so-called 'salad bowl', telephoned Basil Hicks.

Backbencher Goleby was a committed Christian and he had struck up a close friendship with Premier Joh Bjelke-Petersen. It was Goleby who had put the Premier and Alec Jeppesen together just a couple of months earlier. Now he asked if Hicks would also confidentially meet with the Premier.

It was a curious period for Commissioner Terry Lewis and his top brass. Lewis had been diligently running the police force as per the Premier's wishes. He was, for example, immediately acquiescent when it came to enforcing the anti-protest legislation, among other things. At the same time he had done everything in his power to hose out any remnants of the Whitrod era. He had demoted, moved or forced the resignation of Whitrod loyalists. He had dismantled many of Whitrod's initiatives.

Yet less than two years into Lewis's stewardship, Bjelke-Petersen was hearing stories. The Rat Pack was back.

Coupled with cage-rattler Kevin Hooper's ceaseless denigration of the force and its implicit corruption on the floor of Parliament House, there was an odour about the police that resembled the days of Frank 'Big Fella' Bischof. Given that the corrupt Bischof had mentored Lewis, the Premier and some of his trusted National Party colleagues began making their own enquiries.

On Monday 4 September, Hicks joined Bjelke-Petersen and Goleby at the Zebra Motel on George Street in the heart of the city, opposite the government's Executive Building.

Commissioner Lewis had no idea of the meeting. Earlier that day he had spoken at length on the telephone to Stan Wilcox, the Premier's personal secretary, about a variety of matters including Bjelke-Petersen's security, bail for demonstrators and the 'transfer of Insp. Jeppesen'.

The Premier made it patently clear to Hicks that he was worried that Superintendent Tony Murphy was 'going to get involved in prostitution again', and it concerned him. It was mildly ironic that the Premier had to seek advice from one of ousted Commissioner Ray Whitrod's most trusted lieutenants, rather than his own Police Commissioner.

Bjelke-Petersen said he planned to move Murphy out of the CIB. The Premier was tired of Lewis never allowing him to make any decisions when it came to the police department. Would Hicks replace Murphy and take over the running of the CIB?

Hicks agreed. He added that when news leaked out – which it inevitably would – 'they' would launch a monumental smear campaign against him. Hicks would be painted as 'the greatest villain in the world'.

Did either man know that that campaign was already in train? Commissioner Lewis had been aware since April that there were suggestions that Hicks might replace Murphy.

Bjelke-Petersen asked Hicks to bring the necessary transfer papers to him in person. Hicks planned to do that on Thursday 7 September.

Incredibly, given the only participants were the Premier, Goleby and Hicks, the meeting in the Zebra Motel was leaked. Less than 48 hours after Hicks and the Premier talked, and the day before the transfer papers for Hicks were to be delivered to the Executive Building, Deputy Commissioner Vern MacDonald recorded in his diary for 6 September that he had been visited in his office by jailed prostitute Katherine James who made a further statement about having sex with Hicks.

Prison records confirmed that James indeed visited police head-quarters on 6 September. There were no records for her alleged earlier visit to Deputy Commissioner MacDonald's office in late April.

Why would James make a statement in the first week of September, when Commissioner Lewis had already received her statement about the Hicks scandal in April? Was Lewis lying in his diary or was MacDonald?

As promised, on the night of Thursday 7 September, Hicks dropped off the transfer papers to the Premier's office.

On the Saturday night he received an anonymous phone call at home to be told 'a job had been done' on him, and on Monday, officer Noel Creevey informed Hicks that a statement from a prostitute called Katherine James, outlining a sexual relationship with him, had been shown to the Premier.

That Monday night, according to Lewis's diary, the Commissioner met with Superintendent Tony Murphy to discuss 'Juvenile Bureaux and B & E of Surveyor-General's office'. They no doubt had a quiet word about Basil Hicks.

Lewis and company had worked swiftly and efficiently to snooker the Hound.

Hicks, in turn, had only one option. He needed to go to Brisbane Prison and meet face to face with the prostitute Katherine James.

A Delegation

Lorelle Saunders, like many other policewomen in the force, had been appalled at Tony Murphy and Brian Marlin's so-called 'Lesbian Investigation'.

She was also generally dismayed, since the exit of Whitrod, at the lack of opportunities for female police officers. Although she had just been transferred to a new and exciting unit – the Regional Task Force, set up to handle the protestors and civil libertarians who were pitting their war for basic human rights against Premier Joh Bjelke-Petersen on the streets of Brisbane. It may have emboldened her.

Just as she did with the petition over the wearing of slacks, she went into action. Along with Constable Judy Newman, Sergeant Evelyn Hill and Senior Sergeant Bill Hannigan, Saunders took her delegation to meet with none other than Robert Sparkes, President of the Queensland National Party, and Charles Holm, the vice-president.

At the meeting, a wide range of issues were talked about, including the lesbian inquiry and the rights of female officers compared to their male counterparts. Thinking the meeting was confidential, Saunders also discussed aspects of police corruption she'd come across or been told about. She let the political heavyweights know that massage parlours in Fortitude Valley were being protected by the Licensing Branch in exchange for money. She mentioned the World by Night strip club (run by the Bellinos). And she dropped the name Jack Herbert in the mix.

The inspector in charge of the task force was Sergeant First Class Allan Lobegeiger. One of Saunders' first duties was to drive Lobegeiger around, particularly on Friday and Saturday nights. When Lobegeiger was chosen to attend the superintendent's course at the Australian Police College in Sydney, he was required to complete an assignment. He gave it to Saunders to do for him.

After her top-level delegation with the National Party brass, Lobegeiger gave her several warnings.

'Lobegeiger often told me that the current police administration regarded me as "highly dangerous" due to my knowledge of certain corrupt officers and practices and believed that I was a member of a group of dissident officers who had sworn to bring about the downfall of the current administration,' she later recalled.

'He repeatedly asked me the identity of a group of dissident officers known in the press as the "Committee of Eight". It was believed I was secretary to the "Committee of Eight".

'He also told me to stop attending political meetings and criticising the police administration.'

On 14 September 1978, Lewis noted in his diary: 'Allen Callaghan phoned re 3 p/women having deputation to Mr. R. Sparkes.' Four days later he telephoned his Police Minister, Ron Camm, to discuss the same matter.

Less than three weeks later Lewis had a meeting with the Premier about the general running of the force and other matters. They also talked about Lorelle Saunders: '… Hannigan and 3 P/W seeing R. Sparkes; and P/W L. Saunders being member of the Nat. Party. Premier said to transfer her.'

Lewis didn't, though. He may have thought back to when Whitrod had transferred him and Tony Murphy to Charleville and Longreach respectively, and how, in the end, it was a tactical error by the former commissioner, giving both men an opportunity to campaign out of sight against Whitrod.

Still, Lewis was concerned about this mythical Committee of Eight and he saw Saunders as a potential problem.

Good Fun at the Belfast

So long as Barry Maxwell was behind the beer taps at the Belfast Hotel, he was assured of an enthusiastic police patronage, especially now that his old friend Terry Lewis was the big boss.

Indeed, the Belfast had many years earlier usurped the former police pub – the National Hotel – since the royal commission into police conduct at the National in 1963–64, and the retirement of former commissioner Frank Bischof.

The shadows that extended from the National Hotel inquiry were long. For some senior police who were involved, it might almost prove a jinx to grace its doorways again. But that didn't stop the National owners, the Roberts brothers, from drinking at their rival – the Belfast.

'I met old Rolly Roberts on a couple of occasions,' says a former manager at the Belfast. 'He used to come down and see how our business was going. Maxwell didn't like Rolly.

'I think I might have seen Herbert and Hallahan in the early days … Murphy and Lewis … I might have seen all four of them up in the old cocktail bar before we renovated.

'Tony [Murphy] would come in while he was on duty. He'd say hello to Barry and have a couple of drinks. He never discussed police work. Maxwell was always trying to get something out of him; he liked the mystery and excitement of it all.'

There was serious talk, and there was plenty of hijinks too. 'I'll never forget one night, Lewis was there and he would have been Commissioner,' the manager remembers. 'He had another copper with him. They were walking into the Moon Bar; it had a big round doorway, something you'd see on a spaceship. There were plastic chairs, the latest from Sweden or somewhere. Lewis and this poor copper were standing there [when suddenly] Maxwell went, "Is this real?", and pulled his [the policeman's] gun out, full of piss.

'The copper said, "Mr Maxwell, I'll have to ask you to give me my gun back."

'Tony would stay and I think I might have seen Tony a bit pissed but I don't think I saw Terry pissed. Maxwell just drank five-ounce beers.

'I used to appreciate the police coming in. All the detectives used to come there. I'd shout them tea. I said, "You buy the wine and I'll buy the tea." I used to pick the most expensive bottle of wine to get some money out of them. I think probably Barry used to shout all the coppers. His father was a policeman in his day. He always used to think he would be a good cop.'

The manager didn't see much of Jack 'The Bagman' Herbert. He and his wife, Peggy, would sometimes drop by. 'Peggy always came across as a lady to me, but they told me she was red-headed and fiery,' the manager recalled. 'I saw her at a couple of functions they had at the pub.'

While Murphy might not have shared stories of his fascinating life as a top-rate detective with Maxwell, he did with the manager. 'He showed me this new drug – LSD. It was in a matchbox … looked like bits of blotting paper. He sat and talked to me and told me about different things,' the manager says.

'Down on Wharf Street there were the old doss houses full of derros living in there. He told me that they raided one of the houses and found a girl there laying on a mattress naked, with blokes hitting her with drugs and other blokes paying two dollars to have sex with her.

'There was another case. A murder. A lady, a cockie's wife, they found her dead and she'd been raped. They shot her eyes out. It was a really bad crime. It might have been out west, out Toowoomba way.

'Well we were standing in the bar one night – this was shortly after the murder – and Tony was there and he hadn't slept in two days or two nights. He got a phone call and I always let them come into the office at the pub. He still had half a beer there but he said to his mate, "Let's get out of here."

'They got this guy, the murderer, at Coober Pedy. He was brought back to Brisbane. They charged him with the murder.

'Tony Murphy said, "We questioned him all the way back and the poor prick kept falling out of the Jeep on the way back." They must have beat him to get a confession.

'Tony Murphy was a good cop, he would not let anything rest.'

Lewis has fond memories of Maxwell and the Belfast.

'Barry Maxwell – we'd met over the years. He'd worked in hotels, he ended up being the licensee down there,' says Lewis. 'The police used to go upstairs usually. You could get into, not a corner, but one area of it. When I became Commissioner I used to go down there. Barry would call me to come down to lunch. Sheilagh was a lovely woman. They were nice people.'

Lewis remembers that when he was in the Consorting Squad in the 1950s they'd call into the Transcontinental and have two beers, and then might drop into the Sportsmen and have a couple more there, then go on to dinner. But in the 1970s they remained loyal to Maxwell and the Belfast. 'A lot of well-to-do businessmen drank there. You wouldn't have struck any wharfies or painters and dockers,' says Lewis.

The Belfast and its reputation as home away from home to the Rat Pack was not just confined to police gossip. Word had gone further afield. Licensing Branch head Alec Jeppesen had started taping confidential interviews with SP bookmakers into 1978 and a pattern of police graft and corruption was beginning to materialise. One informant told Jeppesen that Tony Murphy and Jack Herbert were 'ruthless bastards' who stressed that bookies 'pay up or fucking else'.

The informant confirmed that 'Terry' and 'Tony' drank with Herbert at the Belfast. 'They all get down there drinking with Terry and Tony and all the boys down at the Belfast,' the informant said on the tapes. 'It's all the same bloody clique, you know.'

One informant talked of bribe money being paid to Brian Hayes, who was promoted to Assistant Commissioner in mid-1978. 'Brian would take an empty bottle. Take anything,' the informant said. 'Well apparently Terry – well I don't know whether it's Terry or whether it's Tony – but they are pushing to get him [Hayes] up. Tony's a rather ruthless bastard. He'd just cut anyone's feet from under them.

'But Terry Lewis, he's got plenty of principles. He's not like Tony.'

Hicks Goes to Gaol

On Thursday 21 September 1978, Commissioner Terry Lewis was facing a day of relatively light duties. As was his custom, he was in his office around 7.15 a.m. and first up had a quick phone chat with the parliamentarian Dr Llew Edwards.

He then proceeded to the Greenbank Military Range, the Australian Defence Force's 4500-hectare live training facility near Logan, 25 kilometres south-west of the Brisbane CBD. There he delighted in a 'display of The American 180 Weapon System'. Then he enjoyed lunch with friends at the Queensland Cricketers' Club over at the Gabba grounds in South Brisbane.

As Lewis socialised, Basil Hicks and Detective Saunders drove out to the Brisbane Prison, signed the Prison Visitors Book, were issued passes and then met the prostitute Katherine James near one of the prison dormitories. Hicks and Saunders were finally at the epicentre of the attempt to destroy The Hound's reputation and his police career.

Hicks had known that Saunders was a good operator and could be trusted from their days working together in Whitrod's Crime Intelligence Unit.

'I considered that she was a mature policewoman,' Hicks later said. 'There were some young ones there at the depot. I knew that she'd been in the army before she came into the police ... I knew that I was exposing her to very, very grave consequences.

'One, because she was coming over to the gaol with me and she was going to witness something that – well, at that time I didn't know what she was going to witness. And two, I was going to expose her to a lot of danger, because she was going over there to the gaol.'

Hicks introduced Saunders to James. 'At first she did not want to talk and after a short while Inspector Hicks left us alone,' said Saunders. 'I recall that Inspector Hicks had a tape recorder in his hand but I cannot say whether it was going or not. He did leave me with the tape recorder while I had a conversation with James.'

Saunders told James about the allegation that she [James] had been told by police to say that there were photographs in existence of her and Hicks having sex. 'I told her he was a happily married man and that this could wreck his family life and that she had better tell us now if it was not true. James told me that the photographs did not exist,' said Saunders. 'She told me that she had been approached by [Tony] Murphy ... to say that they did exist.

'James told me that Basil Hicks was too honest and was causing problems and had to be stopped because he arrested people who were being looked after. She told me that she had to do it or they would put more charges on her and this would affect her parole.'

James admitted to Saunders that in the past photographs had been taken of her in a compromising position with a male. That person was not Basil Hicks.

'Saunders had a conversation with her in which she [James] told Saunders that the whole thing was a set-up and that she'd never had anything to do with Hicks,' says journalist Ken Blanch. 'By the time they got back to the city one of the prison officers had phoned Tony Murphy and told them what they'd done at the gaol.'

Saunders returned to the offices of the Regional Task Force, to which she had recently been seconded, and Hicks went back to Mobile Patrols. Hicks may have been satisfied that he had obtained vindication from Katherine James, but their brief visit to Boggo Road would set in motion a sequence of events that would destroy both of their careers in a way so extreme and calculating, and in such abject disregard to human civility and the sanctity of law, that it made the Rat Pack's previous forays into discrediting people's reputations look harmless in comparison.

The moment Saunders returned to her office she was confronted by her boss, Inspector Lobegeiger. 'What the hell do you think you are doing, antagonising them, going out there with Hicks?' he asked.

Lobegeiger told her she was not to leave the area of the Task Force without his 'express approval'.

He said all hell had broken loose over the visit to Boggo Road to see James. 'He then instructed me to inform him of the full details of the visit to the prison,' Saunders later said. 'I refused. I told him I was acting under the direct orders of a senior officer and if they wanted to know they could ask Inspector Hicks. I refused to discuss the matter with him any further.

'He again demanded the names of the so-called "Committee of Eight". At this point rational discourse ceased and we had a bitter argument over police corruption.'

Word of the prison visit had indeed gotten back to headquarters. The next day Commissioner Lewis recorded in his diary: 'Mr R[on] Borinetti, H.M.Prison, phoned re Insp B. Hicks and a P/Woman seeing Mrs [James] on 21st and inquiring as to who had visited her.'

On the following Monday, Tony Murphy phoned Lewis to discuss the Hicks and Saunders matter.

Around this time, Hicks bumped into Murphy in the street. 'He [Murphy] was coming from the CIB building, I presume, downtown, I was going back up to the depot, and we were approaching each other,' Hicks later recalled. 'We could see each other from some distance away, and he had a big grin on his face, and I admit I was very angry at that time.

'He came down the street and … we just about met, and he walked towards me and said something.'

Hicks didn't quite catch Murphy's quip. It may have been about the prison visit, but he was so enraged with Murphy he didn't respond and kept walking.

'I went back up to the depot, and about … a quarter of an hour to half an hour later I got a phone call,' said Hicks. '[They] didn't say who they were … but the voice, I'd say that it was Murphy rang me up, and he asked me what was I doing taking the policewoman over to the gaol. Why did I take the policewoman over to the gaol?

'I said, "I'm minding my own business." And then he said – I can't remember the exact words, but [he] asked about her [Saunders]. And he said, "I'll deal with her later." That was the end of the conversation.'

And it was the end of Hicks and Saunders.

One Shot to the Head

On Sunday 15 October 1978, Senior Constable Desmond John Connor, stationed in Mareeba, a small town on the Atherton Tablelands in Far North Queensland, was enjoying a day off. Connor, 36, had a lot of things on his mind, most particularly the outfall from allegations that he and fellow officers on the Tablelands were involved in the illicit drug trade.

Mareeba, just over 400 metres above sea level and situated where the Barron River meets Granite and Emerald creeks, was garnering a reputation as a drug capital to rival Griffith in New South Wales.

The allegations against Connor and others stemmed from the arrest in April 1976 of Roland Lawrence Magro and Enea Cardelli. Later that year both were convicted of the cultivation and possession of large quantities of cannabis. Magro got five and a half years in prison; Cardelli copped four. Out of that successful prosecution came rumours that there was police involvement. Namely, that police at one time had taken pay-offs from Magro.

As a result, the rumour and innuendo was investigated by the

Internal Investigation Section of the force down in Brisbane, conducted by Superintendent C.D. Dwyer and Inspector M.H. Stephens. Their confidential report was subsequently presented to Deputy Commissioner Vern MacDonald, who forwarded it to the Solicitor-General. Was there enough evidence to lay charges?

Advice was given on 1 June 1978 that there was insufficient evidence to proceed with charges against officers Connor, Sergeant First Class John Milner of the Atherton police and Detective Senior Constable R.C. Bevan.

Despite being cleared, however, Milner and Connor were to return to uniform duties at Mobile Patrols in Brisbane – a demotion marginally above being sent to Police Stores – while Bevan was to take up a position in a suburban station in the capital.

In the end, Milner's transfer was stopped and he remained in Far North Queensland. He was apparently saved by deputations from prominent local citizens who appealed that he be retained in the region.

Interestingly, on the afternoon of Tuesday 26 September – just a few weeks earlier – Commissioner Lewis had flown to Cairns and then on to the remote Aboriginal community of Kowanyama, on the western edge of the Cape York Peninsula, to open a new police station. While he was at Cairns Airport, waiting for a connecting charter flight to Kowanyama, Lewis's diary recorded: 'Met Hon. Camm [Minister for Police], messrs Armstrong and Tenni, M's.L.A, and discussed transfer of Sgt. 1/C Milner.'

There was no mention of Connor, who had even formally appealed to Premier Joh Bjelke-Petersen to have the transfer reversed.

A royal commissioner would later assess the impact of Milner's transfer being blocked. He noted: 'An unfortunate implication of this change was … that a number of people saw in the change, and in Sergeant Milner's continued presence and activity in North Queensland, an indication of the influence of drug producers and traffickers.

'There is no evidence … to suggest the slightest foundation for this belief which, albeit unfounded, does affect public confidence in the police.'

It transpired that Milner was a member of the National Party and in the past had been active in raising campaign funds for his local member, Martin Tenni. Milner had also, at one time, held a small amount of shares in Tenni's company, Tenni Hardware.

Connor was upset about the demotion and the move to Brisbane. He had settled well in the small community, and had served in the Mareeba CIB since taking over from Detective Senior Constable Graeme Parker in 1972.

Parker had worked with Jack Herbert from the late 1950s in the Licensing Branch in Brisbane, and was part of The Joke. He had taken up his Far North Queensland posting in 1966. Parker had rented a house – owned by a local businessman called Tom Magro – during his time in Mareeba. Tom ran an illegal game in downtown Mareeba; Parker turned a blind eye.

It was common knowledge around town, too, that Magro was good friends with Griffith winemaker Antonio Sergi who was a regular visitor to the region. When Parker was transferred back to Brisbane in 1972, local uniform police shut down Magro's game. Connor kept it closed. He received threats for his action.

That weekend in October, however, there were strange things afoot in the little township of Mareeba.

It was later revealed that a 'notorious drug racketeer' from the New South Wales Riverina district town of Griffith – a place of national infamy as the home of the Italian Mafia since the disappearance and presumed murder of Griffith identity Donald Mackay in 1977 – had arrived in town the day before and had secretly met with Connor. The racketeer was believed to be Antonio Sergi.

Also, it was later revealed that Brisbane criminal identity Tony Robinson Jnr – son to Commissioner Terry Lewis's friend Tony

Robinson Snr – they had known each other since the 1950s – was also sighted in Mareeba on that same weekend.

On the morning of 15 October, Connor reportedly met up with some colleagues at a hotel with some dynamic news. He told them he was going to make an arrest that would 'shake Australia'. Was his target the so-called Griffith Mafia boss who had been seen around town?

Connor was seen that day in casual clothing. He was also armed with his service pistol although it was supposed to have been under lock and key at Mareeba police station since his suspension over the drug allegations.

But later that night, in the car park of the Mareeba RSL, Connor was found shot dead in his car. The windows to the car were wound up, and it appeared that Connor had put the muzzle of the revolver in his mouth and fired. The bullet exited his skull and went through the roof of the car. It seemed to be a case of suicide.

The press would later report that Connor had killed himself on that Sunday evening, but Lewis's diary records a phone call he received at 10 a.m. on that Sunday: 'Dep Comm Hale phoned re Det Connor, Mareeba, committing suicide.'

The next day, Lewis telephoned Justice Williams, the royal commissioner, about the death of Connor.

A week later on Sunday 22 October, the *Sunday Sun* ran an article on Connor's death and it prompted Bjelke-Petersen's media man, Allen Callaghan, to call Lewis twice that day.

Nine days after Connor's death on Tuesday 24 October 1978, Police Minister Ron Camm rose in the parliamentary chamber at 11.40 a.m. and offered a ministerial statement that attempted to head off what he knew would be suspicions over the death of Connor.

'I would like to make this ministerial statement to the House in order to circumvent any wild accusations or allegations that might be made regarding the death of a Queensland police officer in Mareeba, North Queensland, on 15 October this year,' stated Camm. 'I am sure that all members will appreciate the grief of this police officer's family and friends at his death and it would be totally presumptuous of me or anyone else in this House to make an assumption at this time as to the cause of death.'

Camm then turned the tables and criticised the member for Archerfield, Kev Hooper, and his recent allegations about the force, blaming the working-class firebrand for putting the life of an undercover agent in jeopardy and wrecking a drug investigation with his reckless slander.

Camm also mentioned the internal investigation against Connor and others, and that there was insufficient evidence to proceed against them. 'Therefore,' Camm went on, 'it is absolutely necessary that great care is exercised and careful investigation carried out before any disciplinary action is taken against police officers.

'I can assure all honourable members that the policy of this government is to crack down hard and heavy on any drug-dealing whenever and wherever it may occur.'

It wasn't until the following day that Tom Burns and the Opposition began probing more deeply. During Questions on Notice, Burns put a series of queries before Police Minister Ron Camm.

Burns: Was an Inspector Stevenson of Townsville assigned last year to investigate drug allegations in the Mareeba area concerning the late Constable Connor and another police officer whose name and squad are supplied?

Camm: Yes.

Burns: Following Inspector Stevenson's report, were both Connor and the other officer listed for transfer on 10 June 1978 from Mareeba to the Mobile Squad, Brisbane?

Camm: The commissioner decided to effect the transfers of Connor and the other officer.

Burns: Was he aware that in the *Telegraph* newspaper of 23 October the member for Barron River [Martin Tenni] expressed serious doubts concerning the circumstances of Constable Connor's death?

Camm: I have read Tenni's comments in the newspaper.

Burns: In such circumstances of political interference, would he order an inquiry into strong rumours both in the North and in metropolitan police circles of large payments such as $40,000, which has been mentioned, being made into National Party funds from Mareeba sources for protection against prosecution?

Camm: There is no question of protection against prosecution for any person – police or otherwise.

Burns: Would the Minister investigate urgently reports that a notorious drug racketeer, whose name is supplied, who is from the Griffith district in the New South Wales Riverina and who was questioned before the New South Wales royal commission on huge amounts of unaccounted money, visited the Mareeba area and met secretly with Connor shortly before his death?

Camm was adamant that there was no information whatsoever available to the police department which would suggest that there was a secret meeting between the parties mentioned.

Though a coroner would find that Connor had committed suicide, the case – like that of the late Shirley Brifman – would refuse to settle. It would echo into the future.

An Incident at the Cleveland Sands

The mysterious Constable Brian Marlin – known among some colleagues as The Fish or Fisher – often drank at his local, the Cleveland Sands Hotel at Cleveland in the Redland Shire abutting Moreton Bay, 25 kilometres south-east of the Brisbane CBD.

Built in the 1920s, the hotel sported mature poinciana trees out front. In the late 1970s, the pretty suburb of Cleveland was mainly known as the departure point by barge for nearby North Stradbroke Island, despite its rich history and importance in colonial Brisbane.

Marlin was a curiosity to his colleagues in the Licensing Branch. The young constable had seemingly arrived out of nowhere and constantly boasted of his important contacts, including local MP John Goleby and even Premier Joh Bjelke-Petersen.

Marlin had brokered earlier in the year the two secret meetings between the Premier and Alec Jeppesen, then with Basil Hicks.

Marlin had bragged that if he could prove the powerful Tony Murphy was corrupt and was intending to dismantle the Licensing Branch under Jeppesen, who Murphy saw as a threat and an obstruction to the workings of The Joke, then he would make Queensland police history and vault from constable to commissioned rank in one go. Marlin had proved to be a self-starter. He also had a history of violence.

'It was incredible violence,' remembers former colleague Jim Slade. 'You would have to be very careful of Marlin.

'I was told Marlin was after me at one stage of the game. I can tell you that I would have had no hesitation whatsoever in getting the first shot away because he had a side to him ... I couldn't work out what made that man tick.'

Similarly, another colleague, Bruce Wilby, found Marlin puzzling and at times unstable. 'I stopped him from shooting himself when his wife left him,' Wilby says.

Marlin also used an alternative moniker – he referred to himself as Nestor. Was he referring to Nestor of Gerenia in Greek mythology? The Argonaut with the solid gold shield who fought the centaurs, and was considered wise and hospitable? Or, as a fan of American comics and in particular The Phantom, did he take the name from Nestor Redondo, the graphic artist who in the 1970s illustrated several editions of a comic featuring The Phantom Stranger, a supernatural assistant to superheroes including the Justice League?

Marlin lived in Ormiston, and on the night of Friday 27 October 1978, attended the Cleveland Sands Hotel with Constable C.P. Sidey and an associate, Peter Moore, to meet an informant in relation to a drugs investigation Marlin was conducting. The three men arrived in the lounge of the hotel at about 9.30 p.m.

According to Marlin, the three men sat at the bar and ordered drinks off barman Steven Guthrie. Marlin noticed that sitting at the bar was a man known to him as Brian 'Snowy' Collins – unbeknown to Marlin he was an informant of Tony Murphy's – and an 'assailant' named Ron Morris.

Soon after, Collins supposedly said in a loud voice: 'I know Tony Murphy, Pat Glancy and Alan Barnes, I'll fix these cunts for you if you like.'

Collins then approached the trio. 'You're Licensing coppers, aren't you.'

Marlin then made a decision to leave, and walked out into Middle Street.

'I'm talking to you, cunt,' said Collins, who followed the three men out of the hotel.

As Marlin recalled in an official statement: 'I turned around and saw COLLINS behind me ... he punched me on the left temple and chopped me across the windpipe ... I fell to the footpath, dazed.

'I saw COLLINS strike SIDEY about the head and SIDEY fell to the ground. COLLINS went to the boot of a green Fairlane parked immediately outside the hotel ... he removed a wooden bowling pin from that vehicle and struck me across the chest with it. I fell to the footpath again. COLLINS then knocked Moore to the footpath ... I saw blood coming from MOORE'S ear and temple.'

There followed a monumental struggle between Collins and the two police officers. Marlin described him as 'like a mad bull, he did not appear to feel pain, he was immensely strong and no hold I took on him was able to be maintained'.

Collins then began kicking Marlin in 'the region of the testes' and the officer drew his gun. 'COLLINS on seeing the pistol kicked me in the stomach and the pistol discharged into the air,' Marlin alleged.

Marlin and Sidey eventually restrained Collins at gunpoint and ordered him to lay flat on the footpath.

'That's it boys, I'm out of puff,' Snowy Collins supposedly then said, 'No charges, eh, it was a good blue.'

Marlin handcuffed Collins. 'I found that his wrists were so immense that I could secure the handcuffs only on the first notch and no further,' Marlin recalled in his statement.

Brian George Collins, 35, itinerant nightclub bouncer, was charged with the use of obscene language, assaulting Marlin and Sidey and resisting arrest. Marlin was treated for deep bruising of the right groin and thigh, bruising to the left eye and a lacerated left hand.

At the Cleveland police station later, Collins said he had powerful friends in the police force and any charges against him wouldn't stand up. Marlin alleges Collins said he was prepared to let the whole thing go if the charges were dropped. In exchange, Collins' police friends wouldn't go hard on Marlin and Sidey.

Marlin's superiors, however, were soon to hear a different and more disturbing version of events.

An aggrieved Brian 'Snowy' Collins of 251 Grassdale Road, Gumdale, a short drive from Cleveland, penned a single-page letter to Alec Jeppesen, head of the Licensing Branch, in his bunched hand-writing. He also posted a copy to Commisioner Terry Lewis and Minister for Police, Ron Camm. Collins wanted to explain what had really happened.

Snowy wrote that he was leaving the Cleveland Sands Hotel on that night when Constable Marlin shouted out to him: 'Get here, you.'

'There were a few words said then for no reasons at all he [Marlin] hit me five times in the face,' wrote Collins. 'I then retaliated, knocking him to the ground. Then the second License member … got out of the back of their car and with this other man named Peter set upon me.'

After some scuffling he said Marlin and Sidey drew their guns. 'They attacked me with their guns and boots,' Collins said. 'During the melee three shots were fired. Why they suddenly set upon me I do not now [sic]. I gave them no reason whatsoever. I trust you will look into this …'

Who was telling the truth? If Marlin's version was accurate, why would Collins, almost formally, immediately point out that he was connected with Murphy, Glancy and Barnes? If Collins was right, had Marlin targeted him knowing he was a Murphy informant, and assaulted Collins as a show of strength to Murphy?

Unfortunately for Marlin, the story leaked to the press. A brief piece was published, without a byline, on page one of the *Courier-Mail* on Thursday 16 November. POLICE PISTOL WHIP CLAIM, the newspaper said.

'The Police Department is investigating a complaint that a man was "pistol whipped" by detectives last month,' the report read. 'The incident allegedly happened at the Cleveland Sands Hotel. The man was said to have been in a fight with three detectives from the Licensing Branch. The "pistol whipping" allegedly happened when he appeared to be winning.

'A Police Department spokesman said a formal complaint had been passed to the Commissioner [Mr. Lewis].'

Curiously, the newspaper story intimated that the fight had been triggered by an incident between Snowy Collins and an off-duty policeman the night before. 'The policeman is said to have lost the fight and to have returned the following night with two other police,' the report continued.

Commissioner Lewis made no reference to the incident in his diaries immediately after the event. If it didn't make the diary, it didn't necessarily concern the Commissioner.

Then the matter was raised in parliament.

Raymond 'Joe' Kruger, the ALP member for Murrumba, north of Brisbane city, asked the Premier in question time, if the victim of the police attack had suffered a broken nose, a fractured cheek and other injuries?

He further asked if charges were laid on Collins, if there were witnesses to the incident, and if there were other reports that 'the two policemen involved were guilty of intimidation against women staff members during previous visits to the hotel?' What action was being taken by the Commissioner of Police?

The Premier answered: 'The allegation mentioned is presently being investigated by members of the Police Internal Investigations Section under the direction of the Deputy Commissioner of Police. In the circumstances, it would be improper for me to comment at this stage.'

For Lewis, now that the Cleveland Sands matter had been aired in parliament, everything changed. As it did for Marlin. Without doubt he faced at the very least potential disciplinary charges. He had also antagonised Tony Murphy by brawling with one of his informants – Snowy Collins.

Just two days after Kruger asked his Questions on Notice, the Premier's press secretary, Allen Callaghan, phoned Lewis bright and early at 7 a.m. to talk about various matters including 'information given to Premier from Mr Goleby', and also about 'P.C.Const. Marlin, code name Fisher'.

The day after that – Friday 24 November – Brian Marlin entered the Commissioner's office at around 1.15 p.m. During the meeting he unloaded on Lewis about Licensing Branch chief Alec Jeppesen saying that the whole crew were rotten and corrupt.

Marlin had jumped camps.

Whether Tony Murphy had promised to sort out the Snowy Collins matter if Marlin came on side, or indeed if he had been threatened with violence or warned his career was over, Marlin turned utterly and completely. His information for Commissioner Lewis was almost a confession, an unburdening, and it was everything the likes of Lewis and Murphy wanted to hear against this surviving Whitrod faction headed by Jeppesen.

As Lewis noted in his diary: '... saw P.C. Const. Marlin who said that Insp. Jeppesen and Det Sgt Dautel give Hon [Max] Hodges information which he passes on to K. Hooper, MLA ... Jeppesen and Insp. B. Hicks meet twice a week in McDonnell & East under steps; Jeppesen has latest electronic devices; knows who visits my office; has staff disappeared into private life and not thought to be on official work; Jeppesen, Dautel and Det Sgt Lumsden taking "moeity" money for own use; Marlin and P.C. Const Newman approached to join group; Jeppesen hates Murphy and me; Jeppesen instructs some staff to "brick" suspected S.P.'s; has staff watching Robertson and Pickering and Consorters; Branch is "crumbling" because of attitude of Jeppesen to staff; etc.'

Three days later Marlin was back with the Commissioner with even juicier news. He told Lewis that Jeppesen and another officer were feeding John Goleby information that 'Murphy, Herbert, Freier, Leadbetter, Bellino were involved in drugs and gem racket'. Lewis wrote: '[Marlin] ... said it was a conspiracy to get rid of Murphy and embarrass the Administration.'

On Tuesday 28 November, Lewis 'saw Jack Herbert re moieties generally'. He had also received a call from Sydney businessman Jack Rooklyn enquiring if massage parlours were being legalised. '... I assured him they are not.'

The conversion of Brian Marlin was complete. The information he divulged to Lewis, true, false or otherwise, would trigger the last great assault on Jeppesen and his crew.

The broom was set to go through the Licensing Branch, and with force.

Elvis Has Left the Building

The flamboyant private investigator John Wayne Ryan was feeling the financial pinch in 1978, not the least because the Rat Pack had had him in their sights for some time and did enough to make his life difficult.

He was a tough man of the streets who had only been 'dropped' once in his career – not by another person, but by a tear-gas pen that had detonated in his face when he was showing friends his latest gadget imported from Germany.

He had had a hugely successful private security business with lucrative contracts in excess of $1 million, when a false charge of bribing a public official was mounted against him. By the time the case was thrown out of court, his business had all but evaporated.

Ryan was a danger because, by his very nature, he was a watcher. He looked and absorbed everything. Also, he had walked the line between an upright life and the underworld since the early 1960s. While he would never cross the line and step into the dark, he knew a lot and had seen a lot.

A year earlier, he had witnessed at 142 Wickham Street what happened when you fell foul of The Joke. A fighter himself – he preferred to be known as a 'hunter' – he still remembered the extreme violence he had witnessed when Constable Brian Marlin had bashed Tony the Yugoslav at the door of Bellino's illegal casino. He concluded, rightly, that Marlin was a very dangerous man.

Personally, though, Ryan's life was looking up. After a failed marriage, he had met his new girlfriend, Catharina, earlier in 1978 and saw a future for both of them. But he needed to make money.

He had spent more than a decade working variously as a bouncer and security consultant for nightclubs. He had worked for big-name performing artists. He knew the scene inside out. He also performed himself, for fun. He did Elvis impersonation shows. He called his act 'Forever Elvis'. (The King had died on 16 August 1977.) Ryan was also, at one point, a stunt man and a television extra. He had recently seen the Brisith comedian Dick Emery perform a show at the National Hotel. Why not try to turn a quid as an entertainer?

So when he took Catharina to the Bellino-owned nightclub, Pinocchio's, in Queen Street, the city, later in the year, it was so that she could see him on stage. During the show, Ryan saw a familiar face push through the crowd and take a seat beside Catharina while he was performing his act.

'Marlin was mental – a dangerous, dangerous man,' says Ryan.

Marlin turned to Catharina. 'I love your eyes,' he supposedly said. 'You're with somebody, aren't you? John Ryan?'

'Yeah,' she said.

Marlin paused. 'He's not going to be around much longer,' he said.

When Ryan found out about the conversation he thought long and hard about his future in Brisbane.

'I'm going to go,' he told Catharina. 'Do you want to come with me? You need to leave.'

Ryan was confident that they wouldn't be able to physically harm him. But they could hurt Catharina.

'That was it,' remembers Ryan. 'We left.'

A Tired and Nervous Eagle

A month after the notorious Cleveland Sands Hotel incident involving Constable Brian Marlin, a fatigued Brian 'The Eagle' Bolton, gun crime reporter for the *Sunday Sun* newspaper, wandered into the Albion Health Studio at 281 Sandgate Road, Albion, in the shadow of the grey concrete TAB building.

It was 2.20 a.m. on a Monday in late November. There he met massage attendant Kathryn Lynch. He told her his name was Brian. He asked for a massage and handed her ten dollars. 'He then undressed for a shower [and] as he was undressing he asked me if the boys in blue had been in,' Lynch later said. 'I replied that they don't work on a Sunday, so he went and showered.

'He came back to the room and told me he writes for the *Courier-Mail*. He told me that he was very nervous and asked me to pamper him very softly.

'I told him not to worry and he mentioned that a couple of detectives from [the] Licensing Branch were in big trouble over the incident at Cleveland Sands a little while ago.'

Bolton proceeded to tell Kathryn what he knew of the incident. 'He said [Constables] Sidey and Marlin entered the hotel looking for a guy,' she recounted. 'They picked the wrong guy and falsely accused him of a crime; this guy apparently turned on Sidey and Marlin and won the fight.

'I don't remember if he said that Sidey and Marlin came back that night or the following night with this guy posing as a policeman. Anyway he [Collins] said that Marlin and Sidey pistol-whipped him [the guy wrongly accused].

'A lot of people were supposed to have put this guy up to go to the [news]paper. He said he would be very surprised if ... Sidey and Marlin didn't get the bullet from the police force.'

Bolton paused with his story and asked what other services Kathryn could provide. She said – sex.

'So he gave me $30 – he was very impotent and ended up having hand relief,' she said. 'I asked if he had been drinking and he said he was very nervous about the police coming in.'

Bolton was agitated. He kept talking about Marlin, the 'southern cop'. He told Kathryn 'the incident is a lot deeper than what went down [at] the Cleveland Sands'.

'He said a policeman threw a cup of coffee over a client one night at a studio [he didn't mention what studio] ... this client was one of [former Police Minister] Ron Camm's best mates,' she said. 'He told me not to mention this to anybody.

'I told him that I don't see anybody to mention it to anyone.'

The Purge Begins

In Police Commissioner Terry Lewis's office at police headquarters on 20 December 1978, Inspector Alec Jeppesen, head of the Licensing Branch, was interrogated over the so-called moeity scandal, the bulk of the charges fuelled by Constable Brian Marlin, formerly confidant of Jeppesen and suddenly an agent for Tony Murphy and Lewis.

Present were Assistant Commissioner Brian Hayes, Superintendent Syd 'Sippy' Atkinson, barrister Shane Herbert, solicitor Mark O'Brien and Jeppesen.

'For the record will you please record the time as 10.38 a.m. and those present ...,' Hayes began.

Jeppesen wanted clarification that the investigation into him was being conducted under the provisions of Police Rules.

'Yes,' Hayes confirmed. 'It is being conducted in accordance with the Police Rules, but I also wish to advise you that should any matter of a criminal nature be elicited, you will be given all courtesy and cautioned at the appropriate time.' And then: 'For the record Inspector, what is your full name.'

'William Daniel Alexander Jeppesen,' he replied.

'How long have you been a member of the Queensland Police Force?'

'Since 1948.'

From the outset, Hayes aimed to show Jeppesen who was the boss. 'On last Thursday I saw you at the Licensing Branch and I asked you for your present official diary and you told me it was lost in the shift from Ampol House to the present building,' Hayes said. 'To date, I have not received your official diary. Can you give me any explanation for disobeying my instructions?'

'I have not disobeyed your instructions,' Jeppesen countered. 'I have searched for the diary and I have been unable to locate it ...'

'I have been informed,' continued Hayes, 'that it is rumoured at the Licensing Branch that you burned your current diary after I was at your office on Thursday last. What have you to say to that?'

'That is rubbish,' Jeppesen said. 'I would like to know who supplied that rumour.'

As the interview progressed, the aim of the investigation became clear. Its purpose was two-fold – Lewis, Murphy, Hayes and others wanted to secure the names of Jeppesen's informants and the information they had disclosed to him, and they wanted to get Jeppesen. Hayes cut to the chase when asking about one of Jeppesen's informants.

Jeppesen said: 'The informant supplied valuable information.'

'Of what nature?' queried Hayes.

'I am not prepared to divulge confidential information from an informer,' replied Jeppesen.

'This information cannot be classified as confidential,' Hayes shot back. 'You are not nominating the identity of your informer under Rule 49. I direct you to answer my question.'

Jeppesen declined.

Hayes reminded Jeppesen that he was obliged to promptly obey the lawful orders of a superior officer. 'Are you refusing to obey my instructions?'

'I am not refusing your instructions,' Jeppesen answered. 'I don't consider it a lawful instruction.'

'I again instruct you to answer my question.'

'I decline to divulge confidential information of that nature.'

Hayes moved on to discuss raids that Jeppesen and his men had effected at Bellino's gambling joint at 142 Wickham Street, and Roland Short's Matador Club in South Brisbane, as well as Short's Koala Club on the Gold Coast and a unit in the Golden Gate building on the Gold Coast where Short was running illegal games and prostitution, and an illegal game in a unit on the 26th floor of the Condor building on Riverview Parade in Surfers Paradise.

Both Hayes and Atkinson argued that Jeppesen had used no outside informants to assist with information and access for the raids. That, in turn, put into question moeity payments the Licensing Branch had made to these mythical informants on those specific jobs. (A moeity was a percentage of a fine imposed on a convicted person and paid as a reward to a successful informant.)

In effect, Hayes and Atkinson were accusing Jeppesen of inventing informants and pocketing the moeity money.

The accusers praised Constable Brian Marlin. Atkinson said: 'Information received by us is to the effect that after a report was submitted by Sergeant DAUTEL of your branch, explaining the difficulties involved in obtaining evidence to raid these premises at Condor and in which he recommended that a competent undercover officer such as Plain Clothes Constable B.R. MARLIN be used to teach a police agent seconded from another section especially to cover this work on the Gold Coast and as a result of the acceptance of those recommendations, MARLIN and a Constable WHITBREAD were the police agents responsible for infiltrating the premises by way of a key … what I'm saying is that we have been advised that no outside informer was used and that the prosecution was successful through the actions of the police officers themselves. What do you say about that?'

Jeppesen confirmed that outside informants were used in the Condor operation.

They asked him what he had to fear by disclosing the names of his informants.

'Threats have been made by Constable MARLIN I understand to kill another police officer, and his information, which you are relating to me, is not a truthful account of the entry to those premises,' Jeppesen responded.

They assured him any names offered would be treated confidentially.

'It is with great regret that I cannot accept your assurances,' he said.

Jeppesen said he trusted his staff. Hayes and Atkinson then asked if he had trusted Brian Marlin up until very recently.

'I don't want to enter into any defamatory matters, but I consider that he has not told me the truth about an incident at the Cleveland Sands Hotel,' Jeppesen replied cautiously.

Monuments

At the end of 1978 the Queensland National Party, forever faced with dwindling coffers, contacted accountant and fundraising expert Everald Compton for advice.

The Brisbane-based Compton was known about town as the 'Mr Millions' of charity fundraising. In his late forties, he had raised, by his own calculation, over $40 million for various sporting bodies, political parties of all persuasions and charities since he became a full-time fundraiser in the early 1960s.

He had just published a book – *Ten Steps to Successful Fund Raising*, in which he declared: 'Nice guys never win. Leaders win. Be one.'

Compton came to the attention of the Nationals as early as 1974, when he successfully marshalled $750,000 for the building of the new ALP headquarters – John Curtin House – in Canberra. Now Robert Sparkes and the Premier's loyal supporter, the recently knighted Sir Edward Lyons, wanted to establish a secure financial base beneath Premier Joh Bjelke-Petersen and the National Party.

Mr Millions' company, Compton Associates, was approached to assess the success or not of a fundraising campaign centred on the Premier. Everald Compton, as it turned out, had a long association with the Premier's wife, Florence. As youngsters they had attended the same church together – the old red-brick St Andrews Presbyterian Chruch at the corner of Creek and Ann streets in Brisbane city.

'I knew her as Florence Gilmore, and she was a leader of a group at the church around 1946–47,' Compton remembers. 'Then Joh turned up and married her. We kept in touch down the years. In the 1970s I had raised some money for the establishment of John Curtin House in the days of Whitlam and Hawke.

'Joh rang me up and said, "If you can raise money for those socialists you've got to be able to raise millions for me."

'A few days later Sir Robert Sparkes phoned me and I went and met him. He had one of the most astute political minds I'd ever seen.'

Compton was signed up to raise $2.5 million for what would be known as the Bjelke-Petersen Foundation. When the idea was first mooted, a newspaper described the foundation as 'an ambitious scheme to use the cult-worship of the Queensland Premier' to fill the Party's bank account. Compton was given a 12-month contract to bring in the loot.

Compton reportedly said: 'There is [sic] a lot of people out there who think Joh is God – his philosophy is what they want. The reason they are giving to this foundation is because they strongly believe Queensland will be no good without him. They are investing in the future.'

The plan was to delineate regions across the state with an executive of 25 financially influential people in each region. That executive in turn would be responsible for soliciting major gifts to the foundation. State electorates held by the Nationals were given an initial $60,000 target.

Teams of National Party supporters would then blitz Queensland, lining up potential donors and organising fundraising functions. They would be fully trained by Compton Associates.

The Liberal Party saw it as an alarming development. It argued that a political party with such a comprehensive money-making net in the name of Bjelke-Petersen could turn itself into an 'institution', and one that could put in jeopardy the careers of people and financial futures of businesses that did not contribute to the Joh fund.

The money was supposedly being raised to build nine National Party local headquarters buildings.

The press revealed that a $100,000 donation would get your name on one of the buildings, an honorary life governorship of the foundation, life membership of the National Party, and a private dinner with the Premier. It also bought you a scroll, personally signed by Joh.

For $50,000 you got the lot except the building named after you. 'People like kudos for what they do,' said Compton. 'They get a plaque or a building named after them. It's something they can point to.'

The establishment of the foundation was bound to be a political headache. The opportunity for the Opposition to point to it repeatedly as an instrument of corruption and a focal point for the purchase of 'jobs for the boys' would, as it ultimately transpired, be impossible to resist.

Just months into the fundraising, Liberal Party State Director, Stephen Litchfield, said the National Party and the foundation were using 'standover tactics' to secure donations. No money, no government business.

Compton replied that 'each fundraiser had given an assurance that no standover tactics or any offer of kickbacks would be made'. Early in the fundraising, he guaranteed the people of Queensland that everything was above board after the *Telegraph* reported that a company had offered $250,000 to the foundation hoping for government kickbacks and favourable treatment.

'But it took Sir Robert Sparkes and myself only 30 seconds to reject the donation,' Compton reportedly said.

Compton says the offer of the massive donation came from 'one of those White Shoe Brigade men on the Gold Coast who wanted to get into mining'. 'It was a mate of Russ Hinze,' he recalls. 'There were a few others like that who had a go. There were graziers who put money in to try and get their leases extended and we had to tell them to drop dead too.

'In my presence, old Joh never, ever took money from anyone. He kept his hands clean of it.'

Compton says he received some bad publicity over the project. 'When you do political fundraising, you're at risk,' he says.

It was a measure of the National Party's hubris that criticism of the foundation was meaningless to power players like Sir Robert Sparkes and Sir Edward Lyons. Both men at this time were vying for the Premier's attention, and both were drivers of the Bjelke-Petersen Foundation.

As Bjelke-Petersen later said: 'Because it was felt that the Party was investing too much money in property and other assets, I was used as a medium to raise money for what came to be called the Bjelke-Petersen Foundation.

'I went around like a show pony with Bob Sparkes at the height of my career during the Whitlam years [it was actually the Malcolm Fraser years]. I made the speeches and Bob Sparkes raised the money.

'Sparkes seemed to resent the fact that Lyons had grown so close to me.'

So who was Sir Edward Houghton Lyons, and how had he managed in a handful of years to become probably the Premier's closest and most trusted advisor?

Lyons was born in Brisbane in 1914 and was schooled at St Joseph's College, Nudgee. He worked for International Harvester before joining the finance company Industrial Acceptance Corporation (later to become Citicorp).

In something of a surprise move, in the early 1960s Lyons joined the Katies fashion group. His business acumen turned Katies into a major fashion label and retail concern with stores across Australia. He became company chairman in 1971, when Bjelke-Petersen's premiership was in its infancy.

Around that time, the Premier was addressing a business function in Brisbane when the Liberal-voting Lyons approached him afterwards. 'I just wanted to tell you I've been watching you for a long time,' Lyons told him. 'I like you, your attitude and your policies. I'm on your side now, and I'm going to help you.'

It would be a mutually profitable friendship, but Lyons was not so revered with staff trying to get the Bjelke-Petersen Foundation off the ground. One staff member, who declined to be named, says Lyons was one of the first, and most persistent, at utilising the foundation for personal gain and that of his business associates and friends.

'Every dodgy mate of Sir Edward Lyons was turning up,' the staff member recalls. 'He was not the sort of bloke you'd invite home for dinner. There were a few dust-ups with him. He was the most difficult bloke to work with.'

New Year's Death

Commissioner Terry Lewis, after a long year, was looking forward to 33 days of annual leave, beginning Monday 1 January 1979.

Firstly, he had an appointment to see Dr. R.M. Goodwin for a check-up. He would lunch at the famed Milano's Galleria, owned and operated by Gino Merlo, whose restaurant cellar contained over 30,000 bottles of wine, many from Italy, and some chardonnays from California. The dishes on the menu included ravioli stuffed with minced chicken and Moreton Bay bugs in cognac with macadamia nuts. It was the place to be 'seen' with the city's politicians, businessmen and lawyers.

Lewis and his wife, Hazel, would then make their traditional pilgrimage to the Gold Coast. They would take lunch at Sea World with entrepreneur Keith Williams (who would, in the very near future, donate $25,000 to the Bjelke-Petersen Foundation) and have dinner at the Southport Yacht Club.

And as ususal, Lewis's voluminous holiday reading would not be for pleasure. It would take in the annual reports for police departments across Australia, the Report of the International Conference on Terrorist Devices and Methods, the Australian Police College Manual for Hostage Negotiation and an FBI report on 'Prevention and Control of Mobs and Riots'. The latter may have helped him with Brisbane's troubling street-march incidents.

But before all this, on New Year's Day he enjoyed an afternoon at the races at Eagle Farm, betting $50 each way on Decimate (it came second) and $25 each way on Ima Cheeta (it won) before heading home to Garfield Drive and the house in the shadow of the concrete water tower on the hill at Bardon.

At 9.45 p.m. he received a call from R. Dunbar, 're John Andrew Stuart found dead in H.M. Prison at 9.37 pm'. A post-mortem examination was expected to be carried out the next day.

On the Wednesday the press reported that the examination had been inconclusive, 'apart from establishing there was no foul play and that violence had not been used. Pathologists who examined his body yesterday established that all marks and scars on Stuart were old ones,' the *Courier-Mail* said.

In the report, Assistant Commissioner Brian Hayes, who along with Syd Atkinson had arrested and charged Stuart for the Whiskey Au Go Go murders in 1973, reminisced about the dead criminal. 'He was given a fair hearing, and a fair trial and made appeals to the highest courts in the land,' Hayes said. 'Now he has gone to a higher jurisdiction.'

Stuart had always protested his innocence and said he had been verballed in police interviews. His statement about the Whiskey, compiled by police after his arrest, was unsigned.

On Thursday 4 January 1979, the *Courier-Mail* reported that the Stuart clan wanted a royal commission into the Whiskey murders and Stuart's treatment in gaol.

'Stuart's sister, who asked that her name be withheld, said there were too many unanswered questions on her late brother's trial, and the circumstances of the fire, for the matter to be left to rest,' the newspaper said. 'As long as I've got a breath in my body I'm going to push for a royal commission into this matter,' she claimed.

To protest his innocence during his incarceration, on three occasions Stuart swallowed pieces of wire. He also sewed his lips together with wire to underline that his original confession to police over the Whiskey atrocity had been a police 'verbal', or concocted evidence. His self-harm saw him in and out of hospital.

Stuart's mother, Edna, 65, added: 'I'm not being fanatical. We still don't know how he died. I don't think he committed suicide. He had stomach trouble from all the wire he had eaten. He was under medical treatment all the time.'

The *Sunday Mail* of 7 January declared that an acute heart infection may have killed Stuart. A spokesman for the State Microbiology and Pathology Laboratory told the newspaper that a 'microscopic examination' had revealed Stuart possessed a heart infection, possibly the result of a virus, capable of causing sudden death. Suicide had been ruled out.

'He said chemical tests had shown the only drugs in Stuart's body were those legally prescribed by the prison hospital and they were in normal quantities,' the newspaper added.

In the same article, mother Edna Watts declared her son innocent. 'Johnny told me six months after he started this sentence that he had given his heart to Christ,' she said. 'He told me Christ was his witness when he told me: "Mum, I have never killed anyone in my life."

'I'm not pretending he was a saint. He fought all his life. But he wasn't a killer.' She said she wanted to see her son's body before the funeral so she could 'touch him just once'.

On the morning of Wednesday 10 January, a service was held for John Andrew Stuart in the K.M. Smith funeral director's chapel in

Wickham Street, Fortitude Valley. Stuart's death certificate had been released – it stated he had died of natural causes.

After the service, Stuart's casket was taken to the Lutwyche Cemetery, where he was buried with his father, David James Stuart (who had died in 1956) in section nine, grave number eleven.

Many, many questions were buried with him.

Operation Jungle

The trail had been cold for 18 months, but it didn't deter Federal Narcotics Agent John Shobbrook from going after drug dealer John Milligan.

Having flown north to Cairns, Shobbrook and his team immediately began the painstaking task of manually checking hotel and car rental records around the period Milligan was suspected of having taken possession of his parcel of heroin in September 1977.

They soon got a hit. The Narcotics team found a receipt in Milligan's name for a Budget Rent a Car four-wheel-drive in Townsville. The odometer revealed a sum mileage that was consistent with a round trip from Townsville to Princess Charlotte Bay. Townsville hotel records also indicated a link between Milligan and his associate Graham David Bridge. Bryan Parker's and Ian Barron's names were also found on other documents linking them to Milligan during the suspect time period.

The team headed to the little town of Laura, where pictures of the alleged conspirators were identified by Percy Trezise and other residents. In fact Trezise, a former Ansett pilot, offered to fly Shobbrook to remote places in the region where potential witnesses could be interviewed.

The single engine Cessna, however, wasn't a smooth ride. The plane had an oil leak and other alarming idiosyncrasies. 'We also

JACKS AND JOKERS: 1970s

found a hornet's nest in the engine bay; very reassuring,' Shobbrook remembered.

On a return flight to Cairns with Trezise two things stayed with the drugs agent. 'Firstly, I recall every hiccup that Percy's Cessna made (probably a bit of dirt in the fuel line, Percy had explained). Secondly, I became very aware that there aren't too many level emergency landing areas between Laura and Cairns and that there are a lot of rainforest-covered mountains.'

He could visualise the newspaper headlines: FAMOUS NORTH QUEENSLANDER, AND SOMEONE ELSE, DIE IN LIGHT AIRCRAFT CRASH.

On the positive side, the Jungle team eventually collated enough evidence, they believed, to arrest both Milligan and Glen Patrick Hallahan, farmer of Obi Obi and corrupt former Queensland police officer.

Dear Mr Premier

After Brian Marlin had been rescued by Tony Murphy following the shocking incident at the Cleveland Sands Hotel over by the bay, he transitioned his loyalty from Alec Jeppesen. He was now Murphy's boy.

'There is no doubt about it that Marlin and Murphy were really close,' says Jim Slade. 'He thought the sun shone out of Murphy's arse. Murphy was the sort of bloke who could put Marlin in as a bloody spy. This was the sort of person that Murphy was.

'Also, there is no way in the world that a civilian could have the stamp that Brian Marlin had. Even me, who has witnessed every different kind of arsehole, recognised straightaway – here was an arsehole that learned, he learned that from somewhere. You don't learn that coming out of a security company or the army.'

Marlin also knew where his bread was now buttered. To underscore his loyalty to Murphy, Marlin made the extraordinary step of writing a personal letter to Premier Joh Bjelke-Petersen. He had met the Premier during the secret meeting at Lennons Hotel during the winter of 1978 with Jeppesen, John Goleby and Ron Camm. And again a couple of months later at the Zebra with Basil Hicks.

On the morning of Saturday 13 January 1979, Marlin had been on the phone to the Premier. Later that day he penned his letter. It included his home address – 60 Beckwith Street, Ormiston, the next suburb north-west of Cleveland. It would be a fuller, and more elaborate version of what he had relayed to Commissioner Lewis in his office in late November of the previous year.

In his missive, Marlin set out in detail the sequence of events which he alleged had taken place since his first meeting with the Inspector in Charge of the Licensing Branch, Inspector Jeppesen, up to and including the commencement of the current departmental inquiry into alleged moiety fund misappropriation.

Marlin's first target was the former Police Minister under Ray Whitrod – Max Hodges. The police officer had heard that Hodges had attacked him [Marlin] in a recent Cabinet meeting, attempting to 'destroy my veracity, integrity and character', and that it was 'unwarranted, untrue in every detail and nothing more than a deliberate manouvre [sic] intended to refute any evidence I may be called to give in relation to the activities of Inspector Jeppesen.'

Marlin declared that Hodges had aligned himself with officers such as Jeppesen, Basil Hicks, Peter Dautel and other members of the Committee of Eight. He told the premier that any suggestion he had been deliberately placed in the Licensing Branch to gather evidence on behalf of Lewis in relation to Jeppesen was a 'falsehood'. After expressing his disappointments in Jeppesen and his loss of faith in his senior officer he claimed: 'It is a very Bitter Pill to swallow indeed when I proved beyond any doubt that he is dishonest and nothing more than a conspirator and a practising fraud.'

Marlin said in no uncertain terms that after Bjelke-Petersen's meeting with Jeppesen, the latter had become a 'supreme egotist'. 'He and inspector Basil HICKS held clandestine meetings in the underground cafeteria of Macdonald and Easts in George Street, Brisbane, they gathered their fellows and laid plans for the re-structure of the administration.'

Extraordinarily, Marlin claimed to have heard some recorded tapes of these meetings. 'Mr Jeppesen is recorded as having made comments e.g. "I wonder what my Reward will be?"; "Perhaps Basil will get Terry's job and I'll get the 5th Assistant's spot." And to me he said, "How do you reckon I went with old Joh, did I convince him I'm honest?"'

Marlin's conspiracy theories were so completely strangulated and broad-reaching that they were almost comical.

He went on to claim he had evidence that Hicks had indeed slept with the prostitute Katherine James and that the photographs taken of their liaison several years earlier were genuine. This time he introduced Jeppesen into the James fiasco, saying the head of the Licensing Branch had in fact induced a statement from James in Boggo Road prison denying a sexual tryst with Hicks had ever taken place.

Marlin then discussed a secular conspiracy. Jeppesen was a Mason. Hicks was a Catholic and a Mason. Dautel was a Mason in the same Lodge as Max Hodges.

Marlin assured the Premier his change of allegiance had nothing to do with the Cleveland Sands controversy: 'I respectfully draw your attention to the fact that I had reported Inspector Jeppesen's activities well before that matter arose.'

At the end of his long tirade Marlin claimed 'that Commissioner Lewis has been left an unenviable legacy in the wake of the departure of Mr Whitrod, the whole basis of the insurgency by Hicks and Jeppesen is to regain favour and power and there is no doubt in my mind they have utilised every dirty trick in the book to effect this'.

In conclusion he appealed to the Premier: 'Surely Sir, the time has come for the department to present its case against the Inspector openly?'

What would the Premier have made of such a letter?

While it was a further shot across the bow of Jeppesen, it also revealed that in a little over two years of his commissionership, Lewis's administration was one that was still seething with factional disputes between those who were pro- and those who were anti-Whitrod.

To Herbert, Murphy and the other corrupt officers, that the epicentre of this brawl happened to be the Licensing Branch – the heart of the lucrative 'Joke' – was no accident. Jeppesen and his clean-skins had to be removed. The money-making machine of Licensing had to be operated by friends of the corrupt system.

Marlin dropped his letter to Bjelke-Petersen in the post.

The next day, a Sunday, Lewis noted in his diary: 'Phoned Supt. Atkinson, he mentioned that P.C. Const Marlin said he had spoken to Premier re Insp. Jeppesen yesterday.'

The rolling campaign against Jeppesen was gaining traction. Inside the Licensing Branch, the heat was on.

Bruce Wilby says the 'bombshell' was dropped by Brian Marlin in late 1978. 'He tried to bring Alec Jeppesen down with the moiety [money scandal],' Wilby recalls. 'Marlin made out that Alec was pocket-ing the money. It was as far from the truth as ever. The rot started.'

Lewis wrote in his diary for 8 February: 'Hon Camm phoned to say Premier said to transfer Jeppesen.' Then on Monday 12 February: 'Saw Hon. Camm re complaint from Auditor-General re Insp. Jeppesen.' And the next day: 'Phone call from Hon. Camm's office re: Cabinet approval for transfer of Insp. Jeppesen. Phoned P.C. Const Marlin re same.'

It was magnanimous of the Commissioner of Police to keep a lowly constable, registered number 3672, updated on the imminent transfer of one of the most senior and experienced officers in the Queensland Police Force.

A Hat is Lost in King George Square

The government's arcane street-march legislation remained rock solid into 1979, almost 18 months after it had been brought down, and proved a vote-winner for the National Party in the 1977 state election.

Even Bundaberg dentist Dr Harry Akers' brilliant solo demonstration in the rain with his dog Jaffa, highlighting the legislation as a nonsense, had failed to cease the now familiar dance of police and protestor on the streets of the capital.

Yet Brisbane citizens still came out in regular numbers to face Commissioner Lewis's legions of troops and the handiwork of the Special Branch. On Saturday 10 March 1979, a group of 200 women demonstrated on behalf of International Women's Day. They were progressing in an orderly fashion along Adelaide Street in the city, towards City Hall, when the now clichéd direction from the traffic superintendent present was issued – you are taking part in an unlawful procession. There were more than 200 police rostered on to curtail the march that day.

Very quickly the women were virtually surrounded by police. One of the women was Janelle Hurst. On duty that day was her boyfriend, Constable Michael Egan, 21. He wasn't aware she was even marching.

Hurst was questioned by a member of the Special Branch and became upset and agitated. When Egan saw his partner arguing with the undercover officer he threw his police cap in the air and moved in.

'At that time I couldn't stomach any more of what was happening,' he later said. Egan took hold of his girlfriend and told the Special Branch officer to 'leave her alone'. He then walked her a short distance from the melee and calmed her down before he himself was taken hold of by a senior policeman and a policewoman.

They moved Egan past the brass lions and the statue of George V towards the entrance to the old City Hall building.

'Would you come inside, please?' the senior officer asked him. 'I want to talk to you.'

Egan refused. 'If you want to talk to me you can talk to me here,' he replied.

Both officers then marched Egan back to police headquarters in Makerston Street. A short distance away his girlfriend followed. The moment he threw his cap towards the sky his career was over. He resigned that day.

Later, he said: 'I found it difficult to understand why in other States demonstrations were contained by a very small number of police compared to Queensland. And the record of violence in other States was nothing compared to Queensland. There appeared to be unnecessary violence.'

Egan said police were in fact provoking the violence.

Deputy Commissioner Vern MacDonald told the press that the police he had spoken to about the incident were 'annoyed' by Egan's actions. Commissioner Lewis reassured everybody that the situation was an isolated case.

Premier Joh Bjelke-Petersen said it was obvious that Mr Egan didn't want to be a policeman. He hinted that Egan and his girlfriend might have cooked up the whole stage-play for publicity.

A Deadly Tip-off to The Eagle

Since returning from exile in Longreach, and taking charge of the Consorting Squad and the Bureau of Criminal Intelligence courtesy of his friend Commissioner Lewis, Tony Murphy wielded his power with aplomb. In fact, he and his men were verging on reckless.

An intelligent man, Murphy had enough sense to recognise this. Word was out that his attempts to wrest control of SP betting and the massage parlours off the Licensing Branch had reached the Premier's office, and the reaction was not favourable.

Word had also got around earlier in 1978 that Murphy actually held active financial membership with the Australian Labor Party. If true, it was career suicide, so Murphy was forced to write and sign a formal statement, witnessed by a Justice of the Peace, denying any involvement. 'I am NOT a financial member of the Australian Labor Party,' he said in the statement.

He went on to admit that he had been a financial member of the ALP in the later 1950s and early 1960s, and again from 1973 to 1975. 'Resulting from grave injustice done to me by Commissioner Whitrod, I again joined the Labor party while I was stationed in Toowoomba,' he explained of this more recent membership.

Murphy went on to illustrate his stellar career. 'The insinuations levelled at me are in my confirmed opinion designed to injure me in my career,' he concluded. 'I have very firm opinions of who is responsible for making these spurious accusations against me.'

It was a tenuous time for Murphy. So Murphy did what Murphy always did. He offered some scoops to the press that would hopefully divert both public and private attention from his brawl with Licensing, and show yet again what a superlative police officer he was.

The body of Harry 'Pommie' Lewis had been found at Herons Creek near Port Macquarie, on the mid-north coast of New South Wales, on 15 March 1979. Just as Doug Wilson had told Queensland police in his taped interview the year before, Pommie Lewis had been shot in the back of the head.

After Pommie's remains were formally identified, police needed to speak to Terry Clark. (He was tipped off and went underground in Adelaide.) Meanwhile, in Brisbane, the discovery of the body prompted Murphy and other police to seriously reconsider the material given to them by the Wilsons in their record of interview. To date, Queensland investigators had taken much of it with a pinch of salt. Now there was a skeleton with the rear of its skull blown off.

Tony Murphy claimed that five days after the body of Lewis was found, two New South Wales detectives flew to Brisbane as a part of their murder investigation.

Murphy told Commissioner Lewis in a confidential memorandum: '… these New South Wales Police were furnished at my direction with all possible information then available, to the Queensland C.I. Branch, which was material to the possible involvement of CLARKE [sic] and his associates in the murder of [Pommie] LEWIS.

'The New South Wales Police (Detectives WILLIAMS and NUNAN) were supplied with a copy of the transcript of the interview had in Brisbane with the … Wilsons.'

On 23 March, Tony Murphy issued a confidential internal memorandum. 'Forwarded for favour of information,' it read. 'It does appear a reasonable hypothesis under the circumstances, that the body found in the bush near Port Macquarie, may be that of the person Harry LEWIS, mentioned in the attached tape transcript.

'A well-considered press release to the *Sunday Sun* has been made, with a view to eliciting possible assistance from the public …'

The recipient of Murphy's largesse was his mate Brian 'The Eagle' Bolton, the crack police and crime reporter. Bolton had the exclusive that Queensland police were on the scent of a multi-million-dollar international heroin importation racket. Namely, the Mr Asia syndicate run by psychopath New Zealander Terry Clark, the man who had posed as the Premier at the Gazebo Hotel in Brisbane city the year before, and who had been nabbed by police along with two of his drug mules, the heroin addicts Douglas and Isabel Wilson.

Murphy, as head of the Bureau of Criminal Intelligence, had been given the tapes of the extraordinary interviews with the Wilsons, and now it was time to get some kudos.

As Murphy explained to Commissioner Lewis: 'Having regard to the tape reference to the alleged murder by CLARKE [sic] of LEWIS whilst driving from Brisbane to Sydney ... and after a conference with Detective Senior Constable Pickering and also Detective Sergeant Churchill of the Drug Squad, I released such data to Mr. Brian BOLTON, Sunday Sun, as I considered may elicit assistance from the public of Queensland and the New South Wales North Coast in connection with the Port Macquarie murder.'

Murphy was at pains to explain to Commissioner Lewis that he made sure the material given to Bolton was handled carefully, and that Bolton was never made aware of the origin and actual specific substance of the tapes.

Bolton's article appeared in the *Sunday Sun* on 25 March 1979.

'A man whose handless skeleton has been found in a lonely bush grave was tortured and murdered by a mobster on the orders of an international drug running syndicate,' the article stated. 'This is the theory police from two states are working on following the discovery of the grave near Port Macquarie.

'Queensland police have told New South Wales detectives they believe the body is that of a Queensland-based drug courier who disappeared on a drug-carrying mission between Brisbane and Sydney a year ago.'

Bolton's scoop certainly placed Queensland police at the front and centre of this remarkable story. It hinted that Queensland police were also investigating 'drug drops off Noosa beach and other Queensland localities and drug caches hidden in derelict ships around the South Pacific.'

Bolton also reported that police claimed they had 'secret tape-recorded evidence which linked the murder to a massive international drug-running syndicate. Police stressed the tapes were genuine recordings of conversations between syndicate leaders,' Bolton ended his story. 'They did not want to disclose how they obtained them for security reasons.'

A photograph of Tony Murphy was featured with the article.

Cliff Crawford was on a job when the *Sunday Sun* and Bolton's report hit the newsstands. (A version of Bolton's story was picked up by Sydney's *Daily Telegraph* the next day.) 'I'll never forget that morning,' he remembers. 'We pulled into a service station. I saw the headlines and I thought – shit, this is the Wilsons.'

He immediately rang Syd Churchill of the Drug Squad. 'What's going on?' Crawford asked.

'I don't know,' said Churchill. 'It's been leaked.'

'They'll be dead,' Crawford remarked.

It didn't take long for Terry Clark to put two and two together. The Wilsons had sold him out in Brisbane the previous year, when the three of them had cruised up to Queensland to escape the Sydney winter.

On 27 March – two days after the Bolton scoop was published – New South Wales police officers, Detective Sergeant John McGregor and Detective Senior Constable Terry Dawson, interviewed Doug Wilson at his home in Rose Bay, Sydney.

Two days after that, Terry Clark paid the Wilsons a visit.

Doug Wilson rang Detective Dawson to let him know about Clark. The police thought Clark was in New Zealand. Wilson informed them otherwise.

'He was here last night,' Wilson said of Clark. 'He knows I've spoken to Churchill in Brisbane and he knows you've been here. He told Isabel and I that we would end up like Harry Lewis.'

The Madness of Marlin

Alec Jeppesen and his men in the Licensing Branch were seemingly dying a death of a thousand cuts if the drawn-out moeity investigation was anything to go by. Tony Murphy's new best boy in the branch,

Brian Marlin, had wreaked havoc on the unit for six months, following the Cleveland Sands Hotel incident and his recruitment as a mole for Murphy.

On 18 March 1979, Marlin turned the heat up even further. Some of the allegations he provided to Murphy were outrageous and infantile. In a secret report compiled by Marlin, no members of Jeppesen's crew were spared a touch up.

Marlin alleged, for example, that on a trip to Kingaroy, the home turf of Premier Joh Bjelke-Petersen, Licensing Branch officer Bruce Wilby and a convicted criminal, John Joseph Burrows, supposedly picked up a hitchhiker and 'assaulted and robbed him of wallet and money, a .22 rifle and marihuana'.

Jeppesen, Marlin continued, had on another date secured photographs of a brothel madam and a prominent Brisbane solicitor 'in acts of sex' and had used the pictures for blackmail purposes. Another allegation informed Murphy: 'Extensive bugging of telephones and planting of listening devices practised by Jeppesen, Wilby, Dunn, Dautel to obtain information re: S.P. and also in endeavour to disparage present police administration.

'These electronic devices obtained from West Germany, by close associate of Dunn named "Rolf" who is principal of E. & M. Television Services, Capalaba.'

And another: 'Same equipment used by Dawtell [sic] and Policewoman Scott of Licensing Branch at Jeppesen's direction to obtain photographs of young Licensing detectives flagrante delicto with nude poolside parties with massage parlour employees of Madam – Kerry Kent. These photos later used by Jeppesen and Dawtell [sic] to force compliance by young police with unlawful directives of Jeppesen.'

And yet another: 'Jeppesen in possession of a number of tapes which purport to be of Jeppesen interviewing police informants concerning unlawful police activities by C.I.B. and senior police in toleration of unlawful betting and gaming. Voices speaking on tapes with Jeppesen recognised by Const. Marlin as the voices of Dawtell [sic] and other licensing police obviously reading from prepared script.'

Marlin also had some gossip from the pub. He reported: 'Jeppesen when intoxicated made frequent boast of having amassed in four years the sum of $24,000 in the Police Credit Union from monies paid by the department to Jeppesen as Reward monies for informants.'

Marlin's personal letter to the Premier just a couple of months earlier and his compilation of increasingly bizarre claims against Jeppeson and his workmates at the Licensing Branch being fed to Tony Murphy provided the kerosene to the fire that was steadily being built against the branch and its head.

That many of the allegations beggared belief was immaterial. It was important to keep the slander at full bore until the desired objective was achieved. The attack by paper was also followed up with muscle. Murphy investigated Jeppesen's background, and the family pet – a corgi dog – was shot dead. A car seen leaving the vicinity after the gunshot was matched to Marlin's.

In addition, Detective Bruce Wilby's home in Brisbane was raided by police on the suspicion that he had a kilogram of heroin stashed inside.

'At that time we were shifting office from Ampol House to the new police headquarters,' Wilby says. 'We were instructed to take everything out of our lockers and keep it at home for the night. Brian Marlin was there when I was cleaning my locker out. I had two old pistols I'd found in different raids at West End and a little bottle of marihuana seeds. Marlin was the only one to see what I had in my locker.'

The next morning, just on daybreak, police and a special operations unit raided Wilby's house in Ferny Hills, north-west of the CBD. Wilby and his wife and three primary school-age children were inside.

'They sent a fellow who knew me as well as could be, a real decent fellow,' says Wilby. 'There was a carload of special operations fellows parked just up the road. The officer said to me, "There's not going to be any trouble?" They wanted to search the house and said they had information we had drugs.

'I was taken back [to headquarters] and interviewed. They did not search my place. I said the only bastard who knew I had [the guns and marihuana seeds] there was Brian Marlin. The officer who came to the door later warned me – be careful, the top brass are after you.'

Wilby was charged departmentally with failing to furnish reports on the stuff he had in his locker.

On that same day, Licensing officer Peter Dautel started his car and the engine burst into flames.

The elaborate attempt to bring down Jeppesen and his men was not only fierce and broad-ranging, but it was verging on the potentially deadly.

Lewis confirms that the plan was to dismantle the Jeppesen crew: 'The idea was to scatter them, and we did. The moiety thing – they wouldn't cooperate with investigators. The pressure was put on them to get out of the bloody job. I got [Ron] Redmond to do that.'

Approval Withdrawn

Bob Campbell of the Gabba CIB was happily ensconced in the new academic year out at the University of Queensland where he was studying third-year sociology and history when his future plans for a life beyond the Queensland Police Force took a hit.

On 2 April 1979, he was informed that the police approval for his degree had been withdrawn forthwith. He no longer had eight hours free per week to engage in his studies, and 'may continue the course in his own time and at his expense'.

The reason alluded to was Campbell's having reported 'on two separate occasions his intention of terminating service with the Queensland Police Force on the completion of this course of study'.

Campbell, incensed, fired off a letter from his modest Queenslander in Julia Street, Wavell Heights, to the new Police Minister Ron Camm.

> I cannot understand why this particular point of time was used to cancel my concession. I was recently advised that my name had been linked with ex-Constable EGAN [the cause célèbre of the street-march protest just weeks before]. I have never met this person nor contributed to adverse publicity against the Force, however I was never asked to explain my position.
>
> The Police Department seems to display a sympathetic approach to Officers who become alcoholics or are just lazy but cannot find the time to allow people like myself who are interested in improving ourselves to attend lectures and examinations ... The vindictive nature of the campaign against me suggests that I am not dealing with responsible, mature, rational men.

Campbell again asked for permission to speak with the press and to bring publicity to his plight 'to protect myself and more importantly my family'. He concluded: 'I undertake to keep away from any radical groups and avoid publicity if this victimization is discontinued but I will not hesitate to protect myself from these cowardly, malicious people. Thanking you for your time.'

If he wasn't a target before, Senior Constable Bob Campbell certainly was one now. Nevertheless, he would soon grow from a splinter to a thorn in the side of the police department and in particular Commissioner Terry Lewis.

In either an act of suicide or a show of extraordinary resilience, Campbell would soon be lobbing some hand grenades in a counter-attack of ingenious venom that would start as nothing more than a schoolboy-style prank and evolve into a scandal that would, once again, engulf the Queensland Police Force and make it to the feet of the Premier.

Dust to Dust

At around 9 p.m. on the night of Tuesday 17 April 1979, demolition expert George Deen was kicking back watching some television with his family at home in Oxley, 11 kilometres south-west of the CBD, when he noticed a particular newsflash.

The breaking news declared that Premier Joh Bjelke-Petersen and his government planned to demolish the 93-year-old Bellevue Hotel on the corner of George and Alice streets in the city.

The issue of the beautiful but tired three-storey Bellevue, a hotel that had hosted world-famous celebrities and international sporting teams for decades, and had heard its fair share of political skulduggery, being across the street from Parliament House and a regular watering hole and home away from home for country MLAs, had been debated for weeks.

Bjelke-Petersen wanted to obliterate the eyesore and replace it with new additions to what was called the 'parliamentary precinct'. The National Trust, however, had been campaigning strongly for its restoration and had growing public support.

When the hotel first opened for business in 1886, the *Brisbane Courier* was lavish in its praise. It deemed the hotel 'striking' and 'imposing'.

'A better location for a first-class house could not have been chosen, on two other corners of the streets being Parliament House and the Queensland Club and on the third the south-western corner of the Botanic Gardens,' it wrote. It described the ground-floor dining room as 'one of the handsomest rooms in the colony, well lighted and ventilated, and splendidly furnished'. It additionally praised the hotel's use of polished pine and cedar doors.

Despite the National Trust's campaigning, Premier Bjelke-Petersen described the Bellevue as 'a heap of rubbish' and state Government cabinet members approved its demolition 'subject to further discussion'.

Earlier that Tuesday, state Cabinet had ticked off in principle the $35 million 'parliamentary precinct' project. They made no decisions on the fate of the Bellevue, though it was understood that the majority of government ministers from the Premier down believed the building had to go.

Bjelke-Petersen argued that a secret report revealed the hotel's restoration would cost in excess of $2 million. Demolition would cost $40,000.

George Deen of the Deen Brothers, scenting an opportunity with the Bellevue following the newsflash, immediately phoned Parliament House. He told the security guard manning the phone, 'We'll bloody do it' – as in, the Deen Brothers would happily demolish the Bellevue Hotel for the Premier. He left his number.

Shortly after, George Deen received a call at home. It was Premier Joh Bjelke-Petersen. They discussed the secret demolition of the old hotel. It would happen at midnight in three days' time – Friday 20 April.

Also on that Tuesday, Bjelke-Petersen had had a wide-ranging telephone discussion with his Police Commissioner about a permit issued for a street march in Toowoomba, the police at Kingaroy, and Sir David Muir's appointment as Queensland Ombudsman. The Bellevue Hotel was not mentioned.

The next day the government moved swiftly and approved the demolition of the hotel. It was front-page news in the *Courier-Mail* on Thursday 19 April. DOWN IT COMES, the headline read. 'A Sunken Garden in its Place.'

The report said: 'However, in a compromise move to lessen public condemnation of the step, the coalition instructed architects to plan a new building with a Belle Vue [sic] style façade.'

Premier Bjelke-Petersen was quoted as saying: 'The Belle Vue [sic] is not an historic entity but a series of additions to an ill-desgined building. We have set out to protect the real heritage. I support this as my parents were pioneers. We have done what we believe is fair and right for Queenslanders.'

The press and public were made to believe the building would be demolished in a month's time. On that Thursday, however, Lewis recorded in his diary: 'Harold Young phoned re: Premier's direction that Belle Vue be demolished this weekend.'

Down at the corner of George and Alice streets, union officials patrolled outside the old hotel in an attempt to halt any impending demolition. South East Queensland Electricity Board workers had already begun lifting the footpaths in preparation for disconnecting electricity to the building.

Later that day, at the Gaythorne RSL, Lewis was one of the judges of the Lions Youth of the Year awards, along with Sir David Longland.

Come Friday, Lewis received a call in his office from a Detective R. Carter [possibly Bob Carter] 're: Premier's comments on Belle Vue'. That night, hours before the Deen Brothers, with police guard, moved their heavy equipment (six large vehicles and two smaller ones) to the Bellevue Hotel site under cover of darkness, Lewis and his wife, Hazel, enjoyed a farewell dinner for American consulate official Richard C. Dunbar at his home in Alton Terrace, The Gap.

The Bellevue, by this stage, had been surrounded by a barbed-wire fence to separate the Deens from a growing number of protestors. By the time word of the demolition spread across Brisbane, reported on various radio stations, hundreds of protestors had gathered at the corner of George and Alice streets. They shouted 'Save the Bellevue' and waved various placards.

Four Liberal Party MPs – Rosemary Kyburz, her husband Rob Akers, Terry Gygar and Angus Innes – joined the picket.

Down at the Park Royal Hotel in Alice Street and facing the Botanical Gardens, popular Brisbane radio personality Wayne 'Waynee Poo' Roberts was finishing up his act with band Wickety Wak when someone rushed to the stage.

'Hey Poo,' they said. 'They're just about to demolish the Bellevue!'

Roberts announced the travesty to the audience and led them out of the hotel and up the hill to the Bellevue site, still dressed garishly in his stage outfit. On arrival, Roberts hopped onto one of the approaching Deen Brothers trucks and gave the driver 'a gobful'.

'Then a hand grabbed me around the neck and pulled me down from the truck,' Roberts recalls. 'It was a red-headed copper with freckles and he said, "You're under arrest".

'I was shoved into the back of a paddy wagon. I was in my show performing gear – probably a pair of tangerine pants and a bolero-type shirt. I remember shouting through the bars of the wagon to my wife Annette – "Get our solicitor!" And she shouted back, "We don't have one!"'

Rosemary Kyburz, on witnessing the destruction, said: 'This is just too much for the Liberal Party to tolerate.'

The demolition proved to be a difficult job for the Deens. Walls refused to come down, and because of the haste to level the building, the Deens struck other hurdles. 'Right in the middle of the hotel was an electrical substation,' George Deen reportedly said. 'Because of the secrecy and everything else, it was still live. We couldn't get it disconnected. So we worked all the way around it. Luckily it was beneath a stairwell, so when we finished the job and cleaned it all up, the stairwell was left standing. We knocked it all down around it.'

The job took six days to complete.

'People were angry,' George said. 'We had bomb threats on our house. We had police living in our house. Police there 24 hours. Checking around our house. Checking our mail.'

The Bellevue, Deen later rationalised, was riddled with West Indian termite. 'But Joh just wanted it gone,' he said. 'Of course there was opposition from the Liberal Party and everybody else … Joh just wanted to trample everybody and he did it.'

On the Saturday, with the Bellevue in ruins, Commissioner Terry Lewis and his wife, Hazel, headed to the domestic airport at 6 a.m. to catch a flight to Sydney, then on to Adelaide and Perth for a conference and other official police business. They had a suite in the Sheraton Hotel waiting for them.

In Brisbane, though, locals woke to an act of government described by the *Courier-Mail* as one of 'shame' and the latest in several 'hillbilly authoritarian actions that have made this State a national laughing stock'.

Bjelke-Petersen brushed off the wrath of fellow MPs and a confused and bemused public. 'These people with their green bans, their black bans, anything under the sun, must be feeling pretty sheepish,' he defiantly said.

He was also questioned about the tendering process for the demolition contract, organised hastily on the telephone with George Deen just days before. 'I don't know when the tenders were called,' the Premier said. 'It's a matter of checking with the Works Department. Anyway, I'm not concerned with that. That's immaterial.'

Deputy Premier Dr Llew Edwards seemed equally as puzzled by the fiasco. 'I wasn't aware of the decision for contractors to begin work ... and I am concerned that, to my knowledge, the Liberal Party was not given adequate information before demolition began.'

A Works Department source told a reporter the decision to demolish so quickly came from a 'higher authority', but would not confirm or deny that that authority was in fact Bjelke-Petersen.

It was a minor nuisance to the Premier. He would not discuss the tendering process for the job but added that 'all normal procedures had been complied with'. He congratulated the Deen Brothers on a job well done.

Shallow Grave

The bodies of Douglas Wilson, 26, and his wife Isabel, 24, were found on 18 May, buried together in a shallow grave in the holiday town of Rye on Port Phillip Bay, south of Melbourne.

It was later ascertained they were actually executed on 13 April – just 19 days after Tony Murphy's leaked story to Bolton was published. It was also understood Terry Clark was responsible for their deaths.

On hearing news of the murders, drug dealer John Edward Milligan and former Rat Packer and corrupt cop Glen Hallahan had several discussions about who knew what in relation to the murders and how much police knew about the Clark syndicate. There was also talk about Murphy leaking the story to Bolton.

'Tony did Brian a favour,' Milligan said. 'And the result of that anyway [was] the Wilsons were murdered, and he [Bolton] laughed and said, "Well, Tony did have the Wilsons shot".'

Curiously, on 29 May the *Courier-Mail* published a convoluted story out of Melbourne that said the Wilsons, in their interviews with Queensland police in 1978, told them how Clark's massive drug syndicate had an 'inside man' in the Narcotics Bureau in Canberra who had access to a computer, and that the computer may have leaked the information about the Wilsons to Terry Clark, resulting in their murder.

On 1 June, Lewis noted in his diary: 'Hon. Camm phoned re Premier saying that Prime Minister [Malcolm Fraser] has requested an all States Task Force to investigate deaths of Wilsons and others.'

Lewis says he was shocked at the death of the drug couriers and that he drafted a stern rebuke to his old friend Tony Murphy for talking to Bolton.

'That resulted in their murders, no doubt at all,' says Lewis. 'I knew nothing about it until the shit hit the fan. It was a very, very stupid thing to do to ingratiate yourself with the media, to say the least.

'I remember they got Clark. He was wanted in New Zealand. They charged him with possession of a firearm to hold him so they could get in touch with New Zealand and find out what's what. I don't know whether the gun was a present [planted] or he had it with him.'

Lewis ordered Murphy to answer in detail several questions about the Wilsons and the leak of information from the interview tapes to Brian Bolton of the *Sunday Sun*. It was a sharp snub to Murphy. Lewis had rarely, if ever, crossed swords with his colleague and friend.

'I think Murphy might have slowly been wary of me from then on,' says Lewis. 'I was really, really upset about that one. But I always felt that if anybody was prepared to tell police something apart from their own ends, I mean ... these two poor youngsters didn't deserve to be murdered.'

One of the queries Murphy was required to answer was this: 'It would appear that the willingness of the Wilsons to cooperate with the police led to their murders. Please comment on this aspect.'

And Murphy's reply: 'It does now appear as a possibility, that the WILSONS were murdered, because of the information passed on to the Police. If this be a sound premise, the question as to whether it was the initial information to the Queensland Police, the subsequent confirmation of same to the New South Wales Homicide Squad, or the recently alleged leakage from the Customs-Narcotics Computer, which led to their death, is of course a matter for conjecture.

'It also remains open to conjecture, that their untimely ends may have resulted from other nefarious activities, entirely unrelated to CLARKE [sic] and his activities.'

A computer, nefarious activities, even the Wilsons themselves were perhaps responsible for their own murders. But not CIB chief Anthony Murphy.

The Fake Raid

On 8 June 1979, Sir Colin Woods was appointed the first Commissioner of the newly formed Australian Federal Police (AFP). It was expected the force would be operational by 19 October.

At the time of this announcement, Justice Williams' Royal Commission of Inquiry into Drugs had been running since 1977, and was well advanced when Terry Clark's Mr Asia syndicate came onto the radar of authorities courtesy of the Brisbane arrests a year later. It was also sitting when allegations of the involvement of police and parliamentarians in the drug trade were aired on the floor of Queensland parliament.

Parallel to this was Narcotics Bureau Agent John Shobbrook's extraordinary Operation Jungle, and his tracking of John Edward Milligan, a one-time judge's associate and business partner to former detective Glen Hallahan, supposedly farming in Obi Obi on the Sunshine Coast.

By 1979, Justice Williams' disdain for the Narcotics Bureau was gathering a head of steam. He saw the bureau officers as poorly trained and poorly organised. He railed against their work and their defence of their professionalism. With the formation of the AFP, and Williams' public berating of the bureau, the writing was on the wall for the Narcs.

Undercover operative Detective Jim Slade was working happily under the guidance of Tony Murphy at the Bureau of Crime Intelligence, when an extraordinary job came his way.

Slade had been taught well by Murphy, and he loved his work. He was developing rapidly into one of the state's top undercover agents, able to infiltrate anything from criminal gangs to drug-dealing networks. On this occasion, he was ordered to perform surveillance on a house on the Sunshine Coast. The word was that there were enormous quantities of drugs on the premises.

'I don't know why this came about,' remembers Slade. 'I don't know where this letter came from, whether it was sent in from the public or whether it was a letter generated by Tony Murphy, or generated by Justice Williams.

'Williams sent this letter, a copy of the letter, to Tony Murphy, even though Tony knew about it prior to the letter coming, and one to the Narcotics Bureau, and left it at that.

'Justice Williams told Tony Murphy to do a big thing on it and that he would use that as part of [his exposé of the] inadequacies and inefficiencies of the Narcotics Bureau.'

Slade did his job. He conducted surveillance for several weeks and eventually realised that the massive quantities of drugs and human traffic to and from the house, as the intelligence suggested in the letter, were simply not materialising.

Slade claims that senior officers close to Tony Murphy got a raid going. 'They took in the most incredible amount of drugs and busted these people,' he said.

'The whole thing was bullshit. Acting on that, Justice Williams recommended that the Narcotics Bureau be disbanded.

'That whole thing was worked out between Williams and Murphy.'

Big Bucks

Jack 'The Bagman' Herbert was always receptive to some cash in hand, and he struck a mother lode when he went into business with Tony Robinson, described often as Brisbane's most notorious operator of illegal baccarat games.

Tony and son Tony Jnr had entered the gaming machine industry and were looking for someone with enough connections to help them convince pubs and clubs to install in-line ticket machines – a sort of peasant's poker machine, where for a coin the player could yield a piece of paper and the potential to redeem a prize. The prizes were free games on the machine, but it quickly became known that the free games could be exchanged for cash.

Herbert himself saw a cash cow. 'Robinson introduced me to Jack Rooklyn, who ran a company that hired out in-line machines to licensed clubs,' said Herbert. '[He] wasn't a man to fool with. He was the Australian distributor for the American Bally poker machine company, which had links with the Chicago Mafia.

'Soon I started working for Rooklyn, travelling around Queensland putting in-line machines into clubs. The clubs had to get permission to operate them from the Justice Department. The clubs kept 50 per cent of the profits from each machine, and we took the rest.'

The Robinsons' in-line empire expanded and during his working relationship with both men Herbert soon learned they were paying Don Lane, member for Merthyr, a monthly kickback, as he had contacts in the Department of Justice.

Terry Lewis was aware of Lane's relationship with Rooklyn. 'I know Lane knew him,' he says. 'Lane told me he had visited Rooklyn in Sydney and had gone out on his yacht. Apparently Rooklyn had a beautiful mansion overlooking the harbour.

'Lane said if I ever wanted to go out on Rooklyn's yacht and sail around the harbour I should let him know. I didn't.'

Around this time Herbert began to see Lewis again socially, and told him both Lane and a senior public servant with the Licensing Commission were receiving money protecting the in-lines. Herbert, in turn, arranged for Robinson Snr. to meet Lewis who, according to the Bagman, was also put on the payroll. Herbert alleged Lewis received $2000 per month from Rooklyn and Robinson.

(Earlier in the year, Lewis's police diary noted that Robinson came to see him at his office to 'introduce' Rooklyn on 20 March 1978. 'Mr Rooklyn inquired re starting a "Health Studio" on the Gold Coast, informed him if prostitution involved prosecution would be certain.'

Then in late November 1978, the diary stated again: 'Jack Rooklyn called inquiring if massage parlours are being legalised; I assured him they are not.' There was debate in New South Wales at the time over liberalising prostitution laws, resulting in the *Prostitution Act 1979* under the government of Neville Wran.)

While Lewis would later deny knowing Rooklyn, he now says: 'Jack Herbert would have said, "Would you come down and have a sandwich?" I'm sure I saw him at the Crest. Rooklyn, Herbert and me. He [Rooklyn] said he wanted to put poker machines in the Police Club. I said no way in the world. Rooklyn was not a big deal as far as I was concerned.'

Lewis says he had known Tony Robinson since the war days. 'Tony Robinson, I don't know if he's a crook,' Lewis adds. 'I think he was just a ... he had no criminal record – he had one conviction, posses-sion without a licence, concealment of a firearm during the war.

'He had a men's clothing shop in Albert Street ... opposite was the Metro [Theatre] and next to it was a jeweller's shop ... But anyhow, Tony Robinson was known to most of us because he had a flash car and in those days after the war hardly anybody had a flash car and they could park in the city indefinitely. And then when I got on the Consorting Squad I met him because he had a little nightclub down in the Petrie Bight ... La Boheme, or something, anyhow we knew him then.

'He was a smartie, but he was certainly not a bloody criminal. A ladies man of course and bloody dressed like a million dollars and he must have got in with Rooklyn somewhere along the line and Herbert along the line and away it went from there.'

Lewis said he had no idea who Rooklyn was. 'I don't know if he was ever bloody convicted the bastard,' Lewis adds. 'I mean, I did meet him once and he was an unlovable looking bastard ... there's no doubt in the world he was very friendly with Don Lane, and he was very friendly with Jack Herbert as time showed.

'But he was a famous bloody, well, race bloke that had heaps of money apparently … I might be wrong, but I doubt if he had a criminal record. They had an inquiry in Sydney by somebody that showed he was, that's right, he was an associate of some of the Mafia or whatever you like from America. Used to come out and they were friends …'

What was a bigger deal to Lewis was that just four days after the Crest luncheon, it was announced that he had been awarded the Most Excellent Order of the British Empire.

That night – Saturday 16 June – Commissioner Terry Lewis, OBE, and Hazel sat in the special VIP area at Lang Park and enjoyed a rugby league Test between Australia and Great Britain along with 23,049 other punters.

The Kangaroos belted the Poms 35 to nil.

Global Girls

Geoff Crocker was having his ups and downs with his fledgling massage parlour empire in 1979, as were Tilley and Hapeta.

One of the primary reasons was the work of a new Licensing Branch officer, Ron Lewis. Lewis surveyed the landscape and came up with a new way to attack the vice lords. He would go after the owners of the buildings who leased out premises to the likes of Crocker, Holloway, Hapeta and Tilley.

'What I did introduce was – and again you've got to get back to your political masters, they wanted us to "control" [the scene] to a certain degree … so we came up with a control measure,' recalls Ron Lewis.

'We were prosecuting the prostitutes and managers, but quite often the owners of the business weren't touched. If you rented a premises knowing they were used for prostitution, it was considered an offence.'

Ron Lewis soon discovered that the problem with this approach was that if you said to the owner of a building, 'Do you know it's being used for prostitution?', they could defend themselves by denying any knowledge. He started approaching the owners of the brothel buildings and asked them directly: 'Do you know your property is being leased as a brothel?'

'I'd inform them that several prosecutions had taken place on their particular premises, showed them the Act, and told them they were liable for prosecution.

'Six months later I'd come back, produce the convictions that had occurred in the last six months [relating to their property] and charge them.'

The impact was enormous.

Out of the city's 36 or so brothels running at the time, 24 of them shut down after Ron Lewis's blitz.

'They went underground,' Ron Lewis says, 'and formed these escort services.'

That was precisely the direction in which Geoff Crocker headed after being evicted from one of the properties housing one of his brothels, and he'd had enough. 'After all the landlords evicted me and closed them all down I then rented a flat [at 453] Montague Road [West End],' said Crocker. 'One of the girls who was managing one of the parlours for me was pregnant, right, and the parlours had been closed down and she had saved no money and she said to me, "Geoff, can you help me out with a flat?"'

He thought of the possibility of running escorts out of the flat in the three-storey brick block not far from Hill End Terrace and the sharp sweep of the Brisbane River. Crocker installed a couple of phones and Global Girls Escorts was born.

Business grew rapidly. From two girls working, it built to five or six. Crocker drove the girls to their jobs. 'The police used to come in and visit and in them days ... we were [under] the impression we couldn't be busted for escort, like the receptionist couldn't be,' said Crocker.

'I mean, the working girl? She solicited someone in a motel room. I got sort of pretty busy there and people were starting to complain in the other units about the cars coming and going at three or four o'clock in the morning so we moved out of there into a private residence.'

Next up was 27 Sankey Street, Highgate Hill, a large Queenslander on the corner of Dudley Street and opposite a children's playground. Across the park was Paradise Street and the home of the former corruption fighter and fearless parliamentarian, the member for South Brisbane, Colin Bennett. In another era, Bennett had relentlessly pursued the corrupt former police commissioner Frank Bischof and his so-called Rat Pack of bagmen and acolytes – Terry Lewis, Tony Murphy and Glen Hallahan.

It was to the house in Paradise Street that Bennett and his large Catholic family had retreated on 27 December 1959, when little Colin junior had drowned in the Davies Park public swimming pool.

In Sankey Street, Crocker installed up to eight phones, such was the demand for his Global Girls.

Crocker had an aversion to drugs. If any of his girls used, they were sacked on the spot. Besides, he had made a promise to his mother that he wouldn't get involved in that side of the business.

At Sankey Street, Crocker came in contact with an enthusiastic young constable, Sam Di Carlo. Di Carlo had only joined the force in 1975 but had gone to work under Alec Jeppesen at the Licensing Branch and had shown an aptitude for undercover work. Jeppesen encouraged him, describing his charge as 'honest, loyal and dedicated'.

On one of Di Carlo's visits to the premises he got Crocker out in the kitchen on his own. 'Geoff, things are going to get really hot in this business now, we've found holes in the law that we can plug up and you're going to be busted and probably put in gaol,' Di Carlo allegedly told him.

'Oh well, that's how it goes, you know,' Crocker responded. 'You know, there is not much I can do about that, Sam.'

He said he expected Di Carlo to offer him a bribe. The constable didn't. Instead Di Carlo told Crocker his boss said to ask him could 'you guys' look after the branch with information on drugs and SP bookmakers in exchange for some leniency from Licensing?

'Yes, no problem,' said Crocker. 'I hate druggies anyhow so if I can give you a dealer, or even a user, I will.'

He said he offered up to Di Carlo a druggie at a nearby hotel then 'strung him on' for months. 'He came back to being a fair copper,' said Crocker of Di Carlo, 'and not the heavy dude he originally started off to be.'

After Licensing Branch head Alec Jeppesen was transferred, Rigney took his place. He was followed by Noel Dwyer, Ron Lewis's superior.

'Noel Dwyer was a fine family man. That's the way I saw the man,' recalls Ron Lewis. 'Alec Jeppesen was a totally and completely honest man. There was never any suggestion I shouldn't do something [about going after the owners].

'When I went to Dwyer and I tried to get the owners, he didn't think it would do any good but he didn't dissuade me in any way, shape or form.'

Ron Lewis was a tradesman before he joined the police force. He applied the same principles to his Licensing Branch cases – be honest, fair, transparent and work hard. 'One day I was in the office and there was a woman there,' he recalls.

'I was told she worked for a massage parlour. She said, "We always knew where we stood with you, Mr Lewis." I treated them like ladies. I wouldn't take a thing from them. Not even a glass of water. It became a bit of a joke. Sometimes my troops thought I was a bit of an old lady.'

Even so, his dedicated work in the branch didn't necessarily do the diligent officer any favours. Ron Lewis was encouraged to take a job in administration. It was a good position and a sensible step, although he never knew if this encouragement was for the good of his career, or because someone didn't want him to continue working in Licensing.

As for the energetic Italian, Di Carlo, he had admired Jeppesen and felt that Jeppesen had been badly treated. He made no secret of his feelings that Jeppesen had been destroyed by Tony Murphy and Syd Atkinson on the orders of Commissioner Terry Lewis. He aired his theory in the canteen, the Police Union office, and to whichever officers he happened to be with at any given time, irrespective of rank. Jeppesen had been done over.

His self-admitted big mouth would soon land him in the office of the Commissioner of Police. Like Robert Walker, Bob Campbell, Kingsley Fancourt and so many honest officers before him, Di Carlo's commitment to an honest day's work would see him suffer the same time-worn fate – he would be driven from the force in spectacular circumstances.

Goodbye to the Big Fella

In the last week of August 1979 former commissioner Frank Bischof, 74, seeing out his days in his humble home at The Gap, was admitted to the Mater Hospital in South Brisbane having been seriously ill for several weeks.

He died at 8 p.m. on Tuesday 28 August. At 10 p.m. Commissioner Lewis got a phone call at home from one of his inspectors to inform him of Bischof's passing.

The newspapers the next day lauded the Big Fella as a 'good tough cop'. 'Francis Erich Bischof died yesterday and with him died an era of the Queensland Police Force that will be talked of for many years to come,' one said. 'He was outspoken – some thought too much so – and his name was always before the public.'

Bischof was praised for standing up to be counted when it mattered, and for his tireless dedication to the welfare of the state's children. His creation of the Juvenile Aid Bureau – 'virtually a world first and copied by many countries' – was singled out as his lasting memorial. It was noted that the JAB had been the nursery for the current Commissioner of Police.

There was no mention of the closing of the brothels in the late 1950s, his disastrous affair with Mary Margaret Fels, the National Hotel inquiry or his shoplifting charge.

The day after Bischof's death, his protégé Commissioner Lewis addressed members of the 63rd Advanced Training Course at the Police Academy. He no doubt imparted knowledge that the Big Fella had passed on to him.

On Friday 31 August, Lewis and senior officers attended Bischof's funeral service at St John's Cathedral, a few minutes' walk up Clark Lane from the Roberts brothers' National Hotel in the city, where Bischof spent so much of his time in the 1960s and into the 1970s.

Lewis and his officers then proceeded to the Mount Thompson Memorial Gardens in Nursery Road, Holland Park.

After farewelling his old mentor, Lewis went with wife, Hazel, to the Police Academy for lunch with Justice Lucas, then oversaw the induction of 36 fresh constables – the new generation.

Empty Rooms

While Federal Narcotics Bureau Agent John Shobbrook was making huge headway in his pursuit of drug dealer John Edward Milligan, his colleagues in the Brisbane office were running into brick walls all over the place.

Geoff Pambroke had been in the bureau since 1975 and he was getting increasingly frustrated at what he perceived as Commissioner Lewis's men intentionally thwarting the Federal Bureau's cases.

Pambroke, an investigative agent, noticed the same thing when Mr

Asia, Terry Clark, and his couriers, Doug and Isabel Wilson, were brought in for questioning by the state police in 1978.

'If anything, the State police tried to keep us away from them,' Pambroke remembers. 'The hierarchies of the Narcos and the Queensland police were playing games with each other. Lewis didn't like a lot of our blokes. They were worried about what we could do and how well we could do it.

'I remember when the local police were discussing Terry Lewis becoming Commissioner. They said, "This is going to be great. We're all going to be looked after now".'

Pambroke was proud of the work the Federal Narcotics Bureau did, despite the staff being spread thin. With Shobbrook, he would modify vehicles for surveillance work, rigging out Kombi vans for long stretches of undercover work. Both often used their own money to acquit the mechanical changes.

But increasingly that work was all for nought – they went on raid after raid following the exacting gathering of evidence, only to find that the suspects had been tipped off. 'We'd organise a raid on the Gold Coast and there'd be nothing there,' he says. 'Someone had phoned them up. In one case we went into a place and there on a piece of paper were the number plate details of our vehicles.

'If you went through the main street of Surfers Paradise in those days [within view of the offices of Gold Coast state drug squad detectives], then that was the end of it. We had to go in through the back blocks. We did not pull off one successful raid on the Gold Coast.'

The same failure rate was being experienced by the state Licensing Branch. Former Licensing Branch officer Bruce Wilby remembers: 'Everybody knew what the rumours were. In those days ... I had no idea it was as organised as it was. [Syd] Atkinson on the Gold Coast tried to override us all the time. You'd get the message – we'd like you to stay away from this person.'

Similarly, undercover detective Jim Slade faced similar frustrations. He was working on a case involving the Bellino family and their associates when the unthinkable happened. 'I think I did a job with Fred Maynard, we had an undercover officer in there, and the Bellinos just came up to me and said, "We know you're a copper because we've got inside information."

'I was so fucking wild. Here I was, having worked undercover for years, I'd worked with undercover agents, we were so successful with all of our operations, and here was some fucking mongrel, my workmate – someone dobbed us in. That really affected me. I had no time for those bastards.'

Slade would soon be heading to North Queensland to do some serious investigations into the drug trade. He would not forget the Bellino incident. And if the name Bellino came up, he would not hesitate to push the investigation to its very limit.

Wives and Mothers

Despite an emotionally cold childhood, his mother, Mona, having left the family home in Ipswich for the bright lights of Brisbane and its horse racing tracks when he was a boy, and despite prohibitive work hours as Commissioner of Police, Terry Lewis and his wife, Hazel, had established a warm and loving family environment up on Garfield Drive.

Lewis still heard from his mother – an habitué of the Doomben and Eagle Farm tracks – and says he relied on her for racing tips.

'I know, as I worked my tail off and got up another notch, she used to use my name a lot, particularly in the racing fraternity,' says Lewis. 'But Hazel, she was such a gentle, friendly bugger, she'd go and kiss a blackfella if she felt like it.'

Aware of her husband's own upbringing, she encouraged him to be affectionate with his children and would urge Lewis to kiss the children more. 'I'd kiss the two daughters reluctantly for a while there ... only in fairly recent years I kissed the boys when I met them,' he recalls.

'I'd never known it ... I love the kids and I'm sorry I never showed them ... I think my five kids realised what I thought of them.'

In the Lewis household, the children were taught to be frugal. Certainly Hazel and Lewis watched their pennies. At Christmas time, the family arrangement was that no present could exceed $10 in value. For birthdays, Lewis usually got socks, pyjamas, belts or aftershave. With Hazel, it was perfume or nightdresses.

Meals at Garfield Drive were simple and prepared with an eye on the budget. Hazel would prepare ox-tongue, or make pies out of chuck or skirt steak. Chops were braised in gravy and served with carrots, onions and turnips. There were mince-meat rissoles and meatloaf. Hazel always baked her own cakes and biscuits, and occasionally made a tomato relish.

The fresh produce that came into the house was sourced from friends and relatives. The Lewis's received tomatoes, butternut pumpkins, rockmelons and mangoes from a relative's farm. Friends sent pine-apples from Gympie, cabbages, lettuces, potatoes, pumpkins, onions and beetroots from Gatton, apples and oranges from Stanthorpe. Fish was plentiful courtesy of two sons-in-law in the family who liked to throw in a line.

As for household cleaning products, including soaps and deodor-ants, they were at some point supplied free of charge to Garfield Drive because they were damaged goods and unsaleable. So too cooking oil and margarines.

The family had an old Corona motor vehicle. Hazel said a tank of petrol would last her three weeks. 'We went in Terry's office car almost everywhere,' she would later say.

As for entertainment, Lewis as Commissioner had an inexhaustible calendar full of invitations to the theatre, to films, to sporting fixtures and major cultural events, along with a similar number of lunch and dinner requests.

Lewis remembers: 'I was so bloody busy, one day … I got 11 invitations for the one day. Not that that matters now and not because it was me, probably because of my job more than anything else, but I was always getting invited by the banks, the insurance companies, and big, big companies like Mayne Nickless and Rothmans … and I tried as hard as I could to make sure I got to everyone once. You know so they didn't think you were a bit of a twerp.'

If the Lewis's didn't want to cook at home, they didn't have to.

When the Commissioner took his annual leave, the family invariably went down to the Gold Coast at the height of summer and lodged in flats owned by friends. When on holiday they enjoyed staying in and relaxing. It was an opportunity to step off the hectic carousel that was the life of a commissioner of police.

When time permitted, Hazel Lewis occasionally caught up with Jack Herbert's wife, Peggy. The two women had met at a police picnic in Davies Park at West End in the early 1960s. Peggy was a mother, too, and she would often cross paths with Hazel because of the children. They might bump into each other during school holidays on the Gold Coast. Hazel thought Peggy was gracious, gentle, quiet and always a lady. Another good friend to Hazel was Sheilagh Maxwell, wife of Barry Maxwell of the Belfast Hotel.

Still, the life of the wife of a police commissioner was a demanding one too. She viewed her husband's position as a 24-hour-a-day job, and that the family was never free of the rigour of high office. She thought it was stressful, but she loved her family and her husband. She was a police wife, as she saw herself. And a police mother, too.

Up on 12 Garfield Drive, it was Hazel Lewis, by necessity, who held the family together.

As Lewis says: 'There were a couple of ladies in my whole life that I struck that … my wife was one. She went out to help every bugger, black, white or brindle. She used to, well, almost annoy me sometimes. She'd get these black fellows and be shaking hands with them and bloody … Maureen [Tony Murphy's wife] was another. There was a fellow called Sid Currie had a wife, his wife was Hazel, too. She died young but oh, she was a great wife. Some of them were lucky they had them. And some of them didn't deserve them.'

Lewis has a different opinion of Jack Herbert's wife, Peggy. 'I thought she was a bit of a mole,' he reflects. 'I met her, naturally. Can't say I had a lot to do with her. She wasn't a bad looking piece.'

The life of a police family was difficult – temptations were everywhere. 'Men like Merv Hopgood and Abe Duncan, they would never think of betraying their wives and there were many others like that,' Lewis remembers. 'Some of them, I know they did. They were looked upon as pants men, but not looked upon terribly favourably by everybody.

'You had the opportunities insofar as there were pubs everywhere, you walked everywhere a lot … as far as I can recollect, except one at the National Hotel, people working in the pubs were all girls. That was a great chance for them to pick up …'

Lewis himself says he never cheated on Hazel. One woman, though, did catch his eye earlier in his career. It was Yvonne Weier, his partner in the formation of the Juvenile Aid Bureau in the early 1960s. 'If I'd been a single man she'd be one I'd contemplate marrying,' he says. 'Her and Hallahan were friendly for a little while, I don't know what transpired there.

'Her father had been a police officer. I had a good relationship [with her], none of it sexual. She was a really nice person.'

How did Hazel Lewis cope with her husband working in a confined office with an attractive young woman?

'I didn't dare ask her,' he says.

Suite

Now that Jack Herbert had transferred his expertise across to Jack Rooklyn and the Bally Corporation, it may have seemed prudent to try and get his new boss and the Police Commissioner together for a casual chat.

Lewis had supposedly mentioned to Herbert that Premier Joh Bjelke-Petersen was talking a lot about poker machines and whether or not they should be introduced in Queensland. If so, it would be the end of the lucrative in-line machine business. But another door would open up with the pokies. Perhaps bigger riches awaited.

'I told Terry that Jack Rooklyn was anxious to keep in-lines in Queensland and that he'd probably pay $10,000 to secure an adverse report on poker machines,' Herbert wrote in his memoir. 'Terry sent me back to talk to Rooklyn's people. They were worried by an article they'd read in the paper about poker machines coming to Queensland and they asked if Terry Lewis would take $25,000 to keep the pokies out. I knew he'd have taken $10,000 so I didn't need to ask.'

Herbert telephoned Doug Ryan, general manager of the Mayfair Crest Hotel on the corner of Roma and Ann streets to arrange a room for a meeting between Rooklyn and Lewis. Ryan knew Herbert through his brother-in-law, Barry Maxwell, close friend to Terry Lewis. He later described his relationship with Herbert as a 'nodding acquaintance'.

'I do recall on one occasion him [Herbert] ringing me to organise a room in which to have a meeting,' Ryan said. 'This in itself was not out of the ordinary as in our capacity as hoteliers we have been called on by ASIO and Special Branch to let them have the use of a room for confidential meetings.'

Ryan knew Herbert was not a policeman at the time, 'but I had a feeling that he was doing something for the force'.

He added that he didn't remember if the room Herbert was booking was for Commissioner Lewis. 'I'm sure that if he had mentioned that I would have thought it a bit strange that Terry Lewis hadn't rung me as I knew him a lot better than Jack Herbert,' Ryan added.

Lewis's diary entry for Tuesday 12 June 1979, read: 'To Crest Hotel re luncheon re machines in Police Club.' Could this have been the meeting with Rooklyn that Herbert was arranging for the Commissioner?

The maitre d'hotel at the Crest was Serge Pregliasco. He was responsible for the service of breakfast in the hotel's Early American Inn, and lunch in its First Floor restaurant. He had worked at the Crest since April 1977, but had extensive experience in the hotel industry. For example, he had been the maitre d'hotel at the Chandeliers Restaurant in the Chevron Hotel in Sydney for some time. It was there he first met Sydney businessman Jack Rooklyn.

'Mr Rooklyn acknowledged me on occasions when I saw him and attended to him at the hotel,' Pregliasco recalled later. 'Rooklyn is of a very distinctive appearance and is well known in Sydney.'

While Pregliasco had a drinking problem that had come to the attention of his superiors, he was good at his job and well liked by staff.

Then one day he said he was given a special assignment. 'I can remember one occasion when the hotel general manager, Mr Doug Ryan, requested me to take a bottle of wine to one of the two penthouse suites,' he recalled. 'I do not recall whether the bottle was of wine or of champagne.

'It was not a very common occurrence for me, as maitre d'hotel, to take wine up to the rooms as this would normally be done by the room service waiters. However, sometimes with special VIP guests, Ryan told me that it was better to have a more senior man perform this task.'

Pregliasco said he took the bottle to the room. 'When I entered the room I recognised two people,' he later recalled. 'One of these people was Jack Rooklyn, who I recognised from my time in Sydney. The other was ... Terence Lewis. I recognised ... Terence by virtue of the fact that he is a prominent person and you generally recognise prominent people. I had no doubts that it was … Terence. I have a vague recollection there may have been someone else in the room, but I really cannot be certain of this.'

Pregliasco said Rooklyn recognised him. 'You are from Sydney?' he supposedly asked.

'Yes,' replied Serge.

Rooklyn was chuffing on his customary cigar. 'From my observations of Mr Rooklyn when I knew him in Sydney he almost always had a cigar,' the maitre d'hotel said. 'I was not in the room for more than a few minutes. I opened the wine bottle and poured drinks. I think there was already food in the room.'

Herbert later claimed he too was at the meeting, and that he had heard Rooklyn offer Lewis $25,000 for an adverse report.

'Terry nodded and Rooklyn said to him, "Don't let the other side get to you." Terry replied, "I never change horses mid-stream."

'They shook hands.'

Jobs for the Boys

Heading into the winter of 1979, rumour was rife in political and media circles in Brisbane that Premier Joh Bjelke-Petersen's long-time media officer, Allen Callaghan, was to resign. Callaghan had been with the Premier since joining Bjelke-Petersen's personal staff in May 1971, having been an ABC Queensland political reporter. He was 31 years old.

Callaghan had performed miracles with Joh, turning a country bumpkin into a polished, albeit eccentric media performer. The soil of a Kingaroy peanut farm was still in Joh's delivery, but he learned how to be quick on his feet and appealed to the public as a straw-chewing hillbilly who also happened to be a brilliant politician. The ultimate masterstroke, however, was to turn Bjelke-Petersen into a sort of befuddled clown and redneck who had nothing but Queensland at the forefront of his mind.

Joh's comic quips, devoured by the media – particularly in southern states – masked what was really going on in the Sunshine State, and may have contributed to a lack of genuine scrutiny of political, and indeed, police corruption. Joh was just a silly old duffer who didn't need to be taken seriously. Or so it seemed.

Eight years later – his work done – Callaghan had become a little jaded. He needed a change.

Lewis says Callaghan was a 'likeable bloke'. 'I always found him a bloody good brain,' Lewis says. 'I believe he built Joh up. I found Joh a decent bloke but he wasn't the polished bloody politician or performer that I think Allen turned him into. He put words into his mouth. I give him great credit.'

Bjelke-Petersen himself recorded in his memoir: 'Some people have said Allen made me accessible to the media. That is not true – I had always been accessible to the media. What Allen Callaghan did do was to make the media more accessible to me and so help me promote myself.'

The rumours proved to be true.

Callaghan resigned and was almost immediately installed as Deputy Coordinator and Promotions Officer for the Department of Culture, National Parks and Recreation. In Bjelke-Petersen's own words, the Premier had 'found him a senior government job'.

Fortuitously, on 1 July, the Queensland Film Corporation moved from being under the auspices of the Department of the Premier and Cabinet to that of Callaghan's new department. Fulfilling a long-held ambition, he became its chairman. In the arid cultural landscape under the National Party, Callaghan had his work cut out for him.

A Cheery Hello from an Old Soldier

On 27 August 1979, a typed three-page letter landed in Commissioner Lewis's in-tray.

The professional letterhead declared it was from a fibreglass boat-building business called Sea Strike Enterprises, based in Harvey Creek Road, Bellenden Ker, 50 kilometres south of Cairns in Far North Queensland. The author was none other than Gunther Bahnemann – former World War II sniper under Rommel, defector, sailor, author and attempted murderer of Glen Patrick Hallahan.

In 1959, Lewis and Hallahan had been virtual celebrities in Brisbane after they disarmed the 'crazed gunman' Bahnemann one strange night in Lota, east of the city. Both men won the George Medal for Bravery – the state's highest honour for a policeman.

In the struggle to seize the gun off a drugged and drunk Bahnemann, Lewis, Hallahan and two young constables from Wynnum jumped him and the weapon discharged. Bahnemann was found guilty of attempted murder and sentenced to seven years at Boggo Road. He would serve more than half this sentence before being released and would go on to write bestselling books, including *Hoodlum* and *I Deserted Rommel*.

Now, after almost 20 years since the night that changed his life, a hard-up Bahnemann wrote to both friend and foe, Terry Lewis. The lengthy letter, it seems, was prompted by contact initiated by Lewis himself.

Dear Terry,

So many years … was the impression I had when you phoned here. Thank you indeed for your call, Terry, and more so for the most unselfish remark – 'You call me Terry!'. I value that remark of yours, it reminded me of your personal visit to me when I was lodging in the 'Old Roads'. That time I knew that that visit of yours was a sincere action on your part and, it was the kind of 'Moral Guts' visiting the man you helped put away that made me respect you and wanting to be a friend.

Bahnemann filled in the missing years, telling Lewis he had been married to his wife Leonie for 12 years.

Leonie is 33 years of age now, I am 58 years. The age difference caused some remarks at the time we married – It won't work etc etc. Indeed, it did work extremely well despite many hardships ...

They had three children – Tarni, Hagen and young Sonja. 'So you see Terry I do have a fine family, though we were not much blessed with monetary advantage or exceptional luck.'

He explained in detail how his old wooden boatbuilding business went sour after 'fibreglass killed us out', and that he was known by North Queensland police keen on fishing for his exceptional hand-crafted iceboxes.

Then came the real point of the letter. Bahnemann, in a perilous financial state, thought he might be able to do some business with his old nemesis.

When I mentioned boats to you lately, I must admit I had in mind contacting you at a later date since police here showed interest in our craft and thought it would make a marvellous police boat, having the capacity of being the largest trailerable craft made here.

Lewis promised Bahnemann he would drop in to see him on his next commissioner's tour of North Queensland and the boatbuilder said he was looking forward to it.

And please, accept my hand and sincere offer towards whatever help, request, or else is needed, then, should you need it, Terry, just say so, no frills, I am a friend.

PS: Please don't feel obliged to reply, Terry, I just wanted to write this lengthy letter and I feel better for it now.

Why did Bahnemann feel compelled to remain in touch with Lewis? Although a known eccentric, and a man whose financial fortune had always waxed and waned, what was the basis for this so-called friendship based on intermittent letters?

Lewis says he took pity on Bahnemann following his imprisonment all those years ago. Bahnemann may have been keeping his options open. By fate, the man who had helped imprison him was now the most powerful police officer in the state.

To his family, Bahnemann privately and keenly expressed his innocence regarding the shooting incident in 1959, although he offered little in the way of detail regarding his former wife, the prostitute Ada, and the night of his arrest.

Perhaps it was a case of both men – Lewis and Bahnemann – keeping their enemies close.

Medically Retired

Earlier in the year, Lewis had recommended that Jeppesen be transferred out of Licensing. Cabinet overruled it. Just over a month later the transfer was approved.

Immediately following this decision, the ALP's Keith Wright stood in parliament and said he felt impelled to read into Hansard a confidential document he had received. He only referred to the many police and bookmakers named in the document by their initials. In summary, the document detailed how major SP bookmaking syndicates were aware in 1978 that Jeppesen's removal was imminent and that soon they could move their business from Tweed Heads and back into Queensland.

It went on: 'Heads of the SP syndicates in Queensland have made an approach to police officer M with an offer to establish a fund of $60,000 as a pool with all syndicates contributing. This fund was to be sustained in advance and a weekly payment made to the police to protect the operating of SP betting in Queensland again.'

It said syndicate members had been 'hit hard' by Jeppesen and his crew and that the syndicates wanted the Licensing Branch under 'CI branch Superintendent M'.

'I believe there has to be a full inquiry,' Wright added. 'The information I have here is an indictment on this government and on elements in the Police Force.'

There was no inquiry and the Licensing Branch as Jeppesen had assembled it was quickly disintegrating.

Jock Lumsden, a Detective Sergeant (First Class) in Licensing at the time, recalls when things began to fall apart. He says Jeppesen and his team had 'plenty of work and plenty of kills' when the erroneous allegations against Jeppesen and his unit began filtering in.

Lumsden was out at Boggo Road one day and was observed and recognised by an inmate. The next thing he knew he was called in by Murphy and Atkinson for a formal record of interview. 'They suggested I had some knowledge of moieties paid in relation to this inmate,' he says. 'I'm not sure if they were trying to intimidate me. But they seized my official police diary and I never got it back.'

Later in 1979, Lumsden moved back to prosecution.

Jeppesen was medically retired on 6 September 1979, having been transferred to Mobile Patrols earlier in the year.

A month later, Commissioner Lewis would have some good friends to dinner at his home in Garfield Drive – guests included Barry and Sheilagh Maxwell, Jack and Peggy Herbert, and Eric Pratt. He noted in his diary the following week: 'Insp. Jeppesen out medically unfit; transfer of all other Police involved in Lic. Br. Suspect activities; some discontented Police contacting Premier.'

Bruce Wilby was transferred to Clermont, 274 kilometres south-west of Mackay. He had been told by Assistant Commissioner Brian Hayes that he 'needed to remember' he had a wife and three children. Wilby saw it as a direct threat and was happy to be out of Brisbane.

When Lewis again tried to move him without justification to Longreach after just six months, he objected and was summoned to Brisbane for a meeting with the Commissioner and his top men, including Brian Hayes.

They met in a large meeting room in police headquarters. Wilby recalls: 'I let Lewis have his say. "We know you've been bad-mouthing the department," he said. I told him I'd never bad-mouthed the department.

'He said, "As long as you go back up there and keep your mouth shut, you can stay in Clermont as long as you like. Can you do that?"'

The meeting ended, and as Wilby left the room Assistant Commissioner Hayes followed. 'I remember you from Mobile Patrols,' Hayes commented.

'And I remember you from there too, sir,' Wilby said.

'You turned out to be a proper cunt,' Hayes added. 'If it's the last thing I ever do, I'll have you out of this job, Wilby.'

'With all due respect, sir,' Wilby replied, 'I'll still be in this job and I'll piss on your grave.'

Lewis recalls the whole tawdry Jeppesen incident. 'Brian Marlin realised they were working hot ... some member of parliament told him apparently,' recalls Lewis. 'And then he ... must have got in touch with Greg Early and said he [Marlin] wanted to talk to me.

'Anyhow he talked to me one day and said what was going on and wrote out the names of fellows that were "enemies" if you like. And I got some senior officers to investigate the matter and it went on and on.

'They should have been pinched. They were interviewed and refused to answer questions. The file ended up going to the Crown Law office and they came back, and I don't remember this coming back but it would have come back to the deputy saying they can't refuse to answer questions like that.

'They can be forced to answer them but it never got anywhere, never went any further. Jeppesen – he should either have been somehow charged with something or forced to retire if you like, so he went out medically unfit.'

With Jeppesen's squad removed, new officers moved into the Licensing Branch. They were Harry Burgess, Noel Dwyer and Graeme Parker.

Quality Escorts

When Mary Anne Brifman, daughter of Shirley, decided to quietly re-enter prostitution as a young mother, she was fully cognisant of how her mother's tragic past was never that far below the surface in Brisbane.

Terry Lewis, who she claims she remembers as a child occasionally visiting the Brifman home in Sydney in the 1960s, was now the most powerful man in the Queensland Police Force.

Tony Murphy, too, had risen to Inspector and was in charge of the Bureau of Criminal Intelligence, and quite possibly on a level pegging with Lewis despite the disparity in rank. It was evident to some that, in their minds, Tony Murphy actually ran the force.

Still, these two men had been a part of Mary Anne Brifman's life since she was a small child. Now she was retracing her mother's foot-steps, albeit as quietly as humanly possible.

Mary Anne was still working solo out of an escort agency she called Quality Escorts. Despite her low profile she began to meet and get to know other sex industry workers in Brisbane.

'I never, ever paid any graft,' Brifman remembers. 'I knew of Hector Hapeta. I heard a lot of stories about Geoff Crocker from the girls. I didn't personally come across the Bellinos. They had their fingers in prostitution but they were mainly into gambling, that was their big thing.

'Nobody knew I was related to my mother. That was another era, anyway. By this time whole new crews had come on.'

Also, Brifman's marriage to Graham had broken down and she began living in different parts of the city – Lutwyche, Newmarket, then a flat in Kangaroo Point.

Then came the rape by a young police officer in an auto workshop in the city.

'It took courage to report it,' Mary Anne says. 'I didn't want to be known, but I did it because I didn't want it to happen to any other working girls.

'I was back doing what I never wanted to do. I was ashamed of the whole thing. All I wanted to do was get enough money to pay the rent and provide food for me and the kids.

'When the officer raped me it changed me, psychologically. I never wanted to be known as a victim, but the shame, and all those feelings I'd bottled up over the years and never shared … I don't know.'

Milligan Sings

After 14 months on Operation Jungle, an exhausted John Shobbrook got a telephone call in Brisbane from an old mate in the New South Wales Drug Squad. Would he like to know the whereabouts of one John Edward Milligan?

On the afternoon of Monday 10 September 1979, Shobbrook hopped on the next flight to Sydney and proceeded to a block of flats in Edgecliff, four kilometress east of the CBD.

'I knocked on the door and there was John Milligan,' says Shobbrook. 'It was a really strange feeling after working for over a year on the case. He wasn't surprised at all that we were arresting him.'

While Federal Police raided Hallahan's farm in Obi Obi on the Sunshine Coast, Milligan was taken to the imposing Customs House at Circular Quay and placed in an interview room.

Shobbrook told Milligan nothing about the operation he'd been working on. Then Milligan said: 'I know about your little Operation Jungle.'

Milligan expressed no interest in being interviewed.

'I don't need you to tell me anything,' Shobbrook said. 'We've been pretty thorough.'

The Narcotics Agent asked for the whereabouts of Milligan's passport. He said he'd spilled a bottle of ink on it and thrown it away.

Milligan was installed for the night in the nearby four-cell Phillip Street police station. Meanwhile Shobbrook headed across the harbour to Kirribilli where he knew Milligan's sister lived. She handed over the defendant's passport.

In the special Federal Court the next morning Milligan was ordered to surrender his passport. Milligan's solicitor said his client had lost his passport.

'I have it here,' Shobbrook interjected.

Shobbrook recalls Milligan's response: 'If looks could kill, I would have died on the spot. He realised I could be nasty too. That I could think as quickly as he could. He had a disregard for people he didn't think were up to his intellectual capacity.'

Shobbrook told Milligan he'd see him in two weeks at the next hearing.

Milligan hesitated. 'Can I talk to you?'

'No,' Shobbrook said. 'I'm going.'

'You don't know how big this is and who's involved,' Milligan said. 'I've got to talk to you privately.'

Shobbrook and Milligan convened in a nearby solicitor's briefing office and Milligan suddenly started talking about a Queensland triumvirate that consisted of Terry Lewis, Tony Murphy and Glen Patrick Hallahan.

Shobbrook couldn't believe his ears. He knew Milligan was a consummate liar and a great name-dropper. He might have had his little index-card database on every person he ever met to thank for his astonishing ability to credibly mix fact with fiction.

'You're going to have to get me protection,' he told Shobbrook. 'If I go to Long Bay I'll be killed. I'm telling you the truth.'

Milligan was moved to the Holsworthy Army Barracks in south-western Sydney. He was appointed a minder – a senior and experienced Federal Narcotics detective – who drove Milligan to and from Customs House.

'Milligan was a very intelligent person,' the agent recalls. 'I'd pick him up at the gaol every morning and bring him into town. He'd be immaculately dressed and smelling sweet as a lily first thing in the morning, but after a few hours you could smell Milligan's sweat. When we took him back at the end of the day you'd have to wind down all the windows of the car.'

Over three days, Shobbrook interrogated Milligan in Customs House. The interviews were recorded on tapes. 'I did the Operation Jungle record of interview,' Shobbrook says. 'We started talking about a broader area of corruption. As soon as each day's tapes were finished, they were flown straight to central office in Canberra.

'I had established a rapport with John Milligan. I used to sit and cry with him when he got emotional. You get to know them. He had a shoulder to cry on – it kept him talking.'

Milligan, trusting Shobbrook, directed him to a flat in Paddington where numerous documents were discovered, including bank transfer receipts that totalled $26,000, paid by Milligan into the account of former detective and Obi Obi farmer Glen Hallahan.

What Milligan discussed in those 72 hours was explosive. He

alleged that Lewis, Murphy and Hallahan controlled various aspects of crime and corruption in Queensland. 'Glen's the civil arm [of the trio],' Milligan said. 'Tony Murphy is in charge of security. Tony does the dirty work a lot.'

He said businessman, racing yachtsman and Bally poker machine importer, Jack Rooklyn, who had a mansion in Sydney's Darling Point, was one of the few 'heavies' who controlled the police. He said whatever Rooklyn ordered was 'accepted as a directive by Terry Lewis, and by Tony and by Glen in Queensland'.

Milligan had a clear memory of the Rat Pack when he was a young legal associate working in Brisbane in the mid-1960s. 'The Rat Pack was the gang of five. That was Bischof, Bauer, Lewis, Murphy and Hallahan, and they were reputed amongst the legal profession to be the heavies of the CIB and the corrupt characters of the city. Legion were the stories about the corruption and the graft that went on,' Milligan said.

He told in great detail stories of his past, his association with the killer Johnny Regan, his links with the highest echelons of organised crime in New South Wales, and his conversation with Hallahan about the impending death of prostitute Shirley Brifman, just days prior to her actual death by drug overdose.

Milligan admitted that over time he had dropped $26,000 into one of Hallahan's bank accounts and that they had concocted a story that if it was ever queried, the money was for the sale of a parcel of Hallahan's farm to Milligan. (There were never any documents to prove the sale.)

Milligan went on to indicate a conspiracy over the departure of the head of the Brisbane Narcotics Bureau, Max Rogers; Lewis, Hallahan and company had arranged for a former Queensland state police officer, and friend of Hallahan's, to replace him, and that the transition was a 'foregone conclusion'. '… We left it to Terry to do,' Milligan said.

Milligan added if he ever had a query about police he might encounter he always sought counsel from Hallahan to see if 'he is okay or not'.

The drug importer also explained why the Jane Table Mountain importation was finally given the green light. Organisers went ahead 'after the power structure in Queensland had been consolidated after the State election up there [12 November 1977, won by the Nationals on a platform of law and order] and Lewis had been Commissioner for a couple of years so that there could be no immediate allegations against him if anything went wrong'.

There were details, too, of Hallahan arranging for an old friend and police colleague from the 1960s – who had subsequently enlisted in the Commonwealth force – to mock up an investigation into the Jane Table Mountain importation, including a record of interview with Milligan, to hedge off any serious scrutiny of the case prior to Shobbrook's dogged work.

Milligan was under pressure on several fronts, not the least being that the Royal Commission into Drug Trafficking, under Justice Philip Woodward, had wound up and the commission's report was weeks away from being delivered. The royal commission had been sparked by the disappearance of anti-drugs campaigner Donald Mackay on 15 July 1977. The hearings commenced on 10 August that year.

Also, the Williams Royal Commission of Inquiry into Drugs – which had been running since October 1977 and headed by Queensland judge Edward Williams – was set to conclude.

'Why am I talking now?' Milligan asked Shobbrook. 'Because I don't trust Hallahan, because I'm in a great deal of trouble with you people, I haven't been protected from you, I don't trust Hallahan now – I haven't since the royal commission. I've felt that I'm expendable ...'

It was an extraordinary tale. It involved murder, drugs and corruption within most levels of state and federal police departments, the judiciary and government. If true, what John Edward Milligan told John Shobbrook during the three days of interviews in Customs House, Circular Quay, Sydney, exposed corruption on a scale never before revealed in Australia.

As for Queensland specifically, Milligan outlined a deeply entrenched system of corruption that involved police and various members of government, its tentacles going to the very top.

Milligan admitted to Shobbrook that the only reason he embarked on the ambitious Jane Table Mountain drug importation was to earn money for Queensland and New South Wales crime syndicates in the absence of expected incomes from the introduction of poker machines in Queensland. He exposed a long-time underworld campaign to ensure government approval of the machines, and the millions of dollars for Bally Corporation, Bally employee Jack Rooklyn and a host of other well-known crime figures that would follow.

Sydney businessman Jack Rooklyn and his associates, he said, had hoped to have had them installed in the Sunshine State much earlier. There was one major hurdle – Premier Joh Bjelke-Petersen.

'... it was taking so long to get Jo[h] Bjelke-Petersen organised with the poker machine thing ... in fact in the end it was shelved for a couple of years and they're being revived now.

'Jack Rooklyn cracked up on them and said ... and these are the words he used on the telephone, I was there – "It's only a hillbilly State" – anyway and you know the financial return ... it wasn't so great compared with New South Wales that all this hassle and drama sort of continues with the Queensland politicians ... proving too much of an extension for Rooklyn.'

In the end, an impatient Rooklyn decided that if he could stop the introduction of the pokies into Queensland he could protect his investment in his in-line machines.

It was an irony that the Premier and the decision on pokies was proving such a sticking point.

'... they contained Bjelke-Petersen,' Milligan said, going back into recent history since the removal of Police Commissioner Ray Whitrod in late 1976. 'In the areas that they wanted, e.g. the Ministry of Police and the Ministry of Justice they had their men organised and there was such a conspiracy in Cabinet so as to keep Jo[h] Bjelke-Petersen under control in relation only to their matters and I'm particularly here referring to the matter with which I was associated with, e.g. the introduction of poker machines into Queensland.'

Milligan alleged to Shobbrook that prior to the Whitrod coup he was instructed by Glen Hallahan to keep his head down and live quietly in his flat in New Farm until the regime transition had been effected. (Milligan did as he was told, and resided at the Glenfalloch apartments, Unit 1B, 172 Oxlade Drive, New Farm.)

'One of the plans on the drawing board, which I was scheduled for involvement [in] was the introduction of poker machines in Queensland,' Milligan said. 'Jack Rooklyn had already handled the negotiations with San Francisco and they had a situation organised through [William] Lickiss [Liberal Attorney-General appointed in 1976] who was working for them, to arrange to introduce poker machines in Queensland subject to certain conditions and so on and so forth.

'It was a very complicated plot and it was something that didn't come to fruition because they couldn't control Jo[h]. He's just too erratic.'

Another 'friend' was the member for Merthyr, Don 'Shady' Lane.

'He's too tidy and pug,' said Milligan of Lickiss. 'I gather, I haven't anything direct here to prove it but he was going to get a share of the poker machine thing and another one was, um, Lane, the member for Merthyr … ex-policeman … they were very put out when he didn't get a Ministry last time with Bjelke[-Petersen]. Oh, there've been many discussions.'

Shobbrook was incredulous. And Milligan feared for his life.

'I want to live,' he implored Shobbrook. 'I want to get married, I want to have kids; I can't do this for the rest of my life. I can't live the rest of my life getting deeper and deeper, and that's what it's becoming – has become.'

He implied to Shobbrook that nobody had informed on the 'Queensland group' and survived.

Death of the Monster

After receiving his peculiar visitor – Clarence Osborne – at his office at the University of Queensland in 1976, criminologist Paul Wilson became fascinated with the psychopathology of the paedophile despite being disturbed by his physical presence. Wilson had authored many books on a variety of topics, and the Osborne case lured him in. Wilson was astonished at the breadth and range of Osborne's sexual life. He would later write:

> The "boys" he formed relationships with came from diverse back-grounds. While the literature on boys who seek relationships with adult males suggests that they come from working-class homes marked by poverty, violence and general family breakdown, many hundreds, if not a thousand of the boys he had sex with, came from affluent middle-class homes … the rich, prestigious suburbs of semi-tropical Brisbane provided many young men who were, in some cases, to have clandestine affairs with a man who was old enough to be their father and, in some cases, their grandfather.
>
> Unbeknown to the solicitors, doctors and real estate salesmen who lived in the plushness of St. Lucia or Indooroopilly or in the hills of Hamilton, their sons were relating to a small, relatively insig-nificant man (at least as seen by others) with a degree of intimacy that they never manifested towards their socially and economically important fathers.

Osborne, however, was far from a humble 'father figure' to lonely or neglected boys. His life was preying on underage males, so much so that everything in his life outside of his work as a court and then Hansard reporter was fashioned to facilitate his perversions. His house in Eyre Street was just 500 metres from the then main route to the Gold Coast, via Holland Park and Mount Gravatt. Osborne traversed the highway to the coast looking for and successfully picking up hundreds of young male hitchhikers.

Also, he lived a short drive from the Garden City Shopping Centre, opened in 1971 and a magnet for the area's youths. He would photograph boys in and around the complex, and once recorded his eternal gratitude to mothers who bought their sons 'tight shorts'.

Then, in late 1979, fate caught up with Clarence Osborne, world-class shorthand writer, bird breeder and child abuser. A Brisbane mother overheard her son discussing being photographed in the nude by an elderly male. The mother ultimately ascertained that someone called Clarrie Osborne had been taking pictures, not just of her son but other boys who had volunteered to pose naked.

Without approaching the police, the concerned mother happened to mention the situation to the wife of a police officer at a social gathering. A sting was then put into play. The officer organised a stake-out of Osborne and witnessed the Hansard reporter photographing boys in bushland near the city.

As Wilson would later record: 'Police went to Clarence Osborne's house [in Mount Gravatt], searched it thoroughly and took three car loads of tape-recordings, files and photographs, together with Osborne himself, back to police headquarters.

'As the police involved were not from the squad which usually deals with such matters – the juvenile aid squad [sic] – they were reluctant to take further action against Osborne until the material had been more thoroughly perused and legal advice on what Osborne could specifically be charged with was obtained.

'What we do know, however, is that the police were most cooperative with Osborne for reasons that are still unclear. They did, after all, drive him back to his house.'

Extraordinarily, a man found in possession of thousands of photographs of naked children and audio recordings of his sexual encounters with them and who freely discussed with police his predilections and modus operandi during his short interview time with them, was free to go and in fact given a lift home to 54 Eyre Street.

However, former Juvenile Aid Bureau officer Dougal McMillan says the JAB was not informed of the Osborne case on the day he was brought in by CIB officers and questioned. 'They [the original investigating officers] never came near us,' McMillan says. 'I was absolutely stunned when I heard this story. I couldn't understand why the CIB hadn't followed it up and they'd let him go.'

Had the case, of its type unprecedented in Queensland criminal history, been brought to the attention of Commissioner Terence Lewis? With Lewis as the spiritual father of the Juvenile Aid Bureau, as appointed by Frank Bischof, and with the voluminous details of Osborne's activities only just being realised and referred on to the JAB, did word get back to the man at the top?

Not according to his Commissioner's diaries. On Tuesday 11 September 1979, the day Osborne was questioned at headquarters, Lewis does however coincidentally record, as his last business for the day, prior to knocking off at 6 p.m., a call he made to 'Dr Paul Wilson re course for prospective Supt's'.

That night, Osborne, sitting at home in Eyre Street, surrounded by his 'life's work' inside a house rigged with secret microphones and recording equipment, wrote a note explaining he had been questioned by police and that 'this was the best way'.

He then went into the garage down a driveway on the northern side of the house. He hooked a hose up to his exhaust pipe and into the cabin of his vehicle, started the engine and pressed 'record' on the audio equipment he had similarly rigged in the vehicle, and used countless times to record his illicit conversations with boys and the sounds of their sexual trysts.

Osborne, ever the pedant, allegedly recorded his own last words: 'I've been sitting here ten minutes and I'm still alive ...'

Osborne's body was discovered the following day – Wednesday 12 September.

That day, Lewis spoke with a fellow officer about the behaviour of Licensing Branch officer Bruce Wilby, called a Dr Ian Wilkie regarding an upcoming Child Accident Prevention Conference, and attended a cocktail party at the Crest Hotel in the city. Before that, however, he had reason to phone Dr Paul Wilson again regarding the academic's 'biased view and comments' made on a *Nationwide* television report. There is no mention of Osborne or his death, despite talking with Osborne's future biographer twice in two days.

On the Thursday, Lewis again remonstrated with Wilson regarding his 'incorrect claims on *Nationwide*'. Wilson recalls that he later approached Lewis about the possibilities of interviewing detectives in relation to the Osborne case.

Dougal McMillan went out to the Mt Gravatt house after Osborne's body had been removed. He took with him a Justice of the Peace. With Osborne dead, there was no one on whom to serve a search warrant.

'There were stacks of files – some of them quite old – on all sorts of things,' he recalls. 'He'd also been conducting some bodybuilding in the backyard. He really had stuff there that wasn't fit to broadcast. There were many photographs of boys at certain stages of development. They were not appropriate. We found out he'd had a big fire in the backyard on the night that he died.'

The Osborne files were moved to JAB headquarters on the fourth floor of the old Egg Board Building in Makerston Street and secured in a safe. 'My understanding is the case went as high up as the Premier's office because of who Osborne was,' McMillan says.

Osborne was cremated in the last week of September. On Thursday 20 September, a small death notice appeared in the *Courier-Mail*. 'Osborne, Clarence Henry, of Eyre Street, Mount Gravatt. Passed away at home 12.9.79. Sadly missed friend of John and Pauline and "Uncle" of Peter and Geoffrey. There will be no funeral service as requested.'

It wasn't until 30 September that the *Sunday Mail* outlined details of the case of the MONSTER SNARED BY HIS CAMERA.

Detective Sergeant Don Reay, of the Juvenile Aid Bureau, reportedly said it would take three months for three officers to work through the Osborne material, stored in steel filing cabinets. 'There must be a message in all this, but at this stage we can't work it out,' Detective Seargeant Reay said.

He encouraged Osborne's victims to come forward. 'We would like them to witness destruction of their files,' Reay added. The files, he said, would be reduced to ashes following their analysis.

At the time of the 'monster's' death, Dr Paul Wilson was galvanising his idea to write a book on the life and times of Clarence Osborne, having waded through a selection of the eccentric stenographer's photographs, index cards and unpublished memoir. The book – *The Man They Called a Monster* – would be published two years after Osborne's death. It would argue that Osborne had been misunderstood, and that he had basically acted as a father figure to young boys who had little or no meaningful communication with their own fathers.

In one of the notes accompanying the book, Wilson thanks a good friend for his help in being able to interview several detectives in the Juvenile Aid Bureau who worked on the Osborne case.

'The Commissioner of The [sic] Queensland Police Force granted me permission to interview … detectives. His assistance in this respect is gratefully acknowledged.'

Boxes

Jim Slade was finally where he wanted to be.

He was working in the Bureau of Criminal Intelligence, and was being mentored by Tony Murphy, one of the finest police officers he'd ever worked under.

But after almost two and a half years of exciting, non-stop work in the bureau, he began to see things that didn't quite fit. The lifestyles and habits of some of his colleagues weren't matching their salaries.

'Alan Barnes would go in on raids and it was nothing for him to take us all out to dinner later, and for him to sit down and drink two bottles of Dom Pérignon Champagne,' Slade remembers. 'When I found out it was $100 a bottle I nearly died. There was no way in the world he could afford $100 bottles of wine. I knew something was going on there.'

Another officer had a new car every year. Others had boats worth thousands of dollars, purchased without a loan. Some officers regularly bought and sold houses.

'It was quite obvious to me and Norm [Sprenger] that some of them were on the take,' says Slade.

Other officers were often exceedingly violent against certain offenders. One had a depth of violence that shocked even Slade.

'He possessed an incredible violence,' Slade recalls. 'He was a very, very good boxer. He just showed no mercy. Where another police officer would hit once, this guy couldn't stop. He'd absolutely just tear that person down.

'If he was sent to do a job by anyone … whoever he was set upon they'd have to watch their p's and q's.'

To Slade's mind, some of them were not only capable of grievous bodily harm, but murder. 'By that time in life I was able to pick some of the corrupt people, and a most interesting thing came to my attention,' he says. 'Most people that were protégés of most people I knew to be corrupt turned out to be corrupt. But most people who were protégés of people who were honest like Fred Maynard and a few others were never corrupt.

'When I say corrupt I'm talking about going in, picking up a brief-case full of money, and walking out with it and splitting it.

'Another interesting thing I reckoned was that most of those people not corrupt had really strong family backgrounds, the corrupt ones didn't. Maybe the importance of family was a consideration with the corruption side of things.

'I was able to put them in boxes. You work with him? I'm going to have to look out for you. Nine times out of ten I'd be right.'

Slade said he never personally saw Murphy or Barnes take money.

Then again, by his own admission, he wasn't looking very hard. 'I tried to explain to my wife that I was so engrossed in what I was doing – it was nothing for me to have major investigations like Terry Clark, the painters and dockers ... undercover operations where we were running informants for other detectives,' says Slade.

'I cursed myself for not identifying it and doing more about it. But when you're in that situation ... if it's not affecting you, maybe you let it go.'

Spy vs Spy

In the first week of November 1979 an extraordinary collision of events rang alarm bells not just with Lewis and the other members of the old Rat Pack, but within government, both state and federal.

Firstly, Terrance Clark, head of the Mr Asia drug syndicate, was arrested and held in London following the discovery of the handless body of Christopher Johnstone in a quarry in Lancashire. Clark had been wanted for questioning over the Wilson murders, among others, after he had slipped the net in Brisbane.

Secondly, the interim report of Justice Williams' Royal Commission of Inquiry into Drugs recommended that the Federal Narcotics Bureau, described as inefficient and only mindful of its own image, be disbanded and its duties taken over by the new Australian Federal Police Force.

Thirdly, Justice Woodward in New South Wales tabled his own report into drug trafficking, and in it named several major gangs responsible for the bulk of Australia's drug importations. One was 'The Milligan Group'.

Brisbane-based Federal Narcotics Agent John Moller, recuperating from a serious motorcycle accident, was incensed at the proposed dismantling of the bureau, and was nominated by his fellow agents to defend the bureau on a local talkback radio show. He spoke on condition of anonymity. His quotes about Milligan and his links to Queensland police and politicians were subsequently picked up by the *Courier-Mail*.

As a result, the newspaper ran a sensational page-one story on 8 November. POLITICIANS LINKED TO DRUG RINGS, the headline said. 'Narcotics agent tells of secret files.'

The report revealed: 'Several Queensland politicians were named in confidential Federal Narcotics Bureau files as having had connections with people in the drug smuggling world,' a narcotics agent said yesterday. 'We do not have files on the politicians. But they are mentioned on files as being connected with people in a drug organisation.'

That organisation was Milligan's. Moller also revealed that the bureau had recently interviewed 'a former Queensland policeman [Hallahan]'.

'There is no doubt he [the former policeman] was connected with that syndicate and he was assisting them. We know he still has connection with senior police and they have helped certain members of that syndicate to get off charges that they should not have got off.'

Moller, the unidentified source, said the day would come when he could name those involved in the Milligan syndicate, and added: 'People are being killed because they are involved. We're past the days of busting people with deals of grass. We are closing in on the big fish.'

The day after the story was published Detective Sergeant Alan Barnes contacted Commissioner Lewis with some vital information.

Lewis diarised: 'Det. Sgt. Barnes called re John Moller being Narcotics Agent speaking to media; bugging Murphy and Hallahan's phones; Hallahan still claiming friendship with Murphy and me and an anonymous call re me heading Drug Smuggling ring.'

As for Moller, whose identity was so swiftly uncovered and reported back to Lewis, he received a volley of telephone threats at his home in Carseldine in the city's north. 'I had the usual stuff – "we know where you live,"' John Moller remembers. 'But they also told me they knew that my son [Scott, then three] played on a particular footpath of an afternoon.

'They told me to back off.'

Scandal in the House

Hot on the heels of the growing drugs scandal was Labor opposition leader and the member for Mackay, Ed Casey.

After just one year in the job as Labor head, the affable Casey was a competent and steady parliamentary performer without wit or flair, unlike his predecessor Tom Burns.

A former truck business operator and bank clerk, and a keen sportsman in his youth (he would later be a devoted patron of the Queensland Table Tennis Association), the Catholic Casey wanted to capitalise on the Moller revelations and used the privilege of parliament to do so. He thought he had an opportunity to inflict huge damage on the government.

So on Tuesday 20 November, at 11.34 a.m., Casey rose in the House: 'On 7 November 1979, an allegation was made on Brisbane radio that several Queensland politicians were named in Federal Narcotics Bureau files as having had connections with people in the drug-smuggling world.'

Minister for Local Government and Main Roads Russ Hinze immediately rose to a point of order, hosing down Casey. 'I query the authenticity of the document that is being presented to the House by the Leader of the Opposition, and I ask whether he is making a ministerial statement, a personal explanation, or just what he is doing.'

Casey was again permitted to speak, citing subsequent newspaper reports on the narcotics scandal. 'Through resources available to me,' Casey went on, 'I have been able to locate the said Narcotics Bureau agent and have spoken with him on this subject.

'I want to make it quite clear that, as a result of discussions with him, I am satisfied that no member of the state parliamentary Labor Party is named in the files to which he referred and that the parliamentarians concerned are from the Government coalition parties in this House.

'I have learned that the Narcotics Bureau in Sydney possesses the taped record of the interrogation of a notorious international drug runner following his recent arrest. In this taped record of interview, which I understand was also witnessed, I am informed that the drug operator refers by name to a senior member of this Queensland coalition Government.'

The Premier himself rose on a point of order and tried to flip the entire thing back on Casey: 'All I want to say is that the Leader of the Opposition knows that his policy is to legalise the use of drugs.'

Casey ploughed on. He argued that as former Queensland police officers had also been named, the Woodward Royal Commission 'clearly shows that there is overwhelming evidence to indicate the presence of a drug-smuggling ring in Queensland of huge proportions.' He claimed that further evidence would be forthcoming in the impending Williams Royal Commission of Inquiry into Drugs, and called on the Premier and the Queensland Government to set up its own royal commission.

The Speaker interjected and said Casey would not be permitted to make any further personal explanations and was asked to resume his seat. Casey's motion to be further heard on the matter was voted down 49 to 20.

By mid-evening, following the television news where Casey had been interviewed about the drugs scandal, Police Minister Ron Camm stood in the House and fired back. 'Is this another Casey lead balloon? Is this another statement from the Leader of the Opposition that has no substance in fact and cannot be proved by any action that may be taken by the Police Force in this State?'

Deputy Premier and Treasurer Dr Llew Edwards also weighed into the fracas: '... when questioned by the reporter, the Leader of the Opposition refused to give information and squirmed in his seat. He said that he would make it available to parliament tomorrow. For that reason parliament is now giving the Leader of the Opposition and, indeed, all Opposition members, an opportunity to make the allegations now.'

At 10.12 p.m., Casey relished the opportunity to reply to the criticism. 'It was less than 12 hours ago in this Chamber that the very same persons who have tried to make dramatic gestures on this subject were the movers in having me gagged in this parliament. They said absolutely nothing in relation to it.

'Why the turn-around? Why, in this short space of time, has the Government taken the step of holding a special Cabinet meeting and then displaying a complete about-face in this parliament? It is for the simple reason that the Government is absolutely frightened out of its very boots at the public reaction to the way in which it has been conducting the affairs of this State. Very dramatic!'

'Give us the names of the members of parliament. Come on!' the Premier baited.

Casey went on to outline details of the drug trade in Queensland, citing the Woodward and Williams royal commissions and his own sources. Amid constant interjection from the coalition and innumerable points of order, Casey eventually came to the strange tale of John Edward Milligan, former Associate to District Court Justice Seaman.

'On his arrest, Milligan gave long and detailed evidence to the Narcotics Bureau in Sydney. It was very alarming evidence. I am led to believe that the evidence given by Milligan implicated a very senior member of this parliament and also very senior police officers in this state.

'I also believe that Milligan made it quite clear in presenting the evidence to the people doing the interrogation that he had friends in high places, and that the people doing the investigation should be careful. Consequently, a tape-recording was taken in front of witnesses. My understanding is that the tape was then sent to Mr. Fife, the Federal Minister responsible for the Narcotics Bureau. The tape is, or was, in the possession of Mr. Fife.'

After a long, fiery debate, Casey finally put his trump card on the table. He said '… that particular person Milligan did name in that tape the Minister for Justice in this parliament, Mr. Lickiss, as having had some dealings …'

The House erupted.

'I would be a little bit concerned if I were Mr. Lickiss,' said Casey.

'Order! The House will come to order,' shrieked the Speaker.

The debate raged into the early hours of the morning leaving little doubt that Casey's revelations and the bitter debate had its impact on Bjelke-Petersen and the government.

While still baying that the ALP policy was to legalise marihuana, the Premier made an extraordinary concession: 'I have listened with a great deal of interest to the allegations being made by the Leader of the Opposition both within this House and outside it. Mr. Justice Williams is presently commissioned by the Australian Government and four of the State Governments, including Queensland, to inquire into drug trafficking. He is currently finalising his reports to the respective Governments.

'I have asked that he give the highest priority possible to investigating the allegations – not only the allegations mentioned here but anything associated with the Labor Party.'

It was 1.56 a.m., and within a matter of hours the government and opposition would be at each other's throats again.

The Premier was true to his word. Although Justice Williams was tying up his lengthy royal commission into drugs, Bjelke-Petersen wrote to the Secretary of the Commission asking the commission to give priority to allegations that officers of the Queensland Police Force and members of the Queensland Legislative Assembly were involved in the illegal drug trade.

He also asked Justice Williams that all Queensland-related issues that were being dealt with under the umbrella of the commission be deferred until this priority was acquitted. Queensland police officers O'Brien and Pointing were attached to the commission to assist Justice Williams.

Later that month, Milligan came up directly in Lewis's official diary: 'Insp. T. Pointing called re interview with a Mr Milligan wherein he stated that ex-Det. Hallahan said that he would have me give any necessary assistance to Milligan.'

Here was direct evidence that Pointing, working for the commission of inquiry and with full access to confidential Narcotics Bureau data, was surreptitiously reporting back to the Commissioner.

The Milligan allegations were as serious a scrutiny as any previously suffered by Lewis, Murphy and Hallahan. Still, the life of the state's top cop continued as usual. On the day Pointing passed on his drug intelligence to Lewis, the Commissioner and his wife, Hazel, attended a march-past of the 4th Signals Regiment in King George Square, and later that evening the Commissioner went to a Christmas party for the Fraud Squad.

Lickiss Rises

About 11.20 a.m. on 21 November, the MPs, including the Premier, were all back in the chamber in Parliament House at the southern end of George Street, just hours after the previous day's explosive debate that had roared into the early morning.

Naturally, Minister for Justice and Attorney-General Bill Lickiss, the member for Mount Coot-tha, was one of the first to speak.

> Mr. Speaker, as you and other honourable members of this House would expect, I rise to reply to certain allegations raised last night by the Leader of the Opposition,' Lickiss said. 'The honourable Leader of the Opposition has "named" me as being accused of being associated with people involved in drug-trafficking. The accusations are, to say the least, most nebulous and come from sources which are again, to say the least, tainted.

Lickiss was dour and matter-of-fact. It was a quality that had kept him in good stead through a colourful life. He was a navigator with the RAAF in World War II and later a surveyor, map-maker and pineapple farmer. He was awarded a bravery medal following a dangerous incident during the Brisbane floods of 1974. He had been elected to parliament in 1963.

> The source seems to be Milligan who is reported to have claimed that he had friends in high places. Presumably, I am supposed to be one of Milligan's friends. I can say, categorically, that I do not know any John Milligan and certainly am not a friend of the John Milligan who is the primary source of the allegations ...
>
> My reputation for honesty and integrity is such, I believe, that it and any of my dealings with trust accounts or any aspects of criminal investigation and prosecution will stand up to the closest scrutiny.

Fellow Liberal and relative newcomer to parliament, the equally colourful Angus Innes, member for Sherwood, later rose in defence of his colleague.

'The nearest the Minister for Justice would ever have come to drugs would be cutting the grass on his own rider-mower around his home. It was an outrageous proposition, and one that was totally unsubstantiated. He [Casey] did not rely upon any evidence whatsoever,' said Innes.

The House returned to relative calm, debating the Motor Vehicle Safety Bill. During the discussion Don Lane was accused ironically of being a 'big, tough ex-cop', and he in turn accused the Opposition of being 'anti-police'.

In the afternoon, members chewed over the *Port of Brisbane Authority Act* Amendment Bill. Kev Hooper, the member for Archerfield, offered a soft but curious interjection: 'Is there any truth in the rumour that Mr. Max Hodges will be the new chairman?'

It had been only three months since Hodges, the former Police Minister under Commissioner Ray Whitrod, and perhaps his greatest ally, had stepped away from his political career. It was Hodges who had joined forces with Whitrod in attempting to eliminate the Rat Pack in the early to mid-1970s, and who had lost the Police portfolio when he stood up against Premier Bjelke-Petersen over the street-march fiasco, where a young woman was struck on the head with a police baton. He knew of John Edward Milligan's activities, as did former commissioner Whitrod. Now, in the wake of the drug scandal, his name resurfaced.

Again, Hooper's contacts were spot on.

At that, parliament adjourned comparatively peacefully at 5.39 p.m.

The Stranger

Just over a week before Christmas Day 1979, a young man with pitch-black hair, an English accent and spectacles, started work at the Licensing Branch on the seventh floor of police headquarters in the city.

He was Nigel Donald Powell, 28, who had previous experience

with the West Midlands Police, covering Birmingham, Coventry and Wolverhampton in central England.

Powell had joined the Queensland police as a constable on 5 July following his training and was seconded to the City station in Makerston Street. Just days into his new job on 'beat #2' in the CBD, at 10.55 p.m. in King George Square, beneath the giant illuminated clock face of the City Hall tower, Powell came across a dishevelled man who appeared a little worse for wear.

Powell wanted to check if the man was alright. The man became aggressive when Powell enquired about his wellbeing. 'Police here are terrible,' the man said in a European accent. 'You're harassing me!'

'I'm just trying to see if you're alright,' the young constable replied.

The man identified himself as Albert Rosen, chief conductor of the Queensland Symphony Orchestra, and that he was residing at the Crest Hotel. Powell was shocked by the man's reaction to police, something he'd never experienced in the West Midlands.

'I remember going home [to a small flat in Herston] and having a conversation with my wife, Heather, about it,' says Powell. 'She remarked that it appeared people didn't like the police in Queensland. She told me she didn't tell anyone that I worked as a police officer in Brisbane.'

Three weeks later, Powell was on the beat again in the city. He decided to check out the public toilets in Albert Park, a notorious gay beat not far from the police station in Makerston Street. It was 1.30 a.m. on 26 July.

Powell checked the Ladies. His partner went into the Mens, and quickly rushed out.

'I've caught two of them at it,' the young officer said.

Powell then interviewed one of the men, who identified himself as Paul Anthony Griffin, a television broadcaster. (Griffin was in fact an anchor for Channel Nine news in Brisbane. In 1979 he would win a TV Week Logie Award for Most Popular Male Personality in Queensland.)

'Tell me what happened here tonight,' Powell asked Griffin.

'I went to use the urinal and had a torch shone in my face,' the media personality replied.

'You must realise the other officer has seen a circumstance that raises suspicion.'

'I cannot see why.'

Powell asked Griffin about his movements that evening.

Griffin said he had finished work around midnight at the station up on Mount Coot-tha and had dropped into Lucky's pizzeria in the Valley. 'I had a couple of glasses of wine and wanted to go to the toilet before I left so I came here,' Griffin explained.

'Did you see the other gentleman in the toilet?' Powell inquired.

'No, it's very dark in there.'

The media identity refused to go down to the station to discuss the matter, and an inspector was called to the scene. It was the word of two against one police constable, and Griffin was permitted to leave without charge.

Not long after that, on 10 August, Powell arrested a man who had damaged a glass pane and some lights at the Allegro Restaurant in Edward Street. It turned out the offender, who acknowledged he had committed the offence, was detective Sergeant Second Class Peter Reiken of the Fraud Squad. Reiken was taken to the city station and charged on summons.

Powell had unwittingly breached a powerful police code. He had arrested a brother officer. He wasn't made to forget it.

Walking the beat, police cars would cruise by him. 'Are you Powell the Pom?' they'd ask. 'You arrested Peter Reiken?' On other occasions they would simply gawk at him and shake their heads.

On 15 October, Powell was then sent to the suburban station at Nundah – 8 kilometres north-east of the CBD. Just two months later he was informed he'd been transferred to the Licensing Branch. He took up his duties on 17 December.

Unwittingly, Powell was placed in a difficult situation. He was the stranger in town, and he had a natural desire to be liked and accepted.

Powell had come from a comparatively sophisticated police force in the UK. In Queensland he hit an antiquated system head on.

Not only that, he entered a Licensing Branch where inter-personal suspicions and paranoia were literally palpable. There were officers in such a state of nervous disrepair that they could not hold a tea cup steady. The place was paralysed with secrecy.

When Powell was rostered on for a job he would travel to a location with other officers and was only told at the very last minute what the job was, and who or what was the target.

'I wanted to fit in,' he says. 'I went in believing everyone was good and these were the people I wanted to work with. If you walked up on a couple of officers in conversation, they'd just stop. People were paranoid.'

Powell learned very quickly that there appeared to be a number of unwritten rules. There seemed to be an arrangement with the massage parlour girls whereby they were arrested on rotation and invariably pleaded guilty. And when a strip club and brothel called the World By Night, not far from the old National Hotel at Petrie Bight, was raided for illegal sales of liquor, they were back trading as normal an hour later.

Powell, though, was considered a misfit by the older Queensland officers in Licensing. One gnarled detective asked him: 'Are you nationalised yet?' To which Powell replied: 'Don't you mean naturalised?' The young man was instantly labelled a smartarse.

One of his first jobs in the branch was an unusual situation at the Cloudland ballroom at Bowen Hills. On the night of 24 December 1979, Jimmy and the Boys, a shock-rock band headed by outrageous singer Ignatius Jones, described by one music journalist as a 'high voltage package of filth, glorious filth', were performing. Word had gotten out that the band planned to burn on stage an effigy of baby Jesus.

'I was put on the balcony to signal to the guys below when it was about to happen,' remembers Powell. 'The marihuana smoke was drifting up to where I was. I was the lookout with the radio.

'It was bizarre. Almost the entire Licensing Branch was there. It never happened, the burning of the effigy. What were we going to charge them with anyway if it did?'

Still, his outsider status – not just within the branch but to the city's criminal milieu – would prove to be an advantage. It was decided Nigel Powell would be sent undercover.

He quickly grew a beard, suited up in civilian clothes, and began infiltrating clubs, gambling dens and health studios of Brisbane by night.

'Corruption is about the great unsaid to me,' says Powell. 'The only time these things break down is when those involved get a bit confident. They don't think twice that there might be a mole.'

Powell burrowed into the underworld, not knowing that his work and his observations, his keen ear and the joining of a few elementary dots would, in the end, loosen the foundation of a monstrous edifice of institutionalised corruption that had been in full swing before Powell had ever even heard of Queensland.

1980s

A Working Holiday

Just prior to the start of the new decade, Commissioner Terence Murray Lewis gave an interview to the *Courier-Mail* to mark the third anniversary of his being in the top job. Lewis, at 51, told the reporter Jim Crawford that he wanted to remain Commissioner – 'God willing' – until he was 65 years old. That would keep him in the chair until late February 1993.

On 1 January 1980, Commissioner Terry Lewis was back at his desk at 7.20 a.m. If he was anticipating a slow silly season, he would soon be disappointed.

The pressure was on, particularly following the Milligan revelations and with the Williams Royal Commission of Inquiry into drugs set to reconvene. Both Lewis and Tony Murphy were required to give evidence. It would be Murphy's first appearance before a royal commission since the National Hotel inquiry in 1963. The farmer Hallahan was also due down from Obi Obi to give evidence in the District Court.

On 2 January, Lewis recorded in his diary: 'Supt Murphy called re Royal Commission on Drugs.'

Three days later, Lewis paid a visit to Frank Bischof's wife at The Gap 'and collected medals and uniform from Mrs Bischof'.

On Monday 7 January, the day he was set to commence his recreation leave, Lewis was 'interviewed by Messrs T. Wakefield and Bird from ... Royal Commission on Drugs re my knowledge of Hon. Lickiss; G. Hallahan; W. [Sic] Milligan; A. Murphy; resignation of Mr Whitrod; Poker machines; National Royal Comm; and drug increase in Queensland. Off at 10 a.m. With Hazel and [son] John to Faraway Lodge [Gold Coast] on holidays.'

There he socialised with John Meskell, Brian Hayes, Syd Atkinson and other policemen and their wives, all the while conducting police business by phone before returning to Brisbane six days later, then heading back to the coast for another week.

During his break, Lewis read Justice Woodward's 2080-page Royal Commission into Drug Trafficking report.

Then on Monday 4 February, Commissioner Lewis gave evidence before Justice Williams in the District Court. Lewis said of Hallahan: 'He resigned from our force, I understand, in 1972 and I have not seen him or spoken to him or communicated with him in any way since 1972.'

Murphy, in evidence, said he knew of Milligan but didn't know him. Hallahan said he had known Milligan since 1965. He was asked about the $26,000 that Milligan put into his account: 'That was for a small section of my property that I sold to Milligan,' Hallahan said. 'I left it to him to take care of the paperwork.'

Hallahan, one of the state's most feted detectives in his younger days, said he didn't have any idea that Milligan was a drug dealer. Their dealings were purely business. (Shobbrook had already been to the Queensland Land Titles Office and proved there was no deed of sale for the land Milligan supposedly purchased. The Williams Royal Commission made no such investigation and Hallahan's story was accepted.)

Shobbrook was in the court to observe Hallahan take the stand. 'The day that Hallahan gave this evidence to the royal commission was the first time that I had physically laid eyes upon him,' Shobbrook recorded in his memoir. 'The name was so familiar, the face from several black and white photographs was familiar, and there he was – so near and yet so far. Little did I realise at the time that I'd never get closer to him.

'As far as I was concerned I was still compiling a brief of evidence against Hallahan. I had submitted that incomplete brief of evidence to the Commonwealth Crown Solicitor's office ... for an unofficial opinion as to whether a prima facie case existed against Hallahan.

'I was informed that there was already sufficient evidence to lead to a conviction.

'But in spite of the encouragement that I had been given by the Commonwealth Crown Solicitor's office, the case that I had put together against Milligan and Hallahan was being swamped by a torrent of cover-ups, lies and false accusations by my own senior Australian Federal Police officers, by Royal Commissioner Justice Edward Williams ... by Terry Lewis and naturally by Glen Patrick Hallahan.'

Retired assistant commissioner Abe Duncan telephoned Lewis to offer him his knowledge of Milligan that harked back to 1971 when Duncan was interviewing the late prostitute and brothel madam Shirley Brifman. Duncan remembered Hallahan bringing Milligan into the offices of the Crime Intelligence Unit to meet him and Norm Gulbransen.

Murphy again telephoned Lewis: 're aspects of connection by Milligan and Peter Monaghan in Royal Commission Inquiry'. A nervous Police Minister Ron Camm rang, 're Milligan's history'.

Narcotics Agent John Shobbrook, who had chased down Milligan and uncovered what he believed was a massive network of corrupt police in Queensland, was called to give evidence before Justice Williams.

To his shock, Williams was aggressive towards Shobbrook and accused him of making up Milligan's allegations to harm the good name of the Queensland Police Force, and fine officers like Lewis and Murphy. He told Shobbrook: 'If I can prove that you have perjured yourself before this commission then you will be going to gaol.'

'I informed Justice Williams of the reel-to-reel tapes [of the Milligan interviews] but to my knowledge Williams neither subpoenaed the tapes, nor did the Narcotics Bureau Central Office in Canberra, who held the original tapes, offer them to the [commission] to clear the smear of misconduct that Williams was implying against me,' Shobbrook says.

He later bumped into Detective Sergeant Barry O'Brien, one of the Queensland state police seconded to work with the commission, who said to him: 'You are ratshit with the Queensland Police Force.'

Shobbrook desperately sought support from head office in Canberra and his union, the Customs Officers Association. Shobbrook soon realised he'd been hung out to dry.

How could one of the most important investigations into heroin trafficking in Australia to date, allegedly involving senior Queensland police, be cursorily dismissed by Justice Williams, and the investigator himself be accused of making up evidence so he and the Narcotics Bureau would look good?

Shobbrook was an honest officer. He had pieced together the Operation Jungle saga with the utmost diligence and professionalism. How could this be happening?

He more than suspected that dark forces had been at work behind the scenes to, once again, diffuse and derail evidence against the corrupt practices of members of the Rat Pack. His thoughts echoed the suspicions of undercover expert Jim Slade, who suspected his boss Tony Murphy, and Justice Williams, had possibly joined forces in over-blowing a Sunshine Coast drug raid in order to make the Federal narcs look inept.

As for Hallahan, Justice Williams made no adverse findings against him and the allegations he was dealing in drugs with John Milligan. 'The Commission merely records that evidence presently available to it falls short of establishing as even a reasonable possibility, that Hallahan has ever been involved in wrong-doing in connection with illegal drugs,' Williams found.

Hallahan was off the hook. Again.

He told the *Telegraph*: 'I had no doubt in my mind the Commission would come out unilaterally, publicly and absolutely absolving

me ... the suggestion I am still under investigation is wrong ... if there
was any evidence connecting me with any wrongdoing of any sort,
someone would have done something about it by now.'

Somebody did. His name was Douglas John Shobbrook.

But nobody, not even a royal commissioner, wanted to know.

Looking for the McCulkin Girls

Six long years after Barbara McCulkin, wife of local gangster Billy
McCulkin, and her two daughters – Vicky Maree and Barbara
Leanne – vanished without a trace from their Highgate Hill home in
the mid-summer of 1974, the public were finally going to learn the
truth about one of the city's most enduring mysteries.

Police said the McCulkin vanishing rivalled the case of the
Beaumont children in Adelaide who disappeared in 1966.

In fact, police had a theory about the McCulkins that revealed
something far more sinister. They were of the opinion that the
McCulkin girls and their mother, along with the missing prostitute
Margaret Ward, who vanished in 1973, and Vincent Raymond Allen,
a Warwick railway yard worker who disappeared in 1964, were all in
fact murdered by the one killer.

All vicitms had dealings with a man who had a 'heavy' reputation
in the Brisbane underworld. CIB Chief Superintendent Tony Murphy
confirmed that they had a 'very strong suspect'.

Police wanted a joint inquest and were granted their wish. It opened
on Monday 11 February 1980, at the Holland Park Magistrates' Court
before Coroner Bob Bougoure, SM. It would prove to be one of the
most riveting coronial inquests the city had seen in years. The court-
room was heavily guarded by riot police, including an inspector and
three detectives.

One of the first witnesses was well-known criminal identity

Vincent O'Dempsey. He was on remand for another unrelated matter and was handcuffed to the dock, deemed a 'security risk'. He replied 'no comment' to the questions put to him.

Later, Detective Sergeant Trevor Menary told the court that in 1964 Vincent Raymond Allen went on a trip to Sydney with O'Dempsey, and he told police in an interview about the robbery of a jewellery store in Toowoomba.

O'Dempsey was later charged with breaking and entering over the jewellery and granted bail. Allen was set to give evidence against O'Dempsey over the case but disappeared before the matter came to court.

Menary then gave evidence about Margaret Ward, saying she had worked as a prostitute at the Polonia massage parlour in Lutwyche. It was operated by Cheryl Diane Prichard, the de facto wife of Vince O'Dempsey.

In 1973 Ward and Prichard had been charged with prostitution. Both women went to see a solicitor and Ward vanished after the meeting.

Menary, in an interview with O'Dempsey in 1979, had put to him that he had murdered Ward to prevent her giving evidence against Prichard.

As for the McCulkins, Menary would allege that O'Dempsey was seen leaving the McCulkin home in Dorchester Street, Highgate Hill, on the evening of 16 January 1974, in company with a criminal named Gary 'Shorty' Dubois.

Billy Stokes, serving time after being found guilty of the murder of boxer Tommy Hamilton, got a mention early in the inquest. Stokes, in his former publication *Port News*, had accused O'Dempsey and Dubois of murdering the McCulkins.

Billy 'The Mouse' McCulkin – former husband to Barbara – told the Coroner's Court that after his family had gone missing he had warned O'Dempsey that he would blow the heads off anyone who harmed them.

Then Inspector Basil 'The Hound' Hicks took the stand. Hicks said Billy McCulkin had telephoned him at the Crime Intelligence

Unit in 1974 and said he believed his wife and children had been taken and murdered. Hicks said McCulkin was convinced O'Dempsey had murdered them.

At the time, Hicks had interviewed Janet Gayton, a friend of the young McCulkin girls who lived directly across the road. She told him she had seen two men enter the McCulkin house on 16 January and went over and asked the girls who their visitors were. They replied the men were their father Billy's friends Vince O'Dempsey and 'Shorty'.

Another neighbour, Peter Nisbet, told the court McCulkin had complained to him at the time that her husband Billy was giving her a hard time. Nisbet said he had had several conversations with her about the Torino and Whiskey Au Go Go nightclub fires in 1973. Barbara told him she would be able to 'put him away for five years' given the information she had on Billy and the fires.

In the end, the Coroner recommended that O'Dempsey and Dubois be charged with the murder of the McCulkins. He found there was a body of circumstantial evidence sufficient enough for a jury to find the two men guilty of murdering Barbara and the girls.

O'Dempsey told the Coroner: 'I'm not guilty. I've never murdered anyone.'

A year later to the day, the Crown would drop all charges against O'Dempsey and Dubois. Attorney-General Sam Doumany entered a nolle prosequi.

The McCulkins would be added to the police department's already bulging Cold Case files.

Milligan Takes the Stand

In early March in Sydney, Milligan pleaded guilty to the charges laid against him stemming from Shobbrook's investigation. He appeared before Justice Barrie Thorley in the New South Wales Supreme Court.

Shobbrook, presenting the facts and antecedents, made sure Glen Patrick Hallahan's involvement in the case was outlined to the court and entered into the record.

'Has this man Hallahan been charged?' Justice Thorley asked Shobbrook.

'Not yet, your Honour.'

'When he is charged I want him brought before my court.'

The judge asked Milligan if he would prepare a signed statement outlining Hallahan's involvement in his case. Milligan stayed silent.

'Well, Mr Milligan, I will postpone sentencing and remand you in custody for one week while you consider your answer to that question,' Thorley said.

As prison officers prepared to take Milligan back to Long Bay Gaol, he indicated to Shobbrook he would get the statement together. He wrote the statement on 18 March and it was given to Federal Police officer Bill Harrigan.

The allegations in the statement included: that in 1977 Hallahan and Milligan discussed importing heroin into Queensland using light aircraft; that Hallahan provided $1000 to Ian Barron to charter a light aircraft to New Guinea on the first dummy run; Milligan took $3000 from Hallahan to buy the heroin in Thailand; that Hallahan was called on the telephone when the drugs were purchased and the drop was made over Jane Table Mountain; that when Milligan informed Hallahan the recovery of the drugs would be difficult, Hallahan ordered him to continue searching for them; that the single parcel recovered was sold in Sydney, and some of the proceeds were transferred into Hallahan's Commonwealth Trading Bank account in King George Square, Brisbane.

On 19 March, Justice Thorley sentenced Milligan to 18 years' gaol on three heroin charges – two pertaining to a conspiracy to import over the Jane Table Mountain situation, and a third to an unrelated importation involving a female federal undercover agent.

The next morning Milligan was escorted to Brisbane to appear before Williams' inquiry. John Shobbrook was in the public gallery. Milligan asked the commission if his evidence could be heard in camera. Understandably, he felt his life was at risk if he gave evidence against Hallahan in an open court.

Justice Williams replied: 'There has been too much said to this Commission off the record; if you have any allegations to make then you'll make them in public.'

Incredibly, Williams expected Milligan to incriminate Shobbrook about the fabrication of the Operation Jungle evidence.

Milligan lied and told the commission he knew nothing of Hallahan's involvement in drug trafficking. It may have saved his life.

Milligan was then asked to confirm that Shobbrook was lying. Instead, the convicted drug importer said: 'It is unfair to Shobbrook to say anything that infers that we concocted a story or he was concocting a story. He believed that what he was doing was in the best interests of the Bureau and was honest. So it is untrue to say that ... he wanted as much information as I could give him.'

Milligan said he did not invent things.

'You are not saying he [Hallahan] ever had anything to do with drugs are you?' he was asked.

'Well, I don't wish to answer that question,' Milligan replied.

One investigator attached to the commission reflects: 'Milligan made some very serious allegations against Lewis, Murphy and Hallahan going back to the 1960s. Those allegations were swept under the carpet by the Williams Royal Commission.'

Milligan was again asked if he had any information relating to Hallahan and drug trafficking.

'No,' he said.

'No further questions.'

Shobbrook was flummoxed. He was shocked that the five-page statement of allegations against Hallahan, ordered to be produced by

Thorley in Sydney, wasn't introduced and that Milligan wasn't asked about it.

Around this time, senior Canberra-based officers for the Australian Federal Police flew to Brisbane to 'counsel' Shobbrook. In short, he was told to lay off Hallahan and the entire investigation.

Shobbrook broke down. His work had been for nothing.

Within a couple of months he would be superannuated out of the force, deemed 'medically unfit'. He was 32.

In 1981 Justice Williams would be knighted.

Super Saturday

Constable David Moore was doing such a good job in public relations that he was put in charge of the unit.

He designed posters that depicted police officers as human beings, and began to modernise school presentations about 'stranger danger' and other important educational messages. He produced pamphlets and eye-catching stickers. The PR office was next door to the Crime Prevention Bureau down in Makerston Street, and the small unit used to have a few laughs at the 'hick show' their office neighbours put on week after week.

Moore, in turn, was given a 'long leash', and his class presentations in schools across Brisbane were proving popular. The police force was getting some substantial congratulatory feedback courtesy of Moore's initiatives.

One day he was summoned to Ron Redmond's office.

'What are you doing on Saturday?' Redmond asked Moore.

'Why?'

'You're going up on television,' Redmond said.

'No, I'm not,' he replied emphatically.

Producers of the popular children's program, *Super Saturday*, hosted by Fiona MacDonald, television celebrity Jacki MacDonald's sister, wanted a policeman to appear in a small slot.

Moore, contrary to his outgoing character, hesitated. He was a bit cautious of the television medium. Still, he did as he was ordered, and appeared on the show.

During his segment he was paired with the show's wildly popular and satirical puppet Agro, a cross between a Muppets character and a bath mat. Agro was witty, cynical, and managed to extol humour that simultaneously appealed to children and adults. Agro was the mischievous imp, harassing the show's host, eating flies and committing naughty acts.

'They put him [Moore] on TV with him. At that time Moore was a Constable First Class,' recalls a colleague. 'This was a one-off. They wanted someone to talk about stranger danger or road safety. So he sat there. Agro came on. He absolutely took the piss out of Moore.

'He [Agro] called him "Constable Economy" because he was Constable First Class. He [Moore] thought, you little bastard. He gave it back to him.

'The thing was Moore could speak; he wasn't the perception of a dumb cop.'

The episode descended into chaos.

'At one point Moore was breaking up with laughter so much he couldn't breathe,' the colleague recalls. 'Everyone was in fits of laughter. In the end the producer came up to Moore and she said that that was the most fantastic thing. All weekend he worried about it. He thought he was going to be in trouble.'

Host Fiona MacDonald remembers Moore as a good-looking, likeable young man. 'He was a charming and gregarious young policeman,' she says. 'He had a very easy-going way about him and he was eager to chat. We all liked him a lot.

'He was a great communicator. He shared a lot of interesting information and stories. He was Mr Nice Guy.'

On the following Monday, Moore was summoned to his superior Sergeant Ross Melville's office. 'You're going back up there again next Saturday,' Melville told Moore. 'The switchboard lit up. You were a huge hit and they want you back.'

'Constable Dave' was born. He appeared with Agro every Saturday and ultimately presented his own segment about police work.

'He started to involve other police,' Moore's colleague said. 'He would take traffic branch police up. He even had John "Bluey" O'Gorman up there, blowing up a piece of mince wrapped in alfoil in the bush outside the studios to demonstrate how you don't play with bombs or firecrackers.

'It was every Saturday of his life. He couldn't do anything. A taxi would take him up and bring him back.'

Then Moore had a masterstroke idea. Why not induct Agro as a police constable? 'He approached Terry Lewis,' the colleague said. 'By this time Moore had quite a lot of contact with Terry Lewis. He needed permission to do stuff. What could he do or say, what couldn't he do or say on television?

'Moore went to Greg Early and Greg would ring him back and say – the boss has approved that. He had direct access to Early and often the boss would be there and he would come out and speak with Moore about what was happening.'

Fiona MacDonald says the program also began to develop a strong relationship with Commissioner Lewis. 'Lewis was close to us,' she recalls. 'I remember him being up in the studio a lot. It was very good publicity for the police image.'

Constable Dave quickly became a celebrity in small-town Brisbane and soon started working on local radio. It was here he would meet and befriend the popular and successful ABC broadcaster, William Hurrey.

Another Briefcase Full of Cash

In the lead-up to the 1980 state election in late November, Dr Denis Murphy, newly elected Queensland President of the ALP, received a remarkable communique from Premier Joh Bjelke-Petersen.

Bjelke-Petersen suggested they meet on some urgent political business, and Dr Murphy obliged. He met the Premier in his office in the Executive Building on George Street.

Denis Murphy was an extraordinary conciliator as well as a respected academic and author. He had managed to negotiate an internal reorganisation of the Labor Party – the change from the Old Guard to the New Guard – without much long-standing fallout or enmity, and was determined to not only modernise and replenish the Party's finances but to make the ALP a viable election force. But nothing could have prepared him for the offer Bjelke-Petersen was about to put on the table.

The then Federal Leader of the Opposition, former Queensland police officer and minister during the Whitlam era, Bill Hayden, was keeping an eye on Labor candidates for the state election when his attention was drawn to the Party's man standing for Ipswich – Joe Sciacca. Sciacca was up against the formidable Llew Edwards.

'I didn't give him much chance of beating Edwards because Edwards was very highly respected and popular, although he wasn't a populist sort of political operator,' says Hayden. 'He [Joe] was a very private person. And the family had a coal mine ... a coal miners' background. His father worked in the mines. They'd been busted by the Depression.

'All of a sudden Joe's spending money, got a TV company in. And I thought, Jesus, this is going to be costly. And I said, "Where are you getting that money from, Joe?" And he said, "It's coming from head office. I don't ask any questions. I just take it." And it'd be thousands.'

Hayden was nonplussed, so he paid Dr Murphy a visit.

'Denis Murphy ... told me that Bjelke-Petersen had contacted him and offered him so many thousands,' Hayden recalls. 'It was a ... five figure amount and a very big five figure amount. And he [Murphy] went up and had a talk with [Bjelke-]Petersen and [Bjelke-]Petersen said, "Well, we'll give this money to you but you've got to spend it on these campaigns." They were all ... seats that the Liberals held. Edwards was one and I don't know who the others were, but Joh wanted to get rid of them.'

According to Hayden, Denis Murphy was to proceed to the offices of broking business Bain & Company to pick up the money. He was then handed a cheque.

'[Dr Murphy] said, "Oh, no. I'm not going to accept a cheque. I want money in a ... in a briefcase. I want new notes",' Hayden recalls. 'And he told me he got all that money later in notes in the brief-case. And ... he said, "I couldn't take bloody [ALP State Secretary] Manfred Cross. He's been a boy scout for too long. He won't be part of this."

'And when this came out, but no one knew the detail, Manfred said, "I think they're trying to blame me as going with Murphy." He said, "It's just not true. I know nothing about it."'

Hayden says: 'But that was the depth of animosity between the coalition parties ... [Bjelke-Petersen] wanted to get rid of the ... he would rather have a Labor man in Ipswich than Llew Edwards.

'So he was ... Joh Bjelke-Petersen was fighting on two fronts. Basically within his coalition he was fighting the Liberals and he was fighting the Labor Party on the other front.

'I honestly don't think he took Labor too seriously. I think he thought he'd get away with it. There was arrogance there. Been running around for a long time doing all of these Machiavellian deals. You know, they were pretty ruthless bastards ...'

Legendary ALP figure Manfred Cross confirms the cash transaction: 'It was a secret deal. We were offered money. I have no doubt it happened. It was not out of character for Denis – he was very prag-matic. He might have gone to pick up the money on his own. I don't think the Administrative Committee knew about it.'

Hayden's story would later be supported by another anecdote from farmer and grazier and the member for Callide, Lindsay Hartwig.

'It was an August evening just prior to my overseas trip to Zambia [in 1980, three months before the state election],' he recalled. 'I was sitting in the [parliamentary] dining-room – I can show honour-able members the table – when the member for Archerfield [Kevin Hooper] walked in.

'I was the only member in the dining-room at that time and the honourable member made to go to the area in which the Labor Party usually sits.

'I said, "Kevin, come over here and sit with me. There are two of us here; let's talk, even though we are on opposite sides of the fence."

'Within a few minutes we were joined by the Premier. I am prepared to go on any lie-detecting machine that anybody can bring forward and I am prepared to swear an oath on the Bible that in the ensuing minutes the Premier and the member for Archerfield discussed ways and means of defeating Liberal Party members at the coming election.'

Hartwig said independent Labor members were mentioned. 'I heard the Premier say, "Kevin, we have to seek ways and means of defeating these Liberals." I don't tell lies, but I kept that a secret. As a matter of fact, I went outside and had a good vomit.'

Commissioner Lewis was fully au fait with who the Premier liked and disliked in the Liberal Party. Bjelke-Petersen had a particular enmity for Treasurer Llew Edwards, according to Lewis.

'You couldn't trust Llew in any shape or form,' Lewis says. 'Even old Joh, he was a condescending fellow if you like … [he said] when Llew's around you sleep with one eye open.

'Joh tolerated him because he had the brains if you like to be Treasurer, plus the fact that in those days the National Party had to live with the Liberal Party … what he [Edwards] put up they had to accept. I'm sure he [Joh] didn't like him.'

There were possible reasons, too, for Lewis disliking the Treasurer and Deputy Premier. Around this time Edwards had been told by a member of the Liberal Party Executive that Commissioner Lewis was 'unhappy about my leadership of the Liberal Party' and that it needed a change of leadership.

Edwards got on the phone to Commissioner Lewis. 'He denied that he had ever told anybody this and that I had his full support,' Edwards would recall later. 'I indicated to him at this time that it was none of his business to be involved in politics. He assured me that he was not involved in any way.'

A mutual distrust was developing.

Edwards called the Commissioner again not long after, saying he had heard that Lewis, while attending a Police Union meeting, had told those present that the department's diminished funding rates and subsequent low staff numbers were the fault of Treasurer Llew Edwards.

'He categorically denied that he had said this and he informed me that he thought I was doing my best to get money for the police force and that my story was totally inaccurate,' Edwards remembered.

Llew told Lewis he thought morale was low in the force because some specific commissioned officers had been given rapid promotions. 'I particularly mentioned Mr. [Tony] Murphy, Mr. [Ron] Redmond and Mr. [Syd] Atkinson as having received rapid promotion whilst Mr. [Basil] Hicks, Mr. [Noel] Creevey and Mr. Tom Pointing had indicated to me their fairly stationary position,' Edwards said. 'He assured me he would investigate those matters and report back to me and he also indicated to me that I should not advise the Premier of our conversation on that date and I told him I had already advised the Premier of my intended conversation [with Lewis] …'

It didn't end there. As Edwards was also the Racing Minister, he was concerned about illegal SP bookmaking.

To counter this thriving trade, Edwards thought of establishing a special squad of police, 'hand-picked and trusted', who would work with Racing Department officials to knock SP gambling on the head.

'... I raised this matter with the Premier who indicated that it would be a good idea but before he did anything about it he would speak to the Commissioner of Police,' said Edwards.

'Within 24 hours of my raising this issue with the Premier I received a telephone call from the Premier indicating that he had discussed the matter with Terry Lewis and he said that both he and the Commissioner would not support any moves in this direction because they wanted the police force to remain as one unit.

'I never had any direct conversation with ... Lewis about this proposal.'

Justice Williams Reports

After Premier Joh Bjelke-Petersen had implored Justice Williams to explore allegations that some Queensland police and politicians were involved in the illicit drug trade following an explosive parliamentary debate in late November 1979, the good Justice's special 30-page Report to the Queensland Government on Matters of Particular Relevance to the State of Queensland was completed in April and tabled in the House.

Justice Williams dismissed many allegations raised by Opposition leader Ed Casey during that debate as being based on hearsay. He said North Queensland most certainly had 'attractions in terms of geography, climate and population distribution to those who illegally import, produce and traffic in drugs' for the supply of larger southern markets, as in Sydney and Melbourne.

'An example of activities so organised and controlled – in this case from Sydney – is provided by the activities of John Edward Milligan and his associates … which so excited the interest of Mr. E.D. Casey, Leader of the Opposition.'

More importantly, he reported that the public in North Queensland had a 'loss of confidence' in the enforcement of the criminal law dealing with drugs.

'There is no question of recrimination in respect of this loss of confidence,' Williams concluded. 'Its causes can be identified and steps can and should be taken to regain it. Reasons for it include the circulation of the stories of police involvement and corruption earlier referred to. Pressure of demand on police resources and on policemen are another reason.'

Justice Williams recommended that 'a number of police officers of drug squad experience' be stationed in North Queensland. 'These officers would also be available to assist other police in the area in their efforts against criminals engaged in illegal drug trafficking and be free to concentrate a proportion of their activities on identifying and dealing with, either alone or in conjunction with other police forces, large scale activities in the area.'

It was a recommendation that the government and police took seriously. By the end of the year, Commissioner Lewis's chief fixer – Tony Murphy – would be deployed to Cairns to try and take control of a rampant drug problem. He would be followed shortly after by crack undercover operative Jim Slade.

One-Armed Bandits

One of the vexing problems for the pious Premier Joh Bjelke-Petersen into 1980 was whether or not to introduce poker machines into the state's pubs and clubs.

The issue had been debated in the media, and the Registered and Licensed Clubs Association in Queensland was lobbying hard for pokies, given New South Wales and the Australian Capital Territory already had them. But the government had yet to take the bull by the horns.

It did, to a degree, on 26 May.

In what was to be Cabinet Decision No. 32985, it was determined: 'That a Departmental Committee be established comprising representatives of the Departments of Police, Justice, Welfare Services and Culture, National Parks and Recreation to examine the detrimental effects on the community of poker machines and that a report be submitted to Cabinet as soon as possible.'

A week later Lewis wrote to the various departments asking for the names of their representatives on the poker machine committee. He also penned a memo to Assistant Commissioner Brian Hayes, nominating him as chairman of the committee and asking him to ultimately 'furnish a report to me for submission to the Minister in terms of the Cabinet Decision.'

Commissioner Lewis made no mention in his diary of the decision to form a committee on pokies for more than a week, despite direct contact with his Minister, though common sense would dictate that poker machines were discussed, however informally.

It wasn't until Friday 6 June, in a meeting with the Premier that the 'cabinet minute of poker machines' was discussed, along with a report on the activities of 'International Socialists', Australian Federal Police 'intrusions' and 'our next minister'.

The following day – a Saturday and Lewis's day off – he read the 147-page 'Report by Justice Moffitt, Royal Commissioner on "allegations of crime (organized) in clubs".'

The committee on pokies consisted of chairman Hayes, one of Lewis's trusted right-hand men; Colin Pearson, Under Secretary for the Department of Justice; Cedric Johnson, Under Secretary for the Department of Welfare Services; and Stan Wilcox, Bjelke-Petersen's former private secretary and the Director of Sport for the

Department of Culture, National Parks and Recreation.

The committee met through June and into July on the tenth floor of police headquarters. Its 18-page report was completed and signed off at the end of the first week of July.

It summarised the detrimental impacts and possible consequences of the legislated introduction of poker machines as: implications for criminal activity (including organised crime); addictiveness associated with the peculiar nature of poker machines; weakened domestic relationships; impaired work effectiveness; and increased alcohol consumption.

It quoted from the report of the Moffitt Royal Commission report, tabled in the New South Wales parliament in 1974, and in particular focused on the Bally Corporation, run in Australia by Jack Rooklyn, the cigar-smoking Sydney businessman who had met Lewis for food and drinks in the Mayfair Crest in Brisbane in 1979.

The Moffitt report said that some club officials in New South Wales were receiving large cash incentives to take Bally poker machines in their establishments. It included other references: 'Our information indicates that large amounts of American currency are being brought into the country illegally and it is this money, when converted, that is used in the payment of secret commissions.

'Rooklyn has stated he believes poker machines will be legalised in Queensland and Victoria within the next two years and he wants to take over the lot.'

The committee was mindful of the welfare of decent, upstanding Queensland families and the possible impact of pokies and their addictive qualities. 'It is the experience of a number of government departments that gambling can be harmful to parents, children and family life and that it can be the catalyst which leads to criminal activity and imprisonment,' their report said. 'If the poker machines receive the cloak of legal respectability, it is possible that the remaining barrier to many social problems may be seriously diminished.'

The committee complained that it did not have enough time to prepare a detailed response to the issue as 'there is very little currently available in published form' on the detriments of one-armed bandits.

'Police enquiries reveal that the various police forces throughout Australia do not have substantive material which may assist in this regard,' the report went on.

'However, it is felt that the contents of this report may assist Cabinet to appreciate the detrimental effects which have been highlighted in papers and articles.'

According to Jack 'The Bagman' Herbert, Lewis gave him a copy of the committee's report.

'I took it down to Sydney to show Jack Rooklyn and I went to his house in Vaucluse,' Herbert wrote in his memoir *The Bagman*. 'I remember he had a swimming pool with a mosaic floor. He read the report while I was there.'

There was a reference to the way Rooklyn did business that Rooklyn didn't appreciate. Herbert said: 'Maybe that had something to do with him trying to renege on the $25,000. He said he only wanted to pay $15,000 and someone else could make up the rest.

'It took a while to bring him around but in the end Jack Rooklyn agreed to pay the whole lot himself. What he didn't know was that Terry was only keeping $15,000. The rest was a kickback for me, which I shared with two of Rooklyn's associates, John Henry Garde and Barry MacNamara.'

Herbert alleged the money was handed over to Lewis during a meeting again at the Crest, and Hebert was later given his share of the money. Lewis supposedly said: 'That should do you.'

'When I got back to the office and counted the money I found there was only $9000,' said Herbert. 'I phoned Barry MacNamara and told him we were $1,000 light. Barry was hopping mad.

'He was all for docking $1,000 from Terry's payment at the end of the month. I knew this wouldn't go down well – it wasn't worth taking on the Commissioner of Police over $1,000 so we agreed to let sleeping dogs lie.'

Lewis denies he had anything to do with a report that would accommodate the needs of Jack Rooklyn in exchange for cash. 'We thought it'd be alright for the government to let poker machines in,' he recalls. 'But I knew what Joh thought … he would have shot me.

'I checked through it [the report]. It went back quite clearly saying – no, no way in the bloody world. If I was friendly with Rooklyn, I would have proposed that it be considered. He was the poker machine man. I would have said that. Why would he give me $25,000 to say no, you can't have them?

'Herbert would have said – leave it to me and we'll get the money to him. The bloody bastard.'

In fact, Herbert would later tell investigators he copied the report in the T&G Building in Queen Street before taking it down to Sydney to show Rooklyn.

'I can't recall whether I allowed Rooklyn to keep a copy against the wishes of the Commissioner of Police because Rooklyn's that sort of person. He's an abrasive sort of chap and gets his own way … but I do remember destroying a copy of the report on my return to the airport.

'I do remember tearing … I tore some up and put it in a bin at Bondi, because I went to Bondi when I left his [Rooklyn's] place because my son had a unit there.'

Herbert said he never kept a copy of the report. 'It was a load of old rubbish as far as I was concerned,' Herbert recalled. 'I knew it was a, well my term was a hoax, more or less, you know. I was firmly of the opinion Joh … wouldn't allow poker machines into Queensland anyway. It [the poker machine report] was just a rort.'

Treasurer and Deputy Premier Llew Edwards was fully cognisant of the public debate on the introduction of poker machines and their possible impact on the community. He was looking forward to seeing the committee's report. He never did.

Edwards later recalled: 'As far as I knew until that time a report had been requested and I had no idea whether or not it had been completed. I am aware that such a report ... was never submitted back to Cabinet.'

Office Romance

On Monday 16 June 1980, a farewell party was held at the Sandgate home of another policeman for Task Force officer Senior Constable Bill Douglas. He had been transferred to Caboolture. Lorelle Saunders was rostered on duty that night. Her boss, Lobegeiger, had instructed that she and other Task Force officers on duty attend the farewell party.

'I may need you as my driver,' Lobegeiger told Saunders. 'I might let my hair down and have quite a few. The bastards want to send me north, after all I've done – then I might just stop working [and] be a drunk like the rest of them.'

The party kicked into the evening. Lobegeiger drank beer. He was ready to leave the party around midnight. They drove to Saunders' home where he was to drop her off. Lobegeiger invited himself into the house in Koola Street, Wishart.

'I agreed and then made coffee,' Saunders said. 'Whilst we were having the coffee he took hold of me and told me he was in love with me and had been for some time.

'We talked about our feelings for each other, he was holding me, kissing me for most of this time.

'He commenced to phone me daily. This was the commencement of a very deep and intimate relationship between us. He asked me not to mention our relationship to anyone in the Department.'

The next month Lobegeiger was transferred to Cairns. He told Saunders he wished she was going with him on the long, lonely drive up to Cairns.

It was, indeed, the beginning of a loving relationship.

Saunders, however, wasn't aware that having visited her for an hour to say 'goodbye', so to speak, he had then driven around to the home of another lover, Cecily Bull, and driven to the Far North with her.

Meeting an Informant

On 22 July 1980, Commissioner Lewis received a phone call from the Honourable Russ Hinze. Police Minister Ron Camm was retiring from politics. Lewis wrote that Hinze called 're possible appointment as our Minister'. Hinze was officially given the portfolio on 28 July.

He began immediate regular contact with Lewis, as was to be expected. For example, on Wednesday 27 August, he called 're any files on Messrs Bishop or White MLA's ...' Both Bruce Bishop and Terry White were members of the Liberal Party.

Bishop was a vociferous critic of the Bjelke-Petersen regime and White had just been elected the year before. So just a month into the job, Hinze was using the police department to gain leverage against his political opponents.

Lewis had considered Camm the best minister he had worked under. Now he had the voluminous and verbose Hinze to contend with. 'Hinze was alright,' remembers Lewis. 'He was good as a minister in this sense – we'd say to him we need more cars, we need more men, and he'd get up in bloody Cabinet ... and he'd pursue things very strongly.

'But he caused you some problems too. Because he knew everybody, he was at the races, he'd get half-full of soup or three-quarters full or whatever. He had horses, he was in everything. You couldn't dislike him but you couldn't sort of take him home to dinner either.'

Lewis's diary for Saturday 4 October records that he 'saw informant Jack'. The 'Jack' was in fact his old friend Jack Herbert. Lewis remembers that Herbert had, for some inexplicable reason, some information to pass on about vice in the city.

'Herbert saw me – it wasn't hard to see me – and said, look, I can give great information to you ... that will help you show your men, you know, what's going on,' says Lewis. 'And of course it was, you know, brothels here, SP betters there, and I wrote down, one ... three, four, five, six, seven, eight, eighteen ... and then put it in the back of a pocket book.

'When the end of the year came up I put it in the back of the pocket book for the next year and then forgot about it because it really didn't come to anything. I suppose I let him think that he was being a good boy and doing things to help.'

The 1980 pocket book was black. (The following year's pocket book was red.) The codes written in the back of the book were either single capital letters or abbreviations. There was a Jack R (Rooklyn?), Tony R (Robinson?), C (Crest Hotel?), FVG (Fortitude Valley game or illegal casino?), Syd (Atkinson, Gold Coast Superintendent?), Brian (Hayes, Assistant Commissioner?), Your H (Home?) and My H (Home?).

Why would the Queensland Commissioner of Police take what purported to be confidential information on the whereabouts of various brothel and illegal gambling activities from Herbert, several years out of the force and himself up to his neck in profiting from brothels and SP bookmakers? Why abbreviate what may have been specific geographic locations? And why would Lewis take the data seriously enough to develop a 'code' system that he kept in a small personal diary over the work and indeed the resources of his own Licensing Branch? Just to make Herbert feel valued?

Lewis complains that as commissioner he was used by many people he thought were friends. 'I'd say Murphy used me, in all due respect,' he reflects. 'There wouldn't be many of the others I'd feel used me. Some were against me … the likes of [John] Huey, [Ross] Dickson and those fellows. But I would think 50 out of 5000 would have been against me.

'I suppose I was overly … too kind to undeserving bastards. I don't regret it. I just wish I'd been a little more forceful in cutting off a few heads. I do feel I could have … if I'd been harder on a few, some of this probably would never have happened.

'My dad was an easy-going … I don't ever remember him raising his bloody voice.'

Murphy to Cairns

Near the end of 1980 Commissioner Lewis sent Tony Murphy, then 53, to take control of the Far Northern Region. He was based in Cairns. The posting was in part a response to Justice Williams' special report to the Queensland Government on the illegal drug trade up north. Lewis says he posted Murphy because he felt it would be good experience for him as a senior officer.

Jim Slade says the drug problem was getting out of hand. 'If you look at the timeline that I'm talking about, it was at that particular time that things were going out of control in the drug scene, and there was massive money,' Slade remembers.

'I'm sure that if you could get all of the information from the Italian desk of the Australian Bureau of Criminal Intelligence down south, and then what the Bellinos were doing, their method of operation and how they were getting crops done, and a couple of the other people that the Bellinos stood on or that Murphy got out of the way, I think you'd start to see a picture of why he went up there. I honestly don't know. There was no reason other than that.'

The *Telegraph* police reporter Pat Lloyd reported on the transfer. His story read: 'Supt Tony Murphy would "tear the heart out" of the drug-running trade in the far north of Queensland, a senior police officer said today.

'The move is seen by police observers in Brisbane as a declaration of war in the worrying "hot spot" of the drug trade.

'As well, police pointed out, success in controlling his first regional appointment would virtually ensure Supt Murphy promotion to Assistant Commissioner in 15 to 18 months.'

In an interview with Ric Allen of the *Sunday Mail* in Brisbane, Murphy said it was time authorities in Australia realised that importers of hard narcotics like heroin were in fact 'murderers'.

'Not a week goes by in Australia without a drug addict over-dosing or over-dosing other people,' Murphy said.

The detective believed that his recent efforts in organising the Bureau of Crime Intelligence in Brisbane had prompted the Cairns transfer and that he was looking forward to the challenge.

He assessed drug operators as the 'lowest creatures in the world. And if we're going to get the big operators then we'll need help from informers.'

A new sheriff was in town.

More of the Same

In the weeks prior to the 1980 state election, there were whispers that Joh Bjelke-Petersen and the National Party had actually done a behind-the-scenes deal with Ed Casey and his Labor colleagues to crush the Liberals.

Curiously, one Liberal might not have had much to be concerned about following the election on 29 November.

On Monday 3 November, Commissioner Lewis had phoned his friend, the Liberal member for Merthyr, Don Lane, and they discussed 'various matters including future Cabinet appointments'.

Did Lewis have the inside rail on the constitution of the future Cabinet?

On 15 November, the Commissioner was up on Mount Coot-tha making an appearance on Fiona MacDonald's wildly popular live children's television show on Channel 7, starring Constable Dave Moore.

On this morning Lewis hitched a ride on his star, swearing in Agro 'as Special Police P.Rel. Officer'.

The day before the election, Lewis received a flurry of election-related calls. One from the Premier. Another from Russ Hinze. With his wife, Hazel, he zipped up to Government House on Fernberg Road for the Royal Humane Society Awards, over to the Queensland Cricketers' Club for lunch, and later to the Park Royal Hotel for a cocktail party.

In the meantime Sir Robert Sparkes phoned to report fraudulent how-to-vote cards discovered in the district of Toowong.

After a bizarre campaign that saw a passive-aggressive Premier first taunt, and then agree to work in coalition with the Liberals, the result looked predictable.

The ALP tried to remind the Queensland voting public of the drama and controversy of the previous three years – the destruction of the Bellevue Hotel, the street marches and thousands of arrest, the special treatment given to the Japanese developer Yohachiro Iwasaki who had bought up land and built a resort near Yeppoon in Central Queensland. The Bjelke-Petersen government had in 1978 introduced the *Queensland International Tourist Centre Agreement Act 1978* that released Iwasaki from several Queensland statutes. It gave Iwasaki the legal right to purchase and lease Crown land. The construction of the resort was well underway.

In the end, the number of National Party seats in the new Parliament remained unchanged. The ALP gained two and the Liberals lost two.

On the day of the election, a bomb ripped through the Iwasaki development in Yeppoon, causing $1 million damage. Two men were charged with the bombing but later found not guilty in court after a key witness appeared to have conspired with police.

Another perfect day in Queensland.

Mona and the Jockey

Mona Ellen Lewis, mother to Commissioner Terry Lewis, must have had a few loves in her life, but at the very top of the list was horse racing. She had, after all, abandoned her husband and young son Terry in dreary Ipswich, and headed back to Brisbane, and in particular to its racing calendar.

Racing, in a sense, was in her blood. She was one of the Hanlon clan. Her father, Bill Hanlon, had been a horse trainer. Her brother Laurie became one too, as did another brother, Peter. Her brother-in-law Noel was a trainer. Her nephew Jim Townsend became a jockey, and two of her nieces' husbands were jockeys.

'My whole life has been closely connected with horse racing,' she would later declare. 'I've grown up with it and I know a lot of trainers, jockeys, owners and officials connected with racing. I believe I am very well known in Brisbane racing.'

Mona Lewis also claimed she had a close relationship with Brisbane trainer Pat Duff and Michael Pelling, a jockey apprenticed to Duff. She said they gave her excellent racing tips. And on many occasions she took those tips and had a little flutter on behalf of her son. She was remarkably successful.

'On many occasions I have placed bets for my son Terry,' she would say years later. 'Usually this would be at my suggestion where I had received a tip or friends or relatives had a horse running.

'I don't think I could say when I first started this but it would certainly go back some years. I think it would at least go back to when Tom Newbery [the former police minister, and Lewis's first on becoming commissioner in November 1976] was alive because I used to bet for him as well.

'Because of my close connection with racing and the people involved in it I have had a very good period of picking winners and I think the horses I backed for Terry or Mr Newbery mostly won or ran a place though, of course, that was not always so.'

She would ring her son and he would 'send over money' to her, or she'd pay and mother and son would 'settle up' later. The bets were usually for $50 – either on the nose or $25 each way.

Curiously, Jack 'the Bagman' Herbert would later tell investigators that Commissioner Lewis had little interest in the track. 'I just know he wasn't a betting man,' Herbert said. 'I'm not a betting man and I dislike being in the company of anybody on a Saturday afternoon that could only talk races and then when it's over they talk about what they should have done and what they are going to bet next week. And he was the same.'

While her son rarely ventured out to the track – except on official visits – Mona went at every opportunity she could, taking brilliant tips from Duff and Pelling and notching up a winning percentage that must have been the envy of every punter. Her tipster Mike Pelling was an outstanding jockey. He prided himself on his honesty and integrity in a game that had its fair share of shadows. He would go on to win the Doomben 10,000 (on Unequalled and again on Laurie's Lottery), the QTC Derby (Mr. Cromwell), the VRC Dalgety Stakes (also Mr. Cromwell) and a host of other races that elevated him to the very elite of Queensland jockeys.

He remembers Mona Lewis as a little old lady who obsessively frequented the track. 'Mona was at the races every day and she'd dress herself up,' remembers Pelling. 'She was a lonely old lady. She ingratiated herself into racing – as if she was part of the race world – because she was the Police Commissioner's mother. Because she was Lewis's mother you had to be respectful. She was riding the coat tails of her son. That's human nature.

'She'd be clapping away if you rode a winner. She didn't do anybody any harm. The place she was living in, the conditions she was living in, were disgraceful. It was a boarding house type of thing, a place cut into four flats at Hamilton.

'If Mona Lewis had $50 in her pocket she would have thought she was a millionaire.'

As for giving racing tips to Mona Lewis, Pelling remains matter-of-fact. 'Pat Duff wasn't a punter, he was not a gambler,' Pelling says. 'I didn't gamble. I never met Terry Lewis. And not once did I ever tip her [Mona] a horse in my life.'

Jack and Jack

Jack Herbert had only worked for Sydney businessman Jack Rooklyn for a handful of months in the 1970s before joining Tony Robinson and his in-line machine venture. He was doing nicely with the machines and also taking money from the illegal gambling joints run by the likes of Geraldo Bellino and Luciano Scognamiglio. But Jack Herbert loved money, and in February 1981, when Rooklyn paid him a visit, he could almost smell the dollar notes coming his way.

'Tony Robinson and Jack Rooklyn appeared to be friendly but really they were great rivals,' Herbert would write in his memoir. 'Robinson's in-line business was prospering at Jack Rooklyn's expense. Rooklyn realised that a lot of this was down to me.

'One morning Jack Rooklyn visited our office above the amusement arcade in Albert Street [in the Brisbane CBD]. Robinson and Rooklyn were sitting at my desk while I was busy answering the telephone. The air was full of cigar smoke.'

Robinson briefly left the office. 'As soon as the door closed, Rooklyn took the cigar out of his mouth,' said Herbert. 'He spoke quickly and to the point. He asked me if I'd leave Robinson and work for him.

He said he'd pay me more than I was getting from Robinson. At that moment the door opened and Rooklyn changed the subject.'

The deal was done, and Herbert took his considerable talents for organisation and identifying the sources and receipt of corrupt monies, over to Rooklyn of the Bally Corporation.

He had established his credentials with Rooklyn through the detrimental poker machine report the year before.

'By now I was amassing large amounts of black money and laundering it through my racing contacts,' Herbert said. 'With this new-found wealth I bought two factories and two home units. One of them was a penthouse in Surfers Paradise.'

He claims he kept on paying Commissioner Lewis $2000 a month.

Slade Travels North

Tony Murphy, in charge of the Far Northern Region, had settled into Cairns and was getting the lay of the land. There were some familiar faces in town. The Bellinos had a nightclub, the House on the Hill, not far from the CBD. And Geoff Crocker, who ran a number of escort services in Brisbane, was also doing a similar brisk trade in this outpost of his empire. But Murphy needed some expert help and he summoned Jim Slade.

'I was called up to Cairns and Tony Murphy said, "Look, we've got this massive area up here and no one's policing it, I want to see what sort of intelligence you can get out of it",' he said.

It was precisely the sort of work Slade relished, and he threw himself into it. 'I had this most incredible friend, Barry Petersen, a most highly decorated soldier in the Australian Army,' recalls Slade. 'He ran undercover for the Australian Army all through the Vietnam days ... an incredible guy.'

Petersen in fact was awarded 13 medals for tours of Borneo, Malaysia and Vietnam, including the Military Cross. He led the mountain tribespeople of Vietnam against the Vietcong, kidnapping and killing Vietcong agents. His guerrilla unit became known as the 'Tiger Men'. As it turned out, Petersen was extremely helpful to Slade.

'I used to go up to Barry Petersen and say, "I'm doing an operation, I need a helicopter, I need fuel and I need four Gerry cans at this map reference and operate out of there for three lots of three hours",' Slade says. 'Barry would have it there, I'd have an Army helicopter, all the Army supplies I wanted. I got on really well with Barry.'

Slade also delineated that the local drug scene had 'gone up a level'. 'By the early 1980s the Bellinos really started changing their interest from gaming and prostitution to drugs,' he says. 'A lot of the work that I did was to identify competition.

'Everything was good until the Bellinos came in and then violence started to really erupt.'

Slade had a huge, and extremely dangerous, job ahead of him.

The Chairman Takes His Seat

There was debate, and a lot of it. Premier Joh Bjelke-Petersen was adamant that his good friend and confidant, Sir Edward Lyons, be made the new Chairman of the TAB.

The Liberals in the Coalition were against it. Just as they levelled criticism at the Bjelke-Petersen Foundation when it was established in 1979, they now viewed Lyons' prospective elevation to the top job as nothing short of nepotism. Indeed, Lyons himself had bragged in late 1980 that he would be the next chairman of the TAB. Seven Liberal ministers refused to sign the Executive Council minute ratifying Lyons' appointment.

It didn't matter. In early May 1981, Governor Sir James Ramsay gave his nod of approval to the appointment. The job came with a $48,000 per year salary.

In parliament on 6 May, Lindsay Hartwig, the independent member for Callide who had been controversially expelled from the National Party earlier in the year over his criticisms of Party president Sir Robert Sparkes, asked a string of questions of Russ Hinze, Minister for Local Government, Main Roads and Police.

What was Sir Edward Lyons' correct age? What was the term of appointment of the new TAB Chairman? Would the compulsion of retiring at the age of 70 years as applied to hospital, electricity and other boards be enforced? And did the Minister agree with a statement made in a newspaper on the weekend of 2 May [1981] by Sir Robert Sparkes that the position of Chairman of the TAB was one of insignificance?

Hinze replied: 'I understand that Sir Edward Lyons is 66 years of age. However, his age is not relevant to the appointment that has been made of Sir Edward as TAB Chairman under the current Act.

'The term of the new board commences on 30 June 1981. Members of such board will continue to hold office until an appointment of members is made under the *Racing and Betting Act 1980–1981*.

'If Sir Robert Sparkes was correctly quoted, I am sure that he was referring to relative significance. The position of chairman is important to me and, I am sure, to the racing industry. I am also sure that Sir Edward Lyons will fill the position with distinction.'

The topic was irresistible to the member for Archerfield, Kev Hooper.

He told parliament: 'With the problems of identity that seem to have arisen in relation to the birth certificate of Sir Edward Lyons, named as the new head of the Totalisator Administration Board, perhaps the Premier, as one of the initiators of his appointment, may be able to clear up the present confusion.

'I now ask the Premier: Is the Sir Edward Lyons named as chairman of the TAB the same person who acted as master of ceremonies at the wedding reception for one of his daughters? Is this Sir Edward Lyons also the same Edward Houghton Lyons who is remembered far from fondly by his old classmates at Nudgee College in the late 1920s as "Mossy" because of his apparent dislike of soap and water?'

While the last question may have amused the House, the Premier was far from pleased.

'Sir Edward Lyons is a very good personal friend of mine, a very fine man, and a man whom the honourable member could, with credit to himself, take as an example.'

Lewis says he too was a close friend to Lyons, and that friendship was mutually beneficial: 'Ted Lyons used to get in touch with me and I'd go down and see him and he was very, very friendly with Joh. So you picked up a bit of information as to who was doing what around the ridges, politically. Not that you needed it.

'But I remember Lyons getting in touch with me once saying he had a problem up in Cairns that they couldn't get a permit to do something, and you'd ring up and it'd be done. Nothing untoward.'

Lewis fondly remembers heading down to Lyons' office in the T&G building on the corner of Queen and Albert streets and having a chinwag.

'Yeah, he was an easy fellow to talk to,' Lewis says. 'I had to go down to the T&G building and have a couple of scotches with him after work. He sort of kept in touch with me and invited me to go down and have a drink and of course I'm always happy to go down and just listen to him ramble on about who he knew and what he knew.'

Just five days later, on Monday 11 May, Lewis saw Lyons and he discussed, according to his diary: 'Kt' [Knighthoods].

Considering Sir Edward already had one, the discussion may have been about a similar accolade for Terry Lewis of 12 Garfield Drive, Bardon.

Shot Dead in Their Bed

It didn't take long for the North Queensland locals to give William Paul Clarke, a former Sydney leatherworker who had settled on a property off Pinnacle Road in the tiny hamlet of Julatten, a nickname. They dubbed him 'Sarky' because of his sarcastic nature.

Despite this character trait, it wasn't hard to miss Clarke, 36, and his Latvian wife, Grayvyda Maria Clarke. Both were unemployed, yet they were often seen buying equipment for their 93-hectare property with rolls of cash.

Julatten, between Mareeba and Mossman, had a general store and a school to service the neighbouring farming community, and was famed for its natural beauty, its birdlife and, by the 1970s, its close proximity to thousands of hectares of illicit marihuana crops.

Sarky, a devotee of antique cars, many of which he sheltered in a shed on his property, was one of the region's major growers. It was said he had a part-interest in another property – a cattle station at remote Portland Roads on Cape York, a former strategic base for United States servicemen during World War II right on the coast, where he grew huge quantities of marihuana in the wild sub-tropical jungles of the region. The crops were then transported by trawler. Clarke supposedly compressed the weed into blocks with a machine normally used to make concrete building blocks, then sealed them in steel drums with false tops, ready for exporting to the south. The A-frame farmhouse on Pinnacle Road was, it was believed, a sorting house for these massive quantities of dope.

On the night of Sunday 24 May 1981, the Clarkes went to bed as usual. They had been to a nearby horse fair that afternoon. Later, neighbours claimed to have heard the roar of a motorcycle echoing through the hills in the middle of the night.

The Clarkes were both shot dead with a shotgun. Doctors later recovered 132 pellets from the lower right-hand side of William

Clarke's chest, and 80 from the body of Grayvyda. The killer or killers then splashed fuel around the house and torched it. The fire was so intense it melted metal and burned off the heads and limbs of the Clarkes.

The murder was investigated by Detective Ross Beer of the Mareeba CIB, under the direction of regional superintendent, Tony Murphy. The case would limp along for years. Again, there were rumours that police had been involved in the double murder. Beer flatly refuted it.

When Beer was transferred back to Brisbane, he took the bulk of the Clarke murder file with him. He explained he did so because nobody was as familiar with the case as he was, and it made sense to have it at hand.

The Seductive Katherine James

In early 1981, after an addiction to heroin, her flight from Queensland and her subsequent imprisonment on drug charges where she had unwittingly been embroiled in the Basil Hicks photograph scandal, the former massage parlour owner Katherine James made a decision to get back into the game.

Things had changed dramatically since the 1970s. In this new world, the prostitution landscape appeared to be dominated by two figures – Hector Hapeta and Geoff Crocker.

'I decided to work for Hapeta because he seemed to be working mainly in escorts,' James said. 'I had been told that the girls in the parlours got booked on an average every four to six weeks, while the escort girls didn't get booked nearly as often.'

She was shocked at how flagrant the industry had become. 'There was not even a pretense of any massage being done,' she said. 'The receptionist was quite open about what was on offer. The parlours were no longer equipped with massage tables. By 1981, there were beds in them and other fairly plush surroundings.'

She first worked for Hapeta and Tilley out of 66 Warry Street in the Valley – a narrow Queenslander on stumps. She also did jobs at the Top of the Valley, and Fantasia at 24 Logan Road, Woolloongabba.

'I came to be a trusted employee of Hector Hapeta and Anne Marie Tilley,' James said. 'This was because I had known Geoff Crocker and Gerry Bellino from the earlier days in the parlours. There weren't very many girls who had the business experience to actually run a parlour, so I was given a position of trust as receptionist/manageress at 612 Brunswick Street, New Farm.'

James was required to attend weekly meetings where the books and the week's earnings were handed over. 'Anne Marie Tilley appeared to be in charge of things,' James recalled. 'Hector's role was not quite so clear – he seemed to be the overseer and he would try to make management decisions, but he really wasn't bright enough. Everyone had to treat him like he was the boss but if anything went wrong you would always go to Anne Marie. Without doubt, Hector held the purse strings.'

Tilley had a different take on Hector Hapeta. She says he was infinitely more involved in the business decisions for their consortium than anybody ever knew. 'Hector ran it,' she says. 'Hector was actually illiterate. He had dyslexia. I was the speller, but he used to plan the business. What we should open, what we should shut. I don't think we ever shut anything, we just kept going. It was sort of ... we both sort of ran it.

'He had the fast brain. Extremely fast. He was faster than most people I've ever met in my life. His brain would go so fast. Extremely fast.

'He was also fast with figures. If you gave him ... this place earned such and such, he'd go, yeah, alright, that's $45,927.65. His brain was in planning ahead.

'If Hector had ever gone to school, he'd probably be running some multinational company. If you don't know something, surround yourself with people that do. He surrounded himself – like the nightclub people, a manager who knew how to run bars, men who knew about the music side of things. That's how smart he was.'

By 1981 the business was extremely lucrative. Tilley and Hapeta ran 15 houses. Each house brought in after expenses – wages for girls and drivers, phone bills and electricity – about $5000 a week. That's $75,000 for the consortium.

James said she witnessed first-hand what happened to prostitutes who wanted to step out on their own. 'Despite the fact that Hector seemed to be getting the lion's share of the profits, it was never possible for girls to go out on their own,' she said. 'I can recall two girls who tried to set up on their own after working for Hector. Chantal tried to set up halfway to the coast, but Hector stopped her. Another girl [Melissa] opened at Kangaroo Point at Seafarer's Lodge. She was assaulted by Hector outside Fantasia's.

'Even if a girl was working on her own, which was not supposed to be against the law, Licensing Branch would harass them.'

During this period word got back to Hapeta and Tilley that a Licensing Branch raid was imminent. Tilley ordered all of her brothels to close for the night.

'She [Tilley] came to Warry Street, rang all the other houses from there and told the manageresses to send all the girls home, that we were being raided,' James later recalled. 'When I asked her who told her she said that Harry Burgess had rung her and just told her to close down for the night.'

James asked if they'd be open the following day.

'It'll be fine,' Tilley replied.

Tilley, James and some of the girls then went to a nightclub for some drinks. James recalled: 'I wanted to know how she was going to open again the next day and continue because if all these raids were planned they would surely plan them the next day and she [Tilley] said, no, that everything had been taken care of ... it was costing them roughly 20 per cent of their earnings to pay police. [Hector] classed that as one of his overheads.'

Burgess was a regular visitor to Tilley. 'Harry used to call around to see Anne [Marie] nearly most Wednesday nights ... and Anne made it quite clear it was going to be Harry; that the money was being paid to Harry and Harry was the one relaying everything back,' said James.

Hapeta called Burgess 'Harry the Bagman'.

So Katherine James was back in business. And it wasn't long after her return to the scene that, while working at New Horizons brothel at 45 Balaclava Street, the Gabba, she first met an energetic young Licensing Branch officer with a Pommy accent by the name of Nigel Donald Powell.

Powell first breached James for using premises for the purposes of prostitution in June 1981. He said that in the presence of men she was 'lethal' – a classic seductress.

'She was quite short; she had a small frame but a big presence,' Powell recalls. 'She prided herself in the fact that no matter what was going on in her life, she could always get a job as a hairdresser. She always dressed well. She was tidy.'

Over time James grew to trust Powell. She confided information that Powell didn't see the significance of at the time.

Besides, he was told by his Licensing Branch mate and partner, Nev Ross, not to pay too much attention to her allegations about the parlour scene in Brisbane and corrupt police. 'He said that it was dangerous, almost stupid to listen to what she had to say,' Powell recalls. 'I didn't really put any of this together.'

What Powell didn't know was that Ross himself was corrupt and a part of The Joke. 'I didn't suspect him for a moment,' says Powell. 'Nev was my mate. I went to see all his relatives out west at St George on my holidays. He confided in me with personal issues.

'Nev was everybody's friend. He would just tell funny stories. We had a great time. I learned later that in every crew there was somebody they [The Joke] had.'

Monster Book

It wasn't until 1981 that University of Queensland academic and criminologist Paul Wilson published his book on the paedophile Clarence Osborne, more than 18 months after the former Hansard reporter had gassed himself in his car in the garage of his humble home in Mount Gravatt. *The Man They Called a Monster* was released by Cassell Australia.

In its introduction, Wilson explained that he felt compelled to write the story in an accurate and fair way, claiming, 'It may not be a happy story, but it is one that must be told.' He added that he had received assistance from various quarters, including several of Osborne's victims.

'Despite the difficulties of writing a book about men who love boys, I received help and co-operation from a number of unexpected sources,' explained Wilson. 'Many of the men who, as youths, had had a relationship with Osborne, recounted their experiences with a frankness and honesty that I found invaluable. While they may have initially come to see me to find out whether the police or I had a record of their association with Clarence Osborne, they soon confided in me and gave me their trust. They can be sure that this trust has been, and will continue to be, respected.'

Wilson also acknowledged thanks for the permission he was granted to interview officers seconded to the Osborne case. 'Some officers went well beyond the call of duty and commented on earlier drafts of the manuscript,' added Wilson. 'To save them embarrassment I will not mention them by name.'

The respected academic took full responsibility for what he must have known would be controversial to say the least. 'In writing about one of our society's most taboo topics I alone must bear the brunt of any criticisms that arise from this book,' wrote Wilson. 'I am, however, satisfied that every effort which was humanly possible has been made to present the reader with an accurate account of what occurred between Clarence Osborne and his youthful partners.'

The book not only presented Osborne's extraordinary story, it also examined issues of consent and power in sexual relationships and whether society itself paid enough attention to the physical and emotional needs of children.

In his memoir, *A Life of Crime*, Wilson noted that the publication of the book caused a 'small storm'. The edition sold out but was never reprinted.

One newspaper article called Wilson 'an indefatigable sociologist with an eye for the commercially successful publication'. It said Wilson, in his book, was trying to make the reader think of Osborne not as a 'monster' but a man in the great tradition of Greek Love.

It went on: 'Wilson seems to be trying too hard with a thesis that might find some narrow academic attraction, but will be regarded with repugnance by the overwhelming majority.

'Had Osborne not killed himself, I wonder whether he would have been received by the inmates of Boggo Road with the same kind of concerned academic detachment that Wilson shows?'

Others said Wilson should never have written the book in the first place.

Into the Valley

Jack 'The Bagman' Herbert's influence on the Queensland Police Force under Lewis went far deeper than helping out an old mate with some tidbits of information about unlawful gaming and prostitution. In fact, Lewis consulted Herbert when it came to transfers and promotions, particularly within the Licensing Branch.

The new head of the branch, following Jeppesen's demise and the temporary appointment of another inspector in charge who did not take Herbert's bait about 'getting something going', was Noel Dwyer, a Catholic and a family man. Herbert approached Dwyer prior to Dwyer's elevation to inspector and asked him if he'd be interested in taking over Licensing.

Dwyer said he would, but asked Herbert why he, a former policeman, was so heavily engaged in state police appointments. Dwyer was told by Herbert to go soft on illegal games in Fortitude Valley.

Prior to Dwyer's appointment, Lewis showed Herbert a list of possible candidates. When Herbert chose Dwyer, Lewis supposedly responded: 'Are you sure this time?'

A few months after Dwyer took up his new post, Jack Herbert had a meal with Geraldo Bellino and Vic Conte in the Swinging Gate Restaurant. Herbert had never met Conte. Bellino, living in Cairns at the time, had flown down especially for the meeting.

Conte offered Herbert $4000 a month to protect the illegal game at 142 Wickham. He and Bellino knew Herbert was 'sweet with Noel Dwyer'.

'I agreed on the spot,' Herbert said. 'Afterwards I told Dwyer and the Commissioner. Fifteen hundred was for the Commissioner, $500 was for me, and the rest was to be split between Dwyer and the fellows in the Licensing Branch.'

Almost two years into the job, Dwyer furnished Commissioner Lewis with an up-to-date report into illegal gaming and prostitution in Brisbane. He said several premises had 'come under suspicion'. They included: upstairs at 142 Wickham Street, Fortitude Valley (with a massage parlour, Bubbles Bath House, on the ground floor); 677 Ann Street (above the Valley Rocks Restaurant), Fortitude Valley; 701 Ann

Street, Fortitude Valley; 648 Ann Street (above Kisses Nite Club), Fortitude Valley; 301 Wickham Street, Fortitude Valley; Corner of Gipps and Ann streets (under Malcolm Sue's Kung Fu School), Fortitude Valley; and the Buffalo Memorial Club, Constance Street, Fortitude Valley.

Dwyer reported that at 142 Wickham, and on the first floor, were premises conducted by 'Vittorio Conte of 116 Sackville Street, Greenslopes'. Conte was also named as the manager of the World By Night club at 546 Queen Street.

Dwyer wrote: 'These premises are used mainly by persons of Italian origin … as a meeting place for social gatherings. It is known that they do play cards on these premises regularly. Members of the Licensing Branch have witnessed this on several occasions.'

He said 'the card games witnessed by members of the Branch have not been of an unlawful nature, and no evidence has been obtained that any percentage was being taken by the house'.

He said attempts to have agents 'penetrate unlawful games on these premises' had been unsuccessful.

The Branch raided 142 Wickham three times between June 1980 and July 1981. Those arrested were charged with the lesser charge of 'playing an unlawful game' under the *Vagrants, Gaming and Other Offences Act* because of lack of evidence, as opposed to being charged under the Gaming Act. All of those charged failed to appear in court and bail was forfeited.

In Dwyer's opinion, he considered the incidence of unlawful gaming at 142 Wickham as 'not very high'.

'It is inaccurate for anyone to suggest that a blind eye has been turned to this matter by the police, as the premises have received considerable attention from members of the Licensing Branch during the period I have been in charge.'

In conclusion, Dwyer reported to his Commissioner that 'unlawful gaming is well contained, not only in the Valley but in other areas of Brisbane'. He also boasted that Brisbane now had only 12 massage parlours, whereas it had peaked at 56 just a few years earlier.

Meanwhile, Nigel Powell, who had taken a short sabbatical in the United Kingdom before returning to the Licensing Branch when Dwyer was in charge, re-entered his work with gusto.

'The big games weren't going on at that stage,' says Powell. 'But there were a lot of games down the Gold Coast. You only went down there if you were "invited" [by Gold Coast police].'

Anne Marie Tilley and partner Hector Hapeta were building their massage parlour empire, while the Bellino and Conte crew controlled gaming. According to Powell's police diaries, and by his calculation, there were 16 massage parlours operating in Brisbane at the time of Dwyer's report. But the young officer observed a turning point in the local prostitution landscape when branch officer Ron Lewis organised a major raid on the Tilley–Hapeta consortium in 1981.

The raid was pencilled in for April of that year. As usual, branch officers were told virtually nothing of the mechanics of a raid until they were physically in the vicinity of the target. In this instance, the men gathered at the branch at 7 p.m. At the same time, Tilley, who had been tipped off, closed her brothels in advance and partied with her employees.

Tilley was summoned to see Dwyer. She was unexpectedly breached and jailed for eight weeks. Meanwhile, Hapeta took off to Melbourne.

Later that year Hapeta came back to Queensland. 'Tilley copped the charge; somebody had to go,' says Powell. 'There was a deal that was done. I am convinced I saw Hapeta come in and see Dwyer [near the end of 1981]. I happened to be there on that night and I saw Hector Hapeta go straight into Noel Dwyer's office.'

After that, Powell says, he sensed a change. Tilley and Hapeta's empire took off spectacularly. He was right.

A week after Tilley was released from prison on 5 June 1981, she went in to see Noel Dwyer at headquarters. A deal was struck.

Tilley remembers meeting Dwyer: 'Ron Feeney and his wife Jenny were coming to Brisbane from Melbourne to see Noel Dwyer about opening a club. This encouraged Hector to do the same. Dwyer said it was okay.

'I went and saw Dwyer and said, "How come Jenny Feeney can have a [massage] parlour and I can't?"

'"I'll send someone to see you," Dwyer said.'

Dwyer told Tilley that the man he would send would have a packet of Marlboro cigarettes. A couple of days later Tilley was in the lounge room at home in Spring Hill when someone came to the door. It was Vic Conte.

'I'm not going to work with these Italians,' Hapeta later told her. Until then Tilley thought Conte and the Bellinos were just nightclub owners in Brisbane and in northern Queensland.

In the meantime, Dwyer made contact with 'The Bagman', Jack Herbert. According to Herbert, Dwyer took him aside and asked him if he wanted to make a 'red shilling', or kickbacks from prostitution. 'Dwyer told me Tilley would pay me $5000 a month. He said I shouldn't worry about the details; he'd look after everything. All I had to do was make arrangements to collect the money,' Herbert recalled.

Tilley went back to see Noel Dwyer and told him she didn't want to work with people like Conte and the Bellinos. Dwyer told her he'd send somebody else 'called Tom'. Tilley was told to wait for a phone call.

When 'Tom' eventually made contact they arranged to meet at the Coca Cola factory (a bottling plant in James Street, New Farm) in the Valley. He had a little van.

'It was Jack Herbert. I always called him Tom. I didn't know who he was. He spoke with an accent that I had to listen really hard to,' recalls Tilley.

'Okay, we will have to do some business here,' Herbert said. 'You can open up your places again – and you pay me so much a month.' Tilley recalls the amount was about $4000 a month.

Herbert said to her: 'You either pay this and you go and open your businesses and you can stay in Queensland and you won't go to gaol. Just bring me the little bag.'

They made plans to meet once a month at the same time and place. 'He would ring and arrange to meet,' Tilley says. 'We paid in cash. He had the same sort of humour as me. That's what it was. They called it The Joke. We never did. But our life was like a joke.'

Tilley was immediately resigned to paying Herbert for protection. She called it the 'funny money'. 'It was a shitload amount of money,' she recalls. 'Sometimes we made no money. You'd sort of offset it.

'The nightclub [Pharaoh's] was making very good money, maybe $5000 to $10,000 a night. One of the parlours might have gone broke. We'd offset it. I had this accountant who reckoned ... when I think back, it was absurd. He reckoned that in one year we paid $40,000 in taxation. I just gave that to him in a cheque – there's $40,000.

'None of it ever went to taxation. I thought I was sweet, that I'd paid tax. That was it.'

Herbert later alleged: 'I gathered that Dwyer had been doing business with Tilley for some time and that the reason I was invited into the prostitution side was to pay the commissioner. I had a feeling Dwyer was trying to cover himself – that he was worried we'd find out if he didn't include us in the system.

'I took it for granted that Terry would be interested in the money. I told him it came from a respectable businessman who'd just started running escort services and massage parlours. Terry was quite happy about that. I didn't give him a name and he didn't ask for one.'

If Herbert was telling the truth, he was proposing, without realising it, a curious historical parallel. In the late 1950s and through the 1960s, Commissioner Frank Bischof had had his alleged bagmen in the Rat Pack. Now, two decades later, this construct was mirrored with Lewis, who having been a supposed bagman to Bischof, now had his own in ex-cop Jack Herbert.

Were corrupt police simply in parity with the Bjelke-Petersen government and, in particular, the mood engendered around the Bjelke-Petersen Foundation and the supposition that it existed to buy favours from government? Wasn't that another form of The Joke, where favours were bought for cash? Were Herbert, Lewis and company, simply reflecting the zeitgeist?

In Bischof's day it had been common knowledge that the police, going right to the apex of the pyramid, were corrupt, and a passive Queensland community accepted it and went about its business. After the departure of former commissioner Ray Whitrod, the return of Tony Murphy to take charge of the CIB, the character assassinations of honest police, the apathy towards the Lucas Inquiry and the unending allegations of police and government corruption in parliament by Kevin Hooper, the public remained unmoved. Why?

The Woolloongabba Worrier

Bob Campbell, still stuck in the Woolloongabba CIB after his study leave had been cancelled, was inching towards completing his university degrees and his resignation from the force. The heavy-handedness of the treatment towards him had rightly ignited a level of vindictiveness towards his superiors.

So, in an act of pique and undergraduate rebellion that may have been inspired by his years on the University of Queensland campus, he helped produce a comedic 'underground' news sheet that lampooned government and police hierarchies. It was called *The Woolloongabba Worrier* – a small, four-page publication printed on both sides of an A3 sheet of paper and folded in half.

Beneath the masthead it stated: 'The official organ of the honest Police Officers attached to the Woolloongabba Police Station.'

The Worrier – which extended to just three editions – was irreverent and cutting. A caption beneath a photograph of the Commissioner, for example, read: 'The Hon. T.M.Lewis, G.M., O.B.E., B.O., D.I.C.K.H.E.A.D., B.A., Dip. Pub. Admin.'

In one issue there is a small article titled 'Racing Guide for Doomben', one of Brisbane's two racecourses.

Some of the horses in a fictional race included Pee in Ashtray ridden by 'Big Russ' [Hinze, the Police Minister], and Graft and Corruption ridden by Tony M[urphy]. In notes on the horses and riders, 'Big Russ prefers Pee in Ashtray due to its convincing win over Chunda in [the] parliamentary annexe last week', and 'Tony M. is convinced that Graft and Corruption is the best bet. Years of experience are behind Tony in his selection.'

Another article spoofs the department's policing priorities:

In his first statement to *The Worrier*, the Commissioner, Mr Bjelke-Petersen, stated today that thanks to the sterling efforts of members of the C.I.Branch, there was now a 100 percent clean-up rate on all criminal activity.

The Commissioner, however, denied that the figures only pertained to breaches of the Liquor and Gaming Acts, which are well policed by members of the C.I. Branch.

The Commissioner said: 'We have not included the figures for minor unimportant activity, which we consider undeserving of Police attention, such as rape, murder, break and enter etc. but certainly include such blatant crime as shoplifting.'

Outside … only minor crime, such as bank hold-ups, balaclava killings and multiple murders are being committed. *The Worrier* praise all these competent detectives for the manner in which they pursue the pensioner shoplifters. Without their competence, our society would not be safe.

The little hand-produced publication caused enough consternation for Lewis to discuss it with the Premier.

An anonymous note sent to Lewis, accompanied by a few editions of *The Worrier*, made a suggestion about what to do with the editors and authors of the newspapers once they were uncovered. 'The writers need a flogging,' the note said. 'Surely some detectives will oblige.'

Campbell's agitation was working. And he had more to come.

Trisha Traffic is Born

Following Constable Dave Moore's successful appearances on children's television, the rest of the city's media began to take notice. Moore was quick, off-the-cuff and had a disarming style. He was funny and not threatening. There was chatter in the city that Moore was in fact a trained actor and not a policeman at all.

Commissioner Lewis and his team also grasped Moore's value. He was generating vast and valuable quantities of positive public relations for the police department. Radio 4BC subsequently approached Moore and offered him a slot doing live traffic reports.

'We had permission to build a little radio studio in police head-quarters and we would broadcast live from there,' a colleague of Moore's says. 'He'd put in his two cents worth, he'd talk about issues and things, about police. Police were now getting publicity on TV and on radio every day of the week.'

Soon Moore was asked to appear on the children's national tele-vision program, *Wombat*. Fan mail for Moore started turning up. The show, produced by BTQ 7 out of Brisbane, aired every weekday after-noon, and later on weekend mornings. Moore found his quest for stardom at Channel 7.

'Seven were good at promoting,' the friend and colleague remem-bers. 'They took him to the Tamworth Music Festival. He presented on stage. There were the huge Christmas programs there. He was a personality.'

Perhaps Brisbane's biggest radio star at the time was Bill Hurrey, over at the ABC. Hurrey grew up by the Murray River in the little northern Victorian town of Cobram, before the family moved to Papua New Guinea in 1965. By 1969 – just as Ray Whitrod was considering relinquishing his position as PNG Police Commissioner and heading to Queensland to take the top job – Hurrey had begun his radio career with the ABC in Port Morseby.

Hurrey moved to Brisbane in 1972 to study law, working in radio part-time, but dropped out and began regularly reading the ABC television and radio news. He was then in his early thirties.

By the early 1980s he was a fully-fledged star as Brisbane's most popular breakfast radio host. His knowledge of music was encyclo-paedic and his record collection unparalleled. He was also wealthy. He lived in an apartment at New Farm, not far from Fortitude Valley, and he was conspicuous around town in his 450SL Mercedes Benz convertible.

Constable Moore knew of Hurrey but had not encountered him socially.

'Hurrey was huge,' says another friend of Moore's at the time. 'He had a huge following. His radio show was probably one of the finest. He had a great talent and his knoweldge of music was unbelievable.'

Hurrey became aware that Moore was doing the traffic reports. One day Moore did a wickedly funny Edna Everage-style report as a joke. It captured the attention of Hurrey, who approached the police officer about a ribald traffic report for his own morning show. Trisha Traffic was born.

'What Trisha Traffic would do was not only traffic reports but she would pick bits out of the newspaper and comment, and some of them were very risqué,' Moore's colleague says. 'One day he was in the conference room at police headquarters, on the phone doing Trisha

Traffic live, and other police were banging on the door waiting to get in. On that day one of the politicians was giving out flowers to people, and Moore said it is probably someone who wants to give him a stalk.'

Nobody knew Trisha Traffic was Moore. But then an article appeared in the *Courier-Mail* that suggested Trisha was believed to be from Terry Lewis's stable.

Moore was such a success on so many media fronts that he began to wonder whether he wanted to be a police officer any longer.

'In hindsight, he [Hurrey] was interested in, fascinated with, young teenage boys,' a friend of Moore's says. 'And young teenage boys became fascinated with him. He would give them presents. CDs had just come in, movie tickets ... and he ... Bill told a lot of lies about things ... Allegedly he was the godfather to [American entertainer] Stevie Wonder's child. There were a lot of lies that he came to believe himself.'

Bill Hurrey began a social friendship with Moore. He met Moore's family.

'Lewis knew about it,' a source says. 'Often Lewis would phone Moore and say, can you ask Bill to get this music or that music or whatever. He would give Moore a list of what he wanted and Bill would record it on tape and Moore would give it to the Commissioner.'

One Transfer Too Many

Whether his superiors were concerned about his involvement in *The Woolloongabba Worrier*, the feisty little spoof newspaper anonymously produced by disaffected young officers at the Gabba CIB, or for some other reason, Senior Constable Bob Campbell was informed once more, in the winter of 1981, that he was on the move again – this time he would be transferred to Townsville.

Campbell, just a few months earlier, had resigned from the Police

Union, then under the presidency of Col Chant. According to Campbell, a rumour came back to him that Chant had been yarning to an officer at the Police Store about the resignation, and that 'Campbell need not come running to the Union for help' if he was transferred.

Campbell believed a transfer was imminent. So he wrote to Premier Joh Bjelke-Petersen to raise his objections about the constant victim-isation against him.

A standard reply came back from the Premier's office. Three weeks later word came through that Campbell was off to the Surplus Depot, Townsville, in North Queensland.

Campbell had just commenced his final semester at university and asked that his transfer be deferred so he could complete his course in Brisbane. The temporary deferment was accepted.

It had been four long years since Campbell had launched on a path to better himself via his degree, and in the process been ground down by a police culture that Whitrod had attempted to eradicate, and that had, under Lewis's watch, returned to the old days.

Campbell was a square peg in a round hole. And he was tired of all the game playing. In October 1981, in response to the latest transfer farce, he also wrote to firebrand politician Kev Hooper, the member for Archerfield. In the letter he described his sorry relationship with the current administration:

Dear Mr. Hooper,

Please take time to read this rather long exposé on the Queensland Police Force.

I have attempted to expose the corrupt practices, such as drug running, bribery, grafting from massage parlours and gambling dens, that are being perpetrated by the Lewis administration.

I have admired what you have been doing to try and clean up the police Force in this State and I am quite sure, from your statements, that you are well aware of the corrupt elements in the Force. Under Whitrod, these elements were suppressed but since Mr. Lewis has come into power they have flourished, understandably.

Massage parlours are thriving, drugs bigger and better than ever, particularly on the Gold Coast and honest Officers are victimized.

Campbell reiterated that as he would be resigning from the police force he had no hesitation in making a stand against corruption. He said he would be happy to give evidence to a royal commission, should one be called, but that if it was appointed by the government it would be a 'whitewash'.

Campbell's summation had echoes going all the way back to the National Hotel inquiry under Justice Gibbs in 1963–64.

I appreciate that I will have to leave Queensland within a short period of time, as I am quite sure I will not be left alone – if you know the method of operation of the Murphys and Curries of this Force, you will appreciate what I mean by this statement. I wish you every success in your endeavours to expose the corruption of the Bjelke-Petersen/police administration coalition. I feel confident that you know of those members in the parliamentary wing of the national Party involved with police in drug activity and I would be delighted to have such people receive their just deserts.

Thanking you for your service to Queensland.

Campbell knuckled down to study for his final examinations at the university. In a matter of weeks an opportunity to humiliate not just the Lewis administration but the entire Bjelke-Petersen government would by fate literally drop into a waste paper basket and find its way into the hands of Bob Campbell.

I See Nothing

In the meantime, Kev Hooper continued his attacks on Police Minister Russ Hinze, Lewis's police administration and the government in parliament. He named three illegal casinos in the Valley and identified Geraldo and Tony Bellino and Luciano Scognamiglio, who had been secretly taped all those years ago at 142 Wickham Street by honest undercover agent Kingsley Fancourt, as the 'Mafia' who ran them.

Hooper had repeatedly driven a sword through police ministers Newbery and Camm. The larger-than-life Hinze would be no exception. Hot on the heels of the letter from the disaffected Bob Campbell, who had walked the beat of Fortitude Valley in his early days in the force, Hooper rose in the House on Tuesday 13 October and fired both barrels.

'Let me talk about 142 Wickham Street, the site of another illegal casino,' he said. 'Business is so good that it has recently been expanded to provide gambling facilities for ethnic Chinese people. They are providing games such as fan-tan, chug-a-lug and the one referred by the Treasurer, pakapoo.

'The ownership of 142–144 Wickham Street, Fortitude Valley, is as follows. It is owned by Sheard Investments Pty Ltd, registered in Papua New Guinea on 20 March 1972. It was registered in Queensland as a foreign company on 10 July 1972. The registered office in New Guinea is care of Wayland and Wayland, Allotment 4, Section 5, Douglas Street, Port Moresby. The Queensland agent is Glenitch Pty Ltd – everyone will love this – care of that fine old establishment legal firm Trout, Bernays and Tingle, solicitors, SGIO Building, Turbot Street, Brisbane. The directors are Lionel Sheard Fox and Shirley Fox, Allotment 11, Section 36, Madang, New Guinea.

'In passing, I would point out that that company is also in breach of the *Companies Act* for not lodging an annual return since 1972.'

Hooper had some excellent intelligence. He was correctly implying, through naming the owners of the premises in Wickham Street, that no authorities – taxation, police or otherwise – had gone near Sheard Investments in more than ten years, despite the inference of the *Companies Act* breach. This establishment could have been shut down at any time in the past decade, Hooper implied. And it hadn't. He went even further.

'Despite the head-in-the-sand attitude of the Bjelke-Petersen Government, it is a fact of life that the lucrative drugs, prostitution and gambling rackets in Queensland have now become a multi-million-dollar industry reaching into all sections of Queensland life and controlled by a Queensland mafia,' said Hooper to an enthralled House. 'The godfathers of the mafia are Gerry, Tony and Vince Bellino, Vic Conte, Luciano Scognamiglio, also known as Lugano Scognamiglio, Cosimo Rullo, alias Tony Shifty, and Dominic Pasano.

'A well-known Brisbane hairdresser and a used-car dealer are alleged to be part of the gang. As I have no firm evidence against them at this stage, I do not propose to name them.'

Hooper stated that Vince Bellino managed the House on the Hill nightclub in Cairns. 'This is reputed to be the headquarters for the Queensland operation. Tony Bellino's girlfriend, known as Monica, works at 142 Wickham Street and she helps rip off the unsuspecting young gamblers. Monica wears a see-through frock, which makes it extremely difficult for the younger gamblers to concentrate. The gentlemen I have named have a fair criminal history between them.'

He singled out 'Luci' Scognamiglio, who he said was 'in charge of the Gold Coast operation of the Queensland mafia. Even though he is alleged to be on a pension, he is the godfather on the Gold Coast and controls all the prostitution and gambling rackets.'

Hooper continued: 'Geraldo, or Gerry Bellino, has been charged and convicted of the following offences: three charges of selling liquor without a licence, two charges of keeping a common gaming-house, two charges of threatening language and assault, one charge of resisting arrest and one charge of obscene language. That is not a bad record for a young lad who is trying to make his way in this very difficult world! These charges are, of course, just the tip of the iceberg. What stands out is the paltry amount of the fines.'

Hooper reserved his finest condemnation for Premier Bjelke-Petersen and the police.

'It is perfectly obvious that all types of vice flourish unhindered and untrammelled in Queensland,' said Hooper. 'I state quite emphatically that crime of this magnitude could not operate without political and police permission at the highest levels.

'I am absolutely disgusted at the "holier than thou" attitude of the Bjelke-Petersen government to vice and crime in Queensland. From my observations, Fortitude Valley makes Kings Cross look like a kindergarten play area.'

The Hooper address had it all – the Mafia, gambling dens, scantily-dressed women, and the implication of corruption in the highest circles of government and law enforcement.

Hooper had hit one out of the park.

It was, naturally, the page-one splash in the *Courier-Mail* the following day – Wednesday 14 October 1981. THREE 'MAFIA' CASINOS NAMED, the headline read.

'A Queensland "Mafia" was operating three illegal casinos in Brisbane's Fortitude Valley, State Parliament was told yesterday,' the newspaper reported. 'The opposition police spokesman, Mr Kevin Hooper, said a lucrative drug, prostitution and gambling racket in Queensland had become a multi-million dollar industry.'

The story quoted Hinze, saying he had discussed the allegations with Police Commissioner Lewis and other senior police. (If Lewis's diaries are to be believed, this was untrue. Lewis's diary reveals that on the Tuesday, as Hooper regaled the house with crime and skulduggery, the commissioner had indeed been contacted by Police Minister

Hinze, but not about the Mafia allegations. Hinze had phoned Lewis 're: son-in-law Alan Power arrested for U.I.L'. That evening, Lewis attended a Lord Mayoral function at City Hall, then finished duty at 7.30 p.m.)

'I am prepared to look into it further,' Hinze reportedly said, 'provided Mr Hooper gives me or the Police Commissioner concrete evidence to back up allegations made under the protection of parliament. Illegal casinos will not be tolerated in Queensland.'

Hinze stressed that allegations of police corruption were 'complete rubbish'.

The newspaper also ran a side colour story by 'a Special Writer' headlined 'Behind the door in the Valley', with a photograph of the secure door of 142 Wickham Street.

'If you know the Valley, the casinos are easy to find,' it read. 'If you don't, ask an understanding cabbie. The Wickham Street premises above Bubbles Bath House is the obvious choice if you're partial to a hand or two of blackjack.'

The writer described the experience as 'not really a bad night out in Brisbane'.

Prostitute Katherine James often went to the gambling joint above Bubbles Bath House after work. 'The number of people present ... would vary – early in the week there might be only 30 people, but on a Saturday night there could be 150,' she said. 'The games which were played at Bubbles were blackjack, Manila and roulette.

'The police would visit whilst I was there and whilst games were in progress. I never saw police take people's names. I never saw police attempt to close the premises ... the house was taking a percentage of 20 per cent.'

That day, with the *Courier-Mail* screaming its Mafia headline, Lewis noted in his diary that he'd received another phone call from Hinze 're contact to be made with Mr K. Hooper'.

Lewis popped out for an Australian Finance Conference luncheon before returning to his office and getting in touch with the renegade Hooper. 'Phoned Mr Hooper M.L.A. at 1.07 pm at Parlt House, said "Does not wish to talk about matter. Will contact me if decides to talk. It's politics at the moment old mate."'

Allen Callaghan was also on the phone to Lewis about the Hooper bombshell.

It didn't end there.

On Thursday 15 October, the *Courier-Mail* kept the saga going on page one: 3 DENY MAFIA CLAIM.

'The doors of Brisbane's "illegal casinos" were tightly closed yesterday as three men denied allegations made in state parliament on Tuesday that they were Mafia "godfathers".'

Gerry and Tony Bellino described Hooper's assertions as 'malicious, unfounded rumours'. Luciano Scognamiglio also denied any association with organised crime. 'We have nothing to do with any of those allegations,' Gerry Bellino said. 'Just because you are Italian, you are Mafia.'

Scognamiglio was nonplussed. 'I have never had anything to do with the Mafia,' he told the newspaper. 'It is a pack of lies.'

The editorial cartoon for that day by the *Courier-Mail*'s Alan Moir would go down in history. It featured a police officer walking down a street in the Valley and passing a vice den ablaze with advertising – ILLEGAL CASINO HERE EVERY NIGHT. GALS GALS GALS.

The officer is wearing dark sunglasses and tap-tapping a white cane as he passes the entranceway.

Commissioner Lewis seemed fairly unperturbed by the mounting publicity and its farcical overtones. On that Thursday he did speak with Ron Edington, former union boss, about Hooper's assertions, who suggested the ALP be rubbished 'for past policies re prostitution'. This approach distilled Lewis's attitude to damning allegations against himself and the force. It was all just politics. Forget suggestions that corrupt police were protecting illegal gaming and prostitution and probably being paid for the privilege. Forget that year after year stories emerged that here was a constabulary rotten to the core. This was just a snarky ALP trying to score points against the National Party.

Hinze did phone about the statement of reply he was going to make in parliament. And that was that.

On that Thursday night, Lewis attended the opening of a new tavern in Carindale, the honours being performed by Dr Llew Edwards. And later he dropped into the T&G Building to have a yarn with his good friend Sir Edward Lyons.

Not only did the story not go away, it intensified.

The Honourable Russ Hinze, a crafty parliamentary performer and not lacking in bluff, bluster and confidence, turned what was already a circus into what the *Courier-Mail* would describe as a comic opera. The front-page headline for Friday, 16 October 1981, said it all: CITY CASINOS 'ALL LIES' SAYS HINZE.

'Anyone who said they had visited an illegal casino in Brisbane's Valley area was "a liar", the Police Minister, Mr Hinze, said yesterday.

'"My police officers don't think there are any illegal casinos," Hinze said during a press conference. "I don't know of any illegal gambling casinos [sic] and I don't know where it is. I don't think it would be beyond Mr Hooper to dream these charges up."'

Several journalists at the media briefing informed Hinze that they had actually been inside illegal casinos in Fortitude Valley.

The Minister was unmoved.

Accompanying the story was another colourful piece, this time by 'a Staff Liar' (actually staff writer Matt Robbins). 'Somewhere in the last two months I have lost several hours out of my life,' the article said. 'I thought I spent the time at an illegal casino, but Mr Hinze assures me that such places do not exist in Brisbane. Now I'm not sure where I was.'

He offered to take Hinze and his staff on a tour of the casinos. The offer was rejected. (Hooper would offer the same thing to Hinze and Lewis, the gesture labelled by Hinze as a 'gimmick'.)

'The illegal casino row could be amusing if it were not so serious a matter,' Robbins concluded. 'Mr Hooper will not name his senior police informant for fear of repercussions. My name does not appear on this article for the same reason.'

That day Lewis met with Premier Bjelke-Petersen to discuss a range of matters, including 'casinos' and 'Kevin Hooper and Ron Edington'.

That night, Don Lane phoned Lewis to discuss the casino saga.

Hinze phoned Lewis again – on the Saturday morning – about comments by the media on 'casinos', and the Commissioner fielded another call, this one from Sir Edward Lyons.

How did this drama get so out of hand? Lewis, if his diaries are accurate, did not seem overly concerned by it all. But Hinze's silly quips didn't help Lewis.

The Commissioner took an unprecedented initiative.

'I said to Hinze, look, what about getting in a car with the head of the Licensing Branch [Noel Dwyer] ... I said not [with] me so that I don't influence you ... and they could show you these places,' Lewis remembers. 'They went and showed him what must have been Wickham Street and something in Ann Street and he didn't walk up the steps of course. It would have been beyond him.

'He visited these casinos. They're just little sleazy gambling joints. I'd never been in one of them ...'

Lewis recorded in his diary for Monday 19 October 1981: '... With D/Insp Dwyer to TAB, then with Hon Hinze to 701 Ann St, 677 Ann St, 648 Ann St, 142 Wickham St, & 121 Brunswick St, and viewed premises re alleged "casinos".'

Hinze's press secretary, Russell Grenning, says he remembered the famous press conference where Hinze said he didn't know of the existence of gambling dens and massage parlours.

'When Hinze – who was no fool – made this comment it was with a wink that would have felled an elephant but winks don't get recorded in transcripts,' Grenning says. 'He knew there were brothels and illegal casinos in the Valley and elsewhere but felt utterly powerless to do anything about it due to Lewis's relationship with Joh.

'There was a mutual loathing between Lewis and Hinze which built up gradually over 1981. Lewis had cultivated Don Lane and Joh so he could – and did – circumvent Russ and frustrate him at every turn. In a sense, it was an affront to him [Hinze] that Joh let Lewis do this.

'Another reason for their mutual loathing was the fact that "Top Level" Ted Lyons was a great mate of Lewis and, of course, Joh. Hinze always regarded him [Lyons] as a malevolent influence on Joh and the whole government.'

Years later, Colin Lamont, the former member for South Brisbane and champion of civil liberties, remembered the flurry of publicity around the non-existent casinos in Fortitude Valley.

'Russ was on the front page of the *Courier-Mail* saying that there was no corruption in the Valley, there was no gambling in Fortitude Valley,' Lamont said in an interview. 'And a friend of mine [asked] if I'd ever been to one of these places and I said, "No". And he said, "Do you want to go?" And I said, "Yes, I'll take the risk." And I did. And this was after I was in parliament.

'We went up the back stairs of this Bubbles Bath House, and up the fire escape and knocked on the door and got in. And the first person I met was Russ Hinze. And he bought me a drink and I said, "Russ", I said, "you ... how can you afford to be here?" He said, "No journalist can get within a mile of this place tonight." And ... there he was in one of these joints that he said didn't exist. The man had, had balls, if nothing else.'

Grenning believes the story to be false. 'Frankly it is absurd to think that Hinze went to Bubbles Bath House – in his own perhaps curious way he had quite old-fashioned views about that sort of thing,' he says. 'In any case, he would have known that if he did anything that stupid it would instantly be known – and not just "alleged" by somebody who demonstrably was relying on hearsay.'

On Monday 26 October 1981, as the story ultimately petered out,

THE RISE OF FITZGERALD

Lewis made a curious note in his diary. '... saw Col Chant [president of the Police Union] ... re S/Const Campbell, W'Gabba informing to K. Hooper MLA ...'

The Rise of Fitzgerald

By 1981 Tony Fitzgerald had more work than he could handle with a busy practice that constantly took him interstate and away from his young family in Brisbane. He was facing a serious quandary – how could he put in the hours that the job demanded and still be an engaged father to small children?

At just 39, an extraordinary offer came his way.

In 1976, Nigel Bowen, barrister and former politician, had set up the Federal Court of Australia and was appointed its Chief Judge (later Chief Justice). Both the *Administrative Appeals Tribunal Act* and the *Administrative Decisions Judicial Review Act* were put in place around the same time. It meant that for the first time administrative decisions could be effectively challenged. It was a fundamental shift in the law.

Bowen was both a popular lawman and politician who had left politics and gone to the Court of Appeal in New South Wales, when he was asked to set up the Federal Court framework. The court initially proved controversial; the states loathed it.

Bowen withstood the barrage. He was soon attracting the very best of the Sydney bar to join the Federal Court. Eventually they approached Fitzgerald and asked him to set up the court in Brisbane. He would become the youngest Federal Court judge ever appointed.

Fitzgerald found space in a Commonwealth building in Adelaide Street. It became a very popular court quite quickly for the local lawyers. It was hated by the local Supreme Court.

Fitzgerald would find that the old legal guard were split down the middle – some treated him decently, others were outwardly difficult.

According to the *Lex Scripta*: 'He was the Federal Court's first resident Judge in Brisbane, and quickly set about establishing the reputation of the Federal Court in this State as a hard-working and efficient outpost of the Federal Court's national network.

'During Fitzgerald's period as the only Brisbane-based Federal Court Judge, the Queensland District Registry constantly out-performed other State Registries in dealing with its judicial workload and producing decisions which withstood appeal.

'At the same time, the then Chief Judge of the Federal Court, Sir Nigel Bowen, held Fitzgerald in such high regard that he frequently sat on the Full Federal Court in other State capitals, where he was allocated the most difficult and challenging appeals.'

Again, his hours were long and his dedication to the task absolute. Fitzgerald, without doubt, was a rising star in the legal profession. But at what cost?

Take It to the Top Level

Who was 'Top Level' Ted Lyons? The man so trusted by Premier Bjelke-Petersen? The man who kept Commissioner Terry Lewis so enthralled with his stories in his business office high up in the T&G Building in Queen Street?

Lyons had certainly made the Katies women's clothing chain a huge success, but he was hopelessly addicted to punting. And, seemingly, to alcohol.

Insiders at Katies said many strange things went on in the office. 'He used to bet with police officer's money and then he would ring the manager at the main Katies store in Queen Street and he'd say to her, "Just keep a cheque out on one side for Sergeant such and such." Which meant he'd lost; he had to pay it.'

There were concerns too within Katies management about Lyons' behaviour. 'Katies organisation wanted him out of the main Queen Street store because of the way he sort of used to treat staff, and have all these people, including ladies, to the top office,' one former manager remembers. 'And you could see the bottle of Scotch.

'He was a horror, a real horror. He'd say would I meet him down at Lennons because the Lennons Hotel was down in the city at that stage. You used to walk into the room and look around like this and find out there was a chair with just room enough for one person.'

She said Lyons used to boast about his close relationship with the Premier. Government money, too, made its way into Lyons' coffers from a number of sources.

Katies at some point was receiving government funds to assist in traning seamstresses. 'It was all a lot of rubbish because all that they'd done was they had borrowed money from the government and they had to show what they were doing [with it],' the former manager recalls. 'And rather than take the blame and do the interviews with the different ones, he pushed me forward to do all that. And I thought, "You so and so", I don't want to end up in gaol for you.'

'He was really corrupt. He would have paid for his knighthood. I can remember a call coming through from Sydney so I just stepped outside from the door but you could hear what was going on. Then I heard the accountant ask what had happened to cheque number such and such to the value of $25,000. And I thought that must be what he paid for the knighthood.'

Lewis's friendship with 'Top Level' Ted also grew over the years. It extended to personal business advice. 'The only two times that he mentioned anything to me was when we sold up ... my wife had bought a house up the road [in Garfield Drive, Bardon, where the Lewises already had a house at number 12], we borrowed the money ... we kept it for four years and doubled the price of it,' Lewis said in an interview with *Courier-Mail* journalists Ken Blanch and Peter Charlton. 'I said to him [Lyons], what's the best place to put this money in until … we were always planning to build a house, and he said Rothwell's.

'Well I did put it in for a while … my wife was always … shaky … and she said, look, I'd sooner have it in the Credit Union where we know it's safe. We may have left it there [with Rothwell's] about 12 months.

'… and the only other time, he said … gold copper would be a good thing for investment … which I did do … and the shares were 30 cents each and they're worth five cents each now …'

The Bikie Bandits

In the early spring of 1981 Brisbane was held both shocked and gripped by a spate of daring armed hold-ups across the city and on the Gold Coast. The strikes on banks began in July. By the third week of September the culprits had hit seven, and absconded with tens of thousands of dollars. Because the robberies all involved two men on a motorcycle they were dubbed by the press the Bikie Bandit Hold-ups.

In a raid on the Commonwealth Bank in Alderley on 11 September, an elderly customer nearly collapsed during the robbery. 'I was just putting my pension cheque in the bank,' Robert Drew, 69, of Bald Hills, reportedly said. 'Then this bloke with a gun said, "Get over to the wall."

'I went over and heard him say, "Fill the bag up." Then I had one of my spells and had to sit down. I reckon my old heart was beating 100 a minute.'

The Bikie Bandits – on a high-powered motorcycle – continued the spree into October, robbing the National Bank at both Newmarket and West End and the Commonwealth Bank in Paddington in the inner-west of the city. They variously used pistols and sawn-off shotguns.

Police expressed a fear that someone could be shot in future hold-ups. As for the banks, they held unilateral meetings to discuss new security measures in the wake of the Bikie Bandits. Crime Prevention Bureau head, Detective Senior Constable John Hopgood said 'public apathy' was assisting the bandits in eluding arrest. 'When an armed robbery occurs it is just impossible in most cases for bystanders to see nothing,' he told the press. 'Any police force needs information to function. An apathetic public makes our job so much harder.'

In the early hours of Thursday 19 November, detectives perpetrated a series of coordinated dawn raids on houses across Brisbane. Two suspects fled in a car and following a high-speed chase through the streets of genteel Ashgrove were arrested at gunpoint. They were Alfred Thompson, 21, unemployed, of Spring Hill, and Steve Kossaris, also 21 and unemployed, of Ashgrove.

The men were taken to the watchhouse and put in separate cells. According to both men, that night they were allegedly taken into a room in the watchhouse where they would make statements to police.

'You both look pretty sick,' a detective told the two heroin addicts. 'I can give you something to fix you up.' The officer then allegedly directed another detective to go and get some heroin for the two defendants.

The senior detective then allegedly told both men: 'You will have to snort the horse' – inhaling, as opposed to injecting. They refused and a syringe was retrieved.

Thompson alleged a detective '... then held my arm while I injected. The heroin was a very good quality. Kossaris then injected himself.'

Meanwhile, the public defender's office sent down two young lawyers to interview Thompson and Kassaris. On completion of the interviews with their clients the lawyers met up again. One said to the other: 'I've just heard the most extraordinary story I've ever heard.'

The lawyer said his client had told him that police had given him a fix of heroin before he wrote down his formal statement as dictated by police. The other lawyer, incredulous, replied: 'I've just had the same experience.'

If true, it gave new meaning to the word 'verbal'. Both men faced a total of 26 charges.

The allegations that police provided heroin and needles to the two men in order to facilitate a confession would not surface until Thompson and Kassaris's trial in the spring of the following year, but it would ignite yet another crisis for Commissioner Lewis and his boys in blue.

Our Bent Friend

On the morning of 18 December, another letter from the 'crazed gunman' of 1959, Gunther Bahnemann, appeared in Commissioner Lewis's in-tray.

Bahnemann, it transpired, had been to see Tony Murphy in his office in Cairns and had shared some intelligence on the drug scene in Far North Queensland.

Gunther told his former foe that he had recently turned 61 and was as fit as a fiddle. He said whenever he saw Commissioner Lewis on television, he couldn't help but notice that the top cop never seemed to age.

'You know, Terry, our "bent" friend Glen [Hallahan] would have sprouted wings had he been in your seat, in fact, he would have been TV's crowning star with a "Kill Sheet" of endless dimensions,' Bahnemann quipped.

He detailed his meeting with Murphy. 'A couple of months ago I had a session and my wife as well with Tony Murphy in his office, subject marihuana plantations and Cape York in general,' he wrote. 'It so happens that up here I am known as an authority on Cape York – offshore, inshore, and interior-wise of this last bit of wilderness.

'Ten years of pearling along the cape coast, croc shooting in the off-season and in 1950 guiding the American Archibald Expedition from the top to Cooktown, having been wrecked twice on its shores left its mark. A professional navigator, its geographical ramifications stay fixed in my mind to day [sic].'

Bahnemann shared his opinions on likely locations of drug plantations with Murphy. He identified the Portland Road area, the Pascoe River, Packers Creek, Lloyds Bay and Cape Grenville. 'I feel Princes [sic] Charlotte Bay is the southern trading post provided by trawlers,' Bahnemann added.

It was an extraordinary supposition on the former German war hero's part. Princess Charlotte Bay was close to Jane Table Mountain, the precise location where drug importer John Edward Milligan had scrambled about in the wilderness searching for two large packages of heroin dropped from a light aircraft in the 1970s.

Bahnemann couldn't have known that their 'bent' friend, Glen Patrick Hallahan – the man Bahnemann had been convicted of attempting to murder in late 1959 – was Milligan's partner in the drug shipment.

'Tony Murphy thinks along my lines, however, geographically and environment-wise he is not too informed, there is a vast difference viewing it from a helicopter or traversing it on the ground,' Bahnemann added.

He ended the letter cheerily. 'All the best for now, Terry, write if the subject is of interest to you. Best of luck. Gunther.'

The Full Fowl

At around 2 a.m. on Friday 18 December 1981, the phone rang up at Garfield Drive. It was Sir Edward Lyons, chairman of the TAB and trustee of the National Party. He was in the city watchhouse having been detained for suspected drink driving.

Earlier the previous night, Commissioner Lewis and his wife, Hazel, had attended a variety of Christmas functions, one being a cocktail party at TAB headquarters at 240 Sandgate Road in Albion, just north of the CBD. Lewis went on to a Police Union dinner, but 'Top Level' Ted had cocktailed on.

Lyons left the party around 1.20 a.m. in his Rolls-Royce and headed across the Story Bridge and onto the South East Freeway heading for his home in Holland Park, just south-east of the CBD.

Sergeant Lennie Bracken and Constable First Class Carmichael were travelling on the freeway in a squad car and noticed the Roller being driven erratically. Lyons was pulled over. When he refused to take a breath test, he was driven back to the watchhouse. Once there, Kathleen Rynders of the Breath Analysis Section certified that Lyons had a blood alcohol content of .12, just under twice the legal limit. His breathalyser ticket number was D57106. Carmichael started writing out a regulation Bench Charge Sheet.

Lyons, 67, asked officer in charge, Inspector Dante Squassoni, if he could make a telephone call. The phone soon started ringing in Lewis's home.

Lewis asked for Squassoni to get on the line. According to Squassoni, Lewis told him: 'You know he's Premier Joh Bjelke-Petersen's right-hand man ... surely you can do something.'

Squassoni got the impression Lewis wanted the charge dropped. Then Bracken got on the phone, and Lewis said: 'Other than my mother, Lyons is the only bloke I'd like to do something for ... take him home.'

Lewis's diary recorded: 'At 2am Sir Edward Lyons phoned re detention for suspected UIL. Spoke to Const. Carmichael, Insp. D. Squassoni and Sgt. L. Bracken.'

Carmichael later claimed either Squassoni or Bracken told him to forget about the incident, and he threw the Bench Charge Sheet and breath analysis certificate in a waste paper bin. Bracken wasn't happy with the result, and told Lyons to drive himself home, he and Carmichael following the Roller to Holland Park. Lyons asked them in for a cup of tea. They declined.

A young constable, Brian Cook, retrieved the documents from the bin and handed them to Senior Constable Bob Campbell, who then passed them on to the tearaway MP Kev Hooper. Hooper, in turn, immediately leaked them to Ric Allen at the *Sunday Mail* newspaper.

That Friday Lewis recorded nothing in his diary about Lyons' predicament even though he had several conversations with his Minister, Russ Hinze. But on the Saturday, he got in touch with Hinze and Bracken again, probably following queries from the journalist Allen.

The *Sunday Mail* ran its extraordinary scoop on page one the next day: KNIGHT FACES DRIVE CHARGE.

Ric Allen wrote that Lyons had been detained by police over suspected drink driving 'but was not charged or arrested'. 'The Police Commissioner confirmed this yesterday, but denied any "cover-up".'

Lewis, through a spokesman, said: 'Sir Edward had to fly to Sydney on urgent business but he will appear in court on the drink driving charge offence.'

The newspaper pointed out that Lyons had not appeared in the Magistrates' Court on Friday and that no record of the incident could be found in the Brisbane watchhouse log book. Lewis said Lyons would be charged by summons.

On the day the newspaper story appeared, Inspector Squassoni was told by Lewis: 'Make sure Carmichael takes out a summons and make sure he is aware this was the intended action all along.'

A report in the Brisbane *Sun* carried the headline: TOP LEVEL TED – FULL AS A FOWL.

The Attorney-General and Justice Minister Sam Doumany immediately ordered an investigation. Hinze said he would have nothing to do with an inquiry into the Lyons matter. Lewis ordered a separate investigation into how the Lyons documents found their way to the media. Constable Cook, who had originally plucked them from the trash, was transferred to Longreach.

Lewis recalls that the issue was blown out of all proportion: 'I'd been to two functions and I think I got home about 11 o'clock or something, again I'd have it written up. Two o'clock in the morning I think it was I got a phone call and I'd had the two functions, I'd had one or two drinks.

'It was the watchhouse, saying he [Lyons] was there, [he'd] been pinched. Little shithouse, too, of a sergeant, the police officer.

'Ted Lyons must have spoken to me too, so they both spoke to me to say that he'd have to be in Sydney that morning for his ... somebody sponsored him. Katies or something that sponsored some art award [the Archibald Prize], and he had to be down there to present it and he had booked on the six o'clock flight or something.

'So I said to this young fellow, which was permissible, "Can you arrange for him to be released?" But they released him without charging him, which is again okay, I mean you can summons a person.

'But why would I tell them to blood test him or whatever it was ... to take his reading before releasing him? I would have said let him out, but they took whatever his alcohol content was, made a note of it, then released him to go and then some policewoman, she came in after that and found out that morning or the next day that they had released him.

'They made a great big story of it, and of course he was summoned to appear before the court later but it appeared that I had said, "Let the bastard, let the fellow go." And you can't do that. I mean if they're at the watchhouse and every bugger and his dog knows it. So they made a great song and dance about that.'

The story quietly fizzled, but it resonated with Senior Constable Bob Campbell. He was fed up with what he perceived was rampant corruption in the force.

On Wednesday 23 December Lewis noted in his diary: '... saw Const R.J. Campbell re transfer and resign. from 28.2.82.'

Had Lewis and others discovered that he had passed on the incriminating Lyons documents to Kev Hooper?

Campbell himself prepared a confidential 11-page statement, witnessed and signed by a Justice of the Peace, to protect himself.

The next Sunday, Commissioner Lewis and Hazel were down at Hinze's Waverley Park horse stud at Pimpama, on the Pacific Highway 30 kilometres north of Surfers Paradise, for lunch. The stud was Hinze's crown jewel – 24.28 hectares of training tracks, stables, squash courts, pool and staff quarters. The Hinzes lived in a two-storey mansion on the property, guarded by two trained Rottweilers.

Lewis's diary revealed: '... spoke to him [Hinze] re Campbell preparing report to Chief Justice re Abuse of Office ...'

Lewis had some time off in the New Year, taking lunch at Eddie Kornhauser's Paradise Centre in the heart of Surfers Paradise on the Gold Coast. Kornhauser was a close friend of Russ Hinze, and at the time was being interviewed as a prospective applicant to build Queensland's first legal casino on the coast.

Lewis entered his sixth year as Commissioner unaware that soon to be retired Bob Campbell was about to tread down that well-worn, ultimately pointless, and often very deadly path of the whistleblower.

Nationwide

In the New Year, young ABC journalist Alan Hall got a call from one of his good contacts, Kevin Hooper, the opposition spokesman on police and prisons. Hooper had been elected to parliament in 1972; it was the same election that the great corruption fighter Col Bennett, having lost his ALP preselection for the seat of South Brisbane, ran as an independent and lost.

Hooper, by generational fate or design, quickly took up Bennett's mantle. Under parliamentary privilege he poked and prodded at the government and in particular successive police ministers. His prized targets, though, were Terry Lewis and Tony Murphy.

Private secretary to Tom Burns, Malcolm McMillan, remembers the atmosphere in Parliament House when it was suspected Hooper was about to lob a grenade within the chamber.

'He glowed, he was luminous,' says McMillan. 'He'd come into the press room clutching an envelope and say: "Boys and girls, have I got a story for you today!"'

Hooper was given the nickname 'Buckets'. He had an interesting tale for Hall, who worked for the ABC television current affairs program *Nationwide*.

Hooper had been in touch with a disaffected Queensland police officer who – incredibly – was happy to go on camera and deride what he saw as institutionalised corruption in the force. The officer had had a 'gutful', his career had suffered because of his honesty, and he wanted to unburden. The prospective whistleblower was Bob Campbell, one of the co-authors of that unsettling in-house news sheet, *The Woolloongabba Worrier*, that had so enraged his superiors, including the Commissioner. Campbell was due to formally resign from the force on the last day of February.

In turn, Hall learned of Kingsley Winston Fancourt – the disaffected Licensing Branch officer who had come close to exposing Herbert and the Rat Pack in the 1970s. It was an irresistible story for the gung-ho Hall, then 23.

Hall tracked down Fancourt in the small western Queensland town of Anakie. He telephoned and left a message at the local hotel.

A few days later, Fancourt entered the public bar. 'I didn't go to the pub all that often but on this occasion I did,' says Fancourt. 'The barmaid gave me a message, which had been sitting there for a few days. It was from Alan Hall.

'I rang him and told him I'd be willing to come down to Brisbane. He sent up a charter flight for me.'

Fancourt flew out of Emerald for Brisbane and was put up in a hotel. In the presence of his lawyer, Dale Smith, he recorded several interviews with Hall for *Nationwide*. He never came in contact with or discussed any matters with Bob Campbell, who was interviewed separately. 'There couldn't be seen to be any collusion,' recalls Fancourt.

Hall was thrilled that the two former police officers were willing to go on the record for the story. 'They'd raised questions internally [within the department] and were told to either shut up or get out,' Hall remembers. 'At first I went and talked to them individually. Fancourt complained about senior police taking pay-offs from criminals. And Campbell had been involved in the Ted Lyons drink-driving incident.

'I eventually compiled the report that alleged widespread corruption that kept pointing towards Tony Murphy and Terry Lewis.'

The program was due to go to air on Wednesday 3 March. As the story was being put together, Lyons was banned from driving for four months and fined $175 over his drink driving charge.

Then on 2 March, Kev Hooper, knowing what was to be broadcast on national television the following night, rekindled the Lyons scandal and tabled two controversial documents – the bench sheet and breathalyser certificate – in parliament.

Hooper said the so-called Lyons and Lewis conspiracy over the matter deserved an inquiry and criminal charges should be laid. When Hinze asked him what he had against Lewis, Hooper replied: 'I've nothing against him personally. I just think he is a corrupt crook.'

It was the perfect build-up to *Nationwide*'s explosive story.

In the segment, Fancourt and Campbell claimed – with either breathtaking courage or naivety – that senior police were involved in the drug trade, illegal gambling and prostitution rackets, and were masterminding much of the state's criminal activity.

On the program, Hooper weighed in on the attack. 'The corruption is in the highest echelon of the force and it is difficult for the honest police officer to carry out his duties.'

Campbell added that he had been threatened by police following an internal complaint he'd made several months earlier. Fancourt went on to allege that pay-offs to police were 'coordinated' by what was known as 'the Rat Pack', which was made up of three senior detectives.

Don Lane MP got straight on the phone to Lewis at home early the next morning. Lewis was at his desk at 7.40 a.m. 'Phoned Hon Hinze re "Nationwide" attack on Police. Discussed matter with Snr Officers. With messrs Duffy, Atkinson, Murphy, Dwyer, Early and Hatcher to Parlt House and saw Hon Hinze and prepared Ministerial Statement. Hon Hinze phoned re D/C Duffy and a Crown Law officer to see Campbell and Fancourt and request signed statements.'

Hinze was initially apoplectic. He called the *Nationwide* segment and the former officers' allegations 'a cock and bull story', and Campbell and Fancourt 'two disgruntled malcontents with a grudge against the police force'.

He called Campbell a 'bludger' and a 'professional student'. He ordered police to locate the two men and 'wait upon them' if they had to. He challenged the two men to come forward with signed statements about what they knew of this so-called corruption.

What the public didn't know was that Hinze was already in possession of Campbell's statement, and he was about to receive Fancourt's, quite literally, in the middle of his parliamentary condemnation of the two former officers.

Fancourt was in Parliament House in George Street that day too, and submitted his signed statement to Hinze's staff. In the middle of the Minister's tirade, the document was handed to him. Hinze briefly paused, tucked it into a folder he was holding, and continued his attack.

'He had the statement right there, handed to him,' Kingsley Fancourt remembers. 'Hinze didn't even mention it.'

Hinze went to town on Campbell and Fancourt. 'I am reliably informed that Robert J. Campbell is the author of an underground newspaper known as the *Woolloongabba Worrier*,' he bellowed. 'This grubby little rag, which has seen three issues, was published anonymously and clearly expounds philosophies that were repeated in last night's scurrilous attack on *Nationwide*.'

Hinze then turned his attention to Fancourt: 'What I would like to know is why it took Mr Fancourt approximately six years to summon the courage to come forward with his allegations. 'As all honourable members would know, Mr Fancourt left the police force before the present Commissioner, Mr Lewis, was appointed. Whilst in the police force he was the mining warden in Anakie and used this position to obtain some of the best mining leases available.'

'What a filthy smear,' Kev Hooper interjected.

'What did you do about it?' asked Tom Burns. 'He did nothing, only tip the bucket over him six years later.'

'As I said,' Hinze continued, 'he used his position as mining warden in Anakie to obtain some of the best mining leases available.'

'So have some of your ministers,' the ALP member for Nudgee, Ken Vaughan, retorted.

In a press conference later, an enraged Hinze faced a barrage of tough questions from Alan Hall. The two men stoushed. Hinze guaranteed he would have Hall 'out of a job'.

Lewis then called in Tony Murphy and they discussed Campbell.

Early the next week, Premier Joh Bjelke-Petersen also phoned Lewis to discuss 'action on Campbell and Fancourt's allegations'.

Predictably, Campbell, married and the father of young children, faced a now familiar counter-attack. His wife and children were threatened by men who arrived in an unmarked CIB vehicle. Campbell fled with his family to Tasmania. Fancourt returned to the gemfields of central Queensland.

Just over a week after the *Nationwide* segment went to air, Lewis had a meeting with lawyer Des Sturgess about a potential defamation writ. Murphy joined Lewis in the court action. Both, in their writs, identified themselves and Glen Patrick Hallahan as members of the so-called 'rat-pack' referred to in the program.

In his statement of claim, Murphy declared: 'Among police officers in Queensland the words 'the Rat Pack' had since the 1960s been used to refer to and include the plaintiff, Terence Murray Lewis and one Glen Patrick Hallahan who served with them in the police force.'

Detective Sergeant Neal Freier also sued, claiming he was an unnamed police officer in the show, and that he had been defamed. Bjelke-Petersen decided the government would financially assist Lewis's and Murphy's legal action.

Hall stood his ground: 'I talked to ABC management and I didn't resile from any of the allegations made by Fancourt and Campbell. As a journalist there was an acceptance that some of the cops were bent. Murphy in particular was the object of many allegations. It always went back to Murphy.'

Nationwide didn't stop. Another story – featuring actors dramatising two more unnamed whistleblowers including a Gold Coast prostitute – aired on 18 March. In that episode there were further allegations that small, entrenched groups within the Queensland Police Force were involved in prostitution, gambling and SP bookmaking. The groups were controlled by 'a high ranking officer'.

The actor relayed one of the male police officers' allegations: 'The people we're talking about are very cunning operators. They're very astute people and very, very intelligent people.' He added they were 'versed in the intricacies of law in Queensland and the criminal mind'. It was a punishing follow-up to the Campbell and Fancourt story.

Hinze immediately told parliament he would ask Cabinet to establish a tribunal to hear complaints against the police from inside and outside the force. While there was no evidence to support allegations of corruption, the media was 'continually bringing up the matter' and it was now time to clear the air.

The loquacious Police Minister described the latest *Nationwide* story as 'a new soap opera', and that it 'would have done proud' the likes of *General Hospital* and *Days of Our Lives*.

Hinze, ever volatile on the floor of the House, declared: 'The allegations were vague, meaningless, non-specific, but successfully cast another cloud over the Queensland Police Force.'

In the aftermath, Bjelke-Petersen banned Alan Hall from any future government-related press conferences. It didn't worry Hall. 'I think I was too young, too excited about doing the job. I had a healthy dose of paranoia to feed on, especially over a few beers in the pub at the end of the day.'

Lewis was furious at the press coverage of the *Nationwide* aftermath. On Tuesday 6 April, he, along with 'all Snr Officers and Supts' arrived at the offices of the *Courier-Mail*, the *Sunday Mail* and the Brisbane *Daily Telegraph*, a rectangular red-brick building beside the railway tracks in Campbell Street, Bowen Hills.

According to his diary, Lewis had 'very frank' discussions with: 'Messrs H. [Harry] Gordon, D. [David] Smith, D. [Doug] Flaherty, K. [Kevin] Kavanagh and snr officials of Qld newspapers re very unbalanced reporting on Police in recent months'.

That night at home, he had a phone call from Jack Herbert over a police inquiry in New South Wales. There is little doubt they discussed this latest media assault on the Queensland force, and ways to make it go away.

A Typical Day for Anne Marie Tilley

Anne Marie Tilley, the young prostitute from Sydney made good, was sitting on a vice empire that was almost gowing too rapidly to contain.

On any given day she would get up, make herself a coffee, and check the rosters for her parlour receptionists. Tilley would then ring each and every parlour to check with the girls and make sure everything was on track. They had developed a special code, so if one of the girls told Tilley 'the kittens have been born', it meant there was trouble and somebody would be dispatched immediately to the parlour.

Tilley made at least 20 to 30 calls, checking up on business from the previous night. If one of the girls was sick, she'd man the reception herself. By nightfall Tilley would do her round of checks again. She would inspect the day books to see how business was going and make sure that all the girls had been paid.

'Work just kept going, you didn't stop,' says Tilley. 'Hec might stay up late, to 4 a.m. or 5 a.m. I might stay up … to make sure everything was okay … it was 24 hours. I was an alcoholic, but nobody ever knew I was drunk, you could never tell. I just drank Scotch one after the other – rum and coke – just one after the other. The old fella was Bourbon and coke. I had my other little bits of pills and stuff, hash oil. Nobody knew I used drugs. If I was overtired, I'd have a bit of hash, relax me down, have a little nap. Anything else, speed, to keep me awake. I never ever had a holiday in 25 years.'

As for Tilley's payments to Jack Herbert, who she knew as 'Tom', the money was always on time and delivered in the same way. 'Payments to Jack were in old folded up paper bags,' she says. 'Plain old brown paper bags. Or occasionally a plastic bag that couldn't be seen through. It was all packed in there.'

Guns and Handcuffs

By March 1982 Detective Lorelle Saunders was still in an on-again, off-again relationship with Allan Lobegeiger. He'd since been promoted to Regional Superintendent of the South East Police Region and was now based on the Gold Coast.

On Sunday 7 March, Saunders and her friend Roy Coomer went out to the Belmont Pistol Club, then had dinner at Toni's restaurant in Logan Road, Mount Gravatt, south of the CBD. They left the restaurant around 9 p.m. and returned to Coomer's car. They discovered it had been broken into and some pretty dangerous hardware had been stolen from the vehicle – Coomer's four handguns and an Armalite rifle.

Saunders made a formal complaint to police then phoned Lobegeiger on his property in Gatton, almost 90 kilometres west of Brisbane in the Lockyer Valley.

'Allan, I've been out to dinner and the car I'm in has been broken into and a stack of guns [have] gone,' she told him.

'Oh, Jesus,' he said. 'Shit, what were you doing at dinner with guns in a car?'

'I didn't know they were there,' she replied. 'I knew there was a rifle but not all the other stuff.'

'What about yours?'

'No.'

'Who were you at dinner with?' he asked.

'Just a friend.'

'That other bastard. You're the one caught out this time, eh?'

'Be serious. I'm worried.'

Both Saunders and Lobegeiger had been receiving a number of threatening phone calls. She had detected late night prowlers near her home and somebody had emptied a large quantity of dog excrement into her swimming pool. In addition, some shrubs in her garden had suddenly died.

Similarly, Lobegeiger had suffered damage to his house in Cleveland, and the police station at Miami on the Gold Coast had been mysteriously damaged.

She wondered if there was a connection between the caller and the gun theft.

Shortly after, Saunders contacted a drug informant, Douglas Mervyn Dodd, and asked him if he could keep his ear to the ground in relation to the stolen weapons.

On 25 March, Saunders was told that her informant, Dodd, had been arrested with a .22 revolver. Its serial number matched one of Coomer's missing guns.

She phoned Lobegeiger about Dodd. He had already heard the news. 'Don't tell the department anything about it or our relationship if they talk to you,' he warned. 'Trust me and my judgement. There's something going on. Just keep a note of any dealings you have with Dodd ...'

The following day Lobegeiger phoned and told her that Dodd was alleging that she had arranged for him to steal Coomer's guns. She agreed to be interviewed over the matter.

Later, Lobegeiger told Saunders he suspected the whole thing was a set-up organised by Tony Murphy. He and Murphy had clashed when they were both working up in Cairns over 'police pay-offs'. Murphy was building a block of units in Cairns with Lobegeiger's ill-gotten gains, Lobegeiger alleged. Murphy was also against Lobegeiger's activities on the Gold Coast as he had been raiding premises and arresting 'protected' people. He believed Murphy might have been trying to get to him through Saunders.

Saunders herself had done enough over the years, however, to raise the ire of Murphy – her visit with Basil Hicks to interview Katherine James being one of them.

Then on Sunday 25 April, Saunders was questioning a suspect at the city watchhouse in relation to a number of criminal charges. Later, back in the Task Force offices, she saw the Sunday newspapers.

She noticed a story by Brian Bolton – Murphy's old mate – that claimed a Queensland policewoman had plotted to murder a senior police officer. It claimed that detectives had uncovered a plot by a criminal and the policewoman to ambush the officer, murder him and dump his body in bushland on the outskirts of Brisbane.

'There were headlines in the [*Sunday*] *Sun* alleging very serious matters were being investigated against a female officer,' Saunders said. 'This was the [only] knowledge I had of any such investigation. I subsequently contacted my solicitor.'

Commissioner Lewis made no notation about such a major story in his diary, nor did he speak to anyone on the telephone about it. On 28 April, however, he did phone 'Sir Robert Sparkes re P/W L. Saunders'.

It was curious timing to be talking with Sparkes about Saunders, because the very next day on Thursday 29 April, Saunders was at home on sick leave and had gone out to the chemist. When she got back, she was confronted by Detective Inspectors Webb and Flannigan and two other officers. She phoned her solicitor and he told her to come to his office immediately.

She was then arrested by Webb. 'I had no knowledge of the charges until arrested,' she said.

The charges were that she had attempted to procure Douglas Mervyn Dodd to steal money; that on unknown dates she attempted to procure Douglas Mervyn Dodd to conspire with another to kill Allan Lobegeiger; and that on 7 March, at Brisbane, she stole a .357 Magnum Smith and Wesson revolver, a .22 Smith and Wesson revolver, a .44 Magnum Smith and Wesson revolver, and an Armalite semi-automatic rifle and a quantity of ammunition, the property of Roy Alfred Coomer.

'On my arrest I handed my locker keys to Brian Webb.'

Bail was refused on the orders of Tony Murphy, who had recently been promoted to Assistant Comissioner (Crime).

Extraordinarily, Commissioner Lewis made not a single notation about the arrest of Saunders in his diaries. The first female detective in Queensland Police Force history is arrested for attempting to plot and murder a high-ranking police officer, and it didn't warrant inclusion.

What Lewis did was head out to Fig Tree Pocket 're function for Emperor of Japan's Birthday'.

To Put the Record Straight

In the fallout from the *Nationwide* fiasco, corruption-buster Kevin Hooper sharpened his knives for the debate in parliament on the Police Complaints Tribunal Bill.

However optimistic Hinze might have been about setting up some form of watchdog to oversee his force, the debate gave the member for Archerfield a fresh opportunity to hammer the Bjelke-Petersen government over years of corruption allegations against the police, and specifically Commissioner Terry Lewis and his Assistant Commissioner Tony Murphy.

On Thursday 1 April 1982, a frustrated Hooper went to town. Police Commissioner Lewis, perhaps acting on a tip-off, was in the House for the debate. Hooper brought attention to a recent survey that revealed the New South Wales force had the lowest credibility rating of all forces in the Commonwealth, but was followed closely by the Queensland force, with a credibility rating only 0.07 per cent higher. He poked a stick at the Commisoner of Police and directly asked about the activities of the Internal Investigations Section, claiming they were focused on anticipating attacks that might be levelled against corrupt senior officers and intimidating potential witnesses rather than protecting honest officers. He claimed that this was being done 'in conjunction with the trumping up of evidence that could be vital in protecting some senior officers who are well aware of the amount of evidence against them'.

He challenged the Police Commissioner by saying 'if he denies it that will vindicate my argument that he does not know what is happening in his own department'.

Hooper dodged and weaved interjections.

'To put the record straight, who are the criminals in the Police Force who are being protected?' Hooper went on. 'They include none other than the Commissioner himself [Mr Terence Murray Lewis], and his Assistant Commissioner [Tony Murphy]. Both officers have had meteoric rises. As boys, they were banished to the bush by a former honest police commissioner for their conduct, but have risen to stardom under this National Party-controlled Government.

'This parliament is well aware of Mr Lewis's conduct.'

Hooper branded Lewis one of the most 'silent' Police Commissioners in memory. Not even Police Minister Hinze, rising to a point of order, could protect Lewis.

'Parliament is well aware of Mr Lewis's conduct in the [Ted] Lyons [drink driving] fiasco,' the member for Archerfield continued. 'It has been well documented by me, I might add, that the Commissioner has never bothered to publicly refute the allegations. He dare not!

'He may yet have to explain under oath his actions that night. If he and Sir Edward Lyons think that that disgraceful performance is gone and forgotten, they are sadly mistaken. I have not forgotten and neither have the people of Queensland. The day of reckoning will arrive.'

Hooper then went into the dark past and brought Tony Murphy along for the ride.

'Mr Murphy is deeply indebted to the Queensland Police Union for its financial support when he was charged with perjury. That charge followed his conduct during the National Hotel royal commission. I might add that he was not convicted.'

Then the ghost of former prostitute and brothel madam, Shirley Margaret Brifman, dead of a drug overdose just weeks before Murphy was to answer perjury charges stemming from the National Hotel inquiry in the early 1960s, stalked the chamber.

'The chief witness against Mr Murphy was Shirley Brifman who was not available owing to her timely death,' said Hooper. 'The anomalies in the police investigation – or should I say the lack of investigations – into the death of Brifman were well documented in 1972.

'They would no doubt have been brought up in a royal commission into the Police Force. His protection of a former police commissioner [Frank Bischof] has also been well documented.

'Who has been singing the praises of Murphy for many years? None other than the Police Minister, Mr Hinze! At page 1057 of "Hansard" dated 13 October 1971 he said – "Everybody knows that Hallahan and Murphy are highly respected police officers."

'High praise indeed. Unfortunately the praise was misplaced and Hallahan was subsequently kicked out of the Police Force because of his criminal activities.'

Hooper's attack on the Rat Pack, while certainly not his first, was excoriating. Under parliamentary privilege, Hooper's historical cry gathered an air of futility and desperation.

'It is now April 1982,' Hooper continued. 'Almost 11 years later, and the same charges are being laid and there is still no investigation.

'Murphy's protection of gambling joints and massage parlours is legend in the Police Force. I suppose this will be denied, as the Minister assures us that they do not exist and are figments of my imagination. It is well known that the Minister was kicked out of the Golden Hands massage parlour for refusing to pay the fee.'

Hinze retorted with a bit of cryptic scuttlebutt: 'What about the little girl in Malaya?'

'I have never been to Malaya,' Hooper replied.

He then branded the proposed Police Complaints Tribunal a 'National Party kangaroo court'.

'The criticism of the Police Force has been so long, so sustained and so well documented that only a royal commission can unearth the true facts.' Hooper concluded: 'For many years the Minister for Police and I have been great protagonists, but I make my next comment as a friend. This sordid episode is clearly his swan-song, so why doesn't he go out gracefully by appointing a royal commission into the Queensland Police Force? Of course, a few of his mates sitting behind him will get a bit of a splash, but so what?'

Later in the debate, Police Minister Hinze rose to counter Kev Hooper. His attacks had the impact of a wet sponge.

'The attitude of the honourable member for Archerfield should be placed on record. I cannot believe that even members of the ALP would want to support his actions. For so long the Police Force has had to take his criticisms.'

Hinze branded Hooper a political coward.

'His hatred for the Police Force is well known,' Hinze continued near the end of the debate. 'He is bordering on complete hysteria. More so than anyone else in Queensland, he has been a vocal critic of the Police Force for many years.

'One could reasonably assume that he would welcome the establishment of a police tribunal in which to air his complaints and give them some credence.'

In the end though, Hooper's tirade hit the mark.

The following day, Lewis noted a phone call from Bob Gibbs, ALP member for Wolston: 're ALP members disassociating themselves from Mr Hooper's remarks'. Former police union boss, Ron Edington, also phoned 'with information to attack Mr K. Hooper's family – I declined'.

That afternoon, unaware of the irony, Commissioner Lewis and his wife, Hazel, proceeded to the Police Academy at Oxley for the institution's tenth anniversary. The celebrations included the unveiling of the R.W. Whitrod chapel, the 'Harry Allsop Library' [in honour of the first director of the Academy] and the 'T.M. Lewis Pool'.

Dave and Bill and Paul

Constable Dave had become famous in Brisbane and beyond. He was also friends with another famous media personality – Bill Hurrey of the ABC.

For Moore, though, the public attention was getting a little frightening. His face was everywhere in the media. Wherever he went he was stopped by fans. In restaurants they'd want his autograph. They'd stop him when he was out shopping. Radio 4BC did a survey on their talent and Moore topped the list as the most popular.

Then a seemingly innocuous incident occurred when Moore was promoting the police force at Careers Week at the Exhibition Showgrounds. The police stand happened to be next to one for the South East Queensland Electricity Board (SEQEB). The workers on the stand were young men in their late teens and early twenties. A friend of Moore's, Paul Breslin, dropped by the stand and asked the SEQEB boys back to his unit for a drink later on.

'He had a pretty smicko unit down on the Botanical Gardens and he invited three of these guys back for drinks, along with Moore,' says a friend of Moore's. 'During the course of the 45 minutes they were there, everybody was always fascinated with police and the police uniform, and so on that occasion one of the young guys tried on Moore's police uniform. Moore put on his SEQEB uniform. And Breslin took a photo.'

It all seemed fairly harmless, but by now word was beginning to circulate within police headquarters that Moore was mixing with characters like Hurrey and a man called Paul Breslin, a former private investigator and freelance journalist who also described himself as a 'businessman'.

Around this time, Moore was ordered to see Deputy Commissioner Syd Atkinson in his office. 'He wanted to talk to Moore about associating with Paul Breslin,' a source said. 'Paul Breslin had started to become noticeable. He was a member of the Police Club pretending to be this and that. Syd Atkinson gave Moore a verbal warning about associating with him.'

Moore also started to distance himself from Hurrey. He was sick of the scene, and the lies. Moore had a premonition – he imagined seeing one of those old metal stands that held the posters for that day's *Daily Telegraph* or *Courier-Mail*, with his name adversely mentioned in the headline.

About this time Commissioner Lewis was also quietly informed that Dave Moore may have been a homosexual and was mixing with some undesirable characters.

'Every bugger liked him,' recalls Lewis. 'And then eventually it did come up to say that, oh, he was suspect. I think David Jefferies [of the Juvenile Aid Bureau and a close friend to Lewis] might have been one of the fellows involved in looking at him.

'I said, "Look, go and find out … check, is he married and that?" Geez, he's married with four children. I thought it's just some bastard jealous because he's on TV … I found it hard to believe. I didn't pick him. I wouldn't have picked him.'

A Telegram from Tony Murphy

Meanwhile, Jim Slade was working diligently undercover for Tony Murphy in Far North Queensland. He was scoping Cape Tribulation around this time with other undercover officers including Stacey Kirmos. It was dangerous work. Slade and his colleagues were starting to infiltrate drug-dealing circles.

'Stacey was with this group who were dealing drugs, quite heavy,' recalls Slade. 'One of them was an ex-SAS guy and we were quite worried about that.'

According to Slade, the operation was going well until he learned something that shocked him to the core. It was, to Slade, the ultimate breach of trust. 'I learned later that a telegram [was] sent by Tony Murphy to this group and they picked it up at the Bloomfield River post office [not far from Cedar Bay]. The telegram told them that Stacey was in there, and the whole thing turned to shit. They took Stacey hostage.

'Someone might have walked back that night from Cape Tribulation to the ferry and we were able to get assistance and get Stacey out. That would have been the first time in my career I had heard Tony getting involved in anything.'

This event coincided with Justice Williams' Royal Commission which was attempting to establish, among other things, whether or not the Federal Narcotics Bureau was worthwhile.

Also, the National Crime Authority had been pushing for a charter in Queensland and Murphy and Lewis resisted it, says Slade.

'Queensland was the only state in Australia where nothing was happening in relation to external agencies.'

The telegram incident made Slade look at his hero Murphy in a different way. Murphy had taught Slade everything he knew.

It did confirm one thing to Jim Slade. You never knew who you could trust.

Tribunal

When the Police Complaints Tribunal Bill was passed through parliament the hunt was on for a respected member of the judiciary to head it — a contentious post by anybody's reckoning.

Whoever got the nod was already going to be behind the eightball. The tribunal's charter, enshrined in legislation, stipulated that any investigative work would be carried out by the police department's Internal Investigation Unit.

The catch-22 was that back in the first few weeks of Commissioner Lewis's administration, in early 1977, he and Tony Murphy had dismantled Whitrod's crack Crime Intelligence Unit and replaced it with the Internal Investigations Unit (IIU). On top of that, Lewis then came to an agreement with the Police Union – the IIU could not use police to investigate other police. On paper, the tribunal, therefore, was already dead in the water before it put up its shingle.

Nevertheless, someone had to run it.

In April 1982, Judge William Joseph Carter was on the court circuit in Bundaberg and was taking breakfast in his motel room. Carter, the son of a barber and hotel keeper, was born in Goondiwindi and schooled in Toowoomba before studying commerce and dentistry at the University of Queensland. These studies were put on hold after he entered the Banyo Catholic seminary for three years. Carter returned to study law at the University of Queensland in Brisbane, graduating in 1959.

He was admitted as a barrister of the Supreme Court of Queensland on 16 December 1959, and took silk in late 1978. He was appointed as a judge of the District Court of Queensland on 4 February 1980. Carter was smart, likeable, honest, and didn't mind a punt on the horses.

He was finishing up breakfast that day in his motel room when the telephone rang. 'Is that Judge Carter?' the caller asked. 'This is Joh Bjelke-Petersen speaking.'

Carter thought it was a practical joke. He had a good friend who was a superb mimic, and responded accordingly. 'Don't give me that bullshit,' he said. 'I'm on circuit. You don't have any respect for me at all!'

The voice responded: 'Judge Carter?' It actually was the Premier.

Carter recalls: 'He rang me and said – it was inappropriate that he did ring me – he wanted me to chair the Police Complaints Tribunal. I told him I couldn't answer that. It was up to the chairman of the court [Bill Grant-Taylor] to decide. I didn't want to be talking one on one to the Premier, or any other politicians for that matter.'

Carter ultimately accepted the role, working with fellow members, magistrate Phillip Rodgers and Police Union president Col Chant. The tribunal met for the first time on 7 May 1982.

Carter says the tribunal was under media scrutiny from the outset. 'We were seen in some quarters as just a lapdog,' Carter remembers. 'I wanted to ensure that wasn't the case.

'Bjelke-Petersen had always said to the Police Union – look, this body, the new Police Complaints Tribunal, it will be investigative but it won't be supported by any other investigators other than existing police. That was all a deal.'

The first job of the tribunal was to investigate the allegations of former police officers Bob Campbell and Kingsley Fancourt that had been aired on the ABC's *Nationwide* television program and induced the furore that had led to the establishment of the tribunal in the first place.

Neither Campbell nor Fancourt wanted to cooperate with the tribunal. 'They tried to get Campbell and Fancourt to come in and deal with us,' Carter remembers. 'They wouldn't. I didn't talk to them personally. They suspected us of being in league with Lewis and Bjelke-Petersen. It was a bloody challenging job in that context.'

Lewis and his sidekick, Syd 'Sippy' Atkinson as he was known in legal circles, dropped in on Carter from time to time. The tribunal had a room in the Executive Building in George Street, away from the city's law courts.

'I was always worried about that and didn't tell them too much,' says Carter. 'I had my guard up.'

Before Yet Another Royal Commission

Assistant Commissioner Tony Murphy surely would have had his guest appearance at the Williams Royal Commision of Inquiry into Drugs the year before on his mind when he stepped up to give evidence before the Stewart royal commission during the first week of July in 1982.

This time, even the resilient Murphy might have momentarily hesitated. Stewart's commission was, after all, looking into the murder of Mr Asia drug couriers Doug and Isabel Wilson in 1979, and the circumstances surrounding their brutal deaths.

Without doubt, he would have refreshed his knowledge and perused the myriad of official memorandums he had been asked to provide to Commissioner Lewis about the story he had leaked to journalist Brian Bolton. The article suggested that secret taped interviews made by police had helped outline Terry Clark's massive international drug-smuggling ring. Who had spoken to police?

Clark deduced it was the Wilsons. They were dead three weeks after the publication of Bolton's article.

Before Justice Stewart, Murphy trotted out the same line he had presented to Lewis in 1979. He said he hoped the newspaper story about the murders might bring information forward from people on the fringes of the drug ring.

Stewart was scathing of Murphy and his actions. 'How is it that you hoped to elicit information from drug offenders by having an article published which indicated clearly what might happen if they should come forward?' Stewart asked, perplexed.

Murphy replied: 'I believed that those people on the fringe could become sufficiently concerned for their safety. I hoped to bring the worms out of the woodwork.'

Justice Stewart reasoned that the article could have led Clark and his gang to believe that police knew more than what they did. It was an easy step for the drug syndicate principals to believe that someone had informed on them.

'There was an investigation going on in New South Wales,' Justice Stewart went on. 'When the misinformation turned up, it could have deluded them into believing that the police were ready to pounce on them. It seems to me to be counter-productive.'

Murphy retorted: 'It was to protect the Wilsons.'

Later, Brian Bolton was called to give evidence. Justice Stewart asked him about Murphy leaking him the story that led to the death of the Wilsons. 'What was Murphy's reason?'

'In order to get publicity and the possible identification of the murder victim [Harry 'Pommie' Lewis] at Port Macquarie,' Bolton answered.

The journalist went on to inform the commissioner that he had subsequently written many accurate stories about the Mr Asia syndicate, including that Clark was carrying $50 million in cash when he was arrested in England for the murder of associate Christopher Johnstone.

'That is a load of twaddle,' Justice Stewart said.

Lewis recalled of Bolton: 'He was a good little bloke if you could ever find him sober, I don't know if he ever was. But he's the one I told you rang me once in the middle of the night from a cathouse in the Valley somewhere or massage parlour. Full of soup of course and probably showing off to the girls that he could ... but I had words with him the next day. No, Brian was, he wasn't a nasty little bugger, in fact he was the one I think that Murphy trusted to write that bloody story about ... that resulted in the death of those two people.'

Just as Glen Patrick Hallahan had his journalist allies in the 1960s, so too did Lewis and Murphy into the 1970s and 1980s.

The member for Archerfield, Kev Hooper, called for Murphy to resign the day after Bolton gave his evidence, saying he was unfit to hold such a senior position in the Queensland Police Force.

It had been a tough year even for someone like Murphy. There had been the storm over the *Nationwide* television program and the allegations of police corruption from former police officers, Bob Campbell and Kingsley Fancourt.

Now Murphy had been criticised in a major royal commission that was being followed by the nation. The assaults on his reputation were starting to take their toll.

The Hound Bows Out

Although he was in charge of the Sunshine Coast police region, Basil 'The Hound' Hicks, at 55, had had enough. He had been transferred to Rockhampton after the various pro-Whitrod purges by Lewis and Murphy in the late 1970s. On his arrival there, the regional super-intendent informed him he'd been contacted by Commissioner Lewis who had branded Hicks a 'troublemaker'.

Even Police Minister Russ Hinze had talked with Hicks and warned him that Lewis would not have him working back in Brisbane. Hicks went back to Nambour to see out his career, not far from the home of farmer Glen Patrick Hallahan.

Hicks, who did not shy away from a verbal stoush, had another blow-up with Lewis in December 1981. It was over. (Lewis's diary confirmed Hicks' visit to his office the year before. Lewis claimed Hicks unleashed a tirade, saying he had lost faith in the police administration. 'Hates A/C A. Murphy and does not trust him,' Lewis recorded in his diary. 'Has spoken to "Joh" and "Llew" on many occasions. Has tapes of many of his converstaions. Union do not want him and they influence me, as does Murphy. Handed me application to retire from 29.6.82.')

Hicks did indeed resign in late June. It had been an extraordinarily tumultuous career, his honesty ruffling the feathers of Hallahan in the late 1960s, the great quest for truth and transparency under the visionary Ray Whitrod, then the return to dark days for Hicks under Commissioner Lewis.

He had suffered meticulous and elaborate plans to bring him down personally and professionally, involving gossip, allegations of sexual impropriety with a prostitute and allegations he was crooked and protected SP bookmakers.

The exact day of his departure did not rate a mention in Commissioner Lewis's diary.

A House on the Hill

Near the end of July, Constable Nigel Powell of the Licensing Branch was told to go home and pack a bag. There was a job on and he'd be heading outside of Brisbane.

At his Jindalee house, Powell was telephoned again by the office. Pack a bigger bag, they said. You might be away for a while.

'They never used to tell us much, but we knew that Nev Ross and Harry Burgess were away. They were somewhere undercover in North Queensland.

'We were all laughing and joking at the idea of Harry Burgess undercover. He was hopeless undercover. We worked out that we were going to Cairns and that it had something to do with the Bellinos.'

It was Saturday 24 July. The team met at the airport and boarded the police plane. 'In the police plane, as you got up the stairs, was a seat facing the door,' remembers Powell. 'It was actually two seats, but the arm rest had been taken out so it became one seat. That was reserved for the Police Minister, Russ Hinze.'

As the plane took off it started heading south. The younger officers on board were confused. The plane was actually flying first to the Gold Coast to pick up the boss, Syd Atkinson.

'He got on board and as we were taxiing on the runway it was like he was going to explode,' says Powell.

'So, do you know where you're going?' demanded Atkinson of the team. 'Has anybody told anybody where you're going?

'There's a game up there [in Cairns]. It's run by guys from Brisbane. We're going to bust some tables.'

Powell wondered about the raging Atkinson and the plan. He didn't think it was good. He didn't think that was the way the Licensing Branch did things. It was too aggressive.

The police plane arrived in Cairns and a meeting was held at the airport. Present was a local superintendent they called 'One Ball' McCall, on account of his peculiarly high voice, as well as Nev Ross and Harry Burgess. The two Licensing Branch officers told the team they'd been in the illegal casino they were about to raid – it was in a building called Traveltown on Lake Street, in the Cairns CBD – and they'd seen the layout. To Powell, the whole operation was a disaster in the making.

Atkinson again 'went mental' and laid down the law about smashing this illegal game.

'We got there with a warrant,' Powell recalls. 'It was upstairs in a shopping centre. They had a roulette wheel in there and some tables. We pinched everybody. There were people from Brisbane that we knew in there. Allan Holloway who ran the World by Night club for the Bellinos in Brisbane. Geoff Crocker and his wife Julie.'

Crocker and Holloway had in fact set up the casino as a sort of joint venture and the first initiative in what they'd hoped would become a financially rewarding collaboration. Holloway came up with the idea of moving out of Brisbane and expanding in Queensland's regional centres. Crocker had always wanted to go to Cairns.

Crocker and his wife rented, then bought a house in Cairns, and set up the Traveltown casino. 'We had a carpenter in there working for us and I decided that Cairns was where I wanted to be and where I was going to stay, so I got the escort agency going and it never went real good but it was alright,' remembered Crocker.

Holloway contacted Vic Conte in Brisbane about the gambling equipment for the illegal game.

Crocker said: 'Holloway come back to Brisbane and seen Vic Conte and arranged for us to buy gear … cards, chips, cloths, all that sort of thing. A couple of days later it arrived up there on air freight and we picked it up. I think Vic even lent us some dealers. We opened up Traveltown and it took a little while but it started going very good.'

A few months later they noticed large numbers of young men trying to get into the casino to play and they grew suspicious. Were they undercover cops? They scaled back the business.

They'd spent $50,000 refurbishing it. Clients could enjoy blackjack, Manila, 'Unders and Overs', baccarat and 'Crown and Anchor'.

What they'd found, eventually, was that the Cairns locals treated it like a nightclub and just preferred to sit around and drink and socialise. The joint was losing money hand over fist courtesy of the complimentary liquor consumption. Importantly, they weren't paying police protection to run the game.

The raid took place just after 8.30 p.m. 'It was pretty early in the evening,' Julie Crocker later recalled. 'When I say early, it was early because there was hardly anybody there. I was behind the bar and the next thing all these police come in, plainclothes police … and just said, "Don't anybody move", and they started taking down names and took everybody down to the watchhouse.'

She recognised at least one of the officers from Brisbane – Harry Burgess. 'I can remember Harry because at one stage I was behind the bar when everybody was coming in and I looked up and I think I smiled at him and he sort of just walked away like he didn't want to know me, so I just didn't worry about it,' she said.

Crocker couldn't understand why the raid had taken place so early in the evening. Everyone was charged and processed, including Holloway and the Crockers. All pleaded guilty and were released on bail.

On the Sunday, the officers spent the day inspecting licensed premises and were off duty by 4 p.m. En masse, the crew then headed to a popular Cairns nightclub called the House on the Hill, a palatial club in an historic building quite literally just out of town and sitting on a hill. It was run by the Bellinos.

'We went in there just as they were closing,' Powell recalls. 'There was half a dozen of us. They were shutting the doors but somebody said we were from the Licensing Branch and we were off duty.

'The next thing out comes Vince Bellino. "No, no, no! Start up the fires again!" he said. We were looked after. We had steaks and drinks. Then we went back to the Railway Hotel where we were staying.'

The team headed back to Brisbane on the police plane the next day. For years Powell mulled over the purpose of the farcical raid.

'They [Crocker and Holloway] hadn't got permission [for the Traveltown casino],' Powell says. 'They'd exceeded their brief. The Licensing Branch was there to tell them that that wasn't on. It's the only explanation I can come up with.'

Bandits on Trial

Almost a year after their terrifying rampage through the streets of Brisbane, the two so-called 'Bikie Bandits' – Alfred Thompson and Steve Kossaris – went to trial in the Supreme Court before Justice Connolly. Both men faced a combined 26 charges for a string of armed robberies throughout the city.

During the two-week trial, Justice Connolly received a death threat. The *Sunday Sun* newspaper revealed that a man had approached a court security officer and warned him that Justice Connolly would be killed with a shotgun.

Counsel for Thompson and Kossaris moved that the trial be stopped. The jury was frightened, they said.

Justice Connolly would have none of it. 'Do you think the administration of criminal law should come to an end just because somebody makes a threat?' Justice Connolly asked. 'Because some little hoon wanders in and makes some wild statement about releasing the judge from this vale to tears with a shotgun, are you suggesting that the trial cannot proceed? It is ridiculous.'

During the trial it was alleged that Thompson was the primary gunman in the armed robberies that had 'sent shockwaves through the entire Queensland banking system' and had induced terror in innocent civilians. Kossaris drove the getaway motorcycle.

The proceeds from the robberies amounted to almost $100,000 for Thompson and $37,000 for Kossaris. Virtually all of the money was spent by both men on heroin.

During the trial, there were extraordinary allegations that police had provided the defendants with heroin prior to their interrogation and the preparation of their formal statements, supposedly dictated by police.

Police said the statements of Thompson and Kossaris were made voluntarily. Justice Connolly dismissed the police evidence and rejected the statements.

Then clinical pharmacologist Dr P.J. Ravenscroft was called. Following the analysis of blood samples, he was decisive – the defendents had heroin in their systems during the time they were incarcerated in the Brisbane watchhouse following their early morning arrests.

Justice Connolly told the court: 'It is, in my opinion, beyond question that both prisoners were injected with heroin between midday and midnight on November 19th [1981].

'The fact that they were injected with heroin while in custody is, of course, a matter for concern, but it by no means follows that I should accept the view that the police are responsible for such a monstrous act as is charged against them.

'I make no finding adverse to the police officers in relation to the heroin, but I repeat what I said earlier, that it is a matter of concern that persons in the watchhouse, or indeed anywhere in custody, could have access to dangerous drugs. No doubt the authorities will give some thought to this situation.'

Both Thompson and Kassaris were ultimately convicted of the offences. The jury took just 20 minutes to find them guilty. Justice Connolly said that despite the fact nobody was injured as a result of the robberies, the weapons used were loaded at the time of the offences. Thompson was jailed for 10 years. Kassaris got eight years.

Immediately after the trial, two senior public servants lodged a complaint about what would come to be known as the Brisbane Watchhouse Heroin Affair to the relatively new Police Complaints Tribunal, presided over by Justice Bill Carter.

'We had dealt with other cases, quite minor stuff,' recalls Carter. 'There is no doubt that this was, I think I can say correctly, the most important case from a public point of view that we had to deal with.

'After the conviction of Thompson and Kassaris, the public defender took the bit between the teeth and made the complaint to the tribunal.

'We had to do our own investigation. I got Frank Clare [of the Crown Law Office] and Tom Pointing [of the police internal investigations section] to do the investigation. It was unprecedented as far as we knew.'

Bill Carter's report would be done before Christmas. And there would be little cheer contained in it for the likes of Commissioner Lewis, Police Minister Russ Hinze and the Bjelke-Petersen government.

Ghosts

Commissioner Terry Lewis had a frenetic August and September in 1982 leading up to the Commonwealth Games being staged in Brisbane. Not only were 46 Commonwealth countries and territories competing, but the Duke of Edinburgh was to open the games on 30 September, and Queen Elizabeth would perform the closing honours on 9 October.

It had been almost 30 years since Lewis first saw the Queen in person. As a young constable he had stood at the corner of Albert and Turbot streets on 17 March 1954, to see the Royal couple passing through the city to the cheers and applause of the people of Brisbane. This time around, his circumstances were completely different.

Still, some ghosts from the same era would appear before Lewis began a whirl of Royal functions, cocktail parties and other Games-related ceremonies where he would rub shoulders with the nation's elite, including Prime Minister Malcolm Fraser.

The first spectre from the past was the sudden death of former care-taker Commissioner Norwin [Norm] Bauer, the man who had taken Rat Packer Glen Hallahan under his wing when they worked together in western Queensland in the 1950s. Bauer had filled in briefly as Police Commissioner following the bizarre exit of the manifestly corrupt Frank 'Big Fella' Bischof.

Lewis recorded in his diary on Saturday 28 August: '... Noel McIntyre phoned re death of Bauer.'

Bauer had apparently been selling raffle tickets in Queen Street when he dropped dead on the spot of a massive heart attack. The funeral service for Bauer was held in St Paul's Anglican Church in East Brisbane. Lewis attended with his sidekick, Inspector Greg Early.

Shortly after the ceremony, Lewis headed across the river to Parliament House where he had a meeting with Premier Joh Bjelke-Petersen, Llew Edwards, Angus Innes, Bill Hewitt and others. They discussed, according to Lewis's diary: '... Crawford Productions, changing ministers, Supreme Court Justices, Max Hodges, arrest over phone threats, majority verdicts for juries, Costigan, Q.C., Labor supporter ...'

On that same day, 'Hon. Hinze phoned re bullet-proof vest ordered for him'. The large Police Minister might have been worried about external threats, but maybe he should have been looking at assassins closer to home.

On Monday 13 September, Lewis had another meeting with the Premier and discussed, as his diary recorded, 'not wanting Hon. Hinze'.

The second ghost appeared on the front page of the *Courier-Mail* on Saturday 18 September 1982. Across the top the newspaper was crowing an exclusive.

Here were the explosive revelations of Sir Thomas Hiley, the former Deputy Premier and Queensland Treasurer under Frank Nicklin. Hiley, once a fancy dresser with a dandy's cane and a flower in his lapel, had decided to speak out in his retirement that he was comfortably acquitting in Noosa Heads, north of Brisbane on the Sunshine Coast.

THE WILD MEN OF BRISBANE, the headline said. EXCLUSIVE: The Hiley File.

In part one of a three-part investigation, journalist and veteran crime reporter Ken 'Digger' Blanch explained that Hiley had finally decided to shine some light into Queensland's shadowy police and political corners as a public service.

Hiley said: '... the public should be reminded of incidents that have occurred here in the last 40 years so that they may appreciate the chances of the same things being repeated on the much-expanded state of today.'

Part one dealt with the deep-seated corruption of Frank Bischof, former police commissioner, who had died in late 1979.

Under another headline on page 21 – THE CASE OF THE CORRUPT COMMISSIONER – Hiley laid out the misdeeds of Bischof in office, especially his extortion of SP bookmakers and his fraudulent behaviour at the racetrack, where he was a compulsive and exorbitant gambler.

As Blanch began: 'Sir Thomas Hiley, former Queensland Treasurer and Deputy Premier, has no trouble recalling his worst mistake in public office. It was, he says, the day he voted for Frank Bischof to become Queensland's Police Commissioner.'

It was only later that Sir Thomas discovered Bischof was bent 'beyond belief'. He told Blanch that he thought the example set by Bischof might still be 'white-anting some levels of the police force'.

Hiley went on to tell the story of the meeting with Premier Frank Nicklin, Minister responsible for Police, Alex Dewar, and himself at Parliament House in the 1960s, where Bischof's corruption was outlined by Hiley. Bischof pledged to reform himself.

Hiley said in the article: 'I have shown how a Police Commissioner was tempted by graft of the order of $400,000 a year. The present assemblage of opportunity could run to millions of dollars annually.

'Some successor to Mr Hinze or Police Commissioner Lewis might find such a temptation irresistible.'

The scoop was a profound one for Ken Blanch, who knew Bischof and the Rat Pack well during the 1950s and 1960s. 'I was up there at Noosa and spent several days with Hiley,' Blanch recalls. 'He told me the Bischof story. You know a lot of people don't believe it but I think he was probably telling me the truth.'

He recalls:

People defended Bischof after this became public. Bischof had died by then, of course. They said ... it's picking on a dead man who couldn't defend himself. They also argued there was no evidence of Bischof having had a lot of money when he died. Well that would be because of his bloody lifestyle, he used to bet on anything.

There were always certain coppers who would tell you the big fellow was bent but I never saw any evidence and without evidence you can't do anything. I had a number of prostitutes contact me and told me they were being stood over for money by Glen Hallahan after the brothels closed [in the late 1950s]. But there again nobody would take any action on the word of a prostitute, that was why they came to the media.

I don't know what I can tell you about Murphy without getting myself killed.

The front-page picture story beneath the Hiley exposé was head-lined LOOK, IT'S JOH COOL.

The report documented Premier Joh Bjelke-Petersen opening the new Corkscrew rollercoaster at entrepreneur Keith Williams' Sea World Theme Park on the Gold Coast. Bjelke-Petersen could be seen stoically gripping the safety rail in the first carriage of the roller-coaster, his stony face unmoved during the ride. Beside him is his pilot, Miss Beryl Young.

He later said: 'It was very good, pretty fantastic.'

He also paid tribute to Keith Williams as a 'man who made things happen ... You have achieved a tremendous amount in your short life,' the Premier lauded the businessman.

Lewis was clearly perturbed by the revelations about his old boss, mentor and father figure, Frank Bischof. On that Saturday he went into the office and stayed there until 3.15 p.m. He received a call from rouseabout journalist Brian 'The Eagle' Bolton regarding the damning article on 'the late F.E. Bischof'. Lewis also phoned his old newspaper mate Ron Richards about the Ken Blanch scoop. Richards was the newly appointed Managing Director of the *Daily Sun/Sunday Sun*, direct competitors to the *Courier-Mail* and the *Sunday Mail*.

The next day Lewis, with wife, Hazel, and son John Paul, headed across the river to Davies Park, home to the Souths Rugby League Club, than back to Lang Park for the local competition's Grand Final.

The Lewises lunched with former Senator and head of Queensland Rugby League, Ron McAuliffe and then watched the big game. Wynnum Manly defeated Souths 17–3.

Lewis's diary noted that he 'visited Souths dressing room' and later had 'drinks with Ron'.

Still, the death of Bauer and then the public flaying of Bischof as a profoundly corrupt public official, must have given Commissioner Lewis pause for thought.

Wrath

If Kingsley Fancourt, one of the whistleblowers on the *Nationwide* television exposé in early 1982, thought his life would resume as per normal after the show went to air, he was sorely mistaken.

The other whistleblower, Bob Campbell, had fled with his family to remote southern Tasmania. Fancourt went back to his property on the gemfields outside Anakie in western Queensland.

Since he'd resigned from the police force in 1976, Fancourt was convinced his name had been blacklisted by both police and government. His suspicions were heightened when he applied for several mining leases outside Anakie. He pegged the lease areas and submitted his applications for the leases, through his solicitor Dale Smith.

Fancourt was swiftly informed that his applications had been unsuccessful. He received a short, personal letter from Mines, Energy and Police Minister Ron Camm that his applications were 'not in the interests of the public'. The leases were granted to another miner. 'They were taken off me,' says Fancourt.

Fancourt was advised by his local mining warden to appeal and the leases would revert to him. At a cost of about $2000 per lease to make the applications to appeal, he backed away. 'It broke me financially,' says Fancourt.

Following his star turn on *Nationwide*, Fancourt found himself under attack on several fronts. He had a small gold lease in Monto, about 500 kilometres north-west of Brisbane. 'I was behind on my rent and I got a phone call to say that all my gear at the mine was being repossessed and auctioned,' says Fancourt. 'Usually when you're behind they just send you dirty letters for two or three years and then everything's fine. But they repossessed everything. I had a 28-ton excavator and a loader and the plant itself. That cost me over $400,000.

'This is how the bastards get to you without pointing a gun and pulling a trigger.'

Gravely, there were four attempts on Fancourt's life after the corruption show aired on national television. On three occasions the wheel nuts on his car were loosened. Twice the wheels flew off when Fancourt was travelling at high speed but he was not injured. The brake lines on one of his trucks were also severed.

In the end, the pressure took a terrible toll on his wife Val and their four children.

The marriage disintegrated.

The Candidate

Towards the end of 1982, ALP chief of staff and mover and shaker Malcolm McMillan received a surprising phone call in his office in the city. At the other end of the line was Assistant Commissioner [Crime], Tony Murphy.

McMillan had encountered Murphy when he had been in charge of the Longreach district, 1176 kilometres north-west of Brisbane, banished there by then Commissioner Ray Whitrod in the early 1970s. McMillan had been visiting the town with MP Tom Burns, when Murphy had shown up at their motel late one night, offering his low opinion of Whitrod and Police Minister Max Hodges.

'He ... just oozed self-confidence,' says McMillan. 'And he oozed guile. He ... was regarded by his contemporaries in the police force as a brilliant detective in the CIB, but had an extraordinary way of engaging.'

In 1982 McMillan says ' ... suddenly out of the blue he called me in my office and said, "Could we have a drink?" When you're in [political] Opposition you talk to everybody.' Information was gold.

McMillan recalls he and Murphy met at a hotel in the Brisbane CBD: 'During that conversation where it was only he and I there, he said to me that he held a silent ALP membership in Toowoomba.

That's a member where you're on the books but you never go to meetings and you never sort of talk about it.'

McMillan says Murphy then surprised him further. 'He said he'd like to run for state parliament at the next election in 1983 and, in particular, against Rosemary Kyburz in her seat of Salisbury,' McMillan says.

Murphy, following a year that punished his reputation, was toying with the idea of resigning from the force. He had always known he would never make Police Commissioner – his past and his reputation for speaking his mind probably precluded him from the top job and over time he accepted his lot.

By calling McMillan with his extraordinary proposal, he may have been planning ahead for future employment. But why the ALP, given his staunch loyalty to Bjelke-Petersen's regime during his time as a senior officer?

The Joke already had an ear in parliament in Don 'Shady' Lane. Was the consortium thinking ahead, hedging its bets, and looking at securing a friend in the Labor Party as well, should they ever take power?

'What do you think my ... chances would be?' Murphy asked McMillan.

The political operative was frank. 'Virtually none,' he told Murphy.

Ultimately, the successful ALP candidate for the seat Murphy had his eye on at the 1983 state election was a lawyer by the name of Wayne Keith Goss.

Slade Gathers Some Dirt

A year after entrenching himself in the Far North Queensland drug rings, Detective Jim Slade was becoming something of an expert on the illicit drug trade. During most of September, Slade had criss-crossed the Far North gathering intelligence. He logged 27 hours of flying time in both light aircraft and helicopters. He logged a further 16 hours in police vessels and private launches around Aurukun, False Pera Head, Lockhart River and the Bloomfield River.

He also spoke to many dozens of people and concluded that Far North Queensland was being used 'extensively for the landing of illegal immigrants and importation of illegal drugs'.

The next month he furnished a report for the sitting Royal Commission of Inquiry into Drug Trafficking, presided over by Justice Donald Stewart of New South Wales. The inquiry, hot on the heels of the Williams Royal Commission, was sparked by the murders of Douglas and Isabel Wilson, and was charged with investigating Terry Clark's so-called Mr Asia drug trafficking syndicate.

In a covering letter to Slade's report, dated 13 October, his boss Tony Murphy affirmed that the information 'would be of vital interest' to Justice Stewart. It was an irony that he would recommend intelligence to the commission, given that it was Murphy's actions in leaking confidential material on the Wilsons to Brisbane journalist Brian Bolton in 1979 that had most probably resulted in their murders.

Murphy had given evidence to the commission three months earlier. As he pointed out in the covering letter: 'I also made certain recommendations to His Honour suggesting ways of introducing a more effective enforcement in the area.'

It was typical of Murphy to counter any criticism of his work – namely the Wilson leak – with direct, forthright, even imposing assistance to the Stewart commission. He had always attacked when he felt threatened.

Slade had some pertinent observations for the commission of inquiry. He recommended the formation of an 'intelligence cell' based in Cairns.

'This could be made up of members of the Queensland Police Bureau of Criminal Intelligence and Customs Intelligence,' Slade wrote. 'This squad would monitor fauna and flora in and out of North Queensland area, illegal drug importation and the movement of local marihuana. This squad would then have the responsibility of farming this information to the areas when it would have the most effect.'

Slade warned that the vast majority of people he'd spoken to in Far North Queensland had never been approached by authorities in terms of the illegal movements of planes and boats. He suggested cultivating a 'network of intelligence gatherers' comprised of responsible members of the community – teachers, nurses, station owners and mission personnel.

He also recommended a complete revision of the current coastal surveillance methods. Slade noted that the amount of intelligence he had gathered from the field was 'staggering'.

Confiding in the Pom

By the end of 1982, the prostitute Katherine James was attempting to set up her own massage parlour – Xanadu – in Stanley Street at the Gabba.

The business would unfortunately be not far from another Hapeta/Tilley brothel, the Cosmo, which was just around the corner and directly opposite the Mater Hospital. They were not happy with the prospective competition.

Come November, James was starting to provide Licensing Branch officer Nigel Powell with some damning intelligence about corrupt payments to police from the brothel and gaming consortiums across the city. She was hearing rumours that her new business would virtually be shut down by police before it had a chance to get going, all because it potentially threatened the Hapeta/Tilley franchise.

At around 8.30 p.m. on Wednesday 10 November 1982, Powell met with James at the Carindale Tavern. They had one drink in the Banana Bar before heading out to the rear car park.

Powell recorded in his police notebook: 'When asked why she trusted me and why she spoke to me – said my name was one of the only ones never connected to anything going on.'

She spoke at length about Sergeant Harry Burgess, one of Powell's bosses in the Licensing Branch. 'She says that Harry Burgess is being paid in money and favours by HAPETA and for TILLEY, but she has no proof. She says that H.B. [and others] … have sex with girls on numerous occasions but obviously only in one another's company or alone or with others who turn a blind eye.

'She says that Hapeta has the majority of the girls terrified in that he threatens to and does beat the girls up if they do the wrong thing or quit when he doesn't want them to.

'She says that both Hapeta and Tilley have openly boasted that "Xanadu" will be closed by means that imply police means initially.'

James was candid. Powell could see the pieces but he couldn't make sense of the big picture. He couldn't believe these machinations were transpiring right under his nose.

James continued on about Harry Burgess: 'She says that H.B. often goes to Fantasia on or off duty and has a "thing" for Tilley and does disappear with her. Also that Tilley besides the normal alcohol provides meals both at the parlour and at the Aquarius restaurant plus girls.'

Tilley confirms that Burgess had fallen in love with her, and was often hanging around the parlours for sex, a drink or a meal. 'My main concern was having the money to pay, and running the places,' she says. 'I really didn't give a shit. It was inferred to me that Terry Lewis was the almighty.

'I never actually gave him [Lewis] the money. Jack Herbert said, "This is going to the top."

'Maybe [Herbert was lying]. They all lie. They were a very dishonest lot, those policemen. They used to run into the parlour, like the [police] TV show on telly; cops always pose. They'd run into parlours and do that.

'I'd say, "There's clients here you know?"'

'I always found the money to pay, no matter what ... It's like any good books – take rent out every week so you've got it. That was my "funny money". It was in a big roll of carpet in my bedroom.'

She recalls an encounter with Nigel Powell: 'I remember Nigel asked me something untoward one night and I said, "Go ask Harry".'

'It was something like, "How does this all keep going?"'

'"I don't know, ask Harry." I walked away from him. I thought, Why ask that? He must know.

'He was in there every night with the rest of them. Nigel got nothing.'

James would later elaborate on the activities of Harry Burgess, courtesy of what she observed and what Tilley told her when she worked for the Hapeta/Tilley consortium at Warry Street and at the parlour at 612 Brunswick Street.

'I was never in a position to see [Harry] Burgess pick up money, but he would often come to Fantasia and have dinner with Anne Marie,' James recalled. 'She would often order a big seafood platter from Aquarius.

'Burgess and Tilley would sometimes go away for the night when he called at Fantasia. If Anne Marie wanted to spend the night with Harry, I would arrange an all-night booking for her and she would have to put the money in so that Hector would not find out.

'The approach taken by the Licensing Branch detectives varied according to who was on the shift. When they came to Fantasia, some of them would go to the rooms with the girls and sit there all night and drink and eat. If sexual activity took place with the visiting detectives, the house would pay the girls at the end of the night.'

In the dark car park of the Carindale Tavern, James confessed her concerns to Powell.

He recorded in his notebook: 'She fears being planted with drugs. She fears an arson attempt on her studio. She says she no longer trusts

Nev [Ross] as she thinks he talks to H.B. She believes he is the main danger [H.B.] to her existence.

'I told her the best she could do was to keep digging for information no matter how minor about H.B., Hapeta, Tilley, [Roland] Short.'

On the night that Katherine James was beginning to give Powell a rudimentary outline of a network of police corruption known as The Joke, Commissioner Lewis was on a few days recreational leave. That evening he took his wife, Hazel, and youngest son John Paul to Hoyts cinemas in the city to see a film called '*The Boat*' [*Das Boot*], the epic U-boat drama written and directed by Wolfgang Petersen. They had supper at Jo Jo's in Queen Street before returning to Garfield Drive.

Xanadu

By late 1982 Katherine James was to learn just how tight a grip Hapeta and Tilley, and the Bellinos, had on the vice market in Brisbane.

Her entrepreneurial initiative, setting up her own parlour Xanadu, coincided with a change of the guard in the Licensing Branch.

She had worked hard at the Balaclava Street brothel and had saved enough money to either open a parlour or a hairdressing salon. She chose the oldest profession in the world.

'I was attracted by the easy money,' James later said. 'At that stage I knew that it would cost a parlour operator about $1000 per week per house [in payments to police] and about $1500 per phone in order to set up a parlour.

'I decided to approach Nev Ross because I knew him well in order to seek permission to open a parlour. He told me that the Licensing Branch was changing its Inspectors and because of my past I would have to wait and see who was appointed.'

Following the resignation of Noel Dwyer, the new Inspector in

Charge of the branch happened to be Graeme Robert Parker, 48, appointed on 20 September.

Parker joined the force as a cadet in 1951 and had an early stint in the Licensing Branch from 1958 to 1964 where he met and befriended Jack Herbert. He maintained a fairly static police career, spending time in North Queensland from the mid-1960s to the early 1970s, before returning to the Licensing Branch in 1980.

Lewis has positive memories of Parker: 'He was a very, very bright fellow and I liked him. He was a real worker. How he got involved with Herbert I don't know.'

By the time Parker took the top job in the Licensing Branch, graft payments taken from prostitution and illegal gaming had lifted by more than 60 per cent over the previous year. The annual income calculated from the two major consortiums was nudging $250,000. The Joke under Jack Herbert was now a huge, efficiently run business.

Meanwhile, James got the go-ahead to set up a parlour in either the Valley or the Gabba. She chose Stanley Street.

'I then had a meeting with Graeme Parker,' James said. 'Parker did not discuss money with me at the meeting although it was an under-standing that money had to be paid.

'I did discuss money with Nev Ross. I was to pay $10,000 in cash to him and then about $1500 to $2000 per week depending on how well the business went. I paid the cash to Nev Ross personally.'

Parker was extremely particular when he laid down the ground rules for James and her new business. 'Parker wanted to know what was going to be put into the parlour and how many girls I was going to employ,' she recalled. 'He wanted to know whether it was to be "on premises" or escorts. He wanted to know how many phones I had. He told me what ads I could put in the paper. I regarded the conversation with Graeme Parker as the "go ahead" for me to begin renovations for Xanadu.'

James spent about $35,000 fitting out the brothel.

She had barely opened her doors for business when she was hit up for more money by corrupt police. Then the pressure accelerated. 'The police came in and harassed the girls and said that if they left they wouldn't get into any trouble,' James said. 'Towels were even taken. Agents were used and police parked outside for days and harassed clients. I tried to contact Nev Ross. He would not return my calls and neither would Graeme Parker.'

James did in fact ring Nigel Powell to try and get through to Ross. She asked Powell to get a message to him.

'I've done it,' Powell later told her. 'I don't know why he hasn't contacted you back.'

Then police came down heavily on James's staff. They were being arrested and taken to the watchhouse.

Had this been a quick cash grab by corrupt police all along? Or was the Licensing Branch making life hell for James at the bidding of Hector Hapeta and Anne Marie Tilley, James's direct competitors?

James was then approached by Hapeta. 'He made me two offers,' James recalled. 'Firstly, he offered to buy the premises outright for $10,000. His second offer was that I stay on as manageress. He told me I better think seriously about it or I'd be closed in less than two weeks.

'I told Hector to forget it and that I wasn't prepared to deal.'

At this time James briefly left the country. 'I left [receptionist] Priscilla in charge, but before I left it was quite bad,' James recalled. 'They [the police] were parking their car on the footpath directly outside the massage parlour and stopping clients from going in, asking them what they were doing there – just generally letting their presence be felt all day.

'When I was overseas I had contact with Priscilla and she said it got gradually worse. As soon as the new girls started they were told to leave, told to go around the corner [to Cosmo] and get a job and they wouldn't be harassed in any way, and in that time the premises were closed.'

The message was powerfully clear. If you threatened the harmony of The Joke, you didn't last long.

Into the Past

By the end of 1982, Mary Anne Brifman was doing her best to raise her children following her decision to work as a prostitute, and coping with a divorce.

She was living in a flat in Kangaroo Point, not far from where Glen Hallahan, the retired detective and member of the so-called Rat Pack, had once had a place of his own. The same man that her mother had been sexually and emotionally attached to in the 1960s.

Being on the game and living in that part of the city must have made her wonder if indeed she wasn't repeating her own mother's life, and quite possibly making the same mistakes.

As F. Scott Fitzgerald ended his novel *The Great Gatsby*: 'So we beat on, boats against the current, borne back ceaselessly into the past.'

Did she remember, too, the early afternoon of 18 August 1971, at age 14, when she had been interviewed at police headquarters in Brisbane by Sydney detectives Doyle and Paull? For months her mother had been interrogated by the police about her allegations made on the ABC's current affairs program *This Day Tonight*. Mary Anne, in turn was questioned by detectives.

'Do you know Detective Sergeant Fred Krahe?' they had asked her at the time. It was Krahe, also one of Shirley Brifman's lovers and recipient of graft from her, who helped torture Brifman before she fled Sydney for the apparent safety of Brisbane.

'I spoke to him on the phone but the only place I have seen him was at my home at Westleigh.'

'Have you spoken to him on the phone …?'

'Yes, he used to ring up for Mum. Not every day, but it all depends.'

'Can you tell us anything about any misconduct committed by any member of the New South Wales Police Force?'

'I know that Detectives were part of some robberies,' replied Mary Anne. 'Because Sonja, my sister, and I were in the room under the bed at home and Mum was talking to a man who looked like a Detective and they started to talk about the robbery of some diamonds and then they heard Sonja and me under the bed and they told us to go outside.'

They asked her if she knew about any other misconduct by police, and Mary Anne volunteered that her mother used to talk a lot about a 'Mr Allan', who often rang the house.

They asked which 'Mr. Allan' she was referring to.

Mary Anne said: 'He is like you only he is the Commissioner.'

She refused to detail what she knew about Norm Allan, New South Wales Commissioner of Police at the time, and any involvement he might have had in crime, because 'he might lose his job'.

'I am not going to ask you anymore questions,' the detective said. 'Do you wish to say anything further?'

'I have got nothing else to say then,' Mary Anne replied.

Mary Anne Brifman had seen a lot and suffered a lot. She had still not adequately processed her mother's horrific death, nor that she had been put on the game by her own parents when she was 13 – an event that precipitated the journey to Shirley's premature death.

There, at Kangaroo Point, she could look across the river to the CBD and know that somewhere in the offices at police headquarters were two men who knew her family's story intimately. That was Commissioner Terry Lewis and Assistant Commissioner Tony Murphy.

And just as her mother had done in 1963, soon she too would once again be flying south – to Sydney. Mary Anne Brifman would not mirror her own mother's short and tragic life, but she would make a career of prostitution, getting to know the main players of the criminal under-world. She would spend decades contemplating her life, reading widely and moving towards a spiritual truth that her past had blinded her from.

Mary Anne Brifman, unlike poor Shirley, would learn about salvation, and she would find it.

Games

In the week leading up to the XII Commonwealth Games – an epochal event for Brisbane – Commissioner Lewis's work patterns were a combination of official festivities and street-level concerns that protests, especially by Indigenous people, might spoil the party.

On his day off on Sunday 26 September, Lewis and wife, Hazel attended a service of worship at the Wesley Uniting Church in Albert Street, in the city, before he 'drove around where crowd gathering in Forum for Black Protest march'. He later checked out Musgrave Park in South Brisbane, 're Aboriginals gathering'.

The next day, Bjelke-Petersen phoned him about 'inciting statements by C. Perkins'. Charles Perkins, the Aboriginal activist, had been invited to Brisbane to lead a series of protests highlighting to the world media the land rights issue and the paucity of personal and political rights in Queensland under the Bjelke-Petersen regime. Lewis and the Premier also discussed Bjelke-Petersen's 'bullet proof vest received'.

Lewis still had time in a busy schedule to open a new 'liquor bar' at the Police Academy and then pick up Hazel and attend the Commonwealth Countries Exhibition of Police at the Myer store in Queen Street.

On the Tuesday, Syd Atkinson and Ron Redmond joined Lewis at a meeting in the office of Police Minister Russ Hinze to discuss 'demonstrations'. Curiously, on that same day he also popped in to see 'Eric Pratt with Hazel and signed Wills'.

Wednesday saw more cocktail parties, a revision of the Premier's security, and a congratulatory call from Hinze, 're march by aborigines going well'.

Finally, Thursday 30 September 1982 arrived, and the opening ceremony awaited Brisbane and the world. As Lewis recorded in his diary: 'With Hazel to QEII Jubilee Sports Centre re opening of XII Commonwealth Games by Prince Philip. Windy but fine. 45 nations paraded. Magnificent spectacle.'

The star of the show was Matilda, the 13-metre mechanised kangaroo mascot that winked at the crowd as it moved around the stadium's ochre running track. That night Lewis attended a government reception at Lennons in the city.

On Saturday 2 October, Lewis was in the crowd at the archery events. Gold was won by England's Mark Blenkarne, with Australian Michael Coen picking up a bronze. None of our women archers won a medal. The next day it was off to the new world-class Chandler swimming and diving centre.

There was a little culture among the sport. On the evening of Tuesday 5 October, in the presence of the Duke of Edinburgh, Terry and Hazel took their seats in the Albert Street Amphitheatre and caught a performance of Shakespeare's *The Tempest*.

Curiously, Bjelke-Petersen rang Lewis in his office the next day stating that Prime Minister Malcolm Fraser wanted 'details on each protestor arrested'. Considering there were hundreds, it might have been a job for the Special Branch.

That day also saw Lewis dropping in on the badminton events at Chandler, boxing at Festival Hall in Albert Street, wrestling at City Hall and back to Chandler for the cycling.

For the next three days Terry and Hazel attended numerous functions in honour of Her Majesty the Queen.

On Saturday 9 October, it was back to Her Majesty's yacht, *Brittania*, the 126-metre floating palace and the Queen's aquatic home away from Buckingham Palace in London on foreign visits. Lewis noted in his diary: 'At 10.45am to Brittania with Royal Tour Directorate where Queen presented various Awards and gifts, I received framed photograph.'

He then witnessed the closing ceremony back at QEII.

There was Commonwealth Games residue to deal with: the Aboriginal protestors in Musgrave Park, South Brisbane. 'Only 5 tents left,' Lewis notated on the Sunday after the closing ceremony had packed up.

The fanfare soon faded and it was back to business. Police Minister Hinze informed Lewis that Judge Carter, Head of the Police Complaints Tribunal, was concerned over the Bikie Bandit case. Lewis's old mate, Eric Pratt, QC, phoned to let him know that he had been offered the position of District Court judge.

On 29 October, Lewis and his wife, Hazel, were present at the Full Court to witness Pratt's crowning as a judge. Lewis recalls his friend from their days as young policemen on interchange in Sydney in 1958:

> He [Pratt] ... didn't have the educational qualifications [to become a barrister]. [He found out] if you went to New Guinea and got a job with, whatever the Crown Law place is up there, he could do it externally at the University of Queensland. So he went up there and got a job ... and did it externally and got somehow, well got friendly if you like with Gerry Brennan [the future Chief Justice of the High Court of Australia].
>
> Young Gerry Brennan, he was very young and I also met Des Sturgess somewhere along the line, I don't know where or how. And I think from what I was told it was sort of Gerry Brennan gave him some advice and after he'd done X amount of study there he moved to Brisbane to do it full-time.
>
> And that's when I sort of got in touch, well he got in touch with me again ... they got their kids to come down to St Peter's College [at Indooroopilly and close to the city] and Hazel used to go out and get them at the weekend and bring them home to let them have some time out. And then when they were coming down Hazel found this

house for them and then he went full-time and became a barrister and I think he must have gone, I don't remember, might have gone straight into private practice. I can't say I wasn't real close to him but I can't say I wasn't either.

He did come to our place I think once for dinner and I sort of went to his place once but it wasn't as if we were in each other's pocket every day.

... he really, really put the work in on me to become a judge. And I didn't mind, I didn't mind asking people if they could help somebody. I mean they'd only do it if they were prepared to do it ... they wouldn't ... and over the years I suppose I helped lots of people do lots of things.

The Pratt issue merely exemplified Lewis's ever-widening influence and power in societal circles that just six years earlier had never heard of him. A relentless networker, it was now a given that he had the ear of the powerful, from the Premier to the powerbrokers to the wealthy and the highest lawmakers.

It must have been almost inconceivable to those who knew Lewis in his previous, not so enchanted life, to see him now in the social pages, meeting royalty and world leaders. It would have been even more surprising to know how the same man was directly influencing the appointments of judges, Cabinet ministers and the like.

It had been a full month of pomp and ceremony.

But political upheaval wasn't far away.

No, Minister

With the rigmarole of the Commonwealth Games over, and the whole extravaganza relegated to the history books, Commissioner Lewis had different fish to fry – namely, his own Police Minister, Russ Hinze.

Lewis had not forgiven Hinze for setting up the Police Complaints Tribunal in the wake of the *Nationwide* television exposé. He saw it as a betrayal of good, hard-working police officers.

There was, too, Hinze's preparations for a Summary Offences Bill to be brought down in parliament in the new year. The legislation would effectively put a pincer on gambling and prostitution.

A flurry of diary entries underlined Lewis's displeasure with his colourful Minister. On 3 November 1982: '... saw Sir Edward Lyons re Cabinet reshuffle'. Then on 25 November: '... phoned Sir Edward Lyons re Ministers'. Again on 1 December: '... to Parlt House where Premier said he would transfer Police to Hon. W.H. Glasson if acceptable to me'.

On the morning of the day he saw the Premier, the National Party had voted for a new Deputy Premier. Hinze was a major contender, but the victory went to Bill Gunn.

Lewis now remembers Russ Hinze as a 'good' Police Minister, despite his concerted attempts to have him replaced. 'We were allocated say 50 extra policemen for the year ... [Leo] Hielscher and others in Treasury didn't want to give you ten quid,' says Lewis. 'Russ said, "Recruit another 50 or 25. I haven't got Treasury approval but that doesn't matter, leave that to me."

'The next minute you had Treasury on your back.'

Lewis attests that Hinze thought nothing of trying to cut a few corners.

'You'd go down there most Monday mornings before Cabinet ... I'd go down to his office in the old Treasury Building,' remembers Lewis. 'You didn't sit around and talk ... from time to time he'd produce a traffic ticket and see if you could get that fixed up.

'Without fail I'd give it to Assistant Commissioner of Traffic and get them to check it in case they'd made a mistake. I don't remember any of his being wiped.

'Say it was a $50 fine. He'd give you $50 to pay it. It wasn't just the fine but added points to your licence. They were always racing people, mainly jockeys. He thought he'd fix up anything. It was, if you like, white collar crime. The rumour was if you wanted anything done you went to Russ.

'There were always rumours [about corruption] and hardly any of them ever got anywhere because bloody politicians and local governments and developers were all mates.'

Lewis claims he also had to be on hand for a secret assignation from his Minister. 'He rang me one day and said, "You're a JP, aren't you? Come down and sign a form for me,"' Lewis remembers. 'It was an application to get married in a church in Ann Street. "I don't want anyone to know," Hinze said.

'The next thing he married Fay. He didn't want the media or anybody to know that he was getting married.'

By the end of 1982, however, Lewis had lost his patience with Hinze. 'He left debris for others to clear,' says Lewis. 'He was a colossus that pushed everything – ethics, other people – aside.

'He totally supported Joh in Cabinet. He was always the first cab off the rank to support him. [But] I don't think he had any respect for his position or anybody else. His way was the only way. He didn't mind being paid for doing favours.

'I said to the Premier, at one stage, we should have a different minister.'

In the end, Lewis won.

On 2 December, the day after Lewis saw the Premier about replacing Hinze with Glasson, the Commissioner's diary noted: 'Hon Hinze phoned re relinquishing of Police portfolio from 6.12.82.'

Russell Grenning, who would later work for Hinze as press secretary and personal assistant, remembers a specific incident that triggered the demise of Hinze as Police Minister. 'As I recall from my many conversations over the years I was with Hinze [which didn't include his term as Police Minister], the final straw in December 1982 was the demand by Sir Edward Lyons that he [Hinze] attend his Christmas

Party,' says Grenning. 'Hinze flatly refused and told Lyons what he could do with his invitation. Lyons replied to the effect that if Hinze didn't come to the party, he would be stripped of the Police portfolio. And a couple of days later that happened.

'Hinze repeated that story several times. In fact, he was glad to be rid of the Police. Joh had already appointed him Racing Minister two years earlier. He was well known as a keen racing man so it appeared reasonable that he should get the portfolio. While Joh was under pressure from Lyons and Lewis to get rid of Hinze, Joh also realised that he could not afford to offend Hinze, who had great popularity among the public and the National Party backbench.'

Grenning says that around election times, if sitting members or candidates couldn't secure a crowd for a fundraising event, Hinze was the next preferred pick.

'It was Hinze's success in getting up the Police Complaints Tribunal in mid-1982 that marked the definite end to any lingering relationship between he and Lewis,' recalls Grenning. 'Lewis told Joh and Hinze he regarded the establishment of the tribunal as a personal affront – saying that he and the force were wonderful ... of course the tribunal was a toothless tiger but it marked a considerable success by Hinze over Lewis.'

He said Hinze suspected that the relationship between Lyons and Lewis deepened considerably towards the end of 1981 and became a love-in during 1982 and mutually very advantageous.

'Hinze told me the pair were always seen out having dinners and drinks,' Grenning adds. 'Lewis had gained a strong ally in Lyons in his campaign to get rid of Hinze. I don't think that there was any specific matter that triggered the final attack on Hinze by Lyons. I think by that time Lyons and Lewis had so poisoned Joh's mind against Hinze as Police Minister that the refusal by Hinze to attend the Lyons' Christmas party was just the pretext they needed.

'And it worked – the irony is that Hinze was very, very pleased with the new arrangement.'

On 3 December, the day after Hinze phoned Lewis and relinquished his portfolio, the *Courier-Mail* ran a page-one story by political correspondent Peter Morley that Buckingham Palace had rejected a nomination from Bjelke-Petersen that Commissioner Lewis be knighted in the New Year's honours list.

The leaked story was hugely embarrassing for the Premier and his government. The reason offered for the rejection was that Lewis had only relatively recently been awarded an Order of the British Empire in 1979.

A source said: 'It is a gigantic bungle, a real blunder that should never have occurred and may mean that the entire Cabinet in future will have an input into recommendations.'

Hinze was straight on the phone to Lewis, 're article in C.M. re Comm Lewis rejected for Knighthood'. Lewis's ally and Knight, Sir Edward Lyons, also phoned to talk about the Morley article.

Hinze called again later in the day, 're Police Union wanting him to remain as Police Minister'.

Lewis wasn't having a bar of it. He went to an Australian Federal Police Christmas Party at an old favourite – the National Hotel – that afternoon.

On Sunday 5 December, Bjelke-Petersen rang Lewis at home in Garfield Drive. They discussed many things, including 'Hon. [Bill] Glasson probably our next Minister'. Lewis added in his diary notation: 'Snr staff at his office prob. responsible for honours leak to C.M.

'Attended to newspaper cuttings.'

The Bikie Bandit Six

The closer Police Complaints Tribunal head Judge Bill Carter got to completing his report on the astonishing allegations that police had given two suspected bank robbers heroin while they were in custody at the Brisbane watchhouse, the more the agitation was building in police and government quarters that went unseen by the public.

During mid-November Commissioner Lewis recorded in his diary that the Police Union was protesting the use of 'outsiders', referring to the investigating team looking into the Bikie Bandit case for the tribunal. The issue harked back to the days of Ray Whitrod, and the police union fury over the former commissioner and his attempts to investigate police corruption and misdemeanours.

But this was worse. Frank Clare of the Crown Law Office was poking around a force miraculously impervious to outside scrutiny. It wouldn't be tolerated.

On Wednesday 17 November Lewis had phoned Police Minister Hinze about the 'outsider' problem, and on Tuesday 23 November, he got a call from Hinze 're: Premier against outside investigators'. Later in the day Hinze phoned again over Deputy Commissioner Syd Atkinson 'and Supt. Pointing to see Premier with him'.

Hinze, Lewis and his senior officers were preparing for the bombshell that would be the Carter report. And they resorted to familiar tactics – they got the Premier briefed and onside before the storm.

On 6 December, Bill Glasson was appointed as the new Police Minister. He was briefed by Commissioner Lewis. When asked to comment on his new portfolio, Glasson said his ambition was to wipe out corruption. 'If I found anyone corrupt,' he said, 'I will have to take steps to rectify that.'

Curiously, on Thursday 9 December, Lewis's diary records that he had a discussion with the Head of the Police Media Unit, Ian Hatcher, about 'C.M. [*Courier-Mail*] story on bikie bandits and heroin'.

That story wasn't in fact published until the next day. The front-page exclusive alleged there had been attempts to shut down Judge Carter's investigation. On Saturday 11 December, the story again dominated the front page of the *Courier-Mail*.

All the conjecture over Judge Carter's imminent report forced Carter to take an unusual step and talk to the press. He stressed the independence of the Police Complaints Tribunal and declared it would not be influenced by any outside interference. 'I want to refute as positively as I can that any pressure is being brought to bear on the tribunal itself,' he said. 'There has never been any pressure whatsoever on this tribunal in relation to any case at all.'

He conceded that the tribunal had 'expressly requested' that a Crown Law officer be involved with the Police Internal Investigation Unit in looking at the matter.

Even the Commissioner, Terry Lewis, was drawn into the debate. He described as a 'heap of rubbish' any suggestions he'd been involved in shutting down the 'Bikie Bandits' investigation, and denied he had spoken to Bjelke-Petersen about it.

With the release of the report just 48 hours away, Lewis did not mention in his interview that he had in fact been to see Justice Carter on at least two occasions during the course of the investigation.

'Let me put it this way,' remembers Justice Carter, 'Lewis and Atkinson – the Commissioner and Deputy Commissioner – I was conscious of the fact that they were keeping an eye on us.

'They both, and at this time in a heightened sense, were anxious to seek meetings with us. Lewis was a pretty smooth character. I think they were keen to find out what they could and what we might be thinking. I can remember being generally alive to that sort of risk.

'There was one or two, probably two meetings with Lewis and Atkinson in the Executive Building where we [the tribunal] used to have out meetings. They said they were really appreciative of the work we were doing and wondered if there was any help they could give us.

'We weren't dills.'

Carter's report was handed to Glasson on Tuesday 14 December. It was dynamite. Six police were named in the heroin investigation – four in relation to the allegations that the two 'Bikie Bandits' had been supplied heroin, and two with regard to perjured evidence given by them over the police interviews with Alfred Thompson and Steve Kossaris back in 1981.

One of the highest ranking police named was Detective Sergeant Ron Pickering, then head of the Special Crimes Squad.

Glasson handed on a copy of the report to the Attorney-General and Justice Minister, Sam Doumany. 'It will be up to the Solicitor-General to decide whether or not there is a case to answer and if so, to take appropriate action,' Police Minister Glasson said.

The Solicitor-General, D.V. Galligan, was then expected to hand his decision to Police Commissioner Lewis, who was then responsible for making the final decision as to whether to proceed with charges or not.

Come Monday 20 December, Glasson announced that five policemen and one policewoman would be charged over the Bikie Bandits investigation. They would appear in a Magistrates' Court in January of the New Year.

Lewis was in for a busy day. He was behind his desk at 7.20 a.m., and after some minor paperwork he noted in his diary that Col Chant of the Police Complaints Tribunal and others called, 're: charging and possible suspension in "Bikie Bandit" case'. Later: 'Hon. Glasson phoned re: report from Crown Law office.'

Then Lewis called Solicitor-General Galligan 'who said summons proper and suspension not necessary'. He also had a 'brief discussion' with soon to be retired Assistant Commissioner Tony Murphy.

Later that day, Commissioner Lewis made it over to the Executive Building for the Premier's official Christmas party, where he had a quiet word with Bjelke-Petersen and Bill Glasson who told him to 'summons and do not suspend'. It had been a baptism of fire as Police Minister for the generally laconic Glasson.

Lewis eventually made his way back to the Police Club, the traditional refuge for officers when, under siege, they needed to gather for private discussions and debate, and to support each other. The 'Bikie Bandit Six' would have their legal funding taken care of by the union. He drank with Noel Dwyer and, of course, Tony Murphy.

The force had been in this position many, many times, since the days of Frank Bischof. And they had always come out on top. Heading into the New Year, there was no reason to think to the contrary.

Another Christmas Card

As was his habit on an almost annual basis, Gunther Bahnemann, living out on Harvey Creek Road in Bellenden Ker, 50 kilometres south of Cairns in Far North Queensland, wrote Lewis a letter in response to receiving one of the Commissioner's Christmas cards.

The year before the card depicted two mounted police. This year it had a German Shepherd police dog.

'Dear Terry, it is just after two o'clock in the morning, so please overlook the typing errors that may occur, one does get a bit dopey in the head around that hour,' wrote Bahnemann.

Apart from the usual pleasantries, Bahnemann had an extraordinary story to tell. He explained to Lewis that his boat building and fibreglass business had recently hit the wall and he had been forced to apply for social security benefits – 'it was that bad, Terry' – only to be told by a young public servant that the dole was not in place to be a crutch for failed businesses and that he needed to sign a Statutory Declaration pledging not to reopen his business.

'I promptly blew my stack and told her I would rob banks first before I signed such defeatist rubbish,' wrote Gunther. 'Leonie [his wife] promptly rang the Whip at Canberra and got onto Senator Flo Bjelke-Petersen. Flo had a twenty minute talk with Leonie and the ball started rolling.'

Gunther explained that a week later the Senator was in Innisfail and rang his wife, 'inviting her for further discussion'.

'We found Flo very efficient and as she mentioned everyone seems to hear about her pumpkin scones – and no one ever hears about her arguments she carries into parliament,' Bahnemann added.

'Anyway, we got back into business and at the moment employ four workers.'

The previous year Bahnemann had an audience with Assistant Commissioner Tony Murphy. And this year he and his wife had a one-on-one with Senator Bjelke-Petersen, wife of the Premier, himself close to the Commissioner of Police, Terry Lewis. For someone with a conviction for attempted murder against his name, and living in remote Bellenden Ker, Bahnemann mixed with some powerful people.

'I do not want to pat you on the back, Terry, however I think you are just about the most efficient Commissioner Queensland [has] had so far and you are very much liked by the police around here amongst which I have many a good friend.'

Bahnemann repeated that Lewis never seemed to age as the years had rolled by, and attributed it to 'excellent grooming'.

'I shall come to Brisbane in March or April,' he signed off. 'Please allow me a half an hour for old times sake talking to you. All the best for now.'

Murphy Resigns

As the end of 1982 loomed, Assistant Commissioner Tony Murphy decided to call it a day and resign from the force.

As a part of the mythical Rat Pack, he had outlasted Glen Patrick Hallahan by ten years. His departure would leave Commissioner Terry Lewis the last man standing from that golden era of policing when Uncle Frank Bischof mentored his boys and they roamed the city like three kings. Murphy's last day on the job would be Tuesday 21 December 1982.

Even for a hard man like Murphy, it had been a rough 12 months, kicking off with the allegations of police corruption by former officers Campbell and Fancourt on the ABC's *Nationwide* program.

In addition, Murphy's involvement with the murder of the drug couriers Douglas and Isabel Wilson saw him admonished by a royal commissioner. (Lewis says Murphy would have had no chance of further promotion with him as Commissioner following the Wilson murders.)

Murphy was just 55 years old.

His wife, Maureen Murphy, recalls: 'He said that he wanted to get away from it all. There must have been a bit of scandal then in the police force. I thought Tony had got to that stage that he just wanted to get away from everything. He was tired of everything.'

Murphy planned to move to a little place he had over on North Stradbroke Island. His idea was to grow Geraldton wax – *Chamelaucium uncinatum* – a flowering plant popular for its hardiness and longevity after cutting. The flowers were ordinarily white and mauve.

'He loved it there,' Maureen recalls. 'The family loved it over there. He wanted to get away from everything.'

Lewis recalls that the resignation could have been linked to some bad press against Murphy through 1982. 'The reason he gave was that he'd got some sort of adverse publicity … whether it was over the murders of those two people … over something … I think he did a report of some sort about saying that, seeing there was this publicity, it would preclude him from becoming a deputy commissioner, so he gave it away,' says Lewis. 'Why give away being Assistant Commissioner, which was pretty good? I think he would have wanted to stay on and become the boss.

'To go from there, down to an island somewhere growing flowers … it was a very strange finale if you like. Being a detective was his life.'

Murphy's good friend, top legal eagle Des Sturgess, says Murphy had grown weary of taking the public hits. 'He retired because he was sick and tired of the abuse he was getting,' Sturgess recalls. 'Comes a stage when you have difficulty standing much more. He'd been in the firing line for too long.

'He went to Point Lookout; he thought he might be able to make a dollar growing Geraldton wax. He reckoned it was a good place to grow Geraldton wax and sell it. It was all bullocky work he did.'

Lewis says Murphy was a superlative detective and had a brilliant police mind. 'I can't criticise him as a working policeman, but what he did outside of … his social activities if you like … I don't know,' says Lewis. 'The only social activities I ever had with him would have been over a drink in various pubs, which we might have met from time to time. He never came to my home for dinner; I never went to his home for dinner. So we weren't … we were friends but not on a family social sort of thing.'

Lewis says Murphy had a valuable criminal informant named Norris who worked very close with Murphy. Lewis found Norris the type of person he himself would have found it hard to tolerate. 'He was a criminal and he was a very, very bloody close informant for Murphy,' Lewis recalls. 'I don't know whether [Shirley] Brifman ever was or whether she was just a bloody sexual object.

'But Norris, I know was, because well I just know. And he was so … I think it was a relative that found out about Norris dogging on people and went to shoot him with a shotgun, and did in fact blow one arm right off but didn't kill him. They're the sort of people that I suppose, the life, the career that Murphy had, they're the sort of people that he got friendly with.

'And Murphy was with Jack Herbert for four years in the frigging Licensing Branch [1966–71]. Herbert says nobody that ever came there knocked him back.'

Lewis says he never saw Murphy take kickbacks but the word was out there. 'It was certainly said by various people that he did take money. But again, I didn't see it. And it was said that he was, when they were probably in the Licensing Branch they had these games going,' adds Lewis.

'Of course, Tony Robinson had a game going and Herbert and Murphy were supposed to be looking after that. But this is what you're told. We were in the CIB or the JAB and you get these stories but you don't follow them up. That's the boss's worry, that's not my worry.

'No, I really don't think he was anybody that went out and black-mailed anybody or stood over people for money. I'd say it was highly likely that in the Licensing Branch like all the others there, he would have got some bloody money. But ... according to Herbert and others, there was a whole heap of them that did.'

Tuesday 21 December was a pretty quiet day for Commissioner Lewis. He had some trivial duties and then went to see his doctor for a check-up. Later, he went and had a late afternoon drink with Sir Edward Lyons.

There were no formal festivities for retired Assistant Commissioner Anthony Murphy that night. A proper farewell befitting the great man would be held in the Police Union Building on the night of Monday 14 February 14 1983 – Valentine's Day. Premier Joh Bjelke-Petersen would be in attendance.

Jim Slade said Murphy was probably the most brilliant police officer he'd ever seen, and probably one of the toughest. In his prime, Murphy radiated power. In the Brisbane underworld they called him 'The Boss'.

Slade says Murphy wasn't a killer, like his counterpart Fred Krahe in Sydney. 'But Murphy would make the bullets,' says Slade.

Murphy may have suspected, on leaving the force, that he was entering the same twilight zone that had been inhabited by former commissioner Frank Bischof, his own mentor from the 1950s and 1960s.

He was born a policeman. There was nothing else in life that even remotely satisfied Murphy the way being a detective did. He absolutely adored the chase. He loved the company of like-minded tough men and he had relished the power the job gave him.

If anyone thought the frightening, feared, sometimes brutal and often begrudgingly respected cop Tony Murphy was walking away from the police force to quietly grow flowers, they had rocks in their heads.

Blue Skies

In the last week of 1982, Commissioner Lewis tidied a few things up before his 28 days' annual leave.

He launched the exciting new 'Kiss a Cop' campaign prior to New Year's Eve festivities and attended the opening of the 13th Australian Jamboree 'by His Excellency Sir Ninian Stephen, Chief Scout for Australia'.

It had been another big year – his sixth as Commissioner. But Lewis could be well satisfied. He had what appeared to be an inviolable friendship with the Premier and had also made powerful friends in Sir Robert Sparkes and Sir Edward Lyons.

He had seen off Police Ministers who didn't sit well with his philosophies and how he ran his ship, the latest being the formidable Russ Hinze. Earlier in the year his Police Force had survived yet another call for a royal commission into its corrupt ways, and Lewis and the government had established a Police Complaints Tribunal that, in the not too distant future, would be put in the hands of his old mate Judge Eric Pratt.

And though it may have taken six years, Lewis had dismantled and in most cases seen off the final clutch of pro-Whitrod supporters – Pitts, Jeppesen, Hicks, Campbell, Saunders and others.

In the world away from his big office in police headquarters and his home up on Garfield Drive, his old smooth-talking friend Jack Herbert had hooked into the Hapeta and Tilley money-making vice machine and was reeling in tens of thousands of dollars in corrupt payments for The Joke. Down at 142 Wickham Street, upstairs in the casino that didn't exist, punters were enjoying the patronage of Geraldo Bellino, the drinks, the girls, and having a flutter into the early hours of the morning.

Commissioner Lewis had unexpectedly lost a great ally in Tony Murphy, a colleague who he had worked alongside and admired from the late 1940s. Murphy had taught Lewis a lot, and had been indispensable in ridding the force of Ray Whitrod and opening the Commissioner's door to Lewis.

And while on paper – certainly according to the department's annual reports – Lewis was doing a stellar job, his administration in the eyes of many still carried about it the stench of corruption.

It was not difficult to understand why.

The 1970s in Queensland, and particularly Brisbane, had seen the evolution of a bona fide underworld, where crime syndicates had formed and carved out their turf. Like anywhere else in the world, criminal real estate was closely protected and transgression from rivals was often met with violence. Quaint little Brisbane, with its jacarandas and poinsettias, its church raffles and hollering paper boys at the main city intersections, had not been spared the growth of the drug and vice trade, and the attendant criminals that presided over it.

Indeed, those involved in the city's underworld in the 1970s and into the 1980s described the local scene, straight-faced, as being just as violent and dangerous as anywhere else in Australia.

The body count was testimony to such observations. In 1973, the Whiskey Au Go Go inferno was the greatest mass murder in the country's history to that point. There was the controversial 'drug overdose' of Shirley Margaret Brifman, the assassination of National Hotel manager Jack Cooper, the murder of boxer Tommy Hamilton, the disappearance of prostitutes Margaret Ward and Simone Vogel, and the vanishing of Barbara McCulkin and her two young daughters. The bulk of these cases, and many others, had attracted the suspicion of police involvement.

When Commissioner Whitrod had moved on the so-called Rat Pack – Lewis, Murphy and Hallahan – he was ultimately removed, fleeing the state in fear of his life.

Case after case in Queensland courts against alleged corrupt police, illegal casino operators or friends to crooked officers fell over like dominoes.

Within the force, police officers who dared voice their opinions against a corrupt regime were forced out of the job and the state, drank themselves to death, or lost their families under the pressure of the need to do what was right. Hundreds of promising careers were destroyed, further perpetuating a cycle of corruption by leaving behind those who toed the line.

And Jack Herbert, master conman and liar, organised supremely a corrupt system that flourished in the Lewis era and proved resilient to everything thrown at it. Over time, its impact was far greater than its original intention – the effort to keep it hidden from sight and the wheels moving smoothly in turn reached into the public service, the judiciary and into the halls of government itself, and began buckling them out of shape.

Lewis's need to please and impress Premier Joh Bjelke-Petersen had worked brilliantly for both men. Within a year of Lewis taking the chair, Bjelke-Petersen controlled a Police State. Ordinary civil liberties disappeared and would only be returned when and if the Premier deemed it appropriate to return them. With the Queensland Police Force covering his back, Bjelke-Petersen was impervious.

On the eve of 1983, Lewis – always a fine details man, always the master of the small picture, of controlling the day to day – may not have understood the bigger mosaic or the part he was playing in changing the direction of Queensland society. In fact, he may have been thinking about renovating the family home up on Garfield Drive, in finally making a house that befitted his status.

And, set to celebrate his fifty-fifth birthday, he may have been thinking about a little unit down on the Gold Coast, a place he loved, where he and wife, Hazel, could spend some quality time together as they approached retirement.

It was blue skies ahead for Lewis. Indeed, he may have been entertaining in his mind informal discussions he had had with Premier Joh Bjelke-Petersen about securing a diplomatic posting in Los Angeles or London when his time as Commissioner of Police was done. Without doubt, a Knighthood had to be in the offing. All in all, Lewis could see nothing but good times stretching before him.

It had taken an enormous amount of work, and there'd been a lot of collateral damage, but he was where he wanted to be – in control and working for a man who was in control. By and large his enemies were behind him, and most importantly he had men he trusted in important positions throughout the force.

On the last day of 1982 – a Friday – Lewis attended to some trivial paperwork then fitted in some revolver practice. It may have been portentous.

Beyond the blue skies, and the curve of the earth, the first scuds of cloud were gathering. Over time they would knit together then gain force before building into a storm of such ferocity that it would destroy everything in its path.

Unlike the thunder and lightning that Lewis had watched as he sat out in the Petrie Terrace police barracks in Brisbane the night before he was sworn in as a young officer in 1949, this storm – a confluence of speed and fronts from unlikely directions – would take years to build.

But it would seemingly have a single target in its sight. And that target was Commissioner Terence Murray Lewis.

Author's Note and Acknowledgments

Following the publication of *Three Crooked Kings* it became apparent that only a trilogy could do justice to the life and times of former Queensland commissioner of police, Terence Lewis, and all the attendant political intrigue and social history of the era. I am once again grateful to Terry for his cooperation and patience. As with the first volume, I have made every effort in *Jacks and Jokers* to offer a balanced story, and with the numerous narrative threads, Lewis was again offered the right of reply.

Again, I thank Doug Hall for his early encouragement.

I want to express my appreciation to current and former State and Federal police officers who gave me their time for this project. They include: Jim Slade, John 'Bluey' O'Gorman, Ron Edington, the family of the late Robert Walker, Barry Krosch, Les Lewis, Keith Smith, Peter Dautel, Dennis Koch, Ken Hoggett, John Huey, Geoff Pambroke, Ron Lewis, Arthur Volz, Bruce Wilby, the late Noel Creevey, Cliff Crawford, John Moller, Ian Hatcher, the late Abe Duncan, Fred Collins, Pat Glancy, Greg Early, Ross Beer, John Paul Lewis, Max Rogers, Brian Bennett and Bill Harrigan.

I am particularly indebted to former Federal Narcotics Bureau agent John Shobbrook for his recollections and also for kind permission to quote from his extraordinary unpublished memoir. Courtesy of this project, I have been fortunate to establish another wonderful friendship with a man of integrity, former Licensing Branch officer Kingsley Fancourt, whose role in this saga has, I hope, been rightfully restored. Kingsley, you're an inspiration, and here's to many long conversations in the future. The Lewis trilogy has attracted many generous friends, none more so than former Licensing Branch detective and key whistleblower prior to the announcement of the Fitzgerald Inquiry in 1987, Nigel Powell. Thank you Nigel for all of your advice, assistance and camaraderie. Your friendship means an enormous amount. And thank you, Georgia.

Similarly, a heartfelt thanks to Mary Anne Brifman and her family for allowing me into their lives and for being so kind and generous.

I'm again enormously grateful to journalists Chris Masters and Phil

Dickie for their epochal work and for their friendship. I would also like to pay tribute to a couple of other trailblazers – Quentin Dempster and Evan Whitton. Cheers also to Peter James, Tony Koch, Alan Hall, Paul Weston, Nan Dwyer, Trent Dalton, Ken Blanch and Michael McKenna. A special thanks to Hedley Thomas and Des Houghton. Thanks once more goes to former colleagues Michael Crutcher and David Fagan of News Queensland for unqualified support, continued with this book through the kindness and understanding of Christopher Dore, editor of the *Courier-Mail* and Peter Gleeson, editor of the *Sunday Mail*.

During the writing of this book, friend and Brisbane-based journalist Tony Reeves died suddenly while on vacation overseas. Mate, you are sorely missed, but live on in your books and your generosity of spirit. And thank you again to another gentleman, Ian Alcorn.

These books have been aided by the recollections and knowledge of an enormous number of people. I would like to pay tribute to: Sir Llewelyn Edwards, Peter Beattie, Mike Ahern, Terry White, Bill Hewitt, Henry Palaszcuk, Russell Grenning, Paul Braddy, Malcolm McMillan, Ross and June Fels, Edgar Bourke, Anne Marie Tilley, Debbie Kilroy, William Stokes, Carolyn Scully, Leonie Bahnemann, former Justice Bill Carter, Des Sturgess, Lee Kear, Richard Spencer, Andre Look, Ken Lord, Ruth Whitrod Blackburn, Ian Whitrod, Mervyn Carey, Jean Hudson, Dr Harry Akers, John Wayne Ryan, Dr Paul Wilson, Fiona McDonald, Terry O'Gorman, Richard Spencer and Jean Bowra, who transcribed the bulk of the Lewis interviews.

I am additionally indebted to: Alex Mitchell, Judith White, Phillip Knightley, Richard Lawson, Ron and Karen Condon, Marsha and Phil Pope and family, John Shakespeare and Anna-Lisa Backlund, Gillian Morris and Geof Hawke, and Gary Morris and Jo Gaha.

Several books and documents have been important to both *Three Crooked Kings* and *Jacks and Jokers*:

The Road to Fitzgerald and Beyond by Phil Dickie, UQP, 1989
In Place of Justice by Peter James, The Shield Press, 1974
The Sundown Murders by Peter James, Boolarong Publications, 1990

The Long Blue Line by W. Ross Johnston, Boolarong Publications, 1992

The Bagman by Jack Herbert with Tom Gilling, ABC Books, 2004

Before I Sleep by Ray Whitrod, UQP, 2001

The Prince and the Premier by David Hickie, Angus and Robertson, 1985

Trial and Error by Don Lane, Boolarong Publications, 1993

The Man They Called a Monster by Paul Wilson, Cassell Australia, 1981

A Life of Crime by Paul Wilson, Scribe, 1990

The Tangled Web by Des Sturgess, Bedside Books, 2001

Reform in Policing: Lessons from the Whitrod Era by Jill M. Bolen, Hawkins Press, 1997

Don't You Worry About That! by Sir Joh Bjelke-Petersen, Angus and Robertson, 1990

Honest Cops by Quentin Dempster, ABC Books, 1992

Crims in Grass Castles by Keith Moor, Penguin Books, 2009

Joh by Hugh Lunn, UQP, 1978

Inside Story by Chris Masters, Harper Collins, 1992

The Hillbilly Dictator by Evan Whitton, ABC Books, 1989.

Selected quotes were also taken from an extensive interview conducted with Ray Whitrod by Robin Hughes for the Australian Biography project, 2000. I am indebted to Malcolm McMillan and Lindsay Marshall for use of quotes from their extraordinary oral history collection, held by the National Library of Australia. Thank you to Bruce Dawe for permission to quote from his poem 'News from Judea'.

My thanks to all at University of Queensland Press for coming along on this ride, especially CEO Greg Bain, the wonderful and courageous Madonna Duffy (Publisher), and Meredene Hill. I am hugely grateful to Jacqueline Blanchard for a superb and (relatively) painless edit. Thank you to both editorial assistant Tonile Wortley for all your hard work, and the great Bettina Richter.

Finally, I owe everything to my family: my wife Katie Kate, and my wonderful children, Finnigan, Bridie Rose and little Olly G. (Oliver George).

Index